MICROECONOMICS SCOREBOARD

EMPLOYMENT BY INDUSTRY, 2005

SOURCE: STATISTICS CANADA, CANSIM TABLE 282-0008.

	THOUSANDS	PERCENT
Total, All Industries	**16 168**	**100.0**
Total, Goods-Producing Sector	**4 002**	**24.8**
Agriculture	344	2.1
Forestry, fishing, mining, oil & gas	306	1.9
Utilities	125	0.8
Construction	I 020	6.3
Manufacturing	2 207	13.7
Total, Services-Producing Sector	**12 167**	**75.2**
Trade	2 575	15.9
Transportation and warehousing	794	4.9
Finance, insurance, real estate, & leasing	988	6.1
Professional, scientific, & technical services	I 050	6.5
Business, building, & other support services	654	4.0
Educational services	I 106	6.8
Health care & social assistance	I 735	10.7
Information, culture, & recreation	735	4.5
Accommodation & food services	I 005	6.2
Other services	693	4.3
Public administration	833	5.2

AVERAGE WEEKLY EARNINGS BY INDUSTRY, 2005

SOURCE: STATISTICS CANADA, CANSIM TABLE 281-0026.

	AVERAGE WEEKLY EARNINGS
Forestry, logging, & support	$ 881.81
Mining & oil & gas extraction	I 302.56
Utilities	I 083.00
Construction	874.05
Manufacturing	874.88
Wholesale trade	816.60
Retail trade	466.19
Transportation & warehousing	766.42
Information & cultural industries	859.05
Finance & insurance	919.78
Real estate & rental & leasing	642.03
Professional, scientific, & technical services	948.91
Educational services	773.70
Health care & social assistance	640.46
Arts, entertainment, & recreation	414.98
Public administration	899.86

Canadian Microeconomics

PROBLEMS AND POLICIES

EIGHTH EDITION

BRIAN LYONS

Sheridan Institute of Technology and Advanced Learning

PEARSON

Prentice
Hall

Toronto

Library and Archives Canada Cataloguing in Publication

Lyons, Brian
        Canadian microeconomics : problems and policies / Brian Lyons—8th ed.

Includes index.
ISBN 0-13-198297-4

1. Microeconomics—Textbooks.   2. Canada—Economic conditions—Textbooks.   I. Title.

HB172.L96 2006   338.5'0971   C2005-906558-3

ISBN 0-13-198297-4

Vice President, Editorial Director: Michael J. Young
Editor-in-Chief: Gary Bennett
Acquisitions Editor: Laura Paterson Forbes
Marketing Manager: Eileen Lasswell
Senior Developmental Editor: Pamela Voves
Production Editor: Joe Zingrone
Copy Editor: Tara Tovell
Proofreader: Joe Zingrone
Production Coordinator: Andrea Falkenberg
Permissions Research: Amanda McCormick
Page Layout: Integra
Art Director: Julia Hall
Cover and Interior Design: Opus House Incorporated/Sonya Thursby
Cover Image: Getty Images/Will and Deni McIntyre

1 2 3 4 5   11 10 09 08 07

Printed and bound in the USA.

For Barb, Amber, Marnie, Brent, Dylan, Liam, Ryan and Brady

Brief Table of Contents

Contents

7 Market Structures ... 128

8 The Costs and Revenues of the Firm ... 157

12 The Government Sector ... 261

15 Into the Future ... 326

16W The Politics of Economics ... 335

"IN THE NEWS" BOXES

"YOU DECIDE" BOXES

Preface

Introduction

Canadian Microeconomics: Problems and Policies, Eighth Edition, is an introductory text that addresses itself to economic issues and problems faced by Canada and Canadians today. This text is not oriented toward rigorous, elegant, or abstract theory, or toward a mathematical approach to economics; most students of introductory economics neither want nor need these. Rather, its approach tends to be practical and based in the real world, using economic theory to develop an understanding of the issues and problems being discussed and the policy choices facing governments in dealing with these matters. This text is ideally suited to a student's first course in economics and has been used in this role at the secondary school, community college, and university levels.

New to This Edition

In this eighth edition, we have tried to *increase the interactivity of the student with the text*. The most visible change is the addition of an **Integrated Study Guide** following the end-of-chapter questions in each chapter. The Integrated Study Guide consists of three types of questions:

(a) **Review Questions** These are based closely on the material in the chapter and are multiple choice or short answer in nature. The answers are provided at the end of the book, making these questions a useful "self-check" for the content of each chapter.

(b) **Critical Thinking Questions** These questions are more complex and lend themselves to discussion and perhaps debate. Some are based on real-world situations; others are based on "what-if" scenarios.

(c) **Use the Web** These investigation/research questions usually require the same thinking skills as the Critical Thinking Questions, but are based on real-world information that can be found on the internet.

Student interactivity is also enhanced by an increase in the number of "In the News" and "You Decide" boxes, most of which are new for the eighth edition. The questions that accompany these boxes also require critical thinking skills and lend themselves to classroom discussion.

Because what is in the news regarding economics changes so rapidly, new questions based on real-world examples, together with questions that encourage critical thinking, will be regularly posted on our Companion Website (**www.pearsoned.ca/lyons**).

In addition to updating the previous edition's material, the revisions for the eighth edition were undertaken with the following goals in mind:

1. To improve the flow of the material, within chapters and from chapter to chapter.
2. To stress and reinforce certain "themes" across various chapters, such as scarcity, opportunity cost, efficiency and effectiveness, etc.
3. To add current and interesting material, through
   - many new "In the News" and "You Decide" boxes
   - new end-of-chapter questions and Integrated Study Guide questions that add interest and relevance to the material
   - many new "sidebar" items in the margins with examples and colourful facts
   - updated coverage of ebusiness, including Chapter 8's questions on how the costs and revenues of ebusiness firms differ from conventional firms, and the problems and opportunities that this creates

Further, this edition contains improved artwork, which makes it more visually attractive and benefits the visual learner (i.e., bolder, clearer figures); as well, various figures have been redrawn and improved.

More specifically, in Chapter 1, the discussion of production-possibilities curves (formerly in an appendix) has been relocated into the main body of the text, which improves the flow of the material; and a new "You Decide" box on using effectiveness and efficiency to measure a school's performance has been added. Chapter 2 provides an improved explanation of the idea that economic reasons underpin a market system's inherent tendency to underproduce key public services, and of how government subsidies can help to remedy this; further, a new "You Decide" box has been added that asks students to decide whether particular public services should be subsidized or not. In Chapter 3, a new "You Decide" box has been added that asks why the Financial Post 500 rankings of General Motors and McDonald's on the basis of sales revenue and jobs are so different.

Chapters 4, 5, 6, and 7 have new examples and illustrations of how markets work. New "You Decide" and "In the News" boxes have been added throughout these central four chapters: in Chapter 4, on using higher taxes to discourage smoking; in Chapter 5, a current example of Tar Sands crude oil to illustrate the concept of price and supply; in Chapter 6, on golf fees in the Greater Toronto Area, on the sharp rise in world oil prices in 2004–05, and on how the internet affects markets; and in Chapter 7, on the 2005 price war in the Voice over Internet Protocol (VoIP) industry and on the world market for coffee.

Chapter 8 now has more on the economics of ebusinesses, including a new box on how the unusual structure of costs for some ebusinesses (high fixed costs and low marginal costs) affects their pricing strategies. In Chapter 9, the coverage of the "efficiency exception" of the Competition Act has been improved, and the current deliberations over revisions to the Act in response to the Superior Propane case have been brought up to date. Also, a new box has been added on promoting competition in the Canadian beer market. Chapters 10 and 11 have been updated significantly, and coverage of the skills pay gap has been strengthened. In Chapter 10, a new "In the News" box on hockey players' salaries has been added, and Chapter 11 now has a new "In the News" box on future changes in the male–female pay gap.

Chapter 12 has been extensively reworked, with new sections on "Budgeting Basics" and "Uses and Misuses of Debt" to set the stage for coverage of government finances. Coverage of the federal deficit reduction program has been condensed, and coverage of alternative uses of the budget surpluses since 1997 has been expanded.

Chapter 12 also contains a new "In the News" box on the government policies intended to ease the economic effects of the aging of Canada's baby boomers.

Chapter 13 includes enhanced coverage of global warming and the greenhouse effect, and two new boxes: one on the merits of higher gasoline taxes to reduce air pollution and global warming, and another on lessons to be learned from China's water crisis. Chapter 14 has updated data on farm incomes and payments to farmers from government programs, as well as improved coverage of the effects of freer trade on Canadian agriculture.

Followers of previous editions will note that the chapter on "The Politics of Economics" has departed from this edition; however, it will be available on the website.

Overall, the result of these changes is a text that is more current and that flows more effectively, providing considerably more opportunities for students to interact with the material.

Features

According to both students and teachers, a major feature of this book is its readability, which helps considerably in the learning and teaching of a subject that has an (undeserved) reputation of being rather formidable. Other aspects of the text include

- **Coverage of "The Basics"** Chapters 1, 2, and 4 through 7 provide good coverage of the microeconomics basics of markets and market structure.
- **Flexibility** In addition to these basics, a variety of other topics can be covered, including marginal cost–marginal revenue analysis (Chapter 8), competition policy (Chapter 9), labour markets and unions (Chapter 10), trends concerning jobs and incomes (Chapter 11), the role of government in the economy (Chapter 12), the economics of the environment (Chapter 13), and agriculture (Chapter 14).
- **Interactivity** The "You Decide" and "In the News" boxes, together with the end-of-chapter questions and Integrated Study Guide, provide extensive opportunities for students to interact with the material, both on their own and in groups, as well as via the internet.
- **Pedagogical Tools** Learning objectives, "You Decide" boxes, "In the News" boxes, end-of-chapter questions, and current issues on our website all help students to focus on and apply the important points in each chapter.

Organization

To a considerable extent, the text consists of two sections, with the section through Chapter 8 covering mostly the basic elements of microeconomics and the second half of the book presenting specific topics, most of which involve data pertaining to Canada's current economic situation. Following the discussion of the basic problems and questions of economics and an examination of the Canadian economy, the text presents the basic tools of microeconomics—demand and supply—and how these interact to determine output and prices under a variety of conditions, ranging from highly competitive to monopolistic industries. In the second half of the book various topics are covered, including government policy toward business, labour markets and labour unions, trends in employment and incomes, government programs, financial problems and policy choices, and economic issues related to the environment and agricultural sector. The text concludes with a short chapter that ties the text together with a review of Canada's past economic directions and a discussion of future trends.

Supplements

The following supplements have been carefully prepared to aid instructors and students in using this edition:

Resources for Instuctors

Instructor's Resource CD-ROM (0-13-199658-4): This resource CD includes the following instructor supplements:

- **Instructor's Solutions Manual** This manual provides answers to all end-of-chapter questions, assignment questions, Integrated Study Guide questions, and answers to boxed questions in the text.
- **Pearson TestGen** TestGen is a testing software that enables instructors to view and edit the existing questions, add questions, generate tests, and distribute the tests in a variety of formats. Powerful search and sort functions make it easy to locate questions and arrange them in any order desired. TestGen also enables instructors to administer tests on a local area network, have the tests graded electronically and have the results prepared in electronic or printed reports. TestGen is compatible with Windows and Macintosh operating systems, and can be downloaded from the TestGen website located at **www.pearsoned.com/testgen**. Contact your local sales representative for details and access.
- **PowerPoints** A collection of transparencies culled from the textbook or specifically designed to complement chapter content, is also available electronically in PowerPoint software on the Instructor's Resource CD-ROM.
- **Image Library** A collection of transparency masters for all the figures, tables, and graphs in the text.

These instructor supplements offered on CD-ROM are also available for download from a password protected section of Pearson Education Canada's online catalogue (**http://vig.pearsoned.ca**). Navigate to this book's catalogue page to view a list of the supplements that are available. See your local sales representative for details and access.

Resources for Students

In addition to the Integrated Study Guide at the end of each chapter in the text, the following online study material is also provided.

- The **Companion Website** (**www.pearsoned.ca/lyons**) includes a chapter outline, self-assessment quizzes, and links to other relevant web sites for each part of the text.

Acknowledgments

Anyone undertaking a project of this magnitude and duration feels indebtedness to many people. In particular, I would like to express my gratitude to Bill Trimble, who said I should do it, Len Rosen, who refused to let me say I wouldn't, and all those teachers and students who used the first seven editions and offered helpful comments and suggestions. I would also like to thank the people whose reviews of all eight editions of the manuscript were so helpful: for the first edition, Ray Canon, Gord Cleveland, Ward Levine, Jim Thompson, and Ian Wilson; for the second, Alan Idiens and Chuck Casson; for the third, Linda Nitsou, Bo Renneckendorf, Gord Enemark, L.W. Van Niekerk, Stephen

Wise, and Ann Dunkley; for the fourth, Carol Ann Waite, Izhar Mirza, John Parry, and Byron Eastman; for the fifth, Valerie Beckingham, Michael Loconte, Pauline A. Lutes, Peter J. MacDonald, Karen Murkar, John Parry, Don Pepper, Judith Skuce, Don Wheeler, and Peter Young; for the sixth edition, Peter Peters, Karen Murkar, Ian Wilson, Don Wheeler, Martin Moy, Bill Gallivan, Terri Anderson, and Jane Taylor; for the seventh edition, Worku Aberra of Dawson College, Frances Ford of New Brunswick Community College (Moncton), Carl Graham of Assiniboine Community College, Donald Howick of St. Clair College, Al Idiens of College of New Caledonia, Peter J. MacDonald of Cambrian College, Raimo Marttala of Malaspina College, Martin Moy of University College of Cape Breton, A. Gyasi Nimarko of Vanier College, John Pirrie of St. Lawrence College, and Charles Walton of Nova Scotia Community College; and for this eighth edition, Aurelia Best of Centennial College, Tatjana Brkic, Allan Green, and Jack Rink of Red River College, Peter J. MacDonald of Cambrian College of Applied Arts and Technology, Martin Moy of Cape Breton University, Ekaterina Gregory, Alan Idiens, and George Kennedy of College of New Caledonia, and Shirley Pasieka of Southern Alberta Institute of Technology.

Finally, I want to express my appreciation to my immediate family—Barb, Marnie, and Amber—who have provided support and understanding over unduly long periods of time.

I have no doubt that there are many improvements that can be made to this book, and welcome suggestions from teachers and students. Please write to me at Sheridan College, 7899 McLaughlin Road, Brampton, Ontario L6V 1G6, or email me at **brian.lyons@sheridanc.on.ca**.

Brian Lyons
January 2006

A Great Way to Learn and Instruct Online

The Pearson Education Canada Companion Website is easy to navigate and is organized to correspond to the chapters in this textbook. Whether you are a student in the classroom or a distance learner you will discover helpful resources for in-depth study and research that empower you in your quest for greater knowledge and maximize your potential for success in the course.

[www.pearsoned.ca/lyons]

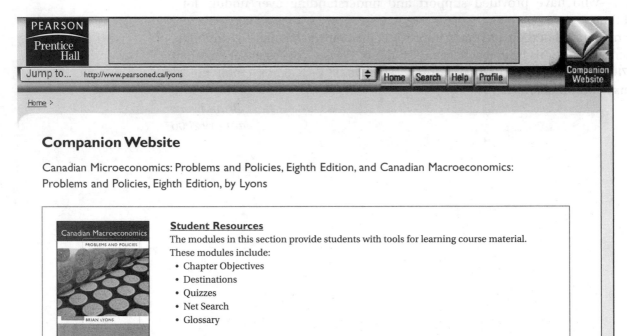

PEARSON
Prentice
Hall

Jump to...   http://www.pearsoned.ca/lyons   Home Search Help Profile   Companion Website

Home >

Companion Website

Canadian Microeconomics: Problems and Policies, Eighth Edition, and Canadian Macroeconomics: Problems and Policies, Eighth Edition, by Lyons

Student Resources
The modules in this section provide students with tools for learning course material. These modules include:
- Chapter Objectives
- Destinations
- Quizzes
- Net Search
- Glossary

In the quiz modules students can send answers to the grader and receive instant feedback on their progress through the Results Reporter. Coaching comments and references to the textbook may be available to ensure that students take advantage of all available resources to enhance their learning experience.

Instructor Resources
Links will direct instructors to a secure, password-protected site that provides access to a variety of teaching aids, including PowerPoint Presentations, downloadable Instructor's Manual, and TestGen test bank. To get a password, simply contact your Pearson Education Canada Representative or call Faculty Sales and Services at 1-800-850-5813.

What Is Economics?

After studying this chapter, you should be able to

1. Explain what is studied in the field of economics.
2. Describe the three basic types of economic resources.
3. Explain the basic *economic problem* of scarcity.
4. Construct a production-possibilities curve from data concerning two products and show on the curve the effect of a change in the efficiency of producing one or both products.
5. Calculate or estimate the opportunity cost of a given economic decision.
6. Define the terms *standard of living*, *productivity*, *efficiency*, and *effectiveness*.
7. Calculate worker productivity in a given situation.
8. Explain how a given decision would affect efficiency and/or effectiveness.
9. Identify the three basic questions of economics.

Living in a world of 24-hour news channels and the internet, it is easy to feel overwhelmed by the constant stream of events being reported to us. Many of these events are of an economic nature, and they are often reported only briefly and with minimal explanations of the *reasons why* they have happened. This often leaves people feeling that economic changes just happen to them, and that they are at the mercy of forces beyond their understanding.

This need not be the case. Economic events don't just happen; they happen because something has *caused* them to happen. And a basic understanding of economics will let you perceive not only *what* is happening, but also *why* it's happening. Doing this does not require mastering difficult economic theories. Much of this book involves organizing things that you already know into a "tool kit," or a framework that can help you to understand the cause–effect connections underlying economic events. And this tool kit will help you not only to understand why things have happened, but also (with a little bit of luck) maybe even to foresee what is likely to happen in the future.

Let's start by getting a clear idea of what economics is all about.

What Is Economics?

Economics means different things to different people. To the householder, economics is the difficult task of balancing the family budget so that there is not too much month left over at the end of the money. To the business leader, economics is the problem of producing a product at a sufficiently low cost to be sold profitably in competition with the products of other producers. To a government leader, economics means making difficult policy choices between goals that often conflict with each other; this makes it impossible to please everyone and difficult to ensure re-election. To the general public, economics is usually associated with vague, incomprehensible, and often contradictory pronouncements by people called *economists*, who many people suspect were created in order to make weather forecasters look good.

Each viewpoint, representing a particular group (householders, business leaders, and government leaders), is only one aspect of the real meaning of economics. To the economist, economics deals with the broader question of how well a society's economic system satisfies the economic needs and wants of its people. Since the basic task of an economic system is to produce goods and services and to distribute them among the people of a society, the most common definition of **economics** is "the study of the decisions a society makes concerning the production of goods and services and how the society distributes these goods and services among its members."

This somewhat dry definition will lead us into considering much more interesting questions about Canadian society, employment, incomes, and government policy, such as

- In what occupations will job opportunities be greatest in the future?
- Should the government control the price of gasoline?
- Why are the wages of unskilled workers falling farther and farther behind the wages of skilled workers?
- Can we have economic growth without destroying our environment?
- Why do some professional athletes earn $10 000 000 per year, while other people earn only $10 000?
- Would a big increase in the minimum wage rate help to fight poverty?
- Why has the number of farmers been decreasing?
- How many Canadians are really living in poverty?

economics

The study of the decisions a society makes concerning the production of goods and services and the division of these among its people.

Some aspects of economic matters, such as those above, raise *philosophical* questions; for instance, is it proper for the government to control apartment rents, or people's wages, or workers' strikes? Other aspects of economics, however, involve more *technical economic analysis*. For example, if the government increased the minimum wage rate by 10 percent, would this cause unemployment to increase by 5 percent? 2 percent? Or 0 percent? Often, economics also becomes involved with *value judgments*. For example, suppose experts agreed that a 10-percent increase in the minimum wage rate would cause youth unemployment to increase by 25 000. *Should* the government increase the minimum wage rate by 10 percent? Some people would favour increasing the minimum wage because of the expected benefits for the *employed*. Others would oppose the wage increase because it would reduce job opportunities for the *unemployed*. There is no "right" answer to this question, because the response to the question depends on the value judgment of the person answering it.

Folklore Versus Economic Analysis (not true)

Probably the greatest obstacle to the effective learning (and teaching) of economics is the fact that many people already think that they know a great deal about the subject. In fact, much of this "knowledge" consists of widely believed but not necessarily accurate ideas such as the following:
- Producers' profits add 20 to 40 percent to the prices we pay for products.
- Canadian companies cannot compete with foreign producers.
- Companies locate wherever wages are lowest.
- The key to increasing Canadians' standard of living is for governments to provide more benefits and services to them.
- A major increase in the minimum wage rate would reduce poverty considerably.
- If the rich paid higher taxes, the rest of us could pay much lower taxes and receive many more government services and benefits.
- A government ban on strikes by labour unions would bring Canada major economic benefits.

None of the above statements *is* true, but many people *believe* them to be true. One key objective of this book, and its companion text, *Canadian Macroeconomics: Problems and Policies*, is to replace such folklore about economics with the tools for accurate analysis of economic issues of importance to Canadians.

The Limitations of Economic Analysis

Because economics deals with the behaviour of people (consumers, business people, government policy-makers), economics cannot be a precise science such as mathematics. Similarly, economic analysis does not provide clear and simple answers to important questions, such as whether the government should increase the minimum wage rate. However, economic analysis can clarify the choices to be made. For example, economic analysis can be used to estimate the benefits and the costs of increasing the minimum wage rate. So, while economic analysis does not provide us with *decisions*, it does provide us with a much better *basis for making decisions*.

Then What Is Economics About?

Economics is about many matters both small and large. On a large scale, *macroeconomics* (after the Greek word *macro*, meaning "big") deals with broad aspects of the performance of the economy as a whole—such as recession, inflation, unemployment, and international trade and finance. These are the subjects of the companion text *Canadian Macroeconomics: Problems and Policies.*

On a small scale, *microeconomics* (after the Greek word *micro,* meaning "small") focuses on particular aspects of the economy such as consumer demand, supply, demand, and prices under various conditions, and the role of big business, labour unions, and government in the economy, as well as the economics of specific industries (such as agriculture) or specific issues (such as the environment). The purpose of this book is to develop an understanding of these microeconomic matters, which are important to all Canadians. Before examining these issues, however, we will consider the basic problems of economics in general. Then, in Chapter 2, we will examine the nature of Canada's economic system.

The Economic Problem: Too Many Wants, Not Enough Resources

The fundamental problem of economics—so basic that it is known as *the economic problem*—is the simple fact that we cannot have everything that we would like. And this reality forces us to make some difficult decisions.

All too often, however, this and other simple but key economic realities become lost in the confusing complexity of our modern economy. And a modern industrial or post-industrial economy can seem very bewildering, because it consists of a myriad of factors such as consumers, small businesses, big businesses, and ebusinesses. In addition, there are labour unions, governments, exports, imports, and the level of output. And to make matters more complicated, there is employment, unemployment, the money supply, interest rates, prices, the international value of the nation's currency, government tax revenues, government spending, consumer spending and saving, banks, profits, stock markets, and many other factors. Furthermore, each of these factors is related to the others in ways that are often subtle and complex. Such complexities often make understanding an issue difficult because they obscure the basic economic principles involved in the issue.

In order to better understand an economic issue, it is helpful to eliminate the many complexities associated with a modern economy, so that we can focus on the basic economic principles involved. As an example of eliminating complexities, suppose that a group of people has been stranded on a deserted island. With none of the complexities of a modern economy to distract us, our group must come to grips with the single most basic economic problem: the people in the group have *economic needs and wants*, but there are only certain *economic resources* available to this particular group. The group needs and wants things such as food, shelter, clothing, security, and so on. To produce these things, the group can use the three basic types of economic resources, or **inputs**—the skills of the people in the group, the equipment they have, and the natural resources of the island.

The Skills of People (Labour)

The largest and most important single economic resource of any society is the skills of its people, which economists refer to collectively as **labour**. Labour includes all the skills possessed by a wide range of people, from manual labourers and skilled workers to managers and research scientists. In our island mini-society, people

inputs

Economic resources, such as labour, capital equipment, and natural resources, that are used to produce goods and services.

labour

The largest single productive input available to any economy, labour includes all of the productive talents of the people of a society, mental as well as physical.

would have various useful and necessary skills such as hunting, fishing, farming, building, planning, and managing.

Capital Equipment

Another vitally important economic resource is society's stock of **capital equipment** (also simply called **capital**), by which we mean its factories, equipment, machinery, computers, tools, and so on. Capital equipment is crucially important because it increases *output per worker per hour*, or **productivity**. And when each worker produces more, the society can enjoy more economic prosperity, or a higher **standard of living**—more goods and services per person. Figure 1-1 illustrates the importance of capital equipment.

Figure 1-1
The Importance of Capital Equipment

Capital Equipment → Higher Output per Worker per Hour (productivity) → Higher Potential Standard of Living (goods per person)

While a modern industrial economy possesses a vast array of factories, machinery, equipment, and tools, our island mini-society will have only a few basic tools, such as spears, fishnets, and plows. So productivity will be low, and the people of the mini-society will have relatively few goods available to them. This scarcity of goods could interest the people in increasing their stock of capital equipment, in order to increase their productivity and their standard of living.

Natural Resources (Land)

The third economic resource available to a society is natural resources, which economists refer to as **land**. In our island mini-society, these natural resources would likely be few and simple—waterways, fish, land, trees, plants, and so on.

People tend to think of natural resources as depletable (and depleting), as is the case with oil. But some natural resources, such as forests and fish, can be renewable if managed effectively, and technology is capable of creating entirely new resources, such as nuclear power and wind power. In a similar way, improvements in technology have helped to make the Athabasca Tar Sands of Northern Alberta an economical energy resource.

The Task of an Economic System

The task of the economic system of any society is to organize and use these economic resources, or productive inputs, to produce goods and services (**output**) of the types and quantities that will best satisfy the needs and wants of the people of the society. This process is shown in Figure 1-2 on the next page.

In our island mini-society, the process shown in Figure 1-2 would be quite simple: people with different skills would use simple tools, such as spears, nets, and plows, to

---

capital (equipment)
The tools, equipment, machinery and factories used to increase production per worker.

productivity
Output per worker per hour; a measure of efficiency.

standard of living
A measure of the economic prosperity of the people of a society, usually expressed in terms of the volume of consumer goods and services consumed per household or per person per year.

land
Short form for all the natural resources available to a society's economy as economic inputs.

output
The goods and services produced by a society using its productive inputs.

"If you were asked to choose just one test of an economy's performance, one of the strongest candidates would be growth in productivity. In the long run, increases in productivity—that is, in output per worker— are the only way for a country to raise its living standards."
— THE ECONOMIST

Figure 1-2
The Basic Operation of Any Economic System

produce products to satisfy basic needs, such as food, shelter, and security. In a modern economy, this process is much more sophisticated, involving a wide range of skills and "high-tech" equipment and resources to produce a tremendous volume and variety of both goods and services. However, the basic task is the same in both economies: to try to use our economic resources to our best advantage.

The Basic Economic Problem of Scarcity

How to use our economic resources to our best advantage is a particularly important question because we do not have enough economic resources to produce everything that we would like to have. This is the basic economic problem of **scarcity**: the economic resources (inputs) on the left side of Figure 1-2 are in *limited* supply, while the amount of goods and services wanted by people on the right side of Figure 1-2 seems to be *unlimited*. Since we cannot have everything that we want, we are forced to *make choices,* some of which might be difficult.

The island mini-economy illustrates this reality particularly clearly, because the choices are so limited. Suppose we have ten people available for work and decide to use five of them for getting food, three for getting fuel, and two for taking care of security by maintaining fences and guarding against certain threatening creatures that roam the island. If we find that we don't have enough food, we can increase food production by 20 percent by *adding* a sixth person to the "food team." However, this addition would require *removing* that person from either the group getting fuel or the group providing security. While we would be better fed, we would have either less comfort or less security. And more of any one of these items means less of another, forcing us to make difficult choices. This forgoing of one thing in order to enjoy more of another is called **opportunity cost** by economists.

We constantly encounter opportunity costs in our lives. Creating your personal budget is an exercise in managing opportunity costs. Since your income can't buy everything that you would like, you have to *make choices* as to what you will have and what you will forgo. Taking that dream vacation would be wonderful, but it will mean that you cannot buy that car that you also really want.

On a broader level, an entire nation, through its government, must come to grips with the same problems. The public wants the best health care and education systems as well as other government services, but governments lack the tax revenues to provide the ideal levels of all services. Since using more tax resources for one service would leave less for other services, the public must accept that each service will not be provided at an ideal level.

scarcity
The problem that, while economic inputs (and thus potential output) are limited in availability, people's wants and needs are apparently unlimited.

opportunity cost
The concept that the real economic cost of producing something is the forgone opportunity to produce something else that could have been produced with the same inputs.

So the basic economic problem of scarcity is a universal one, affecting all societies. This problem is illustrated in more detail by something called a *production-possibilities curve*, discussed below.

YOU DECIDE

The Scarcity Problem on a Personal Level

On a personal level, the problem of scarcity manifests itself in the form of your income. If your take-home pay is $2000 per month, then you have only $2000 (at most) to spend on consumer goods and services each month. If you spend $200 more this month on new clothes, you will have $200 less to spend on, say, restaurant dinners. Just like on the deserted island, enjoying more of one thing means that you must accept less of something else.

Or must you accept less of something else if you enjoy more of one thing? Unlike the unfortunate people on the deserted island, you have a credit card! You can put the $200 for the new clothes on the credit card, and enjoy $2200 of consumer spending this month. Better yet, put the restaurant dinners on the credit card too, and then you can enjoy $2400 of consumer spending—an increase of 20 percent from your monthly take-home pay of $2000. ▪

QUESTIONS

1. Would you recommend this credit strategy to a good friend? Why?
2. If you would not recommend this credit strategy, how *would* you suggest that credit cards be used?

The Production-Possibilities Curve

One way of illustrating the problem of scarcity is with a **production-possibilities curve**. Suppose our islanders can only produce two items—vegetables and fish. If all their economic inputs were devoted to producing vegetables, they could produce 15 kilograms of vegetables daily, but no fish. This option is shown as combination **A** in Figure 1-3, which indicates vegetable production of 15 kg and fish production of 0 kg. If the islanders went to the opposite extreme and used all their productive inputs to produce fish, the result would be fish production of 5 kg and vegetable production of 0 kg, as shown by combination **F** in Figure 1-3 on page 8.

Of course, it is more likely that the islanders would choose to produce some combination of fish and vegetables, such as combination **B** (14 kg vegetables and 1 kg fish), **C** (12 kg and 2 kg), **D** (9 kg and 3 kg), or **E** (5 kg and 4 kg). In making their choice, however, they will be restricted by the limitations of the production-possibilities curve: since their economic resources are limited, *producing more of one product necessarily means being able to produce less of the other*. The islanders may *want* 4 kg of fish and 12 kg of vegetables (combination **X**), but they will not be able to *have* this combination. Resource scarcity dictates that if they want 4 kg of fish, they can only have 5 kg of vegetables, and if they are to have 12 kg of vegetables, fish production can only be 2 kg. So while it is possible to produce 4 kg of fish or 12 kg of vegetables per day, it is not possible to produce this much of both on the same day. The islanders choose among various combinations of products, and the production-possibilities curve reflects the limitations that resource scarcity imposes upon their choices.

production-possibilities curve
A curve that shows the economy's potential output, assuming that economic inputs are fully employed and efficiently utilized.

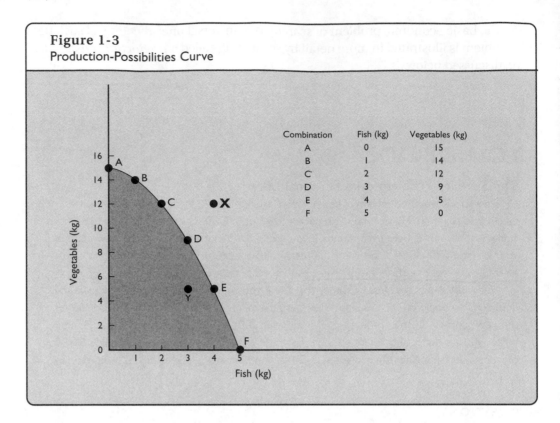

Figure 1-3
Production-Possibilities Curve

Combination	Fish (kg)	Vegetables (kg)
A	0	15
B	1	14
C	2	12
D	3	9
E	4	5
F	5	0

However, the combinations shown by the production-possibilities curve are based on two important assumptions—that the islanders use all of their available productive inputs, and that they utilize them as efficiently as possible. If some of their productive inputs were not used (if, for instance, some of the workers were sick, or one of their fish spears were broken), output would be below the potential level shown by the production-possibilities curve. Point **Y**, at which fish production is 3 kg and vegetable production is 5 kg, reflects such a situation. With fish production at 3 kg, vegetable production could be as high as 9 kg rather than 5 kg, and with vegetable production at 5 kg, fish production could be as high as 4 kg rather than 3 kg. However, if the islanders do not employ all of their productive inputs, their production will be below its potential. In fact, even if all inputs are employed, production may fall short of its potential. If the islanders' inputs (labour and capital equipment) were not producing fish and vegetables as efficiently as possible, production could be below its potential level and the islanders could still wind up at point **Y**.

It is important to recognize that the production-possibilities curve indicates the economy's *potential* output, assuming that economic inputs are fully employed and efficiently utilized. Production can be at any point *on* the production-possibilities curve (if inputs are fully and efficiently utilized) or *within* the shaded area (if they are not), but cannot be *outside* the curve.

However, the islanders need not live forever within the limitations imposed by the curve shown in Figure 1-3. This curve represents the situation at a particular point in time, given the economic resources available to the islanders at that time. If, in the future, they were to add to their economic resources, say, by building new capital equipment or developing new technologies, their potential output of *both* fish *and* vegetables could increase. Figure 1-4 shows the new production-possibilities curve that could be created by additions to or improvements in the islanders' economic resources.

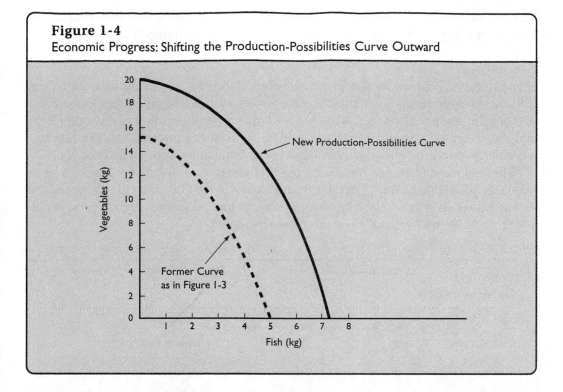

Figure 1-4
Economic Progress: Shifting the Production-Possibilities Curve Outward

The inquisitive reader may wonder why the production-possibilities curve is bowed outward as it is, rather than following a straight line. The shape of the curve reflects the changing efficiency of resources as they are shifted from one use to another. For instance, the table in Figure 1-3 shows that to increase fish production from 0 kg to 1 kg, we must sacrifice only 1 kg of vegetable production, which falls from 15 kg to 14 kg. But as we push fish production higher, we must forgo ever higher amounts of vegetable production to achieve the same increases in fish production. The second kilogram of fish costs 2 kg of vegetables, the third kilogram of fish requires the forgoing of 3 kg of vegetables, and so on.

To produce the first kilogram of fish, we would shift resources (labour and capital) out of their *least efficient use* in vegetable production (say, from the least productive land or using the least efficient capital equipment) into their most efficient use in fishing (say, using the best available equipment to fish the most productive waters). However, as we push fish production higher and higher, the trade-off between fish and vegetable production becomes less attractive. Increasingly, we have to shift labour and capital out of more efficient uses in vegetable production and into less efficient uses in fishing. The fifth kilogram of fish production is particularly costly in terms of vegetable production lost (5 kg of vegetables), as it requires that we shift labour and capital out of our last (and most efficient) use in vegetable production and into our least efficient use in fish production. As a result of these factors, the production-possibilities curve is not a straight line, which would reflect a constant trade-off between fish and vegetable production, but rather a curve which reflects changing efficiencies and trade-offs.

We have used a very simplified situation, involving a production-possibilities curve for only two products, to illustrate the basic nature of the problem of scarcity. While the real world is much more complex, involving many more inputs and outputs, the basic reality shown by our simple production-possibilities curve still exists. Because economic resources are limited, society must somehow make choices between various goods and services. Enjoying more of one thing means having less of something else—we must deal with trade-offs between the things that we want.

Opportunity Cost

These trade-offs shown by the production-possibilities curve bring us back to the concept of opportunity cost that we saw earlier in this chapter. The opportunity cost of using economic resources to produce any item is the amount of any other item that those same economic resources could have produced instead. The production-possibilities curve in Figure 1-3 provides a good visual illustration of this concept.

The opportunity cost of producing the first kilogram of fish is the loss of 1 kg of vegetable production, which declines from 15 kg to 14 kg. The opportunity cost of the second kilogram of fish is the 2 kg of vegetable production lost when their production falls from 14 kg to 12 kg, and so on, as shown in Table 1-1.

Table 1-1
Opportunity Cost

Combination	Fish Production (kg)	Vegetable Production (kg)	Opportunity Cost of
A	0	15	
B	1	14	The 1st kg of fish = 1 kg vegetables
C	2	12	The 2nd kg of fish = 2 kg vegetables
D	3	9	The 3rd kg of fish = 3 kg vegetables
E	4	5	The 4th kg of fish = 4 kg vegetables
F	5	0	The 5th kg of fish = 5 kg vegetables

We can express opportunity cost in terms of vegetable production forgone for *each additional kilogram* of fish, as shown in the table. Alternatively, we can calculate the opportunity cost of *any given amount* of fish production. For instance, the table shows that the opportunity cost of the third kilogram of fish production is 3 kg of vegetables, while the opportunity cost of 3 kg of fish production is 6 kg of vegetables, because if the entire 3 kg of fish had not been produced, vegetable production could have been 15 kg rather than 9 kg.

To calculate the opportunity cost of anything, ask yourself what could have been produced instead of it. For instance, the opportunity cost to society of $3 billion of military equipment is not the $3 billion, but rather the consumer and capital goods that could have been produced by the inputs used to produce the military equipment. And, to a student, the opportunity cost of riotous living on the weekend could be viewed as the 16 extra marks that he or she could have obtained on the economics test if the time had been spent studying.

In summary, scarcity is a basic economic problem that applies to all societies. In the following sections, let's consider some of the implications of the problem of scarcity.

Effectiveness and Efficiency

Because we cannot have everything that we would like, it is very important that we use our scarce economic resources wisely, by producing as much as we can of things that are needed and wanted. These goals are expressed by the terms *effectiveness* and *efficiency*, which are the two most basic measures of the performance of any economic operation, from an individual business to a nation's entire economy.

Effectiveness refers to achieving certain goals, in this case, producing goods and services that are *needed and wanted*. If an economic system can achieve these goals, it is "effective." **Efficiency** refers to using the economic resources available to you to produce a *high volume of output* at a *low production cost per unit*. One common measure of efficiency is *productivity*, or output per worker per hour.

To recap, it is important that an economy be *both* effective *and* efficient. The more efficiently and effectively a society uses its economic resources, the more successful it will be in making available to its people larger volumes of goods and services that are needed and wanted and at lower prices. As a result, its people will enjoy a higher standard of living.

effectiveness
A measure of how well an economy performs in terms of producing goods and services that are needed and wanted.

efficiency
A measure of how well an economy performs in terms of producing high volumes of goods and services at a low cost per item.

YOU DECIDE

Measuring Your School's Performance

Our examples of effectiveness and efficiency in this section have dealt with businesses selling goods and services to consumers. However, the tools of effectiveness and efficiency could also be used to assess the performance of your school.

QUESTIONS
1. How could you measure the effectiveness of your school?
2. How could you measure the efficiency of your school?
3. Explain three ways to increase the efficiency of your school.
4. How would these ways of increasing efficiency affect your school's effectiveness?

The Three Basic Questions of Economics

As we have seen, the task of any economic system is to use its scarce economic resources efficiently and effectively so as to best satisfy the needs and wants of its people. Since economic resources are scarce and we cannot have everything that we want, we are forced to make certain very basic choices:

- What goods and services should we produce?
- How should we produce these goods and services?
- How should we divide up our output of goods and services among ourselves?

These are the three most basic economic decisions that must be made by every society, regardless of its stage of development or its economic system.

What to Produce?

Because economic resources, or productive inputs, are scarce, no society can have all the goods and services it would like to have. Instead, it must make choices or set priorities. For example, the people in our island mini-society would have to decide whether to produce fish, vegetables, shelter, fuel, or equipment such as spears and plows to help them to be more productive.

What makes such choices difficult is that we have to decide not only what *will* be produced, but also what *will not* be produced. If we decide to use six people to farm vegetables, those six people will not be available to catch fish or build shelter. So a decision to produce *more* of one thing necessarily means accepting *less* of other things. This type of decision forces us to set priorities, or decide what is most important to us. Obviously, making decisions relates to the goal of *effectiveness*, as discussed in the previous section, because the priorities we set will reflect our needs and wants, or how much we value each product.

Consumer Goods or Capital Goods?

One of the most basic "what to produce" decisions that must be made is whether consumer goods or capital goods will be produced. Consumer goods (such as food and fuel) can be enjoyed in *the present*, but are used up quickly and do not contribute to longer-term economic prosperity. Capital goods (such as tools and equipment), on the other hand, cannot be consumed and enjoyed *today*, but they will increase our productive efficiency *in the future*. In this way, capital goods will contribute to our production and prosperity in the longer term, by increasing our productivity for the many years that they will last. Figure 1-5 illustrates this choice.

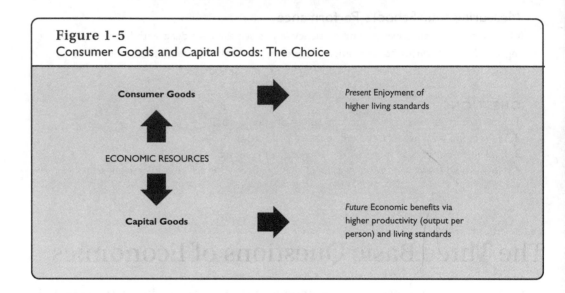

Figure 1-5
Consumer Goods and Capital Goods: The Choice

Consumer Goods → *Present* Enjoyment of higher living standards

ECONOMIC RESOURCES

Capital Goods → *Future* Economic benefits via higher productivity (output per person) and living standards

These decisions will have a crucial influence on the prosperity of a society both in the present and in the future. If our island mini-society emphasizes the production of consumer goods, its people will enjoy a higher standard of living in the present. However, if they emphasize consumer-goods production to the point of neglecting capital-goods production, they will enjoy less prosperity in the future. On the other hand, if its people are willing to do with fewer consumer goods in the present in order to build more capital goods, they can look forward to higher levels of economic prosperity in the future. In the second half of the twentieth century, the greatest economic progress was experienced by nations such as Japan and Germany, which stressed the production of capital goods. Currently, China is making capital goods a top national priority.

How to Produce It?

Once we have decided *what* we want to produce, we must decide *how* each product or service is to be produced. These decisions are a question of production methods: How should we combine our scarce inputs of labour, capital equipment, and natural resources to produce a product or service?

As a simple example, suppose our island mini-society has decided to produce (cultivate) vegetables. The next question is, How should it do this? Should the vegetables be cultivated by hand? Or should people use simple tools such as hoes? Or more sophisticated equipment such as plows? Before the vegetables that the group wants can be produced, the group will have to decide how to produce them.

Generally speaking, our goal will be to develop production methods that result in *higher efficiency* so as to increase our economic prosperity. However, the decision becomes more complicated if we need to use economic resources to build capital equipment in order to increase output per worker. If the amount of capital equipment we can build is limited, would it be better to build a plow for cultivating vegetables or a net for fishing? This decision would be easier to make if we could find a way to measure the *costs* of building the plow and the net (in terms of the hours needed to build each of them) against the *benefits* of each (in terms of the increased output each would bring).

Obviously, in deciding the answer to this question, we are pursuing the goal of *efficiency* as discussed earlier. By being efficient, we avoid wasting our scarce economic resources, and thus increase our economic prosperity.

Most running shoes are manufactured in Asia with low-wage labour, but New Balance also has plants in the United States that use computerized equipment.

Who Gets How Much? (Dividing the Economic Pie)

The last of our three basic questions is this: How will we divide up our output of goods and services among ourselves? Who will receive what share of the output that we have produced?

Should everyone receive an equal share? Or should some people receive more than others? If some are to receive a larger share, why should they get more, and how much more should they get?

We have seen that a society will prosper economically if the work of its people is *effective* and *efficient*. This consideration argues in favour of inequality, with a larger "piece of the pie" providing incentives for people to work more effectively and efficiently. If everyone knew that they were going to receive the same share as everyone else, why should anyone make an extra effort or contribution?

In addition to effectiveness and efficiency, however, there is the goal of *fairness*. How wide a gap between the rich and the poor are we prepared to accept? What if some people cannot produce enough to live decently without help from others? Should the most productive people give up some of what they have produced (earned) in order to help the less productive ones? And if our answer to this question is yes, how much should the better-off people give up in order to help the less fortunate (or less capable)?

This question of how to divide up the economic pie is certainly the most controversial of the three basic economic questions. In a modern economy such as Canada's, a person's share of the "economic pie" depends on his or her *income*. If an accountant's income (*after taxes*, a factor that we will consider in Chapter 12) is twice as large as a labourer's, the accountant's share of the economic pie will be twice that of the labourer.

But by what standards should we *decide* who gets higher incomes and a larger share of the pie? Should NHL hockey players receive a larger share than doctors? Should lawyers have a larger share than social workers? Should firefighters get a larger share than day-care workers? Somehow, every society has to work out the question of how to divide up the economic pie.

Answering the Three Questions

In this chapter we have considered the three basic questions of economics that every society must answer—what to produce, how to produce it, and how to divide it up. Different societies answer these questions in very different ways. In the next chapter we will begin to examine how Canada's economic system deals with these most basic questions.

Chapter Summary

1. Economics is the study of how societies make decisions concerning the production of goods and services and how these will be distributed among its members. The basic task of an economic system is to use its productive inputs (labour, capital equipment, and land) to produce goods and services so as to satisfy the wants and needs of the people of the society. (L.O. 1, 2)
2. This task involves the problem of *scarcity*: whereas society's economic resources are limited in quantity, people's wants and needs are apparently unlimited; thus, not all wants and needs can be satisfied. (L.O. 3)
3. The problem of scarcity and the related concept of opportunity cost can be illustrated with a production-possibilities curve. (L.O. 4, 5)
4. The opportunity cost of producing one good is the other goods that could have been produced with the same resources. (L.O. 5)
5. Scarcity makes it important that economic resources be used both effectively (so as to produce goods and services that are needed and wanted) and efficiently (with high productivity, or output per worker), in order to achieve a high standard of living. (L.O. 6)
6. The task of an economic system is to make the best possible use of its scarce economic resources by providing answers to the following three questions:
   (a) what to produce,
   (b) how to produce it, and
   (c) how to divide it among the people in order to best satisfy the needs and wants of the society. (L.O. 9)

Questions

1. "Every society, regardless of the economic system that it has, faces the problem of scarcity." This statement means that
   (a) all economies have depressions during which scarcities exist.
   (b) there are times when some products can be had only by paying high prices.
   (c) there are insufficient productive resources to satisfy all the wants of a society's people.
   (d) in the beginning, every society faces shortages, but a mature and prosperous economy such as Canada's overcomes scarcity over time.
   (e) None of the above.
   Explain your answer.

2. The economic problem facing any society would be less difficult if
   (a) governments provided more benefits for their citizens.
   (b) human wants were limited.
   (c) economic resources were more abundant.
   (d) technology advanced at a more rapid pace.
   (e) Answers (b), (c), and (d) are all correct.
   Explain your answer.

3. Suppose that in an island mini-economy there were four people working: two people catching a total of six fish per day and two others picking a total of 8 kg of fruit per day. If they decided that they wanted to have three more fish each day, what would be a reasonable estimate of the *opportunity cost* of that decision?

4. John works for 6 hours and picks 12 baskets of berries. Jane works for 4 hours and picks 12 baskets of berries. This means that
   (a) John's productivity and Jane's productivity are equal.
   (b) Jane's productivity is 33 percent higher than John's productivity.
   (c) Jane's productivity is 50 percent higher than John's productivity.
   (d) John takes more rest breaks than Jane.
   (e) None of the above.

5. The following table shows production possibilities for two items—chairs and tables.

Combination	Chairs	Tables
A	0	6
B	8	5
C	15	4
D	21	3
E	26	2
F	30	1
G	33	0

   (a) What is the opportunity cost of producing the first table?
   (b) What is the opportunity cost of producing the third table?
   (c) What is the opportunity cost of producing the sixth table?
   (d) Draw the production-possibilities curve for chairs and tables on a graph, placing tables on the vertical axis and chairs on the horizontal axis.
   (e) If the economy achieved greater efficiency in the production of tables, how would the production-possibilities curve change?
   (f) If a more efficient method of producing chairs were developed, how would the curve change?
   (g) Suppose more economic resources (labour, materials, and capital) became available. How would the curve change?

6. After months of debate over which of its programs should receive more funds, the government decides to spend $2 billion more on health care rather than education, and to allow colleges to increase tuition fees in order to obtain more revenues. Explain the opportunity cost of this decision, from the perspective of:
   (a) college students, and
   (b) society at large.

7. Explain how each of the following management decisions would be intended to affect the *effectiveness* and/or *efficiency* of a company.
   (a) A quality control program under which finished products are inspected more thoroughly in order to ensure that they meet quality standards.

(b) A profit sharing plan, under which a portion of the company's profits above a certain level will be shared with the employees.

(c) A restaurant reducing the number of servers it employs, so that each server has to serve 20 percent more tables than before.

8. In some of the situations in the previous question, a conflict could arise between effectiveness and efficiency; that is, a decision that increases efficiency would decrease effectiveness, or vice-versa. Which are these decisions, and why could such a conflict occur?

9. Visit the website of a newspaper or a news agency such as **www.msn.ca**, and look for news items concerning government policy or business decisions that involve the basic economic concept of opportunity cost. Write a brief explanation of the opportunity cost of the decision that you selected.

Study Guide

Review Questions (Answers to these Review Questions appear in Appendix B.)

1. According to the text, economics deals with
   (a) how to spend money more wisely.
   (b) decisions made by society concerning the production of goods and services.
   (c) decisions made by society concerning how goods and services are to be distributed among its people.
   (d) how a society satisfies the material needs and wants of its people.
   (e) Answers (b), (c), and (d) are all correct.

2. Which of the following are the three basic economic resources (inputs) identified in the text?
   (a) labour, entrepreneurship, money, and credit
   (b) labour, capital, and land (natural resources)
   (c) people, equipment, and money
   (d) labour, capital equipment, and money
   (e) None of the above.

3. The basic economic problem is
   (a) to achieve a more equal distribution of income in order to reduce poverty.
   (b) that economic resources are scarce while human wants are unlimited.
   (c) to establish prices that accurately reflect the relative scarcities of goods.
   (d) to establish a fair system of personal and business taxation.
   (e) to increase your exports so that they exceed your imports.

4. In a country such as Canada today,
   (a) *natural resources* are so plentiful that economists would not consider them to be "scarce."
   (b) *labour* is not scarce—there are over 25 million people of working age, and about one-third of them are not working.
   (c) *capital* is the only economic resource that could be considered to be "scarce."
   (d) all three of these economic resources would be described by economists as being "scarce."
   (e) None of the above.

5. Which is the best description of the opportunity cost of a $200 dinner?
   (a) It is not a serious consideration in the decision of whether to enjoy the dinner.
   (b) It is the nice clothes that could have been bought instead of the dinner.
   (c) It is $200.
   (d) It is only a problem if you don't have a credit card with you.
   (e) It is far too large!

6. The term *standard of living* refers to
   (a) the minimum income that a person or family needs in order to not be poor.
   (b) the average family income.
   (c) the economic prosperity of the people of a society.
   (d) the amount of goods and services consumed by an average family.
   (e) Both (c) and (d) are correct.

7. The most commonly used definition of *productivity* is
   (a) output per worker per hour.
   (b) the total output (gross domestic product) of a nation.
   (c) profit per unit of output.
   (d) the total number of worker-hours worked per year.
   (e) None of the above.

8. A factory employs 20 workers who work 8 hours per day and produce 800 boxes of candles per day. What is the productivity of workers in that factory?
   (a) 800 boxes of candles per day
   (b) 5 boxes of candles per worker per hour
   (c) 40 boxes of candles per worker per hour
   (d) 100 boxes of candles per hour
   (e) None of the above.
   Explain how you calculated your answer.

9. The "what" problem in economics means that
   (a) every society must in some way decide what goods it will produce (and not produce).
   (b) economists should tell us what goods should be produced.
   (c) goods and services should be produced as efficiently as possible.
       society should always produce only those goods that it can produce most efficiently with its technology and resources.
   (e) in every society, the government decides what goods will be produced.

10. In economics, the "how to produce" question refers to
    (a) the decision concerning how to go about marketing a product.
    (b) designing products so as to increase their appeal to consumers.
    (c) how much of each product to produce.
    (d) the decision concerning the production methods to be used to produce goods and services.
    (e) None of the above.

11. In economics, the question of "for whom" to produce goods and services means
    (a) how much should be exported and how much should be kept inside the country.
    (b) businesses must research the market for particular products before they produce and market them.
    (c) how should society divide up its total output of goods and services among the population.

    (d) poor people buy bicycles; rich people buy big cars.

    (e) the more society produces of one product, the less it can produce of other products.

12. A company's decision to introduce a new car that is designed in a manner that will appeal to higher-income women is an example of

    (a) a "what to produce" decision.

    (b) a "how to produce" decision.

    (c) a "for whom" decision.

    (d) a "why to produce" decision.

    (e) None of the above.

13. The following is a table showing the production possibilities for fish and vegetables.

Combination	kg of Fish	kg of Vegetables
A	0	20
B	1	18
C	2	14
D	3	8
E	4	0

What is the opportunity cost of producing

    (a) the first kilogram of fish?

    (b) the second kilogram of fish?

    (c) 2 kg of fish?

    (d) the third kilogram of fish?

    (e) 3 kg of fish?

    (f) the fourth kilogram of fish?

    (g) 4 kg of fish?

14. Imagine a production-possibilities curve for two products. If producers become less efficient at producing both products,

    (a) the production-possibilities curve will shift outward (up and to the right).

    (b) the slope of the production-possibilities curve will become steeper.

    (c) the slope of the production-possibilities curve will become less steep.

    (d) the production-possibilities curve will shift inward (down and to the left).

    (e) None of the above will happen.

15. Imagine a production-possibilities curve for two products. If producers become more efficient at producing only one of the products,

    (a) the production-possibilities curve will not be affected.

    (b) the slope of the production-possibilities curve will change, and become either steeper or less steep.

    (c) the entire production-possibilities curve will shift outward (up and to the right).

    (d) the entire production-possibilities curve will shift inward (down and to the left).

    (e) None of the above will happen.

Critical Thinking Questions (45)

(Asterisked questions 1 to 5 are answered in Appendix B; the answers to questions 6 to 10 are in the Instructor's Manual that accompanies this text.)

*1. Suppose that you had only $200 and your mother was expecting a Mother's Day gift (tickets to yet another Rolling Stones concert) that cost $200; however, your car has just broken down and it will cost $200 to repair it.

    (a) What would be the opportunity cost of buying your mother the gift?

    (b) What would be the opportunity cost of getting your car fixed?

*2. What is the opportunity cost of your attending school this year?

*3. Rajinder wins $1 000 000 in a lottery. Does this mean that Rajinder no longer has to be concerned about the economic problems of scarcity and opportunity cost?

*4. Explain how each of the following management decisions would be intended to affect the *effectiveness* and/or *efficiency* of a company.
   (a) A plan whereby the company's sales representatives provide feedback and suggestions to management based on their experience with customers.
   (b) The introduction of a piece rate incentive plan under which workers are paid $2 for each of the first 50 products they produce, and $3 for each product beyond 50.
   (c) The use of industrial robots that are programmed to perform production tasks repetitively and with great precision.

*5. Explain whether each of the following is mainly intended to improve either the effectiveness or efficiency of a college, and how it is intended to do so.
   (a) a Key Performance Indicator survey of college students asking for their views regarding the quality of the education and services they are receiving.
   (b) an increase in class sizes at a college.

6. How could having an internet website improve the effectiveness and the efficiency of a business firm's operations?

7. The question of how to divide the economic pie can be a difficult one.
   (a) In some societies, old people who are unable to work any longer are given *no* share of the economic pie and are left to die. What economic factors might explain such a custom?
   (b) How does the custom referred to in part (a) compare to Canada's attitudes toward those who are unable to support themselves? What might explain this difference?

8. Regarding the question of how to divide up the economic pie, it has been suggested that the highest paid people in industry and government should receive no more than two-and-a-half times as much take-home pay as the lowest-paid workers. Do you agree with this suggestion? Why? What do you believe would happen if such a policy were implemented?

9. The text notes that although some of the Earth's resources can become depleted, new resources can also be created.
   (a) How can new resources be "created"?
   (b) If you had to pick only *one* new resource that could be created this way, which one would you choose? Why?

10. A common criticism of government departments and agencies is that their operations are *inefficient.*
   (a) What might explain why government operations are often inefficient?
   (b) What is the opportunity cost of any such inefficiency?

Use the Web (Hints for this Use the Web exercise appear in Appendix B.)

1. Visit the website of a newspaper or a news agency such as **www.msn.ca**, and look for news items concerning government policy or business decisions that involve the basic economic concepts of effectiveness and efficiency. Write a brief explanation of how the decision that you selected affects effectiveness and efficiency.

www.msn.ca

2

Canada's Economic System

LEARNING OBJECTIVES

After studying this chapter, you should be able to

1. Explain how a market system economy provides answers to each of the three basic questions of economics.

2. Explain how profits and the profit motive contribute to the effective and efficient use of economic resources.

3. Explain how competition contributes to the effective and efficient use of economic resources.

4. Identify the major strengths of market system economies.

5. Identify three types of problems that tend to occur in market system economies.

6. Describe how a command system operates, and compare its performance regarding effectiveness and efficiency to the performance of a market system.

7. Explain why Canada's economic system is appropriately described as a mixed free-enterprise system.

8. Describe three major types of roles played by government in the Canadian economy.

To overcome the problem of scarcity that we saw in Chapter 1, a society must make the best possible use of its limited economic resources. It must address the three basic questions of what to produce (and not produce), how to produce it, and how to divide it up among the people of the society. To deal with these questions, a society has to use its economic resources (labour, capital equipment, and natural resources) *effectively* (produce things that are needed and wanted) and *efficiently* (produce them in high volume and at low cost and price), thereby generating economic prosperity for its people.

This goal is no small challenge. The Canadian economy—the ninth largest in the world—comprises over 32 million consumers with their own wants and needs, more than 2 million business establishments using a vast array of capital equipment and producing millions of different goods and services, and a labour force of more than 17 million people with a wide variety of skills. How, then, does the Canadian economy organize all these economic resources to produce over $1.3 trillion ($1 300 000 000 000) of goods and services, and in the process succeed in providing its people with one of the highest standards of living in the world? How does it make the billions of economic decisions required to achieve this success?

The Market System

Most of Canada's economic system is organized according to a market system. In the **market system** (also known as the *free-enterprise system*), privately owned businesses (*free enterprises*) produce goods and services for a profit, in response to the demand of buyers. Nearly 80 percent of the total output of the Canadian economy is produced by such businesses, which are collectively known as the *private sector*. In the private sector, the key economic decisions are made by consumers and businesses.

In addition to its private sector, the Canadian economy has a substantial *government sector*, in which the key decisions are made by governments. The government sector accounts for about 20 percent of the output of the economy, consisting mostly of public services such as health care, education, and public security. In addition, governments play a number of other important roles in the economy, which we will examine later.

First let's examine what a market is and how it operates. Then we can see how a market system functions.

market system
An economic system in which economic decisions are made mainly by consumers and privately owned producers, in a decentralized manner.

What Is a Market?

Simply stated, a *market* is where buyers and sellers come together to exchange goods and services for money, or to buy and sell things. Figure 2-1 on the next page illustrates this concept a little more formally, using the market for pizza as an example.

Figure 2-1 shows that the market for pizza consists of

(a) a number of sellers offering to sell pizzas, in competition with each other (economists call this the *supply side* of the market), and

(b) a number of buyers offering to buy pizzas, in competition with each other (economists call this the *demand side* of the market).

In Figure 2-1, the interaction between buyers and sellers in the marketplace determines that the price of one pizza is $15.00 and 100 000 pizzas are sold each week. But if the willingness of buyers to buy pizzas (demand) or the willingness of sellers to sell them (supply) were to change, the price and sales of pizza would also change.

Figure 2-1
The Market for Pizza

How Do Markets Work?

Markets respond to changes in buyers' demand. For instance, if the demand for pizza increased (because there were more buyers, or buyers had more money, or they just liked pizza more than before), the increased demand would cause the price of pizza to increase, say, from $15 to $18 per pizza. This higher price, together with higher sales, would make it more profitable to make pizzas. Existing producers would increase their output, and new producers might start up, so that pizza production might increase from 100 000 to 110 000 pizzas per week.

In the same way, if the demand for pizza were to decrease, then the price would fall, making it less profitable to make pizza. With lower prices and lower sales, producers would make fewer pizzas, in response to the lower demand of consumers.

The "classic" form of market is a farmers' market or a flea market, where many producers and consumers come directly together to buy and sell various products. However, markets take many other forms. To most people, the most familiar market is at the retail level, where consumers buy goods and services from retailers. In addition, there are wholesale markets and commodity markets (where the buyers are businesses that bid for the products in an auction environment), labour markets (where people's time and skills are purchased and the price paid is a wage rate or salary), capital markets (or markets for loans, where the use of someone else's money is purchased and the price paid is the interest rate), and stock markets (where the shares of corporations are bought and sold).

Some markets are conducted over the internet. For examples, visit www.trader.ca and www.expedia.ca.

Some markets, such as the market for babysitters, are extremely local in nature, while others, such as the market for wheat or oil, are worldwide in scope. In many markets buyers and sellers deal face to face, while in e-markets they deal over the internet without ever seeing each other. Regardless of its particular form, however, each market consists of a supply side and a demand side, as shown in Figure 2-1. In Chapters 4 to 6 we will examine the operation of markets in more detail.

Because demand is such a basic force in markets, the market system is sometimes said to be *demand-driven*. And because of the key role played by prices and price changes in adjusting production to demand, the market system is sometimes referred to as the *price system*.

How a Market System Type of Economy Is Organized

Figure 2-2 illustrates the operation of a market system. The upper flows in Figure 2-2 represent consumers buying goods and services from businesses. These flows

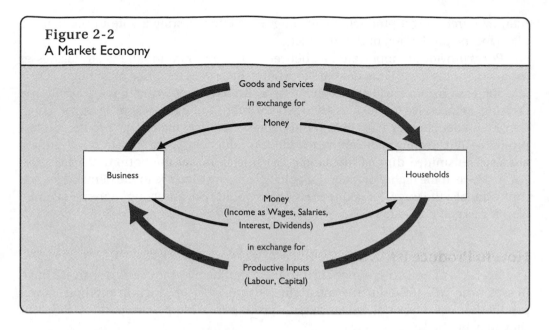

Figure 2-2
A Market Economy

Goods and Services
in exchange for
Money

Business

Households

Money
(Income as Wages, Salaries,
Interest, Dividends)

in exchange for

Productive Inputs
(Labour, Capital)

represent many thousands of markets for specific goods and services, in which millions of consumers buy these items at the prices and in the quantities determined in the marketplace.

In other words, the upper flows would consist of the market for hamburgers, the market for CDs, the market for apartments, the market for baseball tickets, the market for haircuts, and all the other markets for all of the other services that consumers buy. And in each of these markets, a *price* is determined for the good or service involved.

The lower flows in Figure 2-2 represent a different side of the economy, in which businesses buy the inputs for producing the goods and services shown in the top flows.

So the lower flows would include markets for factory workers, for retail clerks, for accountants, for professional athletes, and for all of the other job skills that the economy needs. And in each of these markets, a *price*—in the form of a wage rate or salary level for that type of skill—is established. Also, the lower flows would include markets for the capital needed by businesses; for instance, funds being loaned by people to businesses, for a *price*, or an interest rate.

The operation of a market system such as that shown in Figure 2-2 involves billions of individual decisions by consumers, business firms, and workers about consumer purchases, production levels, prices, the numbers of workers to be employed, wage rates, capital investment, and so on. It is through these innumerable decisions, made in countless markets, that the answers are developed to the three basic questions of what to produce, how to produce it, and how to divide it up.

How the Market System Answers the Three Questions

What to Produce?

Consumers play the largest role in deciding what will be produced. Since the basic goal of business is to earn a profit, businesses will produce those goods and services that are in demand. This process is described by the phrases "consumer sovereignty" (meaning that the consumer is "king of the marketplace") and "dollar votes" (meaning that, by purchasing a product, a consumer is in effect casting a vote in the market-place for the production of that product).

Prices provide an important link between what buyers want and what businesses produce. For instance, if the demand for golfing increases, the price of golfing will rise. The increase in price will make operating golf courses potentially more profitable, creating an incentive for businesses to provide more golfing. In a similar way, a reduction in the demand for red meat would depress its price, making its production less profitable and creating an incentive to reduce production. "Price signals" such as these are also transmitted through the labour markets shown at the bottom of Figure 2-2. For instance, if the higher demand for golfing led to an increase in the demand for golf professionals, the wages of golf professionals would rise, attracting more people into working as golf professionals.

How to Produce It?

The decision of how to produce the product is made by producers, or private businesses, who will strive for the most efficient possible production method. Lower production costs not only mean higher profits; in a highly competitive industry, they may be the key to survival.

Prices also help to determine the methods for producing goods and services. In determining the most efficient production methods, it makes obvious economic sense to minimize the use of the most scarce inputs. Prices help to minimize using scarce inputs because the more scarce an input is, the more costly it will be for producers to buy. For instance, if gasoline is scarce, its price will be high. Since it is such a costly input, producers will minimize waste of it, and will use substitutes, if possible. So to maximize their profits, businesses have to manage society's scarce economic resources carefully, economizing the most on the use of the most scarce resources.

How to Divide up the Economic Pie?

As we saw in Chapter 1, a person's share of the economic pie depends on his or her income. For instance, if electricians take home (after taxes) five times as much pay as day-care workers, an electrician's share of the economic pie will be five times as large as that of a day-care worker.

And since your income is really the price of your productive skills, *prices* play a major role in deciding the question of how to divide up the economic pie. Like other prices, people's incomes (or salaries or wages) are mostly determined by the interplay of supply and demand—in this case, the supply of and the demand for your productive skills. For example, if skilled trades workers are in short supply but in great demand, their incomes (and their share of the economic pie) will be quite high. On the other hand, if there is a large supply of low-skilled workers relative to the demand for them, they will have low incomes and a small share of the economic pie.

How Does the Market System Organize the Use of Economic Resources?

As we have seen, organizing the vast and varied economic resources of an economy such as Canada's to produce millions of goods and services effectively and efficiently is an enormous task. On the face of it, the market system might appear to be ill-suited to such a complex task. The market system has no central plan, and seems to lack any organizing or coordinating forces—rather, it looks more like an economic "free-for-all" in which people buy whatever they want to, produce whatever they want to, and work wherever they want to. Millions of consumers and producers make economic decisions, which are decentralized and apparently uncoordinated, rather than organized according to a centralized plan. Nevertheless, the market system has in practice proven to be the best system for achieving both effectiveness and efficiency in the use of economic resources and in providing a high standard of living for its people.

Then what are the forces within the market system that enable it to mobilize economic resources so effectively and efficiently? The two key features of the market system that promote effectiveness and efficiency are the *profit motive* and *competition.*

The Profit Motive

Profits are those funds from a business's sales revenues that are left after all expenses and taxes have been paid. Profits are therefore available for reinvestment in the business or to be paid out as dividends to the shareholders who own the business.

The *profit motive* plays two vital roles in the operation of a market system. First, profits provide incentives for businesses to use economic resources both effectively and efficiently. By producing goods and services that consumers will buy—that is, by using economic resources *effectively*—a business will increase its sales and profits. And by producing those goods and services at the lowest possible production cost—that is, by using economic resources *efficiently*—a business will also increase its profits.

The second important role of profits is that they provide funds for the *purchase of capital equipment.* Each business purchases capital equipment to improve its own efficiency and profitability. But when many businesses do this, the result is improved productivity across the economy, which is the basic source of higher living standards for society generally. So the reinvestment of profits by businesses makes an important contribution to a society's economic prosperity.

In addition, many Canadians have a large stake in the profitability of corporations. Nearly half of adult Canadians own shares of corporations, many in registered retirement savings plans. In addition, about three dollars of every eight in *pension funds* in Canada are invested in corporate shares, so many people who do not think of themselves as shareholders have a stake in the success of Canadian corporations. In fact, millions of Canadians have billions of dollars invested in shares. These people not only receive part of corporate profits as dividends but also depend on the prosperity of those corporations for financial security in their retirement.

Despite the financial importance of profits, there is a great deal of misunderstanding and even hostility among the public concerning profits. The very word *profit* evokes for many people images of exploitation of workers and consumers, or *profiteering.* One misconception concerns the *level* of profits. Many people believe that manufacturers' profits amount to 30 cents or 40 cents per dollar of sales, whereas before-tax profits are actually about 7 cents to 10 cents per dollar of sales, and after taxes, most manufacturers' profits amount to only 4 cents or 5 cents per dollar of sales. Ironically, the public believes 20 cents per dollar of sales to be a "fair" profit, indicating that there is a great deal of confusion regarding this matter.

The public also has misconceptions concerning the *uses* of profits, which are widely regarded as being hoarded away in corporate coffers or being paid out in lavish dividends to vulgarly wealthy shareholders. In fact, about 30 percent of corporation profits goes to taxes, and most of the remainder is reinvested by businesses in capital equipment. Dividends to shareholders generally amount to a modest return on their

---

profits
Those funds left from a business's sales revenues after all expenses have been paid; such funds are therefore available (after taxes have been paid) for dividends to shareholders and reinvestment in the business.

Different Views of Profits
Suppose a corporation has annual sales of $600 million, profits after taxes of $24 million, 4000 employees, and $600 million of shareholders' capital invested in the company.

The *employees* might feel that they are underpaid. If the $24 million of profits were divided among them, each would receive $6000 more ($24 million ÷ 4000).

Consumers might feel that $24 million in profits shows that they are being overcharged by this company. Realistically though, the total elimination of the manufacturer's profits would only reduce prices by 4 percent ($24 million ÷ $600 million).

From the viewpoint of the *shareholders* of the company, their capital is earning a rate of return (after tax) of only 4 percent ($24 million ÷ $600 million). Compared to other investments, this is not a very attractive rate of return.

So while employees and consumers complain about its high profits, investors might be thinking of selling their shares in the company.

investment, and these "capitalist" shareholders include not only the wealthy but also ordinary Canadians. Because of the public's misconceptions about profits and the negative emotional overtones attached to the word, many companies prefer to call their profits *earnings*.

Competition

Competition, which is the other key element in a market system, plays three vitally important roles in a market economy. First, competition forces businesses to provide consumers with what they want in order to increase their sales and profits. In this sense, competition *promotes effectiveness* in the use of economic resources. Second, competition *promotes efficiency* in the use of economic resources. To prosper in a competitive marketplace, a producer must be as efficient as possible. And third, competition forces producers to *keep prices as low as possible*, in order to compete successfully for business. So, competition ensures that the advantages of higher efficiency/lower production costs are passed along to the consumer, allowing the maximum possible number of people to enjoy them.

Competition is closely linked with *information* in the effective functioning of markets. A free marketplace provides a wide variety of goods and services, of various qualities and at different prices. If consumers are well-informed about what items are available and at what prices, they will be better able to take advantage of the opportunities offered by a free and competitive marketplace. By contrast, poorly informed consumers will be more likely to get poor value for their money.

In summary, a highly competitive marketplace pushes private profit-making producers to serve the interests of consumers by being effective and efficient and by keeping prices down. By contrast, in situations in which there is little or no competition, producers tend to be less responsive to consumers' preferences (less effective), to be less efficient than they could be, and to charge consumers excessive prices.

Together, the two incentives of profits and competition tend to push producers to use economic resources both effectively and efficiently. The ability of the market system to coordinate the decisions of millions of businesses and individuals automatically in response to changes in consumer demand has been referred to as "the miracle of the market." As long ago as 1776, in *The Wealth of Nations*, Adam Smith, the earliest advocate of this economic system, described business people as being led by an "invisible hand" (the profit motive) "to promote (the interest of) the society more effectually than when they really intend to promote it."

Figure 2-3 summarizes the market system's powerful incentives for efficiency and effectiveness, which contribute greatly to productivity and prosperity.

> For an indication of the role of information in markets, visit www.trader.ca and "shop" for a used car.

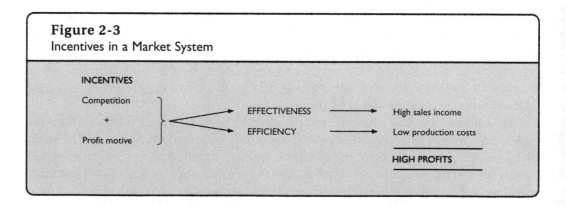

Figure 2-3
Incentives in a Market System

Figure 2-3 also shows how the basic concepts of effectiveness and efficiency relate to the income statement and the profits of a business. A business that is *effective* in the sense of producing what buyers want will enjoy a *high sales income*. If that business is also *efficient*, it will have *low production costs* and other expenses. The more effective and efficient a business is, the higher its profits will be.

Assessment of the Market System

We have seen that about four-fifths of the Canadian economy—the private sector—is organized as a market system. How well does this sector of the economy perform?

According to the criteria of *effectiveness* and *efficiency*, the market system performs very well. With respect to effectiveness, there is no economic system that is more responsive to consumer demand than the market system, which is marvellously flexible in adjusting its production automatically in response to changes in consumer preferences. And with respect to efficiency, no system provides greater incentives for efficient use of economic resources than the combination of the profit motive and competition.

However, the market system also has certain weaknesses. A basic problem is that the market will tend to produce too little of key *public services* such as health care and education. For instance, if college costs $4000 per year, only 100 000 people will attend college, because they consider the high cost of attending college to be justified by the *benefits to them*. However, having more college graduates is of significant *benefit to society*, in the form of more productive and educated citizens. So society would benefit if *more* people attended college, making it logical for the government to *intervene in the market* and reduce the cost of college education, which would encourage more people to attend college. The most common way for government to do this is to operate colleges itself, and finance them partly with grants. Reducing the cost of public services also increases the access of citizens to higher education and health care, which many view as an important social policy.

Another problem that can develop in a market system is **market power**, or monopoly-like power in some markets. Sometimes, producers may be able to band together and agree to limit competition among themselves, resulting in higher prices and profits. In the same way, some workers may be able to band together into labour unions that achieve essentially the same result—less competition and higher prices (wages) for their members. In both cases, an organized group (of businesses or workers) reduces competition in the marketplace for its own benefit, at the expense of others.

And while free markets for labour provide strong incentives for people to acquire skills that are in demand and to work efficiently, it is also true that in a market system there is a tendency for great *inequality in incomes*, as some people enjoy very high incomes, while others live in poverty.

While the profit motive provides strong incentives to be effective and efficient, it also provides incentives to do some things that are less beneficial to society. These things include unfair competitive practices, misleading of consumers, unfair treatment of vulnerable employees, and pollution of the environment.

On a larger macroeconomic scale, another fundamental problem with the market system is *economic insecurity*. Market economies sometimes slump into a **recession**, during which the economy's output falls and unemployment rises. During a typical recession in Canada, the number of unemployed people rises by more than half a million.

market power
The ability to raise one's prices; usually associated with a dominant or monopolistic position in the market.

In 2003, the top 20 percent of Canadian families earned an average income of $150 700 in the marketplace, while the bottom 20 percent of families earned only $8600 on average.

recession
A period during which the economy's output is falling and unemployment is high.

The Command System

command system
An economic system in which economic decisions are made mainly by the government, in a centralized manner.

The major alternative to the market system is known as the **command system**. In a market system, we have seen that the key economic decisions are made by millions of consumers and businesses in a very *decentralized* manner. However, in a command system, all major economic decisions are made in a *centralized* manner, by the government. Government economic planners draw up a central economic plan that maps out all major economic activity for the nation. The economic planners decide what products will be produced and give detailed instructions to plant managers, telling them what to produce. Since the government owns all major production facilities, the planners also choose the production technology and methods. And since the government is the only employer, the planners also can decide the incomes of various groups, and thus how the economic pie is divided. The most famous example of a command system was, of course, the economy of the former Soviet Union.

The command system seems simple in principle, and organizing all of society's economic resources according to a central economic plan sounds attractive. But this system ultimately proved to be a failure. By the time of the collapse of the Soviet Union in the late 1980s, its command system was failing miserably to produce goods and services efficiently and effectively, and the standard of living of the people had been falling for some time. Since then, the countries of the former communist bloc have mostly abandoned their command systems in favour of the market system approach.

Probably the most serious shortcoming of the command system was its lack of incentives. Without competition and the profit motive, producers tended to be both ineffective and inefficient in their use of economic resources. As a result, shortages of many goods were common, and most of the goods that were available were of low quality and of limited usefulness.

Ultimately, the command system proved incapable of organizing and coordinating through a central planning process the millions and millions of decisions needed to run a complex modern economy. The central planning process was simply unable to deal with the gigantic task of organizing the resources of such a vast economy. As one Soviet economic planner said as the system was collapsing, "The latest index of products has 20 million articles. The plan can't detail that amount."

The Ubiquitous Nature of the Market System

A strong argument can be made that markets are a natural aspect of human behaviour. People have different abilities, needs, and wants, so it is only natural for them to exchange (buy and sell) what they produce. For instance, when the former Soviet Union's command system failed to produce the goods wanted by consumers, an illegal but very active black market for many such goods developed. Some of these were smuggled into the Soviet Union from Western nations—for instance, a Sony Walkman would sell for over US$600 on the street in Moscow. Other goods were produced illegally by Russians themselves in secret plants and sold to consumers through the underground economy. In both cases, the unfulfilled demand of Soviet consumers created a market opportunity for enterprising (and risk-taking!) Soviet "entrepreneurs."

"Unofficial" markets also developed in the industrial sector of the Soviet economy. Often, the central planning system would fail to deliver the materials needed by plant managers for their operations—sometimes managers would get too little or none at all, while at other times they would receive more materials than they needed. In order to meet their production quotas, plant managers set up a "parallel market," through which managers would trade surplus materials with each other, receiving in return materials that were needed or credits for future materials when these became available.

The Market System in Perspective

Perhaps the most outstanding feature of the market system is the high degree of *economic freedom* for both consumers and businesses. This freedom underlies the key strengths of the market system, such as the ways in which its incentives of the profit motive and competition drive producers to be both efficient and effective managers of economic resources. The result is that market economies tend to be the best at generating high levels of productivity and a high standard of living.

Ironically, this freedom also underlies the most serious weaknesses of the market system. If producers are free to dominate industries and markets, the problem of market power (or monopoly power) will tend to arise in some situations. Because individuals and groups are free to earn (take?) as big a share of the pie as they can get, some can wind up with a very large share of the pie, while others get only crumbs. And because consumers and businesses are free to spend—and not spend—as they see fit, there are times when spending is inadequate and the economy slides into recessions and high unemployment. These weaknesses of the market system have led governments to take corrective action in various ways, as we will see when we look at Canada's mixed economic system.

The Mixed Economic System of Canada

Canada's economic system can best be described as a *mixed free-enterprise system* because, while this type of system is basically a market system, it also includes a large government sector and a great deal of government involvement in its private sector.

The Private Sector

As we have seen, nearly 80 percent of the total annual output of the Canadian economy is produced by the private sector. In this sector, in which the vast majority of Canadians are employed, businesses produce goods and services in response to market demand and for a profit. In the private sector of the economy, households (or consumers) and businesses make the key economic decisions.

The Government Sector

In the government sector, the key economic decisions are made by governments. The government sector accounts for more than 20 percent of the annual output of the economy, most of which consists of public services such as health care and education. In broad terms, governments play three major roles in the economy.

First, governments are major *providers of public services*. From health care, education, and law enforcement, to traffic control, public transit, and postal service, Canadian governments provide the public with a wide range of services in various ways. In most cases, such as health care, police protection, and elementary and secondary education, the public pays for these services with its tax revenues. In effect, then, the government is buying these services collectively on the public's behalf from the government's own employees (such as teachers) and from others (such as doctors) who provide the services. In some cases, governments *operate enterprises* that provide services, including Crown corporations (such as Canada Post and the Canadian Broadcasting Corporation) and public commissions that provide services (such as public transit and hydroelectricity). In many cases, such as public transit and post-secondary education, governments *subsidize public services*. **Subsidies** use tax revenues to pay part of the cost of the service, making the cost to the user lower. The grand total of these government-provided services is impressive—when the services of all government employees are counted as government purchases, Canadian governments account for about 22 percent of all the goods and services produced by the economy. In 2005, this portion amounted to over $297 billion, or over $9200 for every Canadian man, woman, and child.

subsidies
Payments by the government of part of the cost of a service in order to reduce the cost to the user of the service.

YOU DECIDE

To Subsidize or Not to Subsidize?

As noted in this chapter, a market system will tend to produce less than the ideal amount of public services such as education and health care. To correct for this shortcoming, the government can *subsidize* such services, by giving taxpayers' funds to providers of the services. This government assistance permits these organizations to provide more of these services and to reduce their prices, which encourages citizens to make greater use of these services. ■

QUESTIONS

1. What is the opportunity cost of subsidizing public services?
2. If the government had only enough funds to subsidize two of the following services, which ones would you choose to subsidize? Explain the reasons for your answers.
   (a) public transit in a major city
   (b) a city's symphony orchestra
   (c) government campsites at provincial parks
   (d) college programs in business and technology

Second, governments *regulate* in many ways the operations and practices of businesses. For example, government laws or agencies set standards for many products, regulate advertising practices, set employment standards (such as minimum wage rates and safety standards), set rules for the conduct of employer–employee/union relations, regulate the competitive practices of businesses (including the prohibition of monopolistic practices), and set environmental protection standards. In the case of some farm products, government marketing boards regulate the amount that farmers can produce. In addition, many prices are regulated by government, including electrical rates, tobacco and alcohol prices, some transportation rates, and apartment rents in some areas.

The third major area of government involvement in the economy is the *redistribution of income* through programs that transfer income from people with higher incomes to those with lower incomes. These programs include transfer payments such as employment insurance, welfare, old age security allowances, and assistance to farmers and other groups. In addition, various features of the income-tax system (tax credits) reduce the taxes payable by those with lower incomes, or entitle them to tax refunds, such as the GST credits received by many students.

Taken together, these government programs amount to a great deal of government involvement in the Canadian economy. In 2005 the grand total of spending by Canadian governments (on goods and services, transfer payments to persons, and interest on government debt) amounted to 36 percent of Canada's **gross domestic product (GDP)**, which measures the total of goods and services produced and incomes earned in Canada in any one year. When the many government regulations of economic activity as described earlier are added, the Canadian economy is accurately called a "mixed" system—still mostly "market" in nature, but with a large amount of government involvement.

In 2003, government programs increased the average income of the poorest 20 percent of Canadian families from $8600 to $21 500.

gross domestic product (GDP)
A measure of the total value of goods and services produced and incomes earned in a country in one year.

A Preview of Microeconomics

In Chapter 3, we will take a closer look at parts of the Canadian economy, particularly the various forms of business organization, as well as the "small business" and "big business" sectors of the economy. In Chapters 4 through 6, we will cover the basics of demand and supply, and examine how prices are determined in markets. In the ensuing chapters, we will see how demand and supply interact to determine prices and incomes in a wide variety of markets under a wide range of conditions. In Chapters 7 and 8, we will examine how the prices of goods and services are determined in various types of industries, ranging from highly competitive industries that have a large number of small firms to industries with only a few firms, to monopolies. In Chapter 9, we will consider government policy regarding these various types of industries. In Chapters 10 and 11, we will consider markets for labour and trends in the distribution of income and employment, and in Chapter 12 we will examine the role of government in the economy in more detail. This will complete our microeconomic study of the four major sectors of the economy—consumers, business, labour, and government. Chapters 13 and 14 deal with specific industries or economic issues, and Chapter 15 provides a brief look into the future.

Chapter Summary

1. A market system type of economy (also called the price system and the free enterprise system) operates through markets. In these markets, what to produce is decided by consumer demand, how to produce it is decided by producers, and the division of the economic pie is decided by people's incomes. (L.O. 1)

2. Profits play a vital role in the operation of a market system. Profits provide incentives for the efficient and effective use of economic resources and are a major source of funds for capital investment, which contributes to economic prosperity by increasing output per worker. (L.O. 2)

3. Competition is essential to the effective operation of a market economy. Competition keeps prices and profits down and forces producers to be both efficient and responsive to consumers. (L.O. 3)

4. The main strength of the market system is its high living standards, which are the result of the strong incentives this system provides for efficient and effective use of resources. (L.O. 2, 3, 4)

5. The main weaknesses of the market system are its tendency toward periodic recessions, a lack of competition in some markets, and a tendency for incomes to be distributed very unevenly. (L.O. 5)

6. In a command system, the government decides the answers to the three basic questions of economics. Command systems tend to be less effective and efficient than market systems, due to their lack of incentives. (L.O. 6)

7. Canada's economic system is called a *mixed* or *mixed free enterprise* system: while it is basically a market or free-enterprise system, it includes significant elements of government involvement in the economy. (L.O. 7)

8. Major aspects of government involvement in the Canadian economy are the provision of various public services, the regulation of economic activity, and the redistribution of income from those with higher incomes to those with lower incomes. (L.O. 8)

Questions

1. In a *market* type of economic system, the questions of *what to produce, how to produce it*, and *how to divide up the economic pie* are basically decided by
   (a) the people, working consciously for the social good rather than for their own self-interest.
   (b) social custom and tradition.
   (c) the free decisions of households and businesses, made out of self-interest.
   (d) the government.
   (e) economists.

   Explain the reason for your answer.

2. The market type of economic system would correct a shortage of lumber by
   (a) lowering the price of lumber and the profits of the lumber producers who are causing the shortage.
   (b) the government paying a subsidy to lumber producers to encourage them to increase their production of lumber.
   (c) the government instructing producers to increase their production of lumber.
   (d) increasing the price of lumber and the profits of producers of lumber.
   (e) the government establishing a government-owned lumber company.

   Explain your answer.

3. Everyone knows that child care is far more important than hockey, yet hockey players are paid far more than daycare workers. Why is this so?
   (a) Hockey players are really entertainers rather than producers of a service.
   (b) There are fewer professional hockey players than daycare workers.
   (c) Hockey players are more skilled than persons who get less pay.
   (d) The demand for hockey players is greater than for daycare workers.
   (e) Compared to the demand for them, good hockey players are more scarce than daycare workers.

   Explain your answer.

4. Write a paragraph that evaluates the accuracy of the following statement.
   "Profits serve no useful purpose and contribute nothing to society economically. All that profits do is make prices much higher and take vast amounts of money from consumers and give it to businesses and their wealthy shareholders."

5. The sixteenth-century philosopher Michel de Montaigne asserted that, "No man can profit except by the loss of others, and by this reasoning all manner of profit must be condemned." Do you agree with his position? Does every economic transaction necessarily involve a winner and a loser?

6. Explain how a development in communications technology such as the internet could improve the way in which some markets function.

7. Canada has a mixed economic system, in which both the marketplace and government play a role. For each of the following situations, explain why you think that it would be best dealt with by the market, or by government action.
   (a) There are too many restaurants in a town, and several are losing money.
   (b) The gap between the rich and the poor is very wide, and the poorest citizens are unable to afford even the bare necessities of life.
   (c) The largest supermarket chain in the country is planning to buy the second-largest chain, which would give it a near-monopoly in many communities.
   (d) A trend toward healthier eating has driven the price of chicken up so sharply that many consumers are complaining to the government about the increased prices.
   (e) Several manufacturers are cutting costs by dumping waste into a local river.

8. The internet has brought markets into your home as never before. Visit **www.trader.ca** and look for the best price that you can find on a used 2004 Honda Accord V6. Before the internet, how did people shop for a used car? How has the internet changed the effectiveness and the efficiency of the market for used cars?

Study Guide

Review Questions (Answers to these Review Questions appear in Appendix B.)

1. A *market system* type of economy is one in which
   (a) most economic decisions are made by consumers and privately owned businesses.
   (b) most economic decisions are made in a decentralized manner.
   (c) the dominant influence on economic decisions is the government.
   (d) private and government decision-makers have an equal influence on economic decisions.
   (e) Both (a) and (b) are correct.

2. The "what to produce" problem in economics means that
   (a) the government decides what goods will be produced.
   (b) if we produce more of one good, we must accept less of something else.
   (c) goods and services should be produced as efficiently as possible.
   (d) we should produce only those goods that we can produce most efficiently with our technology and resources.
   (e) every society must somehow decide what goods it will (and will not) produce.

3. In a market system type of economy, which of the following best describes how the question of *what to produce* is decided?
   (a) The most important factor is the government, which through its own purchases and the regulations it places on businesses, is the dominant influence concerning what is produced.

(b) Privately owned businesses (producers) make the decisions as to what to produce, in the final analysis.

(c) The most important factor is consumer demand, which influences prices and profits, and thus incentives for businesses to increase or reduce production.

(d) This decision is made by the people, because everybody works consciously for the social good rather than for his or her own self-interest.

(e) None of the above.

4. *Consumer sovereignty* means that
   (a) consumers do not have legal liability for their misuse of products.
   (b) the question of how products are produced is decided mainly by consumers.
   (c) the question of "what to produce" is decided mainly by consumers.
   (d) the customer is always right.
   (e) None of the above.

5. A market system type of economy would correct a surplus (oversupply) of running shoes by
   (a) raising the price of running shoes and the profits of manufacturers of running shoes.
   (b) government instructing running shoe manufacturers to reduce their production of running shoes.
   (c) reducing taxes on running shoes, to encourage people to purchase them.
   (d) lowering the price of running shoes and the profits of their manufacturers.
   (e) None of the above.

6. In economics, the "how to produce" question refers to
   (a) how to design products so as to increase their appeal to consumers.
   (b) decisions concerning how to go about marketing a product.
   (c) decisions concerning the production methods to be used to produce goods and services.
   (d) how much of each product to produce.
   (e) None of the above.

7. In a market system type of economy, which of the following best describes how the question of *how to produce* goods and services is decided?
   (a) Those productive inputs that are particularly scarce will be used more efficiently, because they will cost producers more.
   (b) The actual decisions regarding the production methods to be used are made by producers (businesses).
   (c) The consumer decides this question, through the demand for goods and services.
   (d) The major factor influencing this decision is the government.
   (e) Both (a) and (b) are correct.

8. In economics, the question of "for whom" to produce goods and services means
   (a) businesses must research the market for particular products before they produce and market them.
   (b) how much should be exported and how much should be kept inside Canada.
   (c) how society should divide up its total output of goods and services among the population.
   (d) poor people buy bicycles; rich people buy big cars.
   (e) the more society produces of one product, the less it can produce of other products.

9. In a market system type of economy, the question of *how to divide up the economic pie* is basically decided by
    (a) the social status of individuals and groups.
    (b) the marketing departments of businesses.
    (c) how much income is received by individuals and groups.
    (d) the government.
    (e) economists.

10. In a market system type of economy, *prices* play an important role in determining
    (a) what will be produced.
    (b) the production methods to be used.
    (c) how the "economic pie" will be divided.
    (d) Both (a) and (b).
    (e) (a) and (b) and (c).

11. State whether each of the following assertions regarding business profits is *true* or *false*.
    (a) T or F
        They provide strong incentives for businesses to produce what consumers want.
    (b) T or F
        They provide strong incentives for businesses to produce goods and services as efficiently as possible.
    (c) T or F
        Most profits are paid out as dividends to shareholders.
    (d) T or F
        They are an important source of funds for capital investment, which increases productivity and our standard of living.
    (e) T or F
        They are considerably larger than many people believe them to be.

12. State whether each of the following assertions regarding competition in a market economy is *true* or *false*.
    (a) T or F
        It results in higher profits for businesses.
    (b) T or F
        It promotes the efficient use of economic resources.
    (c) T or F
        It promotes the effective use of economic resources.
    (d) T or F
        It is not considered to be an important element in the operation of a market economy.
    (e) T or F
        It keeps down the prices paid by consumers.

13. State whether each of the following assertions regarding the market system type of economy is *true* or *false*.
    (a) T or F
        It makes effective use of economic resources for meeting the wants of consumers.
    (b) T or F
        It provides strong work incentives for businesses and for people.
    (c) T or F
        It makes efficient use of economic resources (or productive inputs).

(d) T or F

It grows steadily, and is not prone to economic fluctuations and crises, such as recessions or depressions.

(e) T or F

It tends to generate a high material standard of living.

14. Which *one* of the following criticisms of the market type of economic system is *inaccurate*?

(a) It tends to result in a very unequal distribution of income, with a few very rich people and many living in poverty.

(b) It suffers from economic instability—periods of recession and inflation.

(c) It fails to produce goods and services efficiently.

(d) Private economic power groups can become established, and enrich themselves at the expense of less powerful groups.

(e) It tends to create economic insecurity, particularly due to periodic increases in unemployment.

15. In a *command economy*, the questions regarding *what to produce, how to produce it*, and *how to divide it up* are basically decided by

(a) the people, working consciously for the social good rather than for their own self-interest.

(b) tradition.

(c) the free decisions of households and businesses.

(d) the government.

(e) None of the above.

16. Command systems generally use economic resources

(a) less effectively but more efficiently than market economies.

(b) more effectively and more efficiently than market economies

(c) as effectively and as efficiently as market economies.

(d) more effectively but less efficiently than market economies.

(e) less effectively and less efficiently than market economies.

17. A key reason for the situation in the previous question is that

(a) command economies carefully plan the use of economic resources.

(b) command economies lack the incentive of profit.

(c) command economies lack the incentive of competition.

(d) in market economies, producers have the advantage over consumers.

(e) Both (b) and (c) are correct.

18. Canada's economic system is best described as

(a) a command system for capital goods decisions and a market system for consumer goods decisions.

(b) a market system with extensive elements of government involvement.

(c) a market system for capital goods decisions and a command system for consumer goods decisions.

(d) a command system with elements of market involvement.

(e) None of the above.

19. The three major roles played by governments in Canada's mixed economic system are

(a) national defence, health care, and education.

(b) environmental protection, income security, and health care.

(c) income security, health care, and education.

(d) income security, health care, and national defence.

(e) environmental protection, public safety, and gun control.

Critical Thinking Questions

(Asterisked questions 1 to 4 are answered in Appendix B; the answers to questions 5 to 8 are in the Instructor's Manual that accompanies this text.)

*1. Explain why you think that each of the following represents a market or command element of Canada's mixed economic system.
   (a) Growing demand for goat meat causes its price to increase sharply.
   (b) Primary and secondary education is provided at no cost to students and their families.
   (c) An oversupply of computers causes their price to decrease considerably.
   (d) The government stops the largest corporation in an industry from buying its largest competitor.
   (e) The poorest Canadians are able to receive welfare benefits.
   (f) Following a year-long work stoppage, hockey players accept very large pay reductions.
   (g) The 10 percent of Canadians with the highest incomes pay 53 percent of all personal income taxes paid.

*2. Suppose that a manufacturer is selling two products (product A and product B) for $100 each, and is making a profit (before taxes) of $7 on each product.
   (a) If strong demand increases the price of product A by 2 percent, by what percentage will the profits from product A rise?
   (b) If weak demand for product B causes its price to fall by 1 percent, by what percentage will the profits from product B decrease?
   (c) Given these facts, what would be the logical decision for the management of the company to make?

*3. Three of the following are essential to the operation of a free-enterprise market economy; one is not essential. Which one might a market economy operate *without*?
   (a) the profit motive
   (b) markets
   (c) corporations
   (d) prices

*4. In Chapter 9, we will see that Canada's federal government enforces legislation that is intended to promote competition in Canadian markets.
   (a) Why is competition among producers necessary for a market system economy to operate effectively and efficiently?
   (b) What dangers arise if there is a lack of competition in markets?

5. Suppose there were a shortage of apartments.
   (a) How would a market system correct this situation?
   (b) If the government passed a law that made it illegal to increase rents, how would this law affect how the market for apartments worked?

6. Suppose that, due to an interruption of international crude oil supplies, gasoline became so scarce that its price became too high for many people to afford. Suppose that the government decided that instead of letting the marketplace decide through very high prices who would—and would not—get gasoline, it would be fairer to low-income households to use a command approach, by *rationing* gasoline. For a low price, the government would sell each household a limited number of coupons that could only be redeemed for gasoline.
   (a) If you were administering such a rationing system, how would you decide who gets how many gas coupons, and at what price?

(b) Suppose that some people received more gas coupons than they really needed, while others received fewer than they needed. What would probably happen in these circumstances?

7. What do you like the least about how Canada's economic system answers the three questions of what to produce, how to produce it, and how to divide it up? Why do you think this problem exists? What would you do to correct this problem?

8. Explain to someone who lives in a country with a command system why your standard of living is higher because you live in a country with basically a "market system" type of economy.

Use the Web (Hints for these Use the Web exercises appear in Appendix B.)

www.msn.ca

1. Gather some classmates and have a contest. Visit **www.expedia.ca** and see which of you can find the lowest-cost flight from Halifax to Vancouver that flies during the next four weeks. How has the internet changed the market for travel?

2. Think of something that you would really like to have. Now visit **www.ebay.ca** and see if you can find it. Can you find this textbook on eBay? What was the price? How did people shop for used items *before* the internet? (It's okay to ask your parents; this will be regarded as research rather than cheating.)

Business Organization in Canada

LEARNING OBJECTIVES

After studying this chapter, you should be able to

1. Summarize the advantages and disadvantages of the sole proprietorship, the partnership, and the corporation.

2. Describe the importance of small business in the Canadian economy, particularly in terms of producing services and providing employment.

3. Identify three of the most serious problems facing small businesses in Canada.

4. Explain how the Canadian Federation of Independent Business (CFIB) assists Canada's small business community.

5. Describe the importance of the *big business* sector of the Canadian economy, in terms of output, employment, and exports.

6. Define the terms *multinational enterprise* and *corporate concentration,* and describe the significance of each for the Canadian economy.

7. Explain why control of the modern large corporation usually does not lie in the hands of its shareholders.

8. Describe the role of government enterprises in the Canadian economy and assert the arguments in favour of the government retaining them and the arguments in favour of privatizing them.

We have seen that prices are determined by supply and demand, a process that we will examine in detail in Chapters 4, 5, and 6. In this chapter, we will examine some of the structural aspects of the supply side of the economy—the various forms of business enterprise in Canada—to gain more insight into the business sector that supplies most goods and services.

The most common forms of business enterprise are the sole proprietorship, the partnership, and the corporation, each of which has certain characteristics, advantages, and disadvantages. Listing and describing the pros and cons of the different forms of business organization can be pretty dull, so we will illustrate them through the story of Dan's Doughnut Den instead.

Dan's Doughnut Dens

Dan, an enterprising young man employed by a large multinational corporation, decided that he was tired of working for someone else and would go into business for himself. He found it quite simple to start up his own business—after obtaining a licence from the municipal government, he rented an appropriate building and purchased equipment and supplies with $25 000 of capital obtained from his own savings, a small inheritance, and some loans from his relatives. Before long, "Dan's Doughnut Den" opened. The business was a **sole proprietorship**; that is, it was totally owned by Dan.

At first, things went exceptionally well: enjoying his newfound freedom and independence, Dan worked harder than he ever had, and sales were good and the business seemed headed for success. As the business grew more complex, Dan was working very long hours, many of which were spent recruiting, training, and supervising staff, and dealing with his bank manager. Dan found financial matters a continual hassle—his bank manager was reluctant to provide as much credit as Dan felt he needed, and was always pestering Dan for financial information, which Dan was too busy to prepare carefully. Actually, keeping financial records for the business was a constant and time-consuming chore, and one at which Dan was not too skilled. Partly as a result of this problem, preparing his income tax return was a nightmare that tied up much of his time for about a month each year. Finally, he hired an accountant to sort it out, and was horrified to learn that he owed nearly $4000 in taxes, most of which he didn't have—he had invested practically all of the earnings back into the business, including the opening of another Doughnut Den across town. The sales at the new location were good, too, but having two outlets put an even greater strain on Dan's limited time and talents. For Dan, the crunch came when some of his suppliers and the Canada Revenue Agency (CRA) threatened to sue him for unpaid debts and taxes. Upon consulting his lawyer, Dan learned, to his dismay, that as the sole proprietor of a business he was subject to *unlimited liability*. That is, if the business went bankrupt, he could lose not only the assets of the business but also his personal assets, such as his house.

Still, Dan thought, the business had a lot of promise, with strong sales at both locations. What was required, he concluded, was more than just hard work; he needed more management experience and more capital. So Dan decided to change the business from a sole proprietorship to a **partnership**. One of his new partners was Sally, an old high-school friend of Dan's who had a diploma in Business Administration from Sheridan Institute of Technology and Advanced Learning. Due to the sudden accidental death of a relative, Sally was able to contribute $40 000 to the capital of the business. Perhaps more importantly, Sally brought a more systematic approach to the management of the business, which soon began to show up in the profit figures.

sole proprietorship
A business firm owned (and usually managed) by a single person who bears full legal liability for the firm's debts.

partnership
A business firm owned by two or more persons, with each person bearing full legal liability for the firm's debts.

These figures were calculated (much more proficiently) by the other new partner, Ed, who also contributed $50 000 to the capital of the business. Ed kept the books, working on weekends and in the evening after working at his regular job in an accountant's office. Unlike Dan and Sally, Ed took no active part in the management of the business and was therefore a **limited partner**: if the business went bankrupt, his liability was limited—all he could lose was the $50 000 he had invested. Dan and Sally, on the other hand, were **general partners** who had unlimited liability and could therefore lose their personal assets if the business went bankrupt. As is customary in partnerships, all of the partners took out life insurance policies on each other's lives, so that if one died, the others would have sufficient cash from the insurance to buy the deceased partner's share from his or her heirs. This practice ensured that the death of a partner would not force the business to dissolve. The three partners signed an agreement outlining their respective rights and responsibilities, and the proportions of the profits that each would receive.

The infusion of new capital and managerial expertise improved the operation of the business considerably, and things went quite well for a while. However, after a period of time, disagreements began to develop among the partners. Dan continued to work almost as hard as before, and began to resent the share of the profits taken by the others who, he felt, weren't working as hard as he was. He found this particularly hard to accept because he was the one who had undertaken the effort and risk necessary to start the business originally. Sally felt that, if anything, she was contributing more to the business than Dan, due to her superior business knowledge. Sally's increasingly frequent reminders to Dan that her capital and know-how had saved the business only aggravated the situation (Sally's grade in Human Relations at Sheridan had been a well-deserved low D, and she had fought with the teacher over it). Ed was annoyed by these attitudes on the part of his partners: while he didn't work full-time at the business, his after-hours accounting tasks on their behalf made for many a long day for him. Furthermore, he knew that without the accounting data and analysis that he prepared, Sally couldn't manage the business nearly as effectively as she did. Also, he had contributed more money to the business than either of the other two (the $50 000). The disagreements came to a head when, after a heated exchange with Ed, Dan learned that Sally had signed certain long-term contracts on behalf of the business, which Dan believed to be unwise. Since Sally was a partner, there was no way Dan could cancel these contracts—he was bound by Sally's decisions. Worse yet, as a partner, he was personally liable for the debts of the business. Dan was furious that unilateral decisions by someone else could possibly cause the bankruptcy of *his* business and the loss of *his* personal assets. The other two partners threatened to pull out of the partnership, which would almost certainly mean the end of the business. Dan went home that night wishing that there were some way that he could collect on the insurance on the lives of his partners.

Finally, Dan decided that too much was enough; the partnership just couldn't work over the long term. On the advice of his lawyer, Dan decided to change the form of the business into a **corporation**. As his lawyer explained to him, the corporation would be owned and controlled by **shareholders**, and would be a separate legal entity from the shareholders. This meant that if the corporation went bankrupt, the shareholders' liability would be limited to their investment in the corporation's stock. Control of the corporation would lie with its **board of directors**, which would be selected by the shareholders, who would have one vote per share held. As the lawyer pointed out, Dan could control the board of directors, and thus the corporation, by owning (or controlling the votes of) 51 percent of the shares of the company.

The corporation was set up so that Dan and his wife held 85 percent of the shares, with Dan owning 45 percent and the other 40 percent being registered in his wife's

limited partner
A partner who invests in a business but takes no active part in the management of it, and whose liability is limited to the amount invested.

general partners
Partners who take an active part in the management of the business and who have unlimited personal liability for its debts.

corporation
A business firm that is a separate legal entity from its owners, or shareholders, each of whose liability is limited to the amount of his or her investment in the firm.

shareholders
The owners of shares (stocks) in a corporation; shareholders may or may not have voting rights and their liability is limited to the amount invested.

board of directors
A group of people elected by the shareholders of a corporation to provide direction to the management of the corporation.

name, in order to split their dividend income and reduce their total personal income taxes. A few family friends bought the other 15 percent of the shares. The friends were attracted not only by the prospects for the success of the business but also by the limited liability of shareholders and the tax treatment of the gains from their investments, since both dividend income from their shares and any capital gains realized from sale of their shares for a profit would be subject to favourable tax rates. In addition, as the lawyer pointed out, if the business were ever to expand, the corporate form of organization could prove advantageous for raising the necessary capital, because the corporation could sell shares to the public.

The incorporation process was complex and quite costly, but it seemed like an excellent idea. The two partners were bought out, improved equipment was purchased, and the facilities were renovated. A qualified manager was hired, a website and online purchasing system was implemented, and a sophisticated sales promotion campaign was undertaken. Sales and profits rose, and there were bonuses for the managers and substantial dividends for the shareholders. Dan found that incorporation brought tax advantages to the business, too. When the business was first a sole proprietorship and then a partnership, its income (profit) was taxed as personal income, at personal income tax rates, which became quite high as the income of the owners rose. However, the profits of the corporation were taxed at *corporate income tax rates*, which were lower unless profits were quite low. (On the other hand, the shareholders were somewhat disappointed to find that they were subject to "double taxation"—not only were the profits of the corporation taxed, but the dividends they received out of after-tax profits were also taxed, although at reduced rates, as their personal income.) Bank credit became more available as the business prospered, with the opening of three more outlets. After talking to his investment advisor, Dan also considered selling an issue of shares to the public to raise capital to finance expansion into other provinces.

While Dan found being president of a successful and rapidly growing corporation exciting (not to mention financially rewarding), he also found that, as president, he seemed to spend all of his time in his office, doing paperwork and meeting with managers, committees, and lawyers to talk about financing arrangements, short-, medium-, and long-range plans, reorganization plans, controls systems, and seemingly endless government regulations that had to be followed. At times, Dan longed for the days when he worked in the shop, where he had spent time talking with his customers, and when life was simple.

Dan's wishes were soon to be answered. Fed up with Dan's heavy responsibilities and long working hours (as well as impressed by the assets he had accumulated), his wife established a relationship with the manager of Dan's largest outlet (an ambitious young man anxious to get ahead in the organization) and divorced Dan. She then teamed up with the other shareholders (her friends) against Dan at a shareholders' meeting. While Dan's 45 percent of the shares made him the largest single shareholder, the other shareholders (including his ex-wife) were able to outvote him and remove him from the presidency. The new board of directors was kind enough to offer Dan a job as manager of the company's largest outlet (an opening created by the very recent promotion of its former manager to the presidency of the company), but Dan had lost interest in the business. He declined the offer and went to work as a letter carrier for Canada Post, where he had been told he wouldn't ever have to worry about anything. As a shareholder in Dan's Doughnut Dens, Ltd., Dan is entitled to any dividends per share that are paid to the other shareholders, and he lives quite comfortably on this income, plus his Canada Post salary. While he still owns 45 percent of the company's shares, he does not attend shareholders' meetings of the company. Now see the accompanying "You Decide" box for an update to Dan's story.

YOU DECIDE

Update to the Saga of Dan's Doughnut Dens

Recently, Dan has been spending considerable time with Ermyntrude, a former old friend of his ex-wife. Ermyntrude, who has recently had a bitter personal dispute with Dan's ex, owns 5.1 percent of the shares of Dan's Doughnut Dens. ▨

QUESTIONS
1. From the story about Dan's Doughnut Dens, compile a list of the advantages and disadvantages of each of the three forms of business organization: the sole proprietorship, the partnership, and the corporation.
2. What accounts for Dan's new interest in Ermyntrude?
3. What advice would you give Dan if he were just starting his business?
4. Why do you think that virtually all medium- and large-sized businesses are corporations?

Small Business in Canada

Because small business includes a wide range of enterprises, various definitions are used to describe it. According to a definition used by Industry Canada, a small business is any goods-producing firm employing fewer than 100 workers and any service-producing firm with fewer than 50 workers. Firms between these sizes and 500 employees are considered medium-sized, and firms with 500 or more employees are classed as large.

www.industrycanada.ca

In 2004, there were more than 2.3 million business establishments in Canada. Over 1 million of these were *employer businesses* with a payroll of at least one person, and 95 percent of these had fewer than 50 employees. The other 1.3 million establishments did not have any employees registered with the Canada Revenue Agency, so they were obviously also very small.

Small business includes a tremendous variety of individuals, firms, and economic activities: professionals such as doctors and lawyers; farmers; small-scale manufacturers producing toys, boats, clothing, furniture, and a host of other products; retailers such as drug stores, gift shops, grocery stores, clothing stores, bookstores, music stores, and variety stores; service industry operations such as dry cleaning, hairdressing, restaurants, motels, real estate, insurance, services to business, employment agencies, repairs, and landscaping; and construction, which is characterized by large numbers of small contractors and sub-contractors. To gain a quick impression of the small business sector in your community, just leaf through the Yellow Pages of your telephone book.

Small businesses make a big contribution to Canada's economy. The statistics are imprecise, but it would be reasonable to estimate that small businesses account for well over one-third of all jobs, one-quarter of all goods and services produced, and one-fifth of the exports that are so important to Canada's economy.

Small businesses use all the forms of business organization: while over half are sole proprietorships or partnerships, many are corporations. Many of these corporations are **private corporations**, meaning that they have fewer than 50 shareholders. Private corporations are not required by law to publish considerable financial information in the same way as **public corporations** must, because private corporations do not sell shares and bonds to the general public to raise capital.

private corporation
A private corporation has fewer than 50 shareholders.

public corporation
A public corporation has 50 or more shareholders.

Canadian Federation of Independent Business

www.cfib.ca

Until the early 1970s, small business owners in Canada felt that they lacked a voice in the federal and provincial governments. As a result, they believed, government policies were often formulated without consideration of their effects on small business, which was being threatened by the expansion of taxation and regulations, and the proliferation of bureaucratic "red tape" associated with these. In response to these problems, several organizations of small businesses developed, the most important of which is the Canadian Federation of Independent Business (CFIB).

The CFIB was formed in 1971, and by 2005 it included 105 000 small and medium-sized Canadian-owned businesses in its membership. With offices located across the country, the federation employed a staff of about 300, including legislative specialists, economists, and a field staff engaged in selling memberships nationwide. A major function of the CFIB's staff is conducting surveys and other research with the small business membership. The analysis of this information on the views of the small business community provides the basis for the CFIB's presentations to governments.

The CFIB acts as the small business lobby with government, raising issues such as taxation, financing, government regulations, and red tape. It claims to have saved small business several billions of dollars through its influence on government decisions. The CFIB's stated objective is to promote and protect a system of free competitive enterprise in Canada and to give the independent business owner a greater voice in the laws governing business and the nation. With its sizable cross-country membership base and its lines of communication with each provincial government as well as the federal government, the CFIB is by far the most important and influential of the groups representing small business in Canada.

Problems of Small Business

While some 150 000 new businesses start each year, the failure rate is high, especially in the first year of operations. About 15 percent of new firms do not make it through their first year.

One of the main reasons for failures of small businesses is that management is often stretched too thinly. In many small businesses, a single owner-manager is required to perform more functions than time or expertise permit; as a result, the business often suffers from inadequate management.

According to surveys by the Canadian Federation of Independent Business (see Figure 3-1), taxation and government regulation are the major impediments to the operations and growth of small and medium-sized businesses in Canada.

In a 2004 survey of over 21 000 CFIB members, nearly 80 percent of the respondents cited the total *tax burden* as the most important issue facing smaller firms. CFIB research has shown that the burden of the Canadian tax system falls particularly heavily on labour-intensive small businesses, and that small firms actually pay a *higher* percentage of their profits to taxes than larger firms pay. This is largely due to **payroll taxes**, which are calculated as a percentage of a firm's payroll. For a large high-technology manufacturing corporation whose payroll is a relatively small percentage of its sales income, payroll taxes are not too burdensome. But for small businesses in service industries whose payroll is a high percentage of their sales income, payroll taxes such as premiums for Canada Pension Plan, employment insurance, and Workers' Compensation can cut significantly into profits.

Another major concern of small business is *government regulation and paper burden,* as cited by 62 percent of the respondents. For small business owners who

payroll taxes

Taxes paid by employers based on the number of their employees or the amount of their payroll.

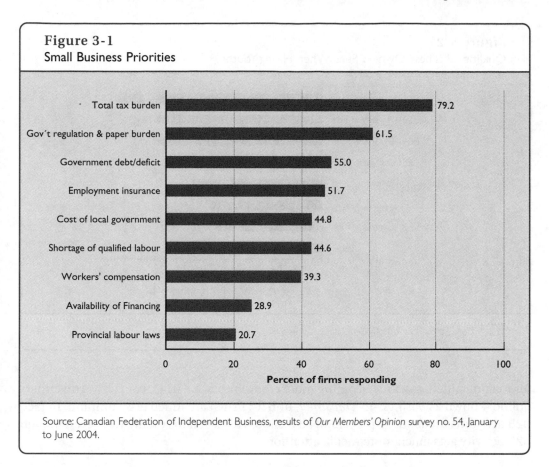

Figure 3-1
Small Business Priorities

Total tax burden — 79.2
Gov't regulation & paper burden — 61.5
Government debt/deficit — 55.0
Employment insurance — 51.7
Cost of local government — 44.8
Shortage of qualified labour — 44.6
Workers' compensation — 39.3
Availability of Financing — 28.9
Provincial labour laws — 20.7

0   20   40   60   80   100
Percent of firms responding

Source: Canadian Federation of Independent Business, results of *Our Members' Opinion* survey no. 54, January to June 2004.

spend a great deal of time managing their enterprise, the time required to fill out government forms relating to statistical information and tax collection (which in many cases consumes 5 to 10 hours per week) can be a real burden.

Financing problems often create serious handicaps. Small firms face considerable problems in attempting to raise sufficient equity and risk capital, and also tend to lack the access that larger businesses have to banks and other credit sources. Not only are small businesses considered by lenders to be a greater risk than larger firms, but also owner-managers of small firms often have difficulty identifying sources of funds.

Shortages of qualified labour are another problem for many small businesses. Small firms have traditionally given young entrants into the workforce their first job. However, for a number of years, small business owners have reported problems with attracting and retaining qualified workers. As Figure 3-2 on page 46 shows, small business owners place strong importance on the attitudes of employees as well as their skills.

Ebusiness and Small Business

Use of the internet by small business more than tripled between 1996 and 2004. A CFIB survey in 2004 showed that over 82 percent of small businesses were actively using the internet. Virtually all firms with more than 100 employees are on the internet, and even among the "micro" businesses with fewer than 5 employees, the internet usage rate is over 60 percent. By far, the most common internet application is email, which is used by virtually every business that is online.

Firms that have a website, buy online, or sell online can be considered to be **ebusinesses**. By far, the most common of these ebusiness applications is operating a website. *Business-to-business* (B2B) transactions, or use of the internet by businesses

ebusinesses
Businesses using processes and activities based on electronic information and data exchanges via the internet and the World Wide Web.

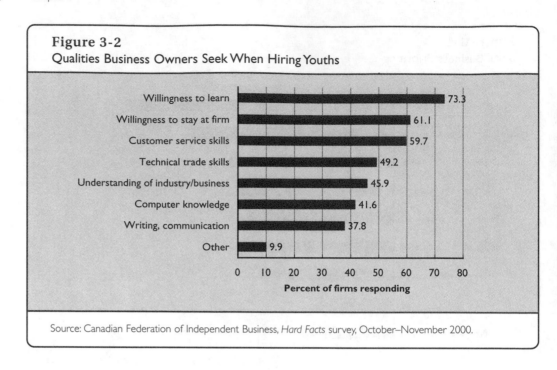

Figure 3-2
Qualities Business Owners Seek When Hiring Youths

Quality	Percent
Willingness to learn	73.3
Willingness to stay at firm	61.1
Customer service skills	59.7
Technical trade skills	49.2
Understanding of industry/business	45.9
Computer knowledge	41.6
Writing, communication	37.8
Other	9.9

Percent of firms responding

Source: Canadian Federation of Independent Business, *Hard Facts* survey, October–November 2000.

for making purchases, are becoming more commonplace. Firms that sell to consumers online (known as *business-to–consumer*, or B2C, firms) are much less common. In fact, B2B accounts for about 90 percent of all business transactions on the web, even though B2C activity gets much more media attention.

Big Business in Canada

As Table 3-1 shows, big business in Canada is a very different world from the small business sector, a world dominated by corporate giants that are household names.

IN THE NEWS

Self-Employment in Canada
According to Statistics Canada (CANSIM Table 282-0012),
- In 2005, 2 512 000 Canadians were self-employed, representing more than 15 percent of the total number of employed people in Canada.
- Self-employment has grown in importance. From 1976 to 2005, the number of self-employed Canadians more than doubled. Over the same period, the number of paid workers not working for themselves grew by a little more than one-half.
- Self-employment is more common among men than women; however, self-employment is growing more rapidly among women. In 1976, 26 percent of the self-employed were women; by 2005 this number had increased to 34 percent. ■

QUESTIONS
1. Why has self-employment been growing so rapidly in recent years?
2. What could explain the increasing participation of women in this trend?
3. Would you expect these trends to continue?

Table 3-1
Canada's 25 Largest Non-Financial Corporations by Sales, 2004

Rank by Revenue 2004	Company	Industry	Sales Revenue $'000s	% sales Outside Canada	Profits $'000s	Major Shareholder(s)	% Foreign
1	General Motors of Canada Ltd.	Vehicle	37 144 552	n.a.	n.a.	General Motors Corp., U.S.	100
2	Alcan Inc.	Mining	32 375 384	96	335 658	Widely held	
3	George Weston Ltd.	Food sell	29 798 000	n.a.	428 000	W. Galen Weston 62.5%	
4	Magna International Inc.	Vehicle	26 869 552	n.a.	900 292	Stronach Trust 66% Class B shares	
5	Imperial Oil Ltd.	Energy	22 408 000	15	2 052 000	Exxon Mobil Corp., U.S.	70
6	Bombardier Inc.	High-tech	20 511 504	34	(110 075)	Bombardier family 58% voting	
7	BCE Inc.	Telecom	19 193 000	2	1 593 000	Widely held	17
8	DaimlerChrysler Canada Inc.	Vehicle	19 151 000	n.a.	n.a.	DaimlerChrysler Corp., U.S.	100
9	Ford Motor Co. of Canada Ltd.	Vehicle	18 127 600	n.a.	n.a.	Ford Motor Co., U.S.	100
10	Onex Corp.	High-tech	16 244 000	82	35 000	Gerald W. Schwartz 68% voting	52
11	EnCana Corp.	Energy	15 364 810	65	4 570 413	Widely held	
12	Petro-Canada	Energy	14 687 000	n.a.	1 757 000	Widely held	
13	Nortel Networks Corp.	High-tech	14 260 007	n.a.	463 069	Widely held	
14	Honda Canada Inc.	Vehicle	13 300 000	67	n.a.	Honda Motor Co. Ltd., Japan	100
15	Wal-Mart Canada Corp.	Merchant	12 500 000	n.a.	n.a.	Wal-Mart Stores Inc., U.S.	100
16	Empire Co. Ltd.	Food sell	11 284 000	n.a.	173 100	Sobey family 72%	
17	Shell Canada Ltd.	Energy	11 228 000	n.a.	1 286 000	Shell Petroleum NV, Netherlands	78
18	Quebecor Inc	Publish	10 982 400	71	112 200	Les Placements Peladeau 65%	
19	Hydro-Quebec	Utility	10 698 000	n.a.	2 435 000	Quebec government	
20	The Thomson Corp.	Publish	10 535 498	97	1 315 311	The Woodbridge Company Ltd. 69%	
21	Noranda, Inc.	Mining	9 078 378	n.a.	716 851	Brascan Corp. 43%	
22	Husky Energy Inc.	Energy	8 440 000	n.a.	1 006 000	UF Inv. 36%, LF Inv. 35%, both Barbados	71
23	Suncor Energy Inc.	Energy	8 087 000	n.a.	1 100 000	Widely held	
24	Costco Wholesale Canada Ltd.	Merchant	7 878 386	n.a.	n.a.	Costco Wholesale Corp., U.S.	100
25	Telus Corp.	Telecom	7 581 200	n.a.	565 800	Verizon Communications, Inc. 25%, U.S.	30

n.a.—Not available/not applicable

Source: Reprinted with permission from National Post Business, *The Financial Post 500*, June 2005.

www.tsx.ca

In 2004, the Ontario Lottery and Gaming Corporation had the 52nd–largest sales revenues in Canada, with $5.7 billion.

www.olgc.ca

All such large businesses are incorporated, mostly in the form of *public corporations* that have the ability to raise capital through the sale of stocks and bonds to the public. Public corporations' shares are traded on stock exchanges such as the Toronto Stock Exchange and the TSX Venture Exchange. Through these stock exchanges, corporations can issue new shares to raise capital, and the investing public can buy and sell shares. The ability to buy and sell corporate shares freely, together with the limited liability of shareholders, makes it possible for public corporations to raise the vast amounts of capital they need, not only from the general public but also from large institutional investors such as pension funds and mutual funds.

The 25 corporations shown in Table 3-1 play a major role in the Canadian economy, with sales amounting to over $407 billion in 2004. This amount represented 32 percent of all the goods and services produced in Canada that year. The column showing each firm's sales outside Canada indicates that several of these largest Canadian firms are major exporters.

Table 3-1 also shows that the ownership of these large enterprises is quite diverse. About half were widely held, meaning that ownership is spread among a large number of relatively small shareholders. In more than half the corporations, control was very concentrated, in the hands of another corporation or a family.

About one-fifth of these largest firms were private corporations. A private corporation has fewer than 50 shareholders and is not required to publish nearly as much financial information as a public corporation. Family-owned firms and subsidiaries of foreign companies often take the form of private corporations, because this form provides greater privacy. Over one-quarter of Canada's largest 25 non-financial corporations were foreign-owned, mostly by U.S.-based parent companies.

Table 3-2 lists the 25 largest employers in Canada in 2004. Each of these firms employs an average of 55 000 people. Altogether, these enterprises accounted for 8.6 percent of all jobs in Canada.

YOU DECIDE

Sales and Jobs
In 2004, General Motors was ranked 1st in sales revenue and 35th in number of employees. McDonald's was ranked 118th in sales revenue and 4th in number of employees. ▪

QUESTION
1. What might explain why General Motors ranks so high in sales and so low in jobs while McDonald's ranks so much higher in jobs and lower in sales than GM?

Table 3-3 on page 50 shows that most of Canada's 10 largest banks and financial institutions are widely held, and none are foreign-owned. Foreign banks have been establishing a growing presence in Canada, and in 2004, 9 of the 50 largest financial institutions were foreign-owned. However, most of them were small compared to those listed in Table 3-3. Foreign banks mainly do commercial lending to businesses, and are therefore not very visible to the general public.

Table 3-2
Canada's 25 Largest Employers, 2004

Rank by Employees 2004	Company	Number of Employees	Revenues per Employee $	Profit per Employee $	FP500 Rank
1	George Weston Ltd.	149 000	199 987	2 872	3
2	Onex Corp.	83 000	195 711	422	16
3	Magna International Inc.	81 000	331 723	11 115	5
4	McDonald's Restaurants of Canada Ltd.	77 000	33 043	n.a.	118
5	Alcan Inc.	73 000	443 498	4 598	2
6	Hudson's Bay Co.	62 394	113 308	957	38
7	BCE Inc.	61 739	310 873	25 802	11
8	Canada Post Corp.	60 000	110 850	2 450	41
9	Royal Bank of Canada	60 000	420 067	46 950	6
10	Wal-Mart Canada Corp.	60 000	208 833	n.a.	23
11	Bombardier Inc.	59 550	344 442	(1 848)	10
12	Quebecor Inc.	47 000	233 668	2 387	26
13	Canadian Tire Corp. Ltd.	45 000	158 969	6 487	36
14	The Bank of Nova Scotia	43 928	375 546	66 723	15
15	The Toronto-Dominion Bank	42 843	373 807	53 918	17
16	Sears Canada Inc.	41 000	151 963	3 139	47
17	The Thomson Corp.	40 000	263 387	32 883	28
18	Mouvement des caisses Desjardins	39 347	214 527	27 245	30
19	Extendicare Inc.	38 000	45 968	3 295	175
20	Canadian Imperial Bank of Commerce	37 281	448 084	58 984	14
21	Nortel Networks Corp.	35 300	403 966	13 118	20
22	Alimentation Couche-Tard Inc.	34 000	172 718	2 338	49
23	Bank of Montreal	33 593	393 177	69 985	22
24	Empire Co. Ltd.	33 000	341 939	5 245	24
25	Four Seasons Hotels Inc.	31 400	10 821	1 058	509

n.a.—Not available/not applicable
Source: Reprinted with permission from National Post Business, *The Financial Post 500*, June 2005.

Multinational Enterprises

Many of the corporations listed in Table 3-1 are what are known as *multinational enterprises*, or corporations that conduct business internationally. Multinational corporations first attracted attention in the 1960s and 1970s; however, following the shift in the 1980s toward freer international trade, their growth became spectacular. Worldwide, there are estimated to be more than 37 000 multinationals with more than 170 000 affiliates, and more than one-third of world trade is conducted between related companies. Over half of all Canada–U.S. trade takes place between multinational affiliates.

The strategic significance of these firms is great: it is estimated that North America's 1000 largest multinationals employ 30 million people and account for about 25 percent of all the goods and services produced in Canada and the United States. Most of the largest multinationals are U.S.-owned; however, approximately 12 percent

Table 3-3
Canada's 10 Largest Financial Institutions, 2004

Rank by Revenue 2004	Company	Revenues $'000s	Assets $'000s	Profits as % of Shareholders' Equity	Major Shareholders
1	Royal Bank of Canada	25 204 000	429 196 000	15.4	Widely held
2	Power Financial Corp.	23 922 000	104 179 000	18.2	Power Corp. of Canada 67%
3	Canadian Imperial Bank of Commerce	16 705 000	278 764 000	16.3	Widely held
4	The Bank of Nova Scotia	16 497 000	279 212 000	19.6	Widely held
5	The Toronto-Dominion Bank	16 015 000	311 027 008	17.1	Widely held
6	Bank of Montreal	13 208 000	265 194 000	18.3	Widely held
7	Mouvement des caisses Desjardins	8 441 000	103 574 000	16.1	Members
8	Fairfax Financial Holdings Ltd.	7 536 172	31 650 222	(0.6)	V. Prem Watsa 55% voting
9	National Bank of Canada	4 771 000	88 807 000	17.5	Widely held
10	Caisse de depot et placement du Quebec	3 859 000	147 200 000	n.a.	Quebec government

n.a. —Not available/not applicable
Source: Reprinted with permission from National Post Business, *The Financial Post 500*, June 2005.

of the top North American firms are Canadian-controlled, providing Canada with a good presence in this large and growing aspect of business enterprise.

Corporate Concentration

In Canada, much business activity is concentrated in the hands of relatively few very large corporations. In broad terms, the largest 25 enterprises (ranked by sales) have tended to control about one-third of all corporate non-financial assets in Canada. In particular industries, such as automobile manufacturing, steel, and breweries, concentration is especially high. This corporate concentration is the result of various factors, including the growth of the sales and assets of the most successful corporations and the tendency of corporations to purchase control of, or merge with, other corporations. As a result, as we will see in Chapter 7, some industries and markets in Canada have come to be dominated by a few large corporations, and to a greater degree than in the United States. When a few firms dominate an industry, concerns are raised about whether there is sufficiently strong competition in the industry. The handful of "competitors" may tend to agree among themselves not to compete too strongly, especially with respect to prices, so that all of them can live together more comfortably and profitably. In these cases, it is viewed as necessary for the government to set down rules for corporate behaviour that, in effect, prohibit anticompetitive practices, as we will see in Chapter 9.

The High-Tech Manufacturing Sector

Table 3-4 shows the top 10 high-tech manufacturers in Canada, ranked by sales revenue. In the late 1990s, investors became very excited about start-up (upstart?) dot-com companies and other internet-related businesses, pouring billions of dollars into new stock issues by these companies. When these funds were spent on electronic equipment and information technology, the sales and profits of high-tech

Table 3-4
Canada's Top 10 High-Tech Manufacturers, 2004

Rank by Revenue, 2004	Company	Revenues $'000s	Profits $'000s	Rank in FP500
1	Bombardier Inc.	20 511 504	(110 075)	10
2	Onex Corp.	16 244 000	35 000	16
3	Nortel Networks Corp.	14 260 007	463 069	20
4	IBM Canada Ltd.	5 500 000	n.a.	57
5	Hewlett-Packard (Canada) Co.	3 200 000	n.a.	99
6	ATI Technologies Inc.	2 657 630	272 587	113
7	Pratt & Whitney Canada Corp.	2 200 000	n.a.	138
8	Research in Motion Ltd.	1 740 726	275 055	176
9	Xerox Canada Inc.	1 220 000	n.a.	211
10	CAE Inc.	1 093 200	64 000	232

n.a. —Not available/not applicable
Source: Reprinted with permission from National Post Business, *The Financial Post 500*, June 2005.

manufacturers soared spectacularly. However, most of the dot-com firms had failed to develop business models that would generate sales and earn profits, so when they had used up their investors' funds, their purchases of technology and equipment plunged drastically. To make matters worse for the high-tech equipment manufacturers, over-investment had created a surplus of bandwidth that killed off spending in that area. The effects of these developments continued through 2004, when the sales revenues of the top 10 high-tech companies were almost 17 percent lower than they had been in 2001.

Who Controls the Modern Large Corporation?

In theory, this is a simple question, since the shareholders of a corporation vote to elect the board of directors, which in turn selects top management and directs them as to the corporation's objectives and the policies to be followed. In reality, however, the matter is often not so simple. In many large corporations, the shares are so widely held that the shareholders are too numerous and too dispersed to exercise any effective control. A typical shareholders' meeting of a large corporation attracts only a handful of shareholders, few of whom ever seriously question or challenge the executive officers of the corporation.

If the small shareholders are often not in a position to exercise control over the large corporation collectively, then who does control it? Given the importance of large corporations in the economy, this is an important question. Unfortunately, the answer is not always clear, since it depends on the circumstances.

If the corporation's stock is so widely held that there is no major shareholder or organized group of shareholders, it will be impossible for the shareholders to exercise control through their meetings. Rather, control will often fall to the *top management* of the corporation, which can control the shareholders' meetings through **proxies**. (A proxy is a legal instrument whereby a shareholder, in effect, delegates to another person authority to vote on his or her behalf.) Under these circumstances, the top

proxies
Legal instruments that allow a shareholder's right to vote at shareholders' meetings to be delegated to another person, either with or without specific instructions as to how that vote will be exercised.

management of a corporation can control the firm, even to the point of nominating and selecting the members of the board of directors to which top management reports. In such cases, the management of the corporation can usually retain control as long as the corporation performs well enough to keep the shareholders content. Those shareholders who disagree strongly with management's decisions will generally sell their shares rather than engage in a struggle for control that will probably prove futile.

In Canada, it is widely accepted that, in many large corporations, the *board of directors* takes a more active part in company policies and decisions than is suggested in the preceding paragraphs. Sometimes such control is exercised through boards of directors by majority shareholders, such as family interests or other corporations that own a majority of the shares. However, the situation is not always so clear-cut—under certain conditions, a group of shareholders (individuals or other corporations or investment funds) can exercise strong influence on a corporation's board of directors even though it does not hold a majority of the total shares outstanding. Such control can be achieved through proxy votes or simply through personal relationships between the people involved.

While corporate directorships have in the past been thought of as sinecure positions involving status and perks but relatively little responsibility, the situation has changed. Directors now face significantly increased responsibilities due to changes in the law that place much more liability upon them for their companies' actions. Under a variety of laws (by one count, more than 100 in Ontario alone), directors of companies are now exposed to a wide range of both civil and criminal penalties including claims for employees' wages and infractions of environmental laws. In fact, in recent years there was growing concern that governments had taken the concept of directors' liability too far. In several cases, directors of companies that were in difficulty resigned when the possibility arose that they could be held personally liable for millions of dollars of claims. This event raised the concern that the laws relating to directors' liability could discourage Canada's most capable people from serving on the boards of corporations.

Partly as a result of this concern, and partly in response to increasing concerns that board members be impartial and independent in providing shareholders with information about their companies, corporations are seeking directors with more expertise and dedication than ever before, and are increasingly going outside their own companies for them. So the question of who controls the large corporation is not a simple one. What can be said is that large corporations play a very important role in the Canadian economy, even greater relative to the size of the economy than in the United States, and that in these large corporations, *control is often separated from ownership*. Widespread small shareholders are not in a position to exercise active control. As a result, control tends to shift, depending on the circumstances, to the top management of the corporation or to groups of influential members of the board of directors. Generally, neither top managers nor directors are major shareholders in their corporation; their claim to control over the corporation is based on their expertise rather than on ownership.

Government Enterprises

Crown corporations
Corporations owned by a government and that are ultimately responsible, through a cabinet minister, to that government.

No discussion of big business in Canada would be complete without reference to government-owned enterprises. Comprising about 10 percent of Canada's very large corporations, government enterprises often take the form of **Crown corporations**. Crown corporations, like other corporations, are legally independent, separate entities. However, their shares are owned by a government, and they are ultimately responsible to the government through a cabinet minister. In addition to Crown corporations, government enterprises often take the form of *boards* or *commissions*, such as hydroelectric commissions.

Whatever legal forms they take, government enterprises constitute an important part of big business in Canada. Their largest single activity is the *provision of electricity*: the combined sales of the 10 provinces' electricity utilities would place them among Canada's largest enterprises. Traditionally, government enterprises have also been important in the fields of *transportation and communications* in Canada, including, at various times, Canadian National Railways, Air Canada, Pacific Western Airlines, British Columbia Railway, and Nordair. More recently, government enterprises, such as PetroCan, Atomic Energy of Canada, Eldorado Nuclear, the Canada Development Corporation, and the Potash Corporation of Saskatchewan, have established a presence in the *energy and resources* sector of the Canadian economy. While government enterprises play a smaller role in the *manufacturing sector,* some provincial governments have acted as partners in manufacturing firms in attempts to stimulate growth and employment in their regions. Table 3-5 lists the 10 largest Crown corporations in Canada, ranked by sales in 2004.

The question of government enterprises has been a controversial one in Canada. Supporters argue that government enterprises have contributed enormously to the economic development and unity of the nation. They point out that in a far-flung country such as Canada, the costs of operating such enterprises are so great that it is necessary for the government to subsidize their operation in order to provide a reasonable level of service to all Canadians. Critics of government enterprises stress the fact that their numbers have increased over the years and have come to include money-losing businesses that the government acquired or retained mainly for political reasons—that is, to "save jobs." They point out that many government enterprises pay above-market wages to their employees and/or operate inefficiently, losing money regularly and falling back on taxpayers for subsidies. As the federal government's budget deficits mounted in the 1980s and 1990s, pressures to reassess the government's commitment to many of its money-losing enterprises grew.

Table 3-5
Canada's 10 Largest Crown Corporations, 2004

Rank by Revenue, 2004	Company	Revenues $'000s	Rank in FP500	Owned by
1	Hydro-Quebec	10 698 000	27	Quebec government
2	Canada Post Corp.	6 651 000	41	Federal government
3	Ontario Lottery and Gaming Corp.	5 730 070	52	Ontario government
4	Ontario Power Generation Inc.	4 918 000	64	Ontario government
5	Canadian Wheat Board	4 136 168	73	Federal government
6	Caisse de depot et placement du Quebec	3 859 000	80	Quebec government
7	British Columbia Hydro & Power Authority	3 424 000	92	British Columbia government
8	Insurance Corp. of British Columbia	3 421 000	93	British Columbia government
9	Liquor Control Board of Ontario	3 320 681	96	Ontario government
10	Alberta Gaming and Liquor Commission	3 081 327	104	Alberta government

Source: Reprinted with permission from National Post Business, *The Financial Post 500*, June 2005.

Privatize

The process of selling government enterprises (usually Crown corporations) to private interests.

In 1985, the federal government undertook a critical review of the performance of its Crown corporations. It decided to sell some of them to private interests, or **privatize** them. The privatization program started with the high-profile sale of De Havilland Aircraft of Canada Ltd. to Boeing Corp. of the United States. In 1989, the sale of Air Canada to private interests was completed, and in the 1990s Petro-Canada and Canadian National were privatized.

Governments have also generally owned and operated most educational institutions at all levels. Some people have suggested, however, that this government "monopoly" should be changed to a situation in which schools have to compete for customers in the same ways as other businesses do (see the accompanying "You Decide" box).

To summarize, government enterprises are big business in Canada, many of them being household names and major forces in the economy. The objectives of these enterprises are not only profits—some of them, such as the Canadian Broadcasting Corporation, are intended to provide particular services throughout the country whether doing so is profitable or not, or to aid in the development of particular industries, products, or regions. The matter of government enterprises has always been a controversial one; critics argue that such operations tend to be inefficient and costly because of political interference and the absence of the profit motive, and supporters argue that they are an essential component of the Canadian economy, performing functions that private enterprise would not or could not.

YOU DECIDE

A Competitive Market for Education?

In most elementary and secondary school systems, students have no choice as to which school they will attend—they are assigned to the school in the area in which they live. Some critics would like to see competition introduced into the education "industry." They want the government to give students (or their parents) vouchers for each year's education and allow them to "spend" these vouchers at any school they wish. In such a system, schools would function partly like businesses—the more students (and vouchers) a school attracted, the more revenue it would have. The theory is that this competition would put pressure on schools to improve the quality of their education. ▪

QUESTIONS
1. What advantages do you see in such a system?
2. What disadvantages or potential dangers do you see in it?
3. What would be required for such a system to operate effectively and improve the quality of education?

Big Business, Small Business, Government Enterprises and Prosperity

Together, the three major types of enterprises discussed in this chapter contribute strongly to the economic prosperity of Canadians, with each making its own special contribution. Big business is a particularly efficient *producer of goods* (manufactured goods, food products, energy and resource products, etc.). Such efficient production of goods means that relatively few workers are needed in goods industries, making a high proportion of Canada's labour force available for work in service industries. Meanwhile, efficient production of goods makes their prices low, leaving consumers with ample funds for buying a wide range of services. The small business sector is a major producer of these services (restaurants, entertainment, travel, etc.) that enrich the lives of Canadians, and provides *employment for many Canadians* in the process. Finally, government enterprises support Canadian producers by providing both the required *infrastructure* and *an educated and trained labour force*; these enterprises also provide key *public services* such as health care to Canadians.

Market Structure

In this chapter we have considered the nature of the business sector of the economy, which produces most of the supply of goods and services. In Chapters 4 through 7, we will see how supply and demand interact to determine prices. This task is complicated somewhat by the fact that supply—the production of goods and services by business—occurs under various conditions ranging from industries comprising large numbers of small firms to industries dominated by a few large firms to industries in which there is only one producer (a monopoly). These different conditions—referred to as *market structures* by economists—have a significant impact on the supply of goods and services. If there is only one firm in an industry (a monopoly), it is in a position to control the supply of the product, thereby raising the price of the product and increasing its profits. In industries dominated by a few large firms, it is sometimes possible for these firms to get together to avoid competing on prices and thus increase their profits. On the other hand, in industries in which there are many small firms, such collective action is very difficult or impossible to achieve. As a result, competition in such industries tends to be more intense, and prices and profits are lower than in either of the first two cases. In Chapter 4, we will examine the concept of demand, and then in Chapter 5 we will begin our examination of supply (and its interactions with demand) in those industries that have a large number of small firms—industries that economists call *competitive*.

Chapter Summary

1. The advantages of the sole proprietorship and the partnership are that they are easily formed and provide strong motivation and a high degree of independence. Disadvantages include lack of access to financing, lack of managerial expertise, the unlimited personal liability of the owner(s), and higher tax rates once the income of the business exceeds a certain amount. An added disadvantage of the partnership is the possibility of disagreements among the partners. (L.O. 1)
2. One advantage of the corporation, the typical form taken by larger businesses, is that it can raise larger amounts of capital due to the limited liability of its shareholders. Another advantage is the lower tax rates on income above a certain level. Disadvantages include the initial costs of incorporation and a greater degree of government regulation, especially with respect to public corporations. (L.O. 1)
3. Small business is an important and dynamic sector of the Canadian economy, consisting of many hundreds of thousands of firms and providing over one-third

of all private sector employment and a high proportion of new private sector job creation in recent years. (L.O. 2)

4. Major problems faced by small business include high tax rates, lack of management expertise, financing problems, government regulations and paperwork, and difficulties attracting and retaining skilled employees. (L.O. 3)

5. The Canadian Federation of Independent Business (CFIB) assists the small business community by lobbying with governments and providing research. (L.O. 4)

6. Big business is another major component of the Canadian economy, accounting for particularly high proportions of the country's output and exports. Multinational enterprises are an important aspect of Canada's big business sector. (L.O. 5, 6)

7. While these large corporations are important to the Canadian economy, the domination of some industries by a few large corporations raises questions as to whether such corporate concentration is in the public interest. (L.O. 6)

8. Control of the modern large corporation is not usually in the hands of the shareholders as a group; rather, it tends to rest with top management and/or the board of directors, neither of which are usually major shareholders. (L.O. 7)

9. A significant number of Canada's large corporations are government-owned, particularly in the areas of electrical utilities, transportation and communications, and energy and resources. Advocates of these enterprises argue that they provide important services to the public, while others argue that they are inefficient and ineffective and therefore should be privatized. (L.O. 8)

Questions

1. Which of the following best describes the contribution of small business to the economic prosperity of Canadians?
   (a) They are major producers of goods.
   (b) They are major exporters.
   (c) They have provided most of the employment growth of recent years.
   (d) They provide a wide range of services to consumers.
   (e) Both (c) and (d) are correct.

2. Which of the following best describes the contribution of big business to the economic prosperity of Canadians?
   (a) They are major producers of goods.
   (b) They have provided most of the employment growth of recent years.
   (c) They are major exporters.
   (d) Both (a) and (c) are correct.
   (e) Answers (a), (b), and (c) are correct.

3. Which of the following best describes the contribution of Crown corporations to the economic prosperity of Canadians?
   (a) They are major producers of goods.
   (b) They are major exporters.
   (c) They provide Canadians with various important public services.
   (d) They have provided most of the employment growth of recent years.
   (e) They make no significant contribution to Canadians' prosperity.

4. Large corporations are owned by their shareholders. In most cases, effective control of such corporations tends to be in the hands of
   (a) the president.
   (b) the shareholders.
   (c) the individual owning the greatest number of shares.

(d) the top management and/or board of directors.

(e) None of the above.

Explain your answer.

5. The text notes that many service industries consist of large numbers of small business firms.

(a) Why do you think that this is so often the case?

(b) Name some exceptions to this generality; that is, service industries that are dominated by a few large corporations. What explains why *these* service industries consist of a few large firms?

6. In your opinion, what is the future for small business in Canada? Do you think its importance will grow or decline? Why?

7. What is *industrial concentration*, and why do both consumer groups and economists consider it to be concern? Include in your answer references to the terms *effectiveness* and *efficiency*, and provide at least one example of such concerns.

8. What is meant by *privatization*, and why do critics of government enterprises believe that privatization would improve their performance in terms of both efficiency and effectiveness?

9. Visit the website for the Canadian Federation of Independent Business at **www.cfib.ca**. What issues are currently of concern to CFIB and the small business community? Why are CFIB and its members concerned about these matters?

Study Guide

Review Questions   (Answers to these Review Questions appear in Appendix B.)

State whether or not the story of *Dan's Doughnut Dens* illustrates that each of the following statements is *true* or *false*.

1. T or F

The sole proprietorship often involves a great deal of strain on the owner-manager.

2. T or F

Sole proprietorships are usually very well-managed, because the owner-manager knows the business so well.

3. T or F

It is possible to be a partner in a business and *not* have unlimited liability for the debts of the business.

4. T or F

Partnerships are often subject to severe strains due to differences among the partners.

5. T or F

The corporate form of business enterprise can involve the risk of the original founder/owner losing control of the business.

6. T or F

A risk of the partnership form of organization is that if one of the partners dies, the business has to be sold so that the deceased partner's heirs can receive their share of the firm.

7. T or F

   To preserve the continuity of the firm after the death of a partner, partners often take out life insurance policies on each others' lives.

State whether each of the following statements concerning the sole proprietorship as a form of business organization is *true* or *false*.

8. T or F

   The owner of the business is protected from liability for the debts of the business.

9. T or F

   It provides strong incentives to be effective and efficient.

10. T or F

    It is inexpensive and easy to form and get started.

11. T or F

    It can readily raise capital in order to buy assets and grow.

12. T or F

    It typically has strong management expertise.

State whether each of the following statements concerning the corporation as a form of business organization is *true* or *false*.

13. T or F

    It is inexpensive and easy to form and get started.

14. T or F

    Its owners (shareholders) have limited liability for the debts of the corporation.

15. T or F

    It is able to raise large amounts of capital.

State whether each of the following four statements concerning Crown corporations in Canada is *true* or *false*.

16. T or F

    They are very few in number and therefore not a major part of the Canadian economy.

17. T or F

    Only the federal government has the power to create Crown corporations.

18. T or F

    They are an important part of the Canadian economy, comprising about 10 percent of Canada's very large corporations.

19. T or F

    Their objective is not only to make a profit, but also in some cases to provide certain services for the public.

20. Which of the following problems is/are commonly faced by small businesses?
    (a) financing problems
    (b) lack of managerial expertise
    (c) government regulations and the extensive paperwork associated with them
    (d) difficulties attracting and retaining capable employees
    (e) All of the above.

21. A *multinational* enterprise is one in which
    (a) shareholders are spread throughout many different countries.
    (b) resources are imported from one country to be processed in another.
    (c) business is conducted internationally, in different countries.
    (d) shareholders are Americans and workers are Canadians.

Critical Thinking Questions

(Asterisked questions 1 to 5 are answered in Appendix B; the answers to questions 6 to 10 are in the Instructor's Manual that accompanies this text.)

*1. Small business operators are known for their independent nature. So why does the small business community believe that it needs the Canadian Federation of Independent Business? To illustrate your answer, explain two key functions that the CFIB carries out for its members.

*2. Many small business owners earn less than they could by working for a large corporation. Why, then, do you think that they have chosen to be small business owners?

*3. What are payroll taxes? Why are small businesses particularly concerned about payroll taxes?

*4. What are the key arguments *in support of* government ownership and operation of enterprises such as Canada Post and the Canadian Broadcasting Corporation?

*5. Explain the arguments *against* government ownership and operation of such enterprises, referring in your explanation to *efficiency*, *effectiveness*, and *opportunity cost*.

6. Each year in Canada, many small businesses fail, for one reason or another.
  (a) Provide at least one example of an industry that consists largely of small businesses and has a high failure rate.
  (b) What would explain the high failure rate for smaller businesses in Canada?
  (c) Does the lack of success of so many small businesses represent a failure of our economic system?

7. Explain how your own personal economic prosperity is enhanced by
  (a) big businesses.
  (b) small businesses.
  (c) Crown corporations.

8. Some people propose that community colleges should be operated as private profit-making businesses rather than as government enterprises. State arguments both *for* and *against* privately-run community colleges, and decide whether you think college education should be provided by private firms or by governments.

9. Check the most recent Financial Post 500 listing of the largest Canadian corporations, ranked by sales revenue. What changes in the rankings have occurred since 2004, and what might explain these changes?

www.nationalpost.com

10. Check the most recent Financial Post 500 listing of the largest Canadian high-tech manufacturing corporations, ranked by sales revenue. What changes have occurred since 2004 in the rankings and profitability of these firms? What might explain these changes?

Use the Web (Hints for these Use the Web exercises appear in Appendix B.)

1. Divide your class into teams of three or four students. Each team has $10 000 to invest in shares listed on the Toronto Stock Exchange. Buy $10 000 worth of shares now, and over the remainder of your course, keep track of the changing value of the stocks purchased by each team on the Toronto Stock Exchange website.

2. In 1980, there were only 12 business "incubators" in North America; currently there are more than 900. What are incubators, and what sorts of assistance do they provide to small business? For information on incubators, visit the Toronto Business Development Centre at **www.tbdc.com**.

www.tsx.com

4

The Demand Side
of Markets

After studying this chapter, you should be able to

1. Draw a demand curve for a product, given a demand schedule showing the quantity demanded at various prices, and explain the buyer behaviour underlying the demand curve.

2. Explain the meaning of the term *complementary good*.

3. Explain whether a given event would increase or decrease the demand for a particular product, and show how the event would affect the demand curve.

4. Explain the difference between *elastic* and *inelastic* demand.

5. Calculate whether the demand for a product is elastic or inelastic over a specific price range, given the demand schedule for that product.

6. Use the concepts and tools in this chapter to analyze given situations relating to demand and to elasticity of demand.

Figure 4-1
An Illustration of a Market

In Chapter 2, we saw how markets consist of
- a demand side, or offers by buyers to purchase products, and
- a supply side, or offers by sellers to sell products.

Figure 4-1 illustrates in a general way how, in a market, the supply side and demand side interact to determine the price and sales of a particular item.

In this chapter, we will consider in more detail the *demand side* of markets, or factors that affect the ability and willingness of buyers to *purchase* particular goods or services. In the next chapter, we will cover the *supply side* of markets, or factors that affect the ability and willingness of businesses to *produce and sell* particular goods or services.

Part A: What Is Demand?

Generally, people will buy more of a product if its price is lower, all other things being equal. Suppose we took a survey of all the households in Cantown to determine how many pizzas people would buy each week in March 2006 if the price were $20 per pizza, $16 per pizza, $12 per pizza, $8 per pizza, and $4 per pizza, respectively. While surveys such as this one are an imprecise way of gathering information, especially when they ask people to estimate what they *might* do under different circumstances, we would expect that the results of the survey would show that people would buy more pizza at lower prices than at higher prices, as shown in Table 4-1.

Table 4-1
Demand Schedule for Pizza in Cantown, March 2006

If the price per pizza were	The quantity sold (bought) per week would be
$20	20 000
16	30 000
12	50 000
8	80 000
4	120 000

Table 4-1 shows the relationship between the price of a pizza and the quantity of pizzas sold (bought): as the price *increases*, the quantity demanded *falls*. This drop occurs for two reasons: higher prices cause some people to become *unwilling* to buy pizza, and others to become *unable* to buy pizza. Those who do not buy pizza at the higher prices can either substitute another product (such as submarine sandwiches) for pizza, or they can do without some pizza (that is, buy pizzas less often, or not at all).

This relationship between price and quantity demanded, known as **demand**, can be shown in a table, or *demand schedule* as in Table 4-1, or a *demand curve* as in Figure 4-2. The demand curve is simply another way of showing the same information in the demand schedule. The demand curve also shows that as the price increases, the quantity demanded falls (assuming that no other factor affecting demand changes).

demand

The entire relationship between the various possible prices of a product or service and the quantity demanded at each price, expressed through either a schedule or a graph.

If Dell changes prices on its website, changes in its customers' buying patterns can be seen within a minute.

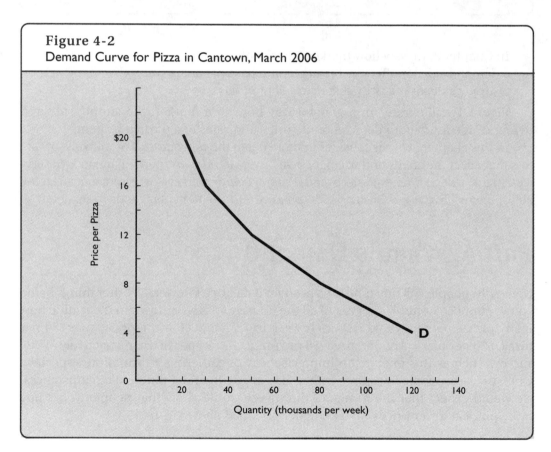

Figure 4-2
Demand Curve for Pizza in Cantown, March 2006

What Demand Is Not

Suppose that, in the example discussed above, the *actual* price of a pizza was $12, and that the *actual* quantity sold was 50 000 pizzas per week. Under these circumstances, it is tempting to conclude that the demand for pizza is 50 000 pizzas, but this conclusion would be incorrect. Demand refers to much more than the *actual* price and quantity bought; it also includes the idea that *if* the price of pizza *had been* higher, less *would have been* sold, and that lower prices would have generated higher sales. When we say "demand," we mean the entire relationship between the *various possible prices* and the quantity demanded at each price. Think of *demand* as the entire results of our hypothetical survey, or as the entire demand schedule or curve, as shown in Table 4-1 and Figure 4-2, respectively.

Shifts in the Demand Curve

In Figure 4-3 the information in the second column of the demand schedule and the demand curve labelled D is the same as that in our previous example. But suppose that some time after we did the original survey, we did another similar survey.

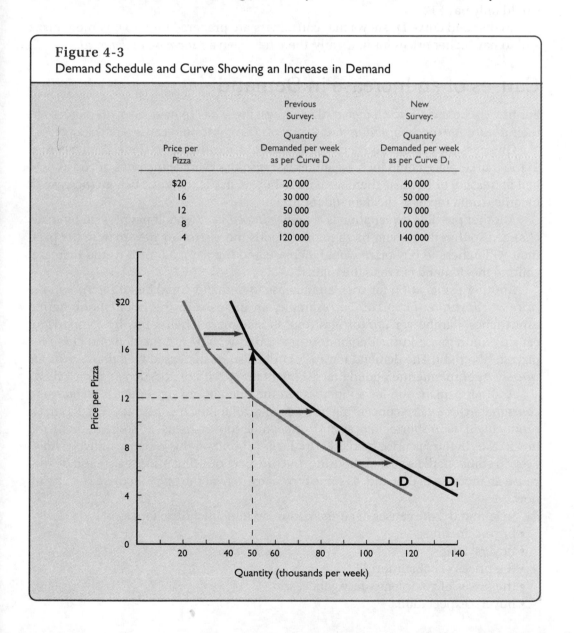

Figure 4-3
Demand Schedule and Curve Showing an Increase in Demand

Price per Pizza	Previous Survey: Quantity Demanded per week as per Curve D	New Survey: Quantity Demanded per week as per Curve D_1
$20	20 000	40 000
16	30 000	50 000
12	50 000	70 000
8	80 000	100 000
4	120 000	140 000

This new survey shows a change in the demand for pizza, which is shown in the third column of the demand schedule. At every possible price, consumers *will buy more* pizza than before. At a price of $20 per pizza, people used to buy 20 000 pizzas per week but will now buy 40 000; at a price of $16, people will increase their purchases from 30 000 to 50 000 pizzas per week; at a price of $12, weekly sales used to be 50 000 pizzas but will now be 70 000, and so on. The demand for pizza has *increased.*

On the graph, this increase in demand causes the demand curve to move to the position shown by the new demand curve D_1. This shift in the demand curve can be seen in two ways. First, as the horizontal arrows show, the demand curve has shifted *to the right*. This shift reflects the fact discussed in the previous paragraph: at every possible price, consumers are prepared to *buy more* pizza per week than before. Second, as the vertical arrows show, the demand curve has shifted *upward*. This reflects the fact that consumers are prepared to *pay higher prices* for pizza. For instance, to get 50 000 pizzas, they will now pay $16 per pizza, whereas before they would only pay $12.

So demand curve D_1 shows that consumers are prepared both to buy more pizza and to pay higher prices for it. Clearly, there has been an *increase in demand*.

Causes of an Increase in Demand

For buyers' behaviour to change in these ways, there has to have been an increase in their *ability* and/or their *willingness* to buy pizza. What could cause such changes?

One possible explanation could be an *increase in consumer income*. Total incomes in the marketplace could increase either because the average incomes of consumers had increased, or because there were more buyers in the market. Such an increase in income would increase the demand for pizza.

Another possible explanation is a *change in people's tastes*. If people's preferences changed so that they prefer pizza to other foods more strongly now than in the past, their willingness to buy pizza would increase and the demand for it would increase, shifting the demand curve to the right.

Another explanation for such an increase in demand could be an *increase in the price of substitutes* for pizza. For example, an increase in the price of submarine sandwiches, hamburgers, or tortillas would make pizza a better buy by comparison, causing an increase in the demand for pizza that would shift the demand curve for pizza to the right. The demand for pizza could also be increased by a *decrease in the price of a* **complementary good** that is bought along with pizza, such as garlic bread.

complementary good
A good that is bought in combination with another good.

Another explanation for an increase in the demand for a product is a *change in consumer expectations* concerning its price or availability. If consumers expect that a product will be in shorter supply and/or become more expensive, some of them will buy it *now*, before its price increases. In the case of pizza, this is pretty unlikely; however, in some markets such as housing, the prospect of rising prices can—and does—cause an increase in demand, as some buyers try to beat the price increases by buying now.

In summary, the causes of an *increase* in demand include changes in
• buyers' incomes,
• buyers' tastes,
• the prices of substitutes,
• the prices of complementary goods, and
• buyers' expectations.

Causes of a Decrease in Demand

Everything discussed in the preceding sections about increases in demand can be reversed for the purpose of discussing decreases in demand. As Figure 4-4 shows, when the demand for pizza decreases, less pizza is bought at every possible price (as shown by the demand schedule), and the demand curve shifts to the left (as shown by the horizontal arrows) to the new location D_2. The change can also be interpreted as a downward shift of the demand curve, as shown by the vertical arrows. This downward shift means that consumers are not prepared to pay as high a price for pizza as they were before.

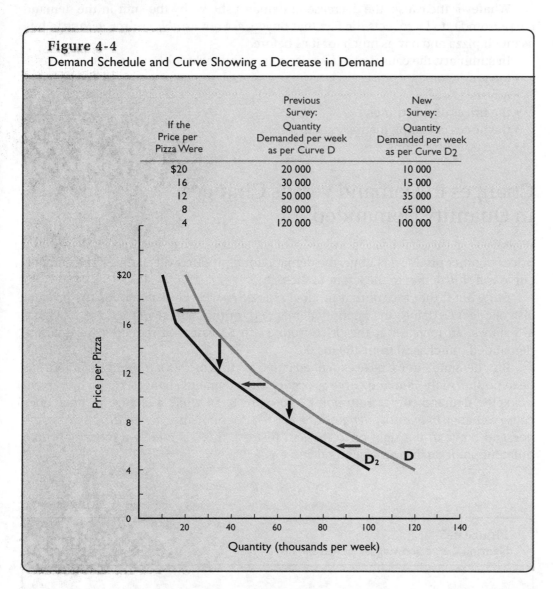

Figure 4-4
Demand Schedule and Curve Showing a Decrease in Demand

If the Price per Pizza Were	Previous Survey: Quantity Demanded per week as per Curve D	New Survey: Quantity Demanded per week as per Curve D2
$20	20 000	10 000
16	30 000	15 000
12	50 000	35 000
8	80 000	65 000
4	120 000	100 000

A shift of the demand curve to the left and down indicates that the factors underlying the demand for pizza have changed in such a way that the demand for pizza has decreased. Such a change can be explained by reference to the same factors discussed earlier. Perhaps people's *incomes have fallen,* leaving them less able to buy as much pizza as before, or perhaps their *tastes have changed,* and they find pizza less attractive than before. Or, perhaps the *prices of substitute products* have fallen—if other foods became less costly, consumers would buy more of them, causing a decrease in the demand for pizza. An increase in the *price of complementary* goods could also cause a decrease in the demand for pizza. Finally, a *change in people's expectations* could cause a decrease in the demand for a product. If people expect lower prices in the future, they may reduce their purchases now, and wait for the lower prices that are anticipated. The housing market provides a better example than the pizza market of the role of expectations. In the housing market, both house prices and mortgage interest rates (the prices of the loans used to buy houses) periodically increase to very high levels, then fall again. When house prices and mortgage rates are believed to be near one of their periodic peaks, many house buyers postpone purchases, expecting that the future will bring lower prices and interest rates.

Whatever the cause, the decrease in demand shown by the shift in the demand curve from D_1 to D_2 reflects the fact that buyers are not as *able* and/or *willing* to buy as much pizza and pay as much for it as before.

In summary, the causes of a *decrease* in demand include changes in
- buyers' incomes,
- buyers' tastes,
- the prices of substitutes,
- the prices of complementary goods, and
- buyers' expectations.

Changes in Demand Versus Changes in Quantity Demanded

We have seen that, if the tastes, incomes, or expectations of consumers change, or the prices of other products change, the demand for a product will change—the demand curve will *shift*, either to the left or to the right.

But what if the *price* of that product changes—will the *demand* for the product also change? Certainly, the quantity demanded (or purchases) will change, as Figure 4-5 shows: an increase in the price from $1 to $3 causes a reduction in quantity demanded (purchases) from 400 to 200.

But "demand," as we have explained it in this chapter, has *not* changed—there has been no *shift* of the demand curve as occurs when demand changes, only a *movement along* the demand curve, from point A to point B. So while a change in price does cause a change in *quantity demanded* (sales), it does not alter *demand*, by shifting the demand curve to the right or to the left. Instead, there is merely a movement to a different point on the same demand curve.

Figure 4-5
Demand Curve Showing an Increase in Price

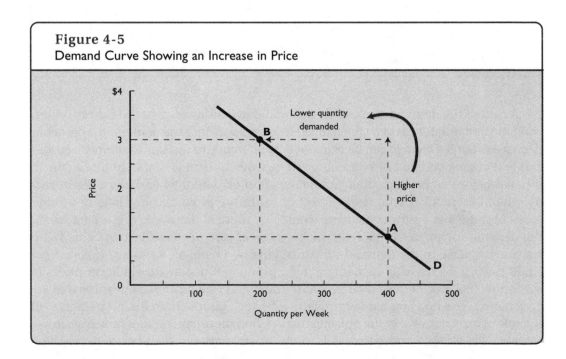

Factors Underlying Demand

In summary, demand is the relationship between the *price* of a product and the *quantity demanded* by buyers. This relationship can be expressed numerically, in a demand schedule, or graphically, in a demand curve. The location of the demand curve for a product depends on such factors as buyers' tastes and incomes, the prices of other products, and buyers' expectations of future price changes. Should these factors change so as to increase the demand for the product, the demand curve will shift to the right and up, whereas changes that reduce the demand for the product will cause the demand curve to shift to the left and down.

Part B: Elasticity of Demand

In Part A of this chapter, we saw that at higher prices buyers will purchase less of a product than at lower prices. A very important question, which we will now consider, is *how much will purchases fall* when the price increases? Since the answer to this question will depend on the nature of a specific product or service, we will examine two different cases.

Elastic Demand

Figure 4-6 shows a hypothetical demand schedule and demand curve for chicken. As the price increases, consumers reduce their purchases of chicken con-siderably—for instance, an increase in price from $0.35 to $0.65 per 100 g will reduce purchases from 500 kg per week to only 100 kg. We could also say that if the price of chicken were to decrease, consumers would increase their purchases of it a great deal.

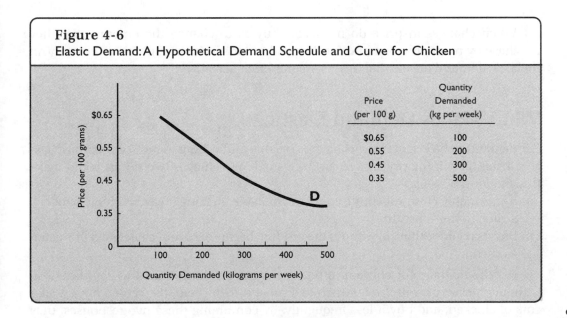

Figure 4-6
Elastic Demand: A Hypothetical Demand Schedule and Curve for Chicken

Price (per 100 g)	Quantity Demanded (kg per week)
$0.65	100
0.55	200
0.45	300
0.35	500

When changes in price cause buyers to make large changes in the amount they purchase, the demand for the product or service is said to be *elastic*. Another way to describe **elastic demand** is to say that buyers are *price-sensitive*.

elastic demand
The term used to describe demand if a price increase causes a reduction in total sales revenue.

Inelastic Demand

Figure 4-7 shows a hypothetical demand schedule and demand curve for gasoline. The demand for gasoline is different: as the price increases, buyers do not reduce their purchases of gasoline by that much. For instance, an increase in price from $0.35 to $0.65 per litre would reduce sales from 325 000 L to 250 000 L per week—a much smaller decrease than in the case of chicken. And if the price of gasoline were to fall, consumers would not increase their purchases of it by very much.

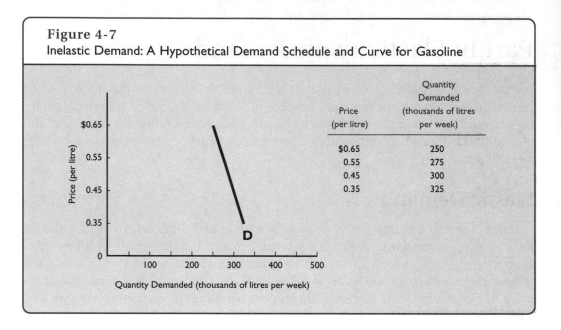

Figure 4-7
Inelastic Demand: A Hypothetical Demand Schedule and Curve for Gasoline

Price (per litre)	Quantity Demanded (thousands of litres per week)
$0.65	250
0.55	275
0.45	300
0.35	325

inelastic demand
The term used to describe demand if a price increase causes an increase in total sales revenue.

When changes in price do not cause buyers to change the amount that they purchase by much, the demand for the product or service is said to be *inelastic*. An **inelastic demand** means that buyers are not price-sensitive.

What Makes Demand Elastic?

For demand to be elastic, buyers have to be able and willing to reduce their purchases substantially if the price increases by a small percentage. Two things could make this situation possible:
(a) a reasonably close substitute could be available, making it easy for buyers to switch to the substitute,
(b) buyers could readily do without the product because it is not a necessity or treated as such.

For the demand for chicken to be elastic, buyers do not need to *completely* do without chicken or *completely* switch to a substitute. Instead, they could buy smaller cuts of chicken, and buy it less frequently. By combining these two responses, they could reduce their purchases of chicken considerably if its price increases by a small percentage, making the demand elastic. But buyers do not necessarily need to make *both* of these adjustments—by *either* substituting *or* cutting back (partially doing without), they can reduce their purchases considerably.

What Makes Demand Inelastic?

If demand is inelastic, buyers will not reduce their purchases by much even if the price increases considerably. They would behave this way because:
 (a) there are no close substitutes available, and
 (b) they are unable or unwilling to do without the product because it is a necessity or is treated as such.

Both of these conditions need to exist in order for demand to be inelastic. For instance, there may be no substitutes for a product, but if buyers can and will do without it, the demand for it would be elastic rather than inelastic.

Also, a product need not *be* a physical necessity for its demand to be inelastic; it need only be *treated* as a necessity. For instance, consumers may be able to survive without colour television sets, but if they *want* them strongly enough, the effect will be the same as if they were a necessity—if the price goes up, people will still buy them.

It is important to be very specific about the product in question when analyzing elasticity of demand. If the price of gasoline *in general* increased, the demand would be inelastic, because buyers need gasoline and there is no ready substitute. However, if the price of a *particular brand* of gasoline rose (and other brands did not), the demand for that brand would be very elastic, because buyers could readily switch to other brands as substitutes.

YOU DECIDE

The Economics of Smoking
It has been estimated that a 10 percent increase in the price of tobacco causes adults to reduce their tobacco consumption by 3 to 4 percent, and causes youths to reduce their consumption by about 8 percent. ■

QUESTIONS
 1. For which age group is the demand for tobacco more inelastic?
 2. What explains the difference in elasticity of demand for the two age groups?
 3. To reduce youth smoking by about half, what sort of price increase would be required?

Defining *Elastic* and *Inelastic*

The preceding examples provide an *illustration* of the concepts of elastic and inelastic demand, but they do not give precise *definitions* of these terms. To define *elastic* and *inelastic* more precisely, we will use as an example the demand for Supersmooth Shaving Cream, as illustrated in Table 4-2 on the next page.

In Table 4-2, we have added a third column—*total revenue per week*, which is the total sales revenue, or price times quantity demanded per week. If we assume that the Supersmooth Shaving Cream Company is currently selling 90 000 cans per week at a price of $1.20 per can, Table 4-2 provides some interesting information.

First, while a price cut from $1.20 to $1.00 would increase sales from 90 000 cans to 100 000 cans per week, it would actually reduce the company's total revenue from $108 000 to $100 000 per week, making such a price reduction an unattractive

Table 4-2
Demand Schedule and Total Revenue for Supersmooth Shaving Cream

Price per Can	Quantity Demanded (thousands of cans per week)	Total Revenue ($ thousands per week) (price × quantity demanded)
$1.80	60	$108
1.60	70	112
1.40	80	112
1.20	90	108
1.00	100	100

decision.[1] On the other hand, a price increase from $1.20 to $1.40 would have the opposite effect: while it would *reduce weekly sales* from 90 000 to 80 000 cans, it would *increase the total revenue* of the company from $108 000 to $112 000 per week.

So, increases in price within the $1.00 to $1.40 price range cause total revenue to increase. Within this price range buyers are not particularly sensitive to price changes—when the price increases, purchases are not reduced by so much that total revenue falls. We have said that when buyers are relatively unresponsive to price changes, demand is said to be *inelastic*. Our formal definition, then, is that

if a price increase causes total revenue to increase, demand is inelastic.

However, increases in the price of Supersmooth Shaving Cream beyond a certain point cause total revenue to *fall*. An increase in price from $1.60 to $1.80 causes total revenue to decrease from $112 000 to $108 000, as this higher price cuts more deeply into sales. In this price range, where buyers are quite sensitive to changes in price, demand is *elastic*. Our definition then is that

if a price increase causes total revenue to fall, demand is elastic.

In summary, elasticity of demand refers to the responsiveness of buyers to changes in price. Demand is said to be elastic if a price increase causes total revenue to fall, and inelastic if a price increase causes total revenue to increase.[2] Similar rules can be worked out for the effects of price reductions, but these tend to be confusing. A simple rule of thumb is that if the *price* and the *total revenue* move in the same direction (up or down), demand is inelastic. These definitions are illustrated in the Supersmooth Shaving Cream demand schedule in Table 4-3.

In the Supersmooth Shaving Cream example, demand is inelastic over the lower price ranges, presumably because at low prices buyers are not very sensitive to price increases. Beyond a certain price, however, the demand becomes elastic, as such high prices drive away more and more buyers. So the elasticity depends on the price range we are discussing. In the real world, when we say that the demand for a product is elastic or inelastic, we are implicitly referring to the price range around its *present actual price*.

---

[1] Note that we say *total revenue*, not *profits*. The effect on profits is more complex—it depends on the combined effect of the increased sales and output on total sales revenue *and* total production costs, respectively. This concept is covered in Chapter 8; however, at this point we can simply assume that higher total revenue means higher profits, and vice versa.

[2] When the price increases from $1.40 to $1.60, total revenue remains unchanged at $112 000. In this borderline case, when the effects of the higher price per unit sold are exactly offset by effects of the reduced number of units sold so that total revenue remains unchanged, we say that the demand has "unitary elasticity."

Table 4-3
Elasticity of Demand for Supersmooth Shaving Cream over Various Price Ranges

Price per Can	Quantity Demanded (thousands of cans per week)	Total Revenue ($ thousands per week) (price × quantity demanded)	Elasticity of Demand (over price range shown)
$1.80	60	$108	elastic from $1.60 to $1.80
1.60	70	112	unitary[a] elasticity from $1.40 to $1.60
1.40	80	112	inelastic from $1.20 to $1.40
1.20	90	108	inelastic from $1.00 to $1.20
1.00	100	100	

[a] Unitary elasticity means there is no change in total revenue as a result of a price increase.

Real-World Elasticity

Elasticity of demand is a very important factor in many business and economic decisions. One obvious area is that of *business pricing policies,* since the elasticity of demand will determine whether a price change will increase or reduce the firm's total revenue. Suppose, for instance, that the Canmore Ice Turkeys hockey team is currently pricing tickets to its games at an average price of $4 each, and that average ticket sales per game are 2400, which is well below the arena's capacity of 3000. Should the Ice Turkeys' management seek to increase ticket sales to 3000 and fill the arena for their games? The answer is not as simple as it seems if increasing attendance requires the kind of price reductions shown in the demand schedule in Table 4-4. If the demand for tickets is as shown, ticket prices will have to be cut to $3 to lure 3000 people to support the Ice Turkeys—a price that would *reduce* the club's total revenue by $600 per game, or more than 6 percent.

Table 4-4
Hypothetical Demand Schedule for Tickets to Canmore Ice Turkeys' Home Games

Average Price per Ticket	Quantity of Tickets Demanded per Game	Total Revenue per Game
$6.00	1650	$9900
5.00	2000	10 000
4 00	2400	9600
3.00	3000	9000

Table 4-5
Another Hypothetical Demand Schedule for Tickets to
Canmore Ice Turkeys' Home Games

Average price per Ticket	Quantity of Tickets demanded per game	Total Revenue per game
$6.00	1500	$9000
5.00	1900	9500
4.00	2400	9600
3.25	3000	9750

In fact, the demand schedule indicates that, financially, the Ice Turkeys would be better off if they *raised* the ticket price to $5, as the loss of sales would be more than offset by the higher price per ticket. Even at a price of $6 per ticket, there are still enough die-hard Ice Turkeys fans to make a nearly half-empty arena more profitable for the club than one with 2400 fans paying $4 each.

On the other hand, suppose the demand schedule is as shown in Table 4-5. In this case, it would pay the club to *reduce* the ticket price. A price reduction would increase total revenue as well as attendance, whereas price increases would have the opposite effect.

Obviously, the Ice Turkeys' management would like to know the elasticity of the demand for their tickets. However, in the real world, sellers do not have neat and precise demand schedules to guide them in their pricing decisions. While the market research departments of larger corporations may expend considerable effort in attempts to estimate the elasticity of demand for their products,[3] many smaller businesses operate on a trial-and-error basis, gaining a rough idea of the elasticity of demand by testing the market with small price increases or reductions. But this lack of a reliable method for determining elasticity of demand does not mean that sellers operate in the dark in their pricing decisions. Large corporations might sense that their position in the market is so dominant that the demand for their product is quite inelastic. And small retailers sense that if their prices increase above those of their competitors, the demand for their products will prove to be quite elastic. For similar reasons, discount retailers operate on the basis that at least a certain segment of consumers is quite sensitive to prices.

In a similar way, elasticity of demand influences the *ability of workers to increase their wages*. For instance, the demand for certain highly skilled workers, such as professional athletes, is inelastic. Such work is in demand, and there is no alternative way of doing it. Consequently, such people are in an excellent position to bargain for higher wages—which they do. By contrast, people in the lawn-mowing industry probably face a more elastic demand since their service is not essential and buyers have the alternative of mowing their own lawns. As a result, the demand for lawn mowing would be more elastic, making it more difficult for people who mow lawns to raise their prices and incomes.

---

coefficient of elasticity
The percentage change in quantity demanded that results from a 1-percent change in price.

[3] Usually, the elasticity is expressed numerically as a **coefficient of elasticity**. For instance, a coefficient of 1.2 means that a 1-percent increase in price causes a 1.2-percent reduction in quantity demanded, while a coefficient of 0.4 means that if the price increases by 1 percent, quantity demanded declines only 0.4 percent. Demand is *elastic* if the coefficient is greater than 1.0 and *inelastic* if the coefficient is less than 1.0. For example, the coefficient of elasticity for food has been estimated at 0.4, while for durable goods the coefficient has been estimated at 1.1.

Elasticity of demand is also an important consideration underlying the *taxation policies* of governments. Three of the most heavily taxed products are alcohol, tobacco, and gasoline. Moral, health, and ecological considerations aside, a major reason for these products being singled out for exceptionally high taxes is that the demand for all three is inelastic, so sales (and tax revenues) hold up quite well even after tax increases have raised these products' prices considerably. There is little point in imposing heavy taxes on products whose demand is elastic, because sales would fall drastically, devastating those industries (not to mention reducing government tax revenues).

Elasticity of demand is also a factor underlying certain social problems, a good example of which is the low incomes of many farmers over the years. Farmers have advanced technologically, raising productivity and the total output of farm products, but most still find themselves in a difficult position economically. While the increased output has depressed farm prices, the lower prices have not led to increased sales of farm products, because the demand for food is inelastic—people do not buy much more food just because it is a bargain. Farmers receive lower prices for their crops, but are unable to sell more crops to offset the lower prices, leaving them with low incomes. Largely as a result of these problems, many groups of farmers have had to rely upon various types of government programs to support their prices and/or incomes, as we will examine in Chapters 9 and 14.

Conclusion

This chapter has considered demand—the first part of the demand-and-supply process that determines prices in markets. In Chapter 5, we will consider supply, and then how supply and demand interact to determine prices.

Chapter Summary

1. A demand schedule or curve reflects the fact that, as the price of a good or service increases, the quantity demanded generally decreases, other things being equal. (L.O. 1)
2. A complementary good is a good that is bought in combination with another good. (L.O. 2)
3. If consumer tastes, incomes, or expectations change, or the prices of other products change, the demand for a product will increase (in which case the curve shifts to the right) or decrease (in which case the demand curve shifts to the left). (L.O. 3)
4. If buyers can do without a product or find a close substitute, a price increase will cause the seller's total sales revenue to fall, and demand will be elastic. (L.O. 4, 5, 6)
5. If buyers cannot or will not do without a product and cannot find a close substitute, a price increase will cause the seller's total sales revenue to increase, and demand will be inelastic. (L.O. 4, 5, 6)

Questions

1. If the incomes of Canadian families increased significantly, how would the demand curve for vacation packages be affected? Explain the reason for your answer.
2. If the price of electricity increased sharply, how would the demand curve for electric heaters be affected? Explain the reason for your answer.

3. How would a significant increase in the price of chicken affect the demand curve for fish? Explain the reason for your answer.

4. Following is the demand schedule for tickets to a show:

If the price were	The quantity demanded would be
$10	700 tickets
9	800
8	900
7	1000

(a) For a price increase from $7 to $8, is demand elastic, inelastic, or unitary elastic?
(b) For a price increase from $8 to $9, is demand elastic, inelastic, or unitary elastic?
(c) For a price increase from $9 to $10, is demand elastic, inelastic, or unitary elastic?

5. State whether each of the following will make the demand for the product or service involved *more elastic* or *more inelastic*, and explain *why* it would do so.
(a) The development of a new good-quality Canadian-produced white wine would tend to make the demand for imported white wine more _____, because _____.
(b) Rising consumer incomes should make the demand for restaurant dinners more _____, because _____.
(c) The use of freezers in more homes should make the demand for foods that can be frozen more _____, because _____.
(d) In the summer, the demand for steak would become more _____, because _____.

6. Which product has the more inelastic demand—barbecues or propane gas for barbecues? Explain the reason for your answer.

7. Ticket prices to Toronto Maple Leafs hockey games are not only the highest in the National Hockey League, but also have increased faster than other teams' prices in recent years.
(a) What makes it possible for the Maple Leafs to charge such high prices, and then increase them even further?
(b) Could a team such as the Edmonton Oilers or Columbus Blue Jackets imitate the Maple Leafs' pricing policies? Why or why not?

8. A customer is about to buy 4 shirts at $20 each. When she finds that they have just gone on sale for $15, she buys 5 shirts instead. Is her demand for these shirts elastic or inelastic? Explain the reason for your answer.

9. Visit the Statistics Canada website at www.statcan.ca and click on, in sequence, *Canadian Statistics Tables by subject Trade Retail trade New motor vehicle sales.*

What has been the trend in the demand for new motor vehicles in Canada over the past five years, and what might explain this trend?

10. Visit the Statistics Canada website at www.statcan.ca and search *The Daily* for "new motor vehicle sales." What have been the most recent developments in the demand for new motor vehicles, and what are the reasons for these?

Study Guide

Review Questions (Answers to these Review Questions appear in Appendix B.)

1. Which of the following portrays a typical demand curve?

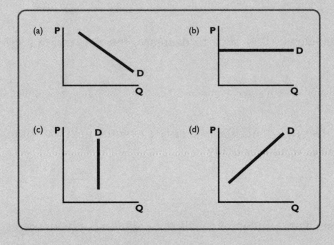

2. The demand curve shows that (for most products), an increase in price causes the quantity demanded to _____.

3. The effect in question 2 happens for two reasons:
   (a) some buyers become _____ to buy as much as before, and
   (b) some become _____ to buy as much as before.

4. Buyers who reduce their purchases have two basic alternatives: they can _____, or they can _____.

5. Following is the demand schedule for rowboat rentals on Lake Canmore.

Price per Day	Quantity Demanded per Week
$30	10
25	20
20	30
15	50
10	70

   On graph paper, draw the demand curve for rowboat rentals on Lake Canmore.

6. If family incomes increased, the demand curve for restaurant dinners would
   (a) shift to the left.
   (b) shift to the right.
   (c) not be affected.

7. If the price of imported wine decreased, the demand curve for Canadian-produced wine would
   (a) shift to the left.
   (b) shift to the right.
   (c) not be affected.

8. As a result of a successful advertising campaign for butter, the demand curve for margarine would
  (a) shift to the left.
  (b) shift to the right.
  (c) not be affected.

9. As a result of an increase in the price of margarine, the demand curve for margarine would
  (a) shift to the left.
  (b) shift to the right.
  (c) not be affected.

10. If sales of sport utility vehicles (SUVs) were to decrease, the demand curve for gasoline would
  (a) shift to the left.
  (b) shift to the right.
  (c) not be affected.

11. If many people expected the price of houses to increase over the next year or two, the demand curve for houses would probably
  (a) shift to the left.
  (b) shift to the right.
  (c) not be affected.

12. If a serious recession caused family incomes to fall, the demand curve for travel to Caribbean resorts would
  (a) shift to the left.
  (b) shift to the right.
  (c) not be affected.

13. As a result of the development of DVDs, the demand curve for tickets to movie theatres
  (a) shifted to the left.
  (b) shifted to the right.
  (c) was not affected.

14. For which one of the following would the demand be *most inelastic?*
  (a) electric heaters
  (b) electricity
  (c) stoves
  (d) lamps
  (e) TV sets

15. In the winter, Canadians' demand for vacations in the south
  (a) becomes more elastic.
  (b) becomes more inelastic.
  (c) Neither (a) nor (b)—elasticity of demand is not affected by the season.

16. Place the following in order of elasticity of demand, the *most elastic* coming first.
  • chocolate ice cream
  • dairy products
  • Neilson's chocolate ice cream
  • ice cream

Critical Thinking Questions

(Asterisked questions 1 to 6 are answered in Appendix B; the answers to questions 7 to 14 are in the Instructor's Manual that accompanies this text.)

*1. Which of these demand curves (**A** or **B**) shows an *elastic* demand? Explain fully the reasons for your answer, and show any calculations that you used.

*2. Following is the demand schedule for a dozen cobs of corn:

If the price were	The quantity demanded would be
$5	20 thousand per week
4	30 thousand per week
3	40 thousand per week
2	50 thousand per week

(a) Over the price ranges shown below, is the demand for cobs of corn *elastic* or *inelastic*?

$2 to $3: _____

$3 to $4: _____

$4 to $5: _____

(b) What could explain the *change* in the elasticity of demand as the price increases?

*3. Explain whether each of the following will make the demand for the product or service involved *more elastic* or *more inelastic*, and *why* it would do so.

(a) At Christmas, the demand for turkey should become more _____, because _____.

(b) The development of DVDs would make the demand for movie tickets more _____, because _____.

(c) The opening of a new pizzeria in town would make the demand for the existing pizzerias' products more _____, because _____.

*4. For each of the following pairs of goods, state which one of the pair has the more *elastic* demand, and explain the reason for your choice.

(a) air conditioners/furnaces

(b) automobiles/licences for automobiles

(c) telephone service/electricity

(d) new automobiles/replacement parts for automobiles

*5. Suppose the price of gasoline were to rise to record levels in the future.

(a) How would this affect the demand curve for SUVs?

(b) What is the economic term for the relationship between gasoline and SUVs?

*6. When the price of gasoline soared in 2005, economists pointed out that a major reason why the price went as high as it did was that the demand for gasoline was inelastic.

(a) Explain the reasoning behind this argument, in terms of the behaviour of buyers.

(b) If the price of gasoline remained high, might the elasticity of demand for gasoline change?

7. By 2004–05, the prospect of higher gasoline prices was generating interest in alternatives such as hybrid engines and alternative fuels. Describe *two* ways in which the development of such alternatives would affect the demand curve for gasoline, and show both of these changes on a graph.

8. If you were selling a product with an *inelastic* demand, what would you emphasize and not emphasize in your advertising?

9. If you were selling a product with an *elastic* demand, what would you emphasize in your advertising?

10. "The dilemma posed by the demand curve is that, to increase *sales*, you must lower your *price*. This means that you will have to charge *less* to some buyers than they would have been prepared to pay, thus forgoing some sales revenue." Is there any way for a seller to get around this dilemma? (*Hint: Think Canadian Tire.*)

11. Many economists (and merchandisers) believe that the demand curve for some products is the type of curve shown in the following graph rather than the simple downward-sloping demand curve discussed in this chapter.

(a) What is the relationship between price and quantity demanded, as shown by this curve?
(b) What could explain this peculiar type of consumer behaviour?
(c) How could merchandisers use this type of consumer behaviour to their advantage?

12. The following graph portrays some very unusual buyer behaviour.

(a) What is the buyer behaviour shown by this graph?
(b) What could explain such unusual buyer behaviour?
(c) Can you think of a product that might have a demand curve like this one?

13. What is the product with the *most elastic* demand that you can think of? Compare your choice with the choices of other students, and debate which choice is the best.

14. What is the product with the *most inelastic* demand that you can think of? Compare your choice with the choices of other students, and debate which choice is the best.

Use the Web   (Hints for these Use the Web exercises appear in Appendix B.)

1. Housing building contractors start building new houses in response to trends in buyers' demand. Visit the Statistics Canada website at **www.statcan.ca** and click on, in sequence, *Canadian Statistics > Tables by subject > Construction > Housing starts and completions > Housing starts, by provinces.*

  (a) What has been the trend in the demand for new housing in Canada over the past five years, and what might explain this trend?

  (b) Has the trend in your province differed significantly from the Canadian trend? If so, what might explain any differences?

2. Visit www.statcan.ca and search *The Daily* for "residential construction investment." What have been the most recent developments in the demand for new housing, and what are the reasons for these developments?

3. Usually, a market transaction is initiated by a seller offering something for sale, after which a buyer makes an offer. On some websites, prospective buyers try to initiate a transaction by stating that they are interested in purchasing a particular item. To see examples of such "demand in action," visit **www.visitmuskoka.com/cottage_wanted.htm** and **www.artspace2000.com/Artspace_II.htm** (click on "Art Wanted").

Appendix 4A
Graphs as Tools

In economics, graphs are frequently used, not only to illustrate statistical data but also as tools of analysis. This appendix is intended to introduce students who are not familiar with graphs to the types of graphs we will use in the remainder of this text.

The simplest and most common graph, and the one with which most people are quite familiar, is the *historical series graph*, which shows the behaviour of a statistic over a period of time. Figure 4A-1 is an example of such a graph. It

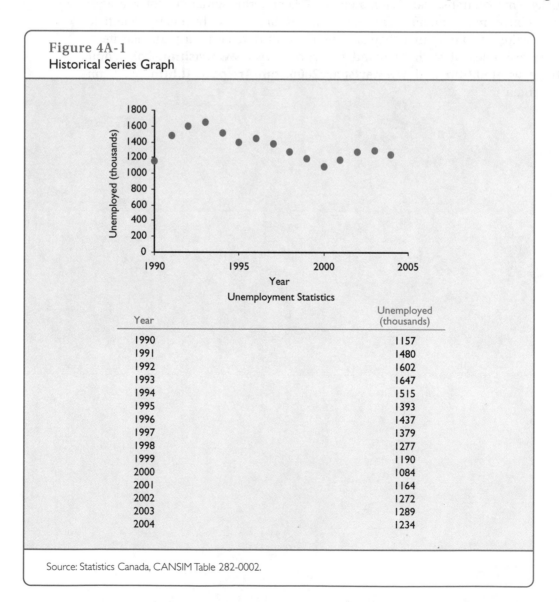

Figure 4A-1
Historical Series Graph

Unemployment Statistics

Year	Unemployed (thousands)
1990	1157
1991	1480
1992	1602
1993	1647
1994	1515
1995	1393
1996	1437
1997	1379
1998	1277
1999	1190
2000	1084
2001	1164
2002	1272
2003	1289
2004	1234

Source: Statistics Canada, CANSIM Table 282-0002.

Figure 4A-2
Descriptive Graph

Source: Statistics Canada, CANSIM Table 282-0002.

shows the fluctuations in the number of Canadians unemployed in each year from 1980 to 2001.

The actual statistics on which the graph is based are shown in the table below the graph.

Since we have only one figure for each year, only the dots can be drawn on the graph with certainty. However, to allow the graph to give us a better visual presentation of the trends it shows, we usually join the dots together as a line, as shown in Figure 4A-2. Because such a time series graph simply describes a trend in a visual manner, it can be called a *descriptive graph*.

There is, however, another type of graph that we use in economics, particularly in microeconomics. Such a graph partly *describes* a situation, but can also be used to help to *analyze* the situation. Suppose that we wish to show how many coats Kathy's Coat Shop could sell at various prices. This information could be shown in a *table*, as in the first part of Figure 4A-3. This table tells us that at low prices, Kathy can sell more coats per week than she can sell at higher prices. The same information can also be shown on a graph, as in the second part of Figure 4A-3. This graph shows the same information as the table does, but this graph shows the information visually. (Again, we have only the five specific pieces of information as shown by the dots, but have joined the dots

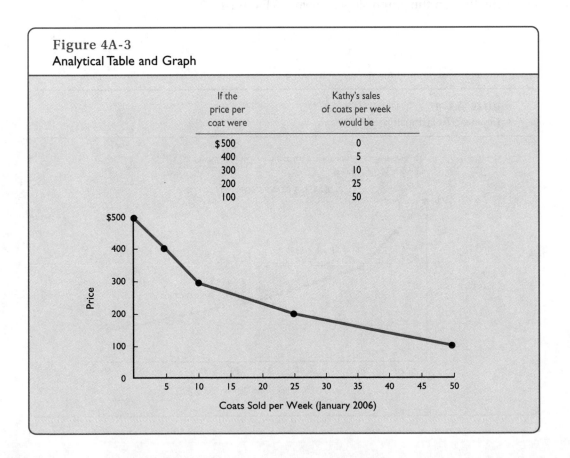

Figure 4A-3
Analytical Table and Graph

If the price per coat were	Kathy's sales of coats per week would be
$500	0
400	5
300	10
200	25
100	50

together as a line to provide a better visual presentation of the information.)

It is important to understand the nature of graphs such as the one in Figure 4A-3, because it is quite different from graphs such as the one in Figure 4A-2. Figure 4A-2 shows the behaviour of unemployment *over a period of time*—the 1990–2004 period, as shown on the horizontal axis. Figure 4A-3, by contrast, shows the relationship between the price of coats and coat sales *at a particular point in time* (January 2006 in our example). As time changes and the behaviour of buyers changes, so will this relationship change—for instance, in July we would expect coat sales to be much lower at each price shown on the graph.

The most important function of graphs such as the one in Figure 4A-3 is to show the relationship between two variables—the price of coats (on the vertical axis) and sales of coats (on the horizontal axis). The two basic types of relationships that can be shown on such a graph are *inverse* and *direct*. Figure 4A-4 shows an inverse relationship—the higher the price goes, the lower the sales go and vice versa. When higher amounts of one variable are associated with lower amounts of the other variable in this way, the line on the graph slopes down

to the right, and we say that the two variables are *inversely related.*

Conversely, if higher quantities of one variable are associated with higher quantities of the other, the two variables are said to be *directly related.* An example of a direct relationship in economics would be the relationship between the wage rate offered for part-time student help by a college's athletic department and the number of hours of work offered by students—the higher the wage rate, the greater the number of hours the students will be prepared to work. Such a relationship is shown in Figure 4A-5.

Finally, while graphs such as Figure 4A-4 and 4A-5 can describe a relationship between two variables, they can also help to analyze, or explain, that relationship. That is, the graph can portray a *cause-and-effect relationship* between two variables such as the price of coats and sales of coats. If Kathy raises her price from $200 to $300, the increase will *cause* sales to decline from 25 coats to 10 coats per week. Because they can be used to analyze relationships in this way, graphs such as Figure 4A-4 and Figure 4A-5 are sometimes referred to as *analytical graphs,* as distinct from the simpler descriptive graphs, such as Figure 4A-3.

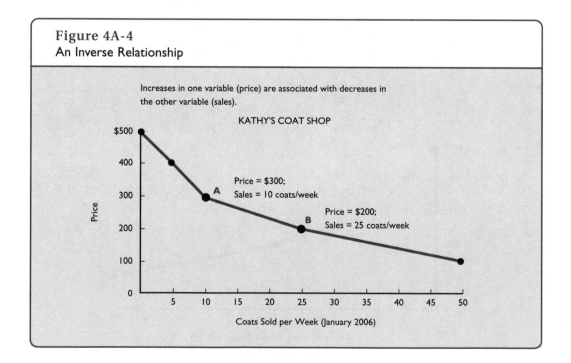

Figure 4A-4
An Inverse Relationship

Increases in one variable (price) are associated with decreases in the other variable (sales).

KATHY'S COAT SHOP

Price = $300;
Sales = 10 coats/week

Price = $200;
Sales = 25 coats/week

Coats Sold per Week (January 2006)

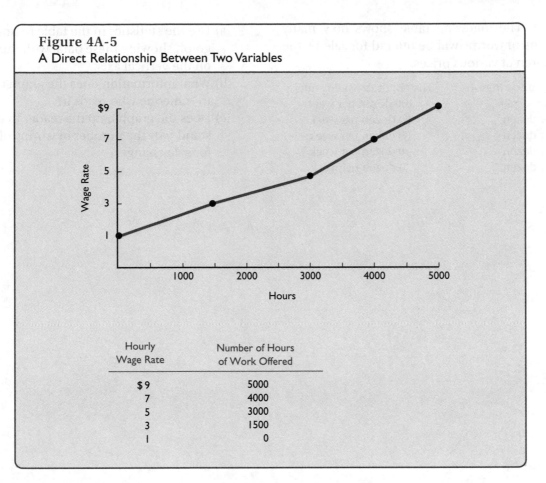

Figure 4A-5
A Direct Relationship Between Two Variables

Hourly Wage Rate	Number of Hours of Work Offered
$9	5000
7	4000
5	3000
3	1500
1	0

Study Guide

Review Questions

(Answers to these Review Questions appear in Appendix B.)

1. The following table shows the number of American travellers entering Canada over a 5-year period.

Year	Number of Travellers
2000	44 million
2001	43 million
2002	41 million
2003	36 million
2004	35 million

   (a) Use the statistics in the table to draw a graph of the number of American travellers entering Canada from 2000 to 2004.
   (b) What information does the graph convey to someone who reads it?
   (c) Does the graph help the reader to understand *why* the number of American travellers entering Canada changed?

2. The following table shows how many tickets people would buy to a concert at various prices.

If the price were	People would buy
$50 per ticket	4000 tickets
40 per ticket	5000 tickets
30 per ticket	6000 tickets
20 per ticket	7000 tickets
10 per ticket	8000 tickets

   (a) Use the statistics in the table to draw a graph showing these data, with the price on the vertical axis.
   (b) What information does the graph convey to someone who reads it?
   (c) Does the graph help the reader to understand *why* the number of tickets sold changes?

3. In a resort area with recreational fishing, children pick worms and sell them at a roadside

stand. The following table shows how many dozens of worms will be offered for sale by the children at various prices.

If the price were	The children would supply
$5 per dozen	100 dozen per week
4 per dozen	80 dozen per week
3 per dozen	60 dozen per week
2 per dozen	40 dozen per week
1 per dozen	20 dozen per week

(a) Use the statistics in the table to draw a graph showing these data, with the price on the vertical axis.

(b) What information does the graph convey to someone who reads it?

(c) Does the graph help the reader to understand *why* the number of worms offered for sale changes?

5

The Supply Side of Markets

After studying this chapter, you should be able to

1. Identify industries as either *competitive* or *concentrated* according to the criteria in the text.

2. Differentiate between the nature of supply in competitive and concentrated industries, using the terms *price-taker*, *price-maker*, and *market power* in your explanation.

3. Draw a supply curve for a product from a supply schedule showing the quantity supplied at various prices.

4. Explain whether a given event would increase or decrease the supply of a particular product, and show how this would affect the supply curve.

5. Explain the difference between *elastic*, *inelastic*, and *perfectly inelastic* supply.

6. Explain why a given event or situation or makes the supply of an item more elastic or more inelastic.

7. Draw the demand and supply curves for an item and show the equilibrium price and quantity, given the demand schedule and the supply schedule for that item.

8. Use the concepts and tools in this chapter to analyze given situations relating to supply and to elasticity of supply.

As we have seen, markets consist of
- a demand side, or offers by buyers to purchase products, and
- a supply side, or offers by sellers to sell products, as shown in Figure 5-1.

In Chapter 4, we saw how, on the demand side of markets, the demand for particular products is determined by the ability and willingness of buyers to *purchase* those products. In this chapter, we will consider the supply side of markets and factors that affect the ability and willingness of businesses to *produce and sell* particular goods and services.

Figure 5-1
An Illustration of a Market

Competitive Conditions

Before we examine how demand and supply interact to determine prices, we have to take a closer look at the supply side of the market—the right panel of Figure 5-1. In particular, we need to examine how different types of industries and firms[1] are organized and operate.

As we saw in Chapter 3, the process that we call *supply* takes place under different conditions. Some industries have many small firms, while other industries are dominated by a few large firms, and in a few markets there is only one producer (a monopoly). These different conditions—which economists refer to as **market structures**—have a significant effect on the supply of various products. There is a great deal of difference between the ways in which a small vegetable farmer and a huge automobile manufacturer make their decisions as to how much output to produce and what price to charge for it.

market structure
Term used to describe the organization and nature of a market or an industry, particularly whether it is competitive or concentrated in nature.

Competitive Industries

One basic market structure consists of what economists call **competitive industries**. Competitive industries have the following two basic characteristics:
- they consist of a large number of small firms, and
- it is easy for new firms to enter (and exit) the industry.

competitive industry
An industry that consists of many small firms and is easily entered by new competitors.

---

[1] The term *firm* refers to a business; the term *industry* refers to the group of business firms producing a particular product or service. For example, Ford is one *firm* in the North American automobile *industry*.

As a result, competition among producers is strong, and the strong competition holds prices and profits down to relatively low levels. If prices and profits *were* to increase to higher levels, new producers would be attracted into the industry, which would increase supply and push prices and profits back downward. While this situation is not to the advantage of the producers in the industry, they are unable to do anything about it; because they are so numerous, it is impossible for them to get together and agree to restrict competition among themselves. And even if they did manage to agree to increase their prices, new competitors would enter their market anyway. Examples of competitive industries include much of the small business sector described in Chapter 3, such as small-scale retail stores, many small agricultural producers, small-scale manufacturing, and many service industries, such as restaurants, barbershops, repair shops, home renovations, lawn care, and so on.

Figure 5-2 summarizes and illustrates the characteristics of competitive industries. In the left panel of the diagram, each circle represents one of the many firms in a competitive industry. The arrow pointing down into the industry shows the "births" of newly established firms entering the industry. The arrow at the bottom illustrates another aspect of a competitive industry—the "deaths" of some firms that fail to survive in such a competitive environment.

Figure 5-2
Characteristics of Competitive and Concentrated Industries

Competitive Industries	*Concentrated Industries*
Producers have very little control over prices and profits	Producers are sometimes in a better position to influence prices and profits
because	*because*
1. there are many small firms in the industry; and 2. it is easy for new firms to enter (and exit) the industry;	1. there are only a few firms in the industry; and 2. It is difficult for new firms to enter;

so that	*so that*
the producers are unable to control the supply—if profits become high, new firms start up, causing supply to rise and prices and profits to fall;	existing producers may be able to reach agreements to limit supply and increase prices;
with the result that	*with the result that*
prices and profits tend to be held down to low levels.	prices and profits tend to be maintained at above-competitive levels.

Concentrated Industries

Not all industries are competitive in this sense; in some industries, a few large firms dominate the market. In these industries, it is much more difficult for newcomers to enter the market, due to obstacles such as the amount of capital required and the established position of the existing firms in the market. Such obstacles put these established firms at a greater advantage than firms in competitive industries. First, because they are few in number, the dominant firms will be in a better position to agree among themselves not to compete vigorously on prices. As a result, profits in such **concentrated industries** are often higher than those in competitive industries. Second, because it is so difficult for new firms to enter the industry, there is much less risk that the industry's high profits will attract newcomers who would increase competition and erode their high profits. Examples of concentrated industries include banking, steel, breweries, and petroleum refining, as well as government monopolies such as Canada Post.

The panel on the right side of Figure 5-2 on page 87 shows the characteristics of concentrated industries. The industry is dominated by a few large firms, and there are few if any "births" of new entrants or "deaths" of firms.

Price-Makers, Market Power, and Price-Takers

Prices are determined by demand and supply. If a group of producers/sellers in a concentrated industry can restrict the supply of their product by agreeing to restrict their production of it, they can increase its price. Sellers who possess the ability to influence the supply of their products are called **price-makers** because they have the ability to determine (or at least influence) the price of the product. Another way of describing this situation is to say that such producers have **market power**. In this way, organized groups have been able to maintain high price levels, at various times, for a wide variety of products, including diamonds, oil, coffee, and eggs.

By contrast, in an industry that is competitive, there are many disorganized sellers and new producers can enter the industry easily, which makes it impossible for producers to control the supply or the price. Such producers are described as **price-takers**, because the market, not the producers, determines the price, and each producer must accept that price. Since each individual producer cannot control the price, the economic incentive is for each producer to produce as much as possible, as efficiently as possible, and sell it for the going price.

Because the production and pricing decisions associated with supply in concentrated industries are different from those in competitive industries, we will consider the two separately. In this chapter, our first look at supply will be limited to the case of competitive industries, which includes a wide range of industries, from farming to small-scale manufacturers to a vast array of services such as restaurants, home repair contractors, barbershops, and so on. Later, in Chapter 7, we will consider the case of concentrated industries.

Supply Under Competitive Conditions

As a general rule, in a competitive industry, an increase in the *price* of the product will lead to an increase in the *quantity supplied*. By making it more profitable to produce the product, higher prices will generate higher output by
- leading existing firms to increase their output, and also
- attracting new firms into the industry, which will also increase output.

concentrated industry
An industry that is dominated by a few large firms and is not easily entered by new competitors.

price-maker
Term used to describe the position of the dominant firm(s) in a concentrated industry, which can influence the price of the product.

market power
The ability to raise one's prices; usually associated with a dominant or monopolistic position in the market.

price-taker
Term used to describe the position of the individual small firm in a competitive industry, which is unable to influence the price of its product and is forced to accept (take) whatever price is determined in the market.

This important characteristic of competitive industries is illustrated in Figure 5-3, in which a price increase from $6 to $8 causes the quantity supplied (offered for sale) to increase from 50 000 units per week to 80 000 units per week.

Finally, it should be clarified that the concept of *supply* does not refer to the physical *quantity* of a product in existence but rather to the quantity of it that is *offered for sale*. For instance, the supply of used 10-speed bicycles in a city is not the 300 000 such bicycles that *exist* there, but rather the number that would be *offered for sale* at various possible prices. And the 1000 used 10-speed bicycles that are presently on the market (offered for sale) is the *quantity supplied* at the current market price of, say, $85.

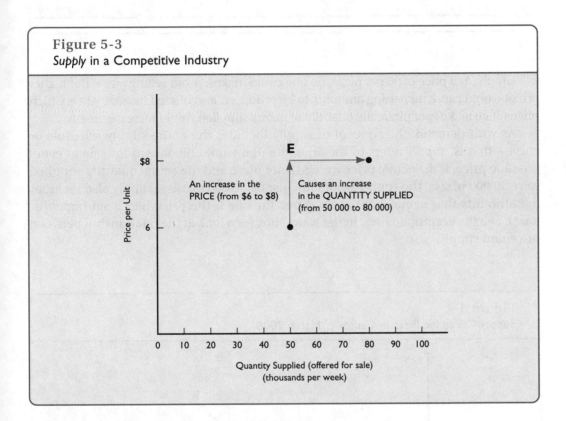

Figure 5-3
Supply in a Competitive Industry

Back to the Pizza Example

Now let's revisit the market for pizza that we used in Chapter 4 to illustrate the demand side of markets. Suppose that the supply side of the pizza market is a "competitive" industry consisting of a large number of pizzerias in competition with each other, and that it is easy to enter the industry. Now suppose that pizza prices *increase*. What effect will this increase have on the amount of pizza offered for sale?

We should expect the higher prices to induce producers to offer *more* pizzas for sale, by making it more profitable to sell pizzas. Existing pizzerias will increase their output, and new pizzerias will start up, attracted by the industry's higher profits.

The supply of pizzas is illustrated in the **supply schedule** in Table 5-1 on the next page, and graphically in a **supply curve** in Figure 5-4 on the next page. Both the supply schedule and the supply curve reflect the fundamental fact that we have stressed: in a competitive market, increases in price will tend to cause increases in the quantity that producers

supply schedule
A table depicting the relationship between the price of a product and the quantity supplied (offered for sale).

supply curve
A graphical representation of a supply schedule.

Table 5-1
Supply Schedule for Pizza in Cantown, March 2006

If the price per pizza were	The quantity supplied (offered for sale per week) would be
$20	100 000
16	80 000
12	50 000
8	20 000
6	0

will supply. At a price of $6 per pizza, no one could make a profit selling pizza. But higher prices would cause increasing amounts to be produced and offered for sale. At very high prices such as $20 per pizza, the quantity of pizzas supplied would increase greatly.

As with demand, the concept of supply includes the entire supply schedule or curve—that is, *supply* refers to the amounts that would be offered for sale at every possible price. If the actual price were $12 per pizza and the actual quantity supplied were 50 000 pizzas, the supply would not just be 50 000 pizzas—supply also includes the amounts that *would have been offered* for sale if the price had been higher or lower. See the accompanying "In the News" box for a look at the relationship between price and supply.

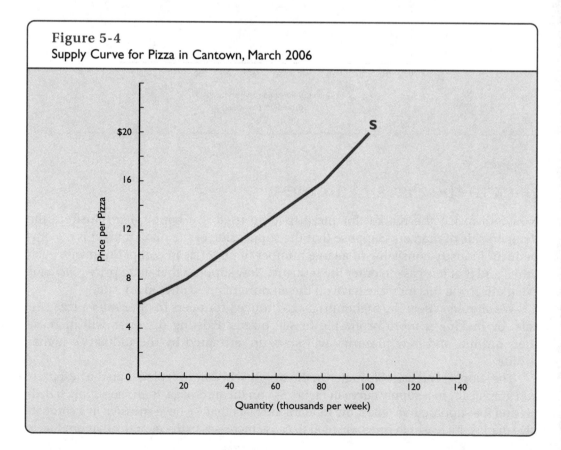

Figure 5-4
Supply Curve for Pizza in Cantown, March 2006

IN THE NEWS

Price and Supply

The oil sands of northern Alberta contain an immense amount of crude oil; however, this oil is much more costly to extract and process than oil from conventional wells.

In 2004, world crude oil prices increased sharply, reaching levels well over $50 per barrel. In March 2005, Suncor Energy announced that it would invest $10 billion in a third oil sands facility that would increase production capacity to about 550 000 barrels of crude oil per day. ▇

QUESTIONS

1. In what way can these events be considered to be an illustration of markets working effectively?
2. What other sorts of developments could be expected as markets make adjustments to higher prices for crude oil?

Changes in Supply

An Increase in Supply

In Chapter 4, we saw that, if demand increased, the demand curve shifted to the right. In a similar way, increases in supply cause the supply curve to shift to the right, as shown by the new supply curve S_1 in Figure 5-5 on the next page.

There are two ways of looking at the changes shown in Figure 5-5:

(a) *Sellers are offering more pizza for sale.* The supply schedule at the top of Figure 5-5 shows that at a price of $20, sellers used to offer 100 000 pizzas for sale, but will now put 130 000 pizzas on the market; at a price of $16, 110 000 pizzas will be offered for sale as compared to 80 000 pizzas before, and so on. At every possible price, sellers are offering 30 000 more pizzas for sale than they did before. On the graph, this relationship is shown by the shift of the supply curve to the right, to its new location, as shown by the new curve S_1. The horizontal arrows pointing in the direction of higher output show this change.

(b) *Sellers are willing to sell pizza at lower prices.* The supply schedule shows that when 80 000 pizzas are offered for sale, sellers used to charge $16 for each pizza, but will now charge only $12. Similarly, for 50 000 pizzas, they used to charge $12, but now their price is $8. On the graph, the vertical arrows pointing in the direction of lower prices show this change.

Causes of Increased Supply

What could *cause* producers to offer more pizzas for sale, and at a lower price than before? One likely reason is *an increase in efficiency*, which would enable producers to *produce more pizza*. Increased efficiency would also *reduce production costs per pizza*, enabling producers to offer pizza for sale at a *lower price* than before. These two effects of increased efficiency are shown in Figure 5-6 on the next page.

Technology often generates increases in supply, both by making it possible to produce more of a product and by reducing production costs per unit. Computer

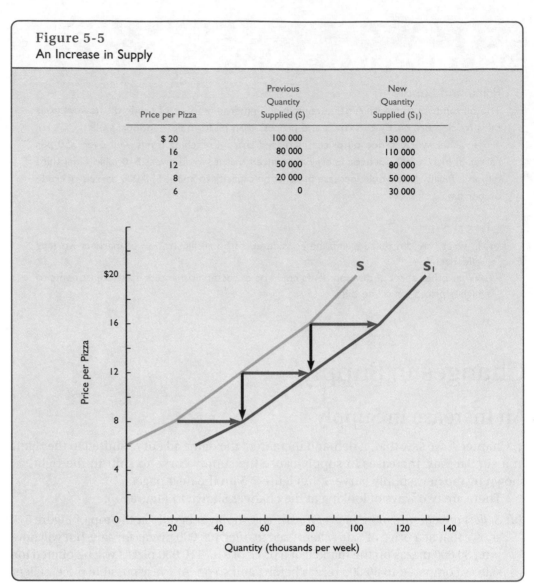

Figure 5-5
An Increase in Supply

Price per Pizza	Previous Quantity Supplied (S)	New Quantity Supplied (S₁)
$ 20	100 000	130 000
16	80 000	110 000
12	50 000	80 000
8	20 000	50 000
6	0	30 000

Figure 5-6
Higher Efficiency as a Cause of Increased Supply

technology was an especially strong force in increasing productivity in various industries in the period following the mid-1990s.

There are various other possible causes of an increase in supply. If *new producers* (either domestic or foreign) were to enter the market, the increased *competition* would bring both a higher supply of the product and lower prices, as has happened recently with freer trade between nations. If the government paid *subsidies* to producers such as public transit commissions, they could afford to expand and charge lower prices, both of which represent an increase in supply. In the case of farm products, weather is a factor, as when a *good harvest* causes an increase in supply. *Expectations* can also affect supply—if higher sales and profits were expected in the near future, existing producers might produce more, and new producers might enter the industry.

In general, anything that increases the ability and willingness of producers to offer more of their product for sale and/or reduce prices will cause an increase in supply. Such factors include the following:
  • increases in efficiency,
  • improvements in technology,
  • increased competition, such as from new firms or imports,
  • subsidies from governments,
  • weather, in the case of agricultural products, and
  • producers' expectations.

A Decrease in Supply

A decrease in supply is shown in Figure 5-7 on the next page. This figure shows the opposite of everything that is covered in the previous section, in terms of what happens and the causes of these changes.

As the supply schedule shows, less pizza is offered for sale at each possible price. This relationship is shown on the graph by the horizontal arrows pointing in the direction of lower output. Also, as the supply schedule and the vertical arrows show, sellers will only sell their pizza at higher prices than before. As a reflection of these changes, the supply curve shifts to the left, to its new location S_2.

Causes of Decreased Supply

Such a decrease in supply would be caused by the same factors that cause an increase in supply, but operating in the opposite direction. For instance, a *decrease in efficiency* in the industry would decrease supply by reducing the amount produced and offered for sale and by increasing production costs per unit of the product and thus prices, as shown in Figure 5-8 on the next page. Also, *higher production costs* (for labour or materials) would push the supply curve upward to S_2 in Figure 5-7, by forcing producers to increase their prices.

A *reduction in competition* in an industry, caused by factors such as the exit of some firms or government restrictions on imports, would cause a decrease in supply. *Taxes* can decrease supply, by forcing producers to require higher prices for their products (for instance, cigarettes), and may even reduce their ability to produce as much. *Government regulations* can also decrease supply; for example, some agricultural marketing boards can actually limit how much farmers produce. In the case of farming, bad weather will decrease the supply of affected crops. And *expectations* can generate a decrease in supply. If lower sales and profits were

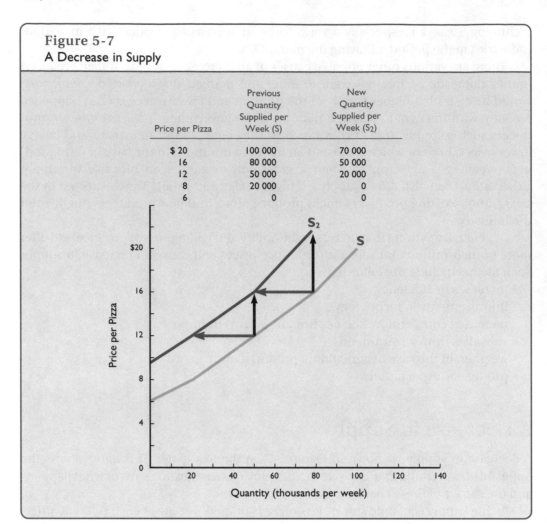

Figure 5-7
A Decrease in Supply

Price per Pizza	Previous Quantity Supplied per Week (S)	New Quantity Supplied per Week (S₂)
$ 20	100 000	70 000
16	80 000	50 000
12	50 000	20 000
8	20 000	0
6	0	0

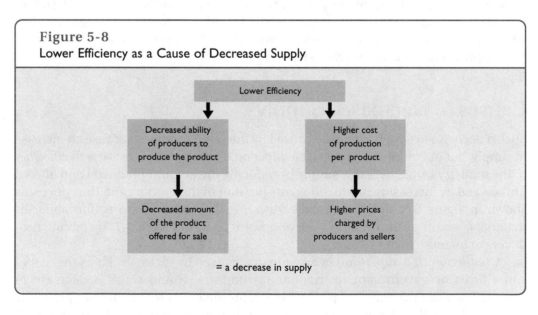

Figure 5-8
Lower Efficiency as a Cause of Decreased Supply

expected, supply might be reduced as firms cut back on output or as some of them even leave the industry.

In general, anything that reduces the ability and/or willingness of producers to produce the product and/or increases their production costs will reduce the

supply of the product, and shift the supply curve to the left or upward. These factors include the following:
- reductions in efficiency and increases in production costs per unit;
- reductions in competition, such as restrictions on imports or firms leaving the industry;
- taxes on the product or the producers;
- government regulations that limit output and/or increase costs per unit; and
- producers' expectations.

Elasticity of Supply

We have seen that, as the price of a product produced in a competitive industry increases, the quantity supplied will increase. We must now consider the question of *how much* the quantity supplied will increase in response to a higher price. In some cases, the higher price will cause prompt and large increases in the quantity supplied, while in other cases, even very large increases in price will not cause the quantity supplied to change significantly, at least in the short run.

Inelastic Supply

If rising prices do not cause significant increases in quantity supplied, supply is said to be inelastic. Figure 5-9 shows an **inelastic supply**: here, even a fivefold increase in price (from $2 to $10) only causes the quantity supplied to increase by one-half (from 40 to 60 units).

    Such an inelastic supply is usually caused by obstacles to increasing production of the product, at least in the short run. These obstacles could include shortages of labour or materials, limited plant capacity, or rising costs such as overtime wage rates. For instance, the supply of strawberries in January would be inelastic: while an increased volume of them *could* be obtained, the amount would be limited and the cost of importing them over long distances would add greatly to their cost.

inelastic supply
A situation in which quantity supplied does not increase readily when the price increases.

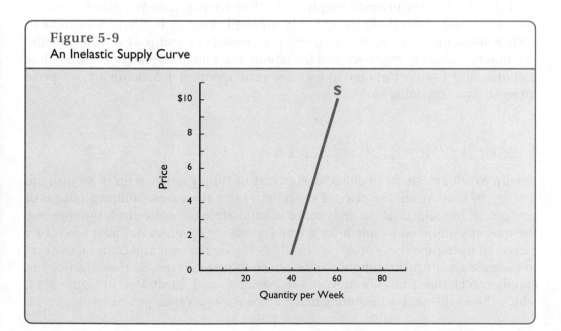

Figure 5-9
An Inelastic Supply Curve

The most extreme case of inelasticity of supply—*perfectly inelastic supply*—is illustrated in Figure 5-10: here, despite very large price increases, *no* increase in the amount offered for sale takes place. The best example of such a situation would be a unique item such as an original work of art—no matter how high the price goes, there can be only one of it.

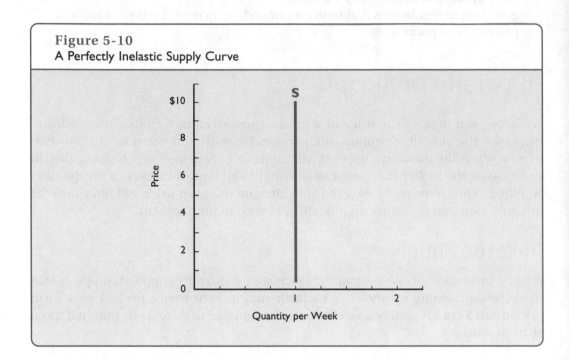

Figure 5-10
A Perfectly Inelastic Supply Curve

Elastic Supply

elastic supply
A situation in which the quantity supplied increases readily when the price increases.

If an increase in price brings forth onto the market a large increase in the quantity supplied, supply is referred to as **elastic supply**.

Figure 5-11 shows an elastic supply curve. Here, tripling of the price (from $2 to $6) causes a fivefold increase in the quantity supplied (from 20 to 100). An example of such a situation could be the production of pencils or compact discs—with the machinery already in existence and the labour and materials readily available, it is a simple and low-cost matter to increase production of pencils or CDs if price increases warrant doing so.

Elasticity of Supply Over Time

Finally, as with elasticity of demand, elasticity of supply tends to increase with the passage of time. When the price of the product first increases, limited amounts of equipment or trained labour may make it impossible (or quite costly) to increase the quantity supplied by much for a while. However, given more time, producers can often overcome these obstacles by obtaining equipment and training workers to increase the quantity supplied in response to price increases. How elasticity of supply can change from the short run to the long run is illustrated in Figure 5-12, which shows the supply becoming much more elastic as time passes.

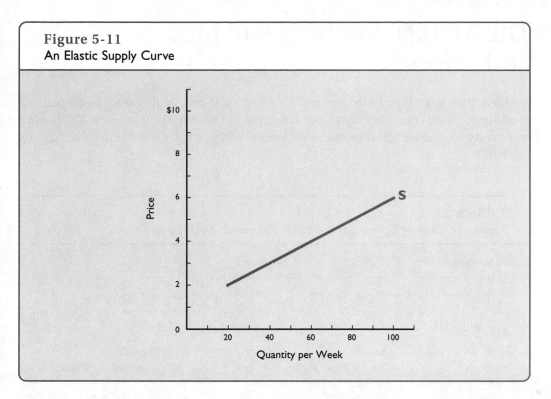

Figure 5-11
An Elastic Supply Curve

What is the actual difference between the short run and the long run? For the production of pencils or CDs, it may just be a matter of days before production can be increased significantly; for annual agricultural products, up to a year. For higher oil prices to stimulate increased exploration, development, and production of oil on a large scale, 10 to 15 years may be required.

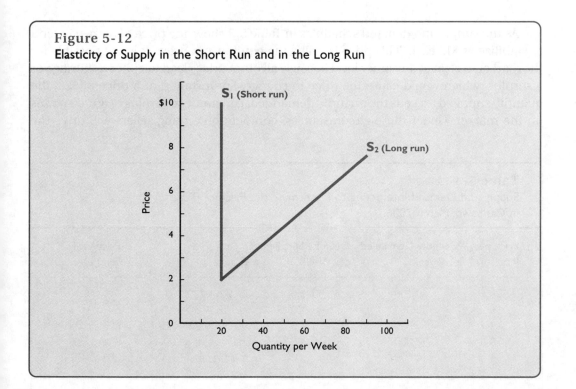

Figure 5-12
Elasticity of Supply in the Short Run and in the Long Run

The Market: Supply, Demand, and Prices

We have now examined both demand (in Chapter 4) and supply under competitive conditions (in this chapter); these two concepts are summarized in Table 5-2. We are now ready to consider how demand and supply interact, by combining them, as in Table 5-3.

Table 5-2
Supply and Demand Schedules for Pizza in Cantown, March 2006

DEMAND		SUPPLY	
The relationship between the price of the product and the number of units buyers will offer to buy.		The relationship between the price of the product and the number of units producers will offer to sell.	
Price per Pizza	Quantity Demanded per Week	Price per Pizza	Quantity Supplied per Week
$20	20 000	$20	100 000
16	30 000	16	80 000
12	50 000	12	50 000
8	80 000	8	20 000
4	120 000	4	0

equilibrium price

A price determined in the marketplace by the interaction of supply and demand.

As the supply and demand schedules in Table 5-3 show, the price of pizza will tend to stabilize at $12 each. This price is called the **equilibrium price**. It is not possible for the market to clear at any other level because all other prices lead to either a shortage or a surplus, which would cause the price to change. For instance, at a price of $20, the quantity supplied exceeds the quantity demanded, generating a surplus of 80 000 pizzas on the market. Under these circumstances, competition among sellers will drive the

Table 5-3
Supply and Demand Interacting to Determine the Price of Pizza in Cantown, March 2006

Price per Pizza	Quantity Demanded per Week	Quantity Supplied per Week	Balance	Price Will Tend to
$20	20 000	100 000	Surplus of 80 000	Fall
16	30 000	80 000	Surplus of 50 000	Fall
12	50 000	50 000	No surplus/no shortage	Remain stable
8	80 000	20 000	Shortage of 60 000	Rise
4	120 000	0	Shortage of 120 000	Rise

price down toward the equilibrium level of $12. Similarly, prices below $12 discourage production but encourage demand, causing shortages on the market. As buyers compete for the limited supply, the price will be bid up toward the equilibrium level of $12. Only at a price of $12 are the actions of both buyers and sellers in harmony so that there is neither a surplus nor a shortage. As a result, the price will tend to settle at the equilibrium level of $12.

The interaction of supply and demand can also be shown on a graph, as in Figure 5-13. On the graph the equilibrium price of $12 is determined by the intersection of the supply curve and the demand curve at the *equilibrium point* (E). The intersection of the curves also determines the quantity that will be bought (and sold), that is, the **equilibrium quantity** of 50 000 pizzas per week.

equilibrium quantity
The quantity sold (bought) at the equilibrium price.

To summarize, the way in which supply and demand interact to determine the price of a product or service can be represented on a schedule such as Table 5-3, or on a graph such as Figure 5-13. Both the schedule and the graph depict the behaviour of buyers (demand) and sellers (supply) in the market for a particular good or service, and the equilibrium price and quantity that will emerge in that market.

Figure 5-13 is a very *static* representation of a market, showing the demand for and supply of pizza *at a particular point in time* (March 2006). In reality, however, markets are very *dynamic,* with constant changes in supply and demand occurring, causing continual changes in equilibrium prices and quantities. In effect, then, Figure 5-13 is a *snapshot* of a dynamic, changing situation at a particular point in time. In the next chapter, we will consider the more realistic situation of how markets change and adjust in response to changes in both supply and demand.

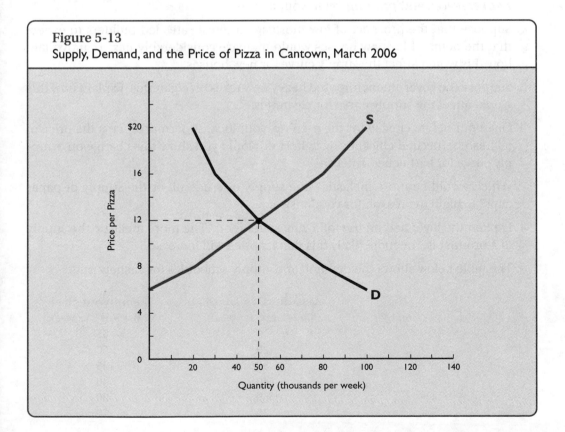

Figure 5-13
Supply, Demand, and the Price of Pizza in Cantown, March 2006

Chapter Summary

1. Competitive industries consist of many small firms and are easy to enter; in concentrated industries, a few large firms are dominant and it is difficult for new firms to start. (L.O. 1)
2. In competitive industries, producers are unable to restrict the supply of the product, so increases in the price of a product will cause increases in the quantity supplied. In concentrated industries, producers may be in a position to agree to restrict output and increase prices. (L.O. 2)
3. Increases in supply will shift the supply curve to the right, while decreases in supply will shift the curve to the left. (L.O. 4)
4. If the quantity supplied does not increase significantly in response to a small increase in price, supply is *inelastic*, while supply is *elastic* if small price increases cause large increases in the quantity supplied. (L.O. 5, 6)
5. In competitive markets, supply and demand interact freely to determine the equilibrium price and quantity, which will change as supply or demand changes. (L.O. 7)

Questions

1. Would economists consider Canada's banking industry to be *competitive* or *concentrated*? Explain the reasons for your choice.

2. Would economists consider the restaurant industry to be competitive or concentrated? Explain the reasons for your choice.

3. Explain why economists consider the distinction between competitive and concentrated industries to be an important matter, using the terms *price-taker*, *market power*, and *price-maker* in your answer.

4. Suppose that the prospect of low mortgage interest rates led builders to expect that the demand for new houses would increase considerably next year. Explain how this would affect the supply curve for new houses.

5. Suppose the government imposed heavy new taxes on cigarettes. Explain how this would affect the supply curve for cigarettes.

6. One hour before closing for the evening, your local supermarket cuts the price of its fresh barbecued chickens by half. How would you show this change on a supply curve for barbecued chicken?

7. Which would be more inelastic—the supply of crude oil or the supply of paper clips? Explain the reason for your answer.

8. Explain the logic behind the following statement: "The more inelastic the supply of a product is, the more likely it is that its price will increase."

9. The table below shows the demand and supply schedules for cashew nuts.

Price per Can	Quantity Demanded ('000s cans per week)	Quantity Supplied ('000s cans per week)
$8	10	55
7	20	50
6	30	45
5	40	40
4	50	30
3	70	10

(a) On graph paper, draw the demand and supply curves for cashews.

(b) What will the equilibrium price of cashews be? Explain why it will be this price, and not any of the other possible prices.

(c) Suppose that, due to increased imports of cashews, the quantity supplied at each possible price increases by 20 000 cans per week. How would the price be affected? Show these changes on your graph.

10. The internet can provide an indication of the number of sellers competing in a market. Visit **www.bizrate.com** and "shop" for a product that is of interest to you. Does this seem to be a competitive industry? How many sellers did you find? What was the range of prices?

Study Guide

Review Questions (Answers to these Review Questions appear in Appendix B.)

1. What are the two basic characteristics that cause an industry to be classified as competitive? (Select *two* answers.)
   (a) There is competition from foreign imports.
   (b) There are many small firms.
   (c) Competing firms do a lot of advertising.
   (d) Most firms in the industry have been in business for a long time.
   (e) It is easy to start up a new firm in the industry.

2. Because of the characteristics described in question 1, in competitive industries
   (a) producers can control the price of their products, but not the supply of them.
   (b) producers can control the supply of their product so as to increase its price and their profits.
   (c) producers are unable to control either the supply of their product or its price, and profits tend to be low.
   (d) product prices tend to be high because there are too many producers in the industry.
   (e) None of the above.

3. Which of the following best describes the characteristics and behaviour of concentrated industries?
   (a) With only one producer in the industry, prices and profits tend to be unusually high.
   (b) With only a few large producers in the industry, prices tend to be lower than in competitive industries, because firms spend less money on competition.
   (c) The few firms in the industry are able to make price agreements among themselves and thus earn high profits, but they are unable to keep out new firms attracted by the industry's high profits.
   (d) Because there are only a few firms in the industry and it is difficult for new firms to enter the industry, producers may be able to agree to avoid price competition and restrict supply, thus forcing prices and profits to high levels.
   (e) None of the above is a reasonable description of concentrated industries.

4. Indicate whether an economist would classify each of the following industries as competitive or concentrated.
   (a) steel manufacturing _____
   (b) window washing _____
   (c) airlines _____
   (d) travel agencies _____

5. Which of the following is the supply curve for a competitive industry?

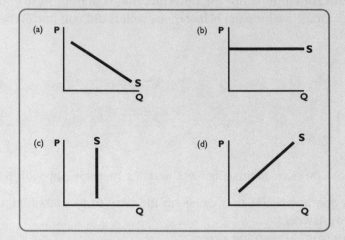

6. The supply curve described in question 5 reflects the fact that in competitive industries, as the price increases, the quantity supplied will
   (a) increase.
   (b) not be affected.
   (c) decrease.

7. The effect described in question 6 takes place because
   (a) when prices increase, producers hold down their production in order to keep prices and profits high.
   (b) when prices increase, the increased profitability of the product gives existing producers an incentive to increase the amount of it that they produce/supply.
   (c) when prices increase, the increased profitability of the product attracts new producers into the industry, which increases the amount produced/supplied.
   (d) an industry can only produce/supply a certain amount of output, regardless of the price of the product.
   (e) Both (b) and (c) are correct.

8. If there were an increase in the cost of the leather from which shoes are made, the supply curve for shoes would
   (a) shift to the right.
   (b) shift to the left.
   (c) not shift in either direction.

9. If there were an influx of low-price imported shoes from Asia, the supply curve for shoes would
   (a) shift to the right.
   (b) shift to the left.
   (c) not shift in either direction.

10. If new technology improved the efficiency of shoe manufacturers, the supply curve for shoes would
    (a) shift to the right.
    (b) shift to the left.
    (c) not shift in either direction.

11. If several shoe manufacturers were to go out of business, the supply curve for shoes would
    (a) shift to the right.
    (b) shift to the left.
    (c) not shift in either direction.

12. If the government restricted imports of clothing from Asia, the supply curve for clothing would
    (a) shift to the right.
    (b) shift to the left.
    (c) not shift in either direction.

13. Supply is said to be *inelastic* if an increase in the price of the product
    (a) causes a large increase in the quantity supplied.
    (b) causes a small decrease in the quantity demanded.
    (c) causes no increase in the quantity supplied.
    (d) causes a small increase in the quantity supplied.
    (e) None of the above.

14. Supply is said to be *elastic* if an increase in the price of the product
    (a) causes no increase in the quantity supplied.
    (b) causes a small increase in the quantity supplied.
    (c) causes a large increase in the quantity supplied.
    (d) causes a small decrease in the quantity demanded.
    (e) None of the above.

15. Supply is said to be *perfectly inelastic* if an increase in the price of the product
    (a) causes a large increase in the quantity supplied.
    (b) causes a small increase in the quantity supplied.
    (c) causes no increase in the quantity supplied.
    (d) causes a small decrease in the quantity demanded.
    (e) None of the above.

16. Which of the following is the best example of a product with a perfectly inelastic supply?
    (a) pencils
    (b) crude oil
    (c) lumber
    (d) an original oil painting
    (e) corn on the cob in January

Answer questions 17–20 on the basis of the following demand and supply schedules for carrots:

Price	Quantity Demanded ('000s kg per week)	Quantity Supplied (per kg) ('000s kg per week)
$5	10	50
4	20	40
3	30	30
2	40	20
1	50	10

17. On graph paper, draw the demand and supply curves for carrots.

18. In the market represented by the above diagram,
(a) the equilibrium price will be $ ___ per kilogram and
(b) the equilibrium quantity will be _____ kilograms.

19. If the price were $4, the result would be
(a) a shortage of 20 000 kilograms, causing the price to increase.
(b) a surplus of 10 000 kilograms, causing the price to increase.
(c) a surplus of 20 000 kilograms, causing the price to fall.
(d) a balance between supply and demand, making the price stable.
(e) None of the above.

20. If the price were $2, the result would be
(a) a surplus of 20 000 kilograms, causing the price to increase.
(b) a shortage of 20 000 kilograms, causing the price to increase.
(c) a shortage of 10 000 kilograms, causing the price to increase.
(d) a balance between supply and demand.
(e) None of the above.

Critical Thinking Questions

(Asterisked questions 1 to 5 are answered in Appendix B; the answers to questions 6 to 10 are in the Instructor's Manual that accompanies this text.)

*1. Suppose that there were large inventories of unsold summer shoes in the hands of retailers in August. How would such a situation probably affect the supply curve for summer shoes?
Explain your answer, and illustrate it with a graph.

*2. Which would be more elastic—the supply of medical doctors or the supply of retail clerks?
Explain your answer fully.

*3. Following are the supply and demand schedules for candles.

Price	Quantity Demanded	Price	Quantity Supplied
$6	20	$6	50
5	40	5	40
4	60	4	30
3	80	3	20
2	100	2	10

(a) On graph paper, draw the supply and demand curves for candles, and indicate the equilibrium price.
(b) Suppose that improvements in efficiency cause the supply of candles to increase by 30 at each price shown. Draw the new supply curve and indicate the new equilibrium price.

*4. The graph below represents the world supply curve for crude oil, in which the current price is $50 per barrel and production is 85 million barrels per day.
Suppose that the current production level of 85 million barrels per day represents the maximum daily production rate from existing oil fields. Additional output could be obtained from more remote and difficult sources; however, the production cost per barrel of such oil would be higher, and it would take time to increase production of it.
(a) On graph paper, draw the supply curve for oil for quantities beyond 85 million barrels per day.

(b) What are the implications of this supply curve for the price of oil if demand increases?

(c) What could prevent the developments in part (b) from occurring?

*5. In 2004–05, the price of gasoline increased faster than the price of crude oil from which gasoline is made. It was then reported that no new oil refineries (which process crude oil into gasoline) had been built in North America for many years. Using the concept of elasticity of supply, explain how this situation could contribute to rapidly rising gasoline prices.

6. A good example of government subsidizing a service is *public transit*. In this case, subsidies keep public transit fares low, with the objective of encouraging the public to use public transit in order to reduce automobile traffic congestion and pollution. These social benefits are the justification for using taxpayers' money to subsidize transit riders.

(a) How would government subsidies affect the supply curve for public transit? Another example of a subsidized public service is *college and university education.*

(b) How does the government subsidize post-secondary education?

(c) What are the social benefits that the public is intended to derive from these subsidies?

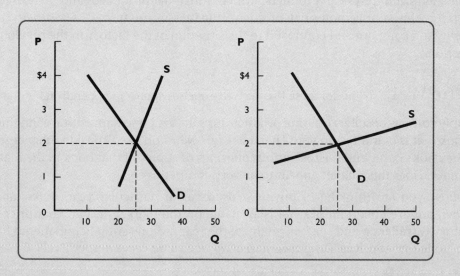

7. In the graphs at the bottom of page 105, the demand curves are identical and the equilibrium price is $2 in each case. However, the supply curves are of different shapes.
   (a) What might explain the different shapes of the two supply curves?
   (b) How would this affect the price of the products if the demand for each were to increase?
   (*Hint: Draw a new demand curve on each graph showing an identical increase in demand.*)

8. The text says that, generally, the supply of a product becomes more elastic as time passes.
   (a) Why would supply become more elastic as time passes?
   (b) Can you think of any exceptions to this generality?
   (c) What would be the implications for the prices of such products?

9. You are managing a factory that is capable of producing a maximum of 100 products per day. If you use overtime labour, you can produce up to 150 products per day. Due to equipment maintenance requirements, 150 products per day is the absolute maximum that you can produce. At present, there is a recession—business is slow, and you are producing only 80 products per day.
   (a) Suppose that sales of your product increase, and so does its price. Your employer asks you to increase production from 80 to 100 products per day. Would the term *elastic* or *inelastic* best describe your ability to supply more of the product? Why?
   (b) Suppose that the economy is booming, unemployment is low, and the sales and price of your product continue to increase. Your employer asks you to increase production from 100 to 150 products per day. How will the elasticity of your supply change, and why? What are the implications of this change for the price of the product?
   (c) Suppose that the sales and price of your product increase even further, and your employer requests production of 180 products per day. What has happened to the elasticity of your supply, and why? What are the implications of this change for the price of the product?
   (d) What can be done to overcome the problems in part (c)?

10. Some ebusinesses produce and sell electronic products, such as software and games. Once the "original" product has been produced, buyers can simply download additional copies of it from the firm's website, without any of the costs associated with physical products, which must be produced and delivered. Describe the supply potential of such ebusinesses in terms of *elasticity of supply*, and compare and contrast it to the situation of the factory in the previous question.

Use the Web (Hints for these Use the Web exercises appear in Appendix B.)

1. Supply consists of sellers offering products for sale. Visit **www.amazon.ca** and find a book that is of interest to you. Then click on "New and used" beside the picture of the book's cover and see the various offerings of copies of that book in the marketplace. Does this market appear to be very competitive?

2. Suppose you are thinking of buying a used car of particular year, make, and model, but are uncertain of what is available on the market and at what prices. Visit **www.trader.ca** and see how many of that car are presently being offered for sale, and at what prices. Does this market appear to be very competitive?

6

The Dynamics of Competitive Markets

After studying this chapter, you should be able to

1. Explain with the aid of a graph how a market will adjust to factors that cause an increase in demand, a decrease in demand, an increase in supply, and a decrease in supply.

2. Explain why a change in supply will have a larger effect on price if demand is inelastic rather than elastic, using a graph to illustrate your explanation.

3. Explain why a change in demand will have a larger effect on price if supply is inelastic rather than elastic, using a graph to illustrate your explanation.

4. Logically determine the changes in demand and/or supply that are occurring in a market, given information on changes in price and sales, plus other market information.

5. Explain with the aid of a graph the effects on a market of a government price support that holds the price above its equilibrium level.

6. Explain with the aid of a graph the effects on a market of a government-imposed price control that holds the price below its equilibrium level.

In Chapter 5, we considered how supply and demand interact in competitive markets to determine equilibrium prices and quantities, using as our example the market for pizza, reproduced in Figure 6-1.

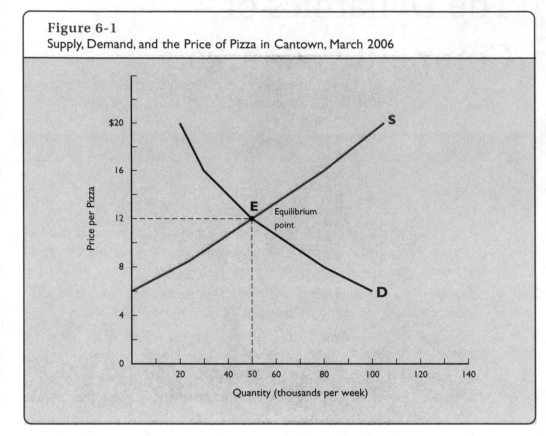

Figure 6-1
Supply, Demand, and the Price of Pizza in Cantown, March 2006

The equilibrium price ($12) and equilibrium quantity (50 000 pizzas) in Figure 6-1 must be interpreted carefully. They do not mean that the "proper" price is $12, or that the price will necessarily *stay* at $12. All they mean is that, given the behaviour of sellers (supply) and buyers (demand) *at that time* (March 2006), the equilibrium price will be $12. However, the behaviour of buyers and sellers does not remain static; rather, it continually changes. As a result, the supply and demand curves in Figure 6-1 are best viewed as a "snapshot" of a dynamic, changing situation. As supply and/or demand change, the supply and demand curves will shift, causing changes in the equilibrium price and quantity. In the following sections, we will consider a few such changes, and in doing so, we will see how competitive markets actually operate.

Changes in Supply and Demand

An Increase in Demand

The demand curve in Figure 6-1 depicts buyer behaviour in March 2006. Suppose that a change in consumers' tastes leads to an increase in demand so that the demand curve shifts to the right, as shown in Figure 6-2. Assuming no change in supply, the new demand curve, labelled D_1, intersects the supply curve at a higher point, resulting in a higher equilibrium price of $14 per pizza. This higher price creates an incentive for pizza-makers to offer more pizzas for sale. As a result, there is an increase in quantity supplied, to 65 000 pizzas. So an increase in demand (without a change in supply) will cause increases in both the equilibrium price and quantity as the market responds to the higher demand.

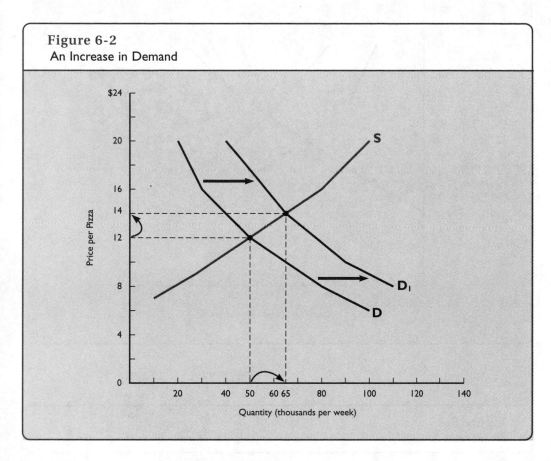

Figure 6-2
An Increase in Demand

In 2005, golfers paid $240 for 18 holes of golf at Glen Abbey Golf Club in Oakville, Ontario (cart included).

A Decrease in Demand

Figure 6-3 on the next page shows the results of a decrease in demand for pizza, such as might occur if consumers switched to buying other types of food that had become more popular. As the graph shows, such a decrease in demand will shift the demand curve to the left (to D_2), causing the equilibrium price to decline (from $14 to $12), and leading pizza-makers to reduce the quantity supplied (from 65 000 pizzas to 50 000 pizzas). Thus, the market responds to a decrease in demand by reducing both the equilibrium price and quantity.

An Increase in Supply

Suppose that, for some reason such as the establishment of new pizzerias, the supply of pizzas increased. Such an increase in supply would cause the supply curve to shift to the right, as shown by curve S_1 in Figure 6-4 on the next page. This increase in supply would decrease the equilibrium price from $12 to $9, and this price reduction would induce an increase in the quantity demanded, from 50 000 pizzas to 70 000 pizzas. So the market's response to an increase in supply is to reduce the equilibrium price and increase the equilibrium quantity.

The decrease in the volume of passenger train service provides a good example of a long-term decrease in demand.

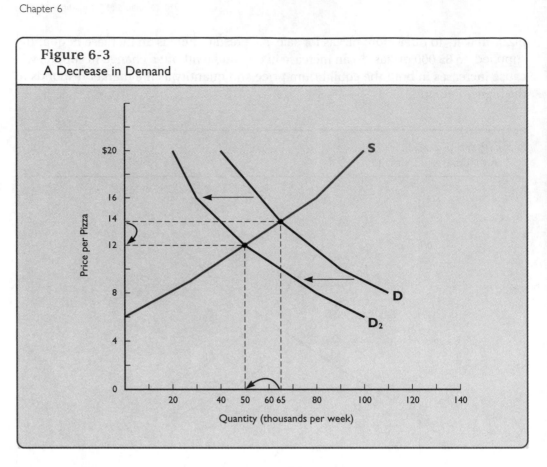

Figure 6-3
A Decrease in Demand

In 2001, excess production capacity and fierce competition in the computer chip industry led to price cuts as large as 30 percent at one time.

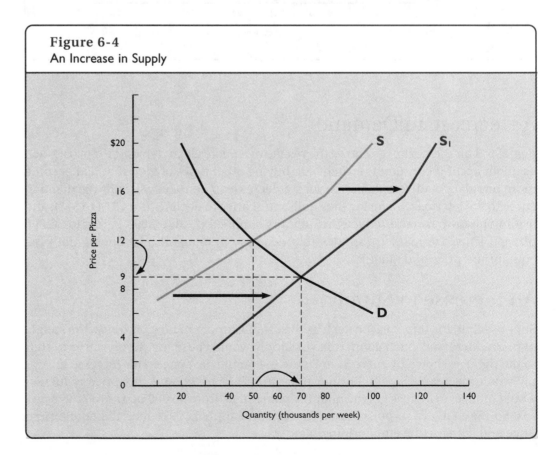

Figure 6-4
An Increase in Supply

A Decrease in Supply

If factors such as increases in production costs led to a decrease in the supply of pizzas, the supply curve would shift to the left, as shown by curve S_2 in Figure 6-5. With the lower supply, the equilibrium price would increase from $12 to $14 and this price increase would induce a reduction in the quantity demanded from 50 000 pizzas to 40 000 pizzas. When the supply of a product decreases, the market's response is to increase the equilibrium price and to reduce the equilibrium quantity.

Bad weather that reduced harvests has in some years caused the price of coffee on world markets to *double*.

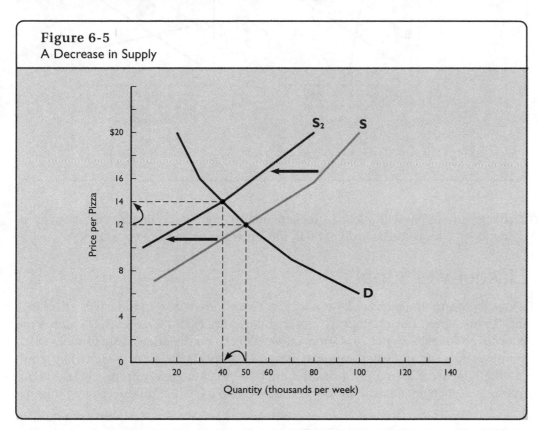

Figure 6-5
A Decrease in Supply

Elasticity

Elasticity—the responsiveness of buyers and sellers to changes in prices—greatly affects how markets respond to changes in supply and demand.

Elasticity of Demand

The importance of elasticity of demand is shown in Figure 6-6 on the next page. When the market is faced with a reduction in supply, the supply curve shifts from S to S_1. If the demand for the product is *inelastic*, as shown in graph (a), the equilibrium price increases a great deal, from $5 to $8. The price increase is so large because demand is inelastic—buyers are unable or unwilling to substitute or do without this product, so they bid actively for the reduced supply, forcing the price up sharply. If, on the other hand, the demand were *elastic*, as shown by graph (b), the situation would be quite different. The same reduction in supply would cause a much smaller price increase, to only $6, because the demand is elastic—since buyers are able to substitute for this product or do without it, they do not bid up its price nearly as much when it is in short supply. So how

In the market for crude oil, the inelastic demand for gasoline is a major contributor to the sharp fluctuations in prices that often occur.

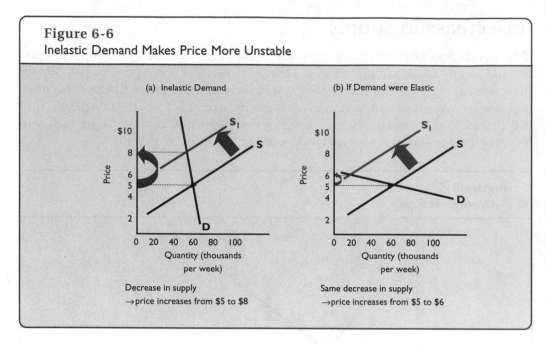

Figure 6-6
Inelastic Demand Makes Price More Unstable

(a) Inelastic Demand

(b) If Demand were Elastic

Decrease in supply
→price increases from $5 to $8

Same decrease in supply
→price increases from $5 to $6

a change in supply will affect price depends to a great extent on the elasticity of demand—the more inelastic demand is, the larger the price changes will be.

Elasticity of Supply

Elasticity of supply also has a large effect on how changes in demand affect prices (see the "In the News" box on page 113 for an interesting example). Figure 6-7 shows the effect of an increase in demand (from curve D to D_1) on the price of the product when supply is inelastic and when supply is elastic. If supply is inelastic, as shown by graph (a), the increase in demand causes the price to increase greatly, from $50 to $80. An example of such an inelastic supply would be crude oil, when producers are pumping

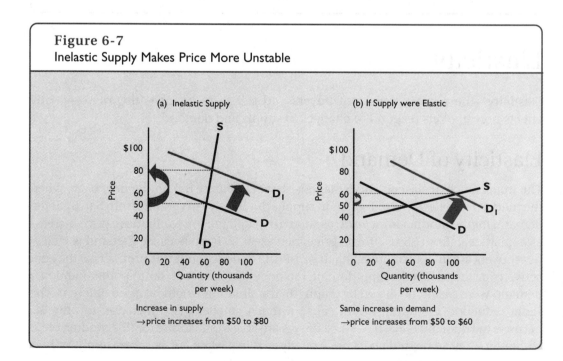

Figure 6-7
Inelastic Supply Makes Price More Unstable

(a) Inelastic Supply

(b) If Supply were Elastic

Increase in supply
→price increases from $50 to $80

Same increase in demand
→price increases from $50 to $60

as much oil as possible and it is difficult to produce more oil, regardless of how high demand and prices go. However, if the supply had been elastic, as shown by graph (b), the price increase would have been much smaller, rising to only $60. The reason for the smaller price increase is that supply is elastic—as the price increases, producers increase the quantity supplied, which holds the price increase down. To continue the example of crude oil, curve S_1 could represent the supply curve after a period of time, when more oil fields had been developed. Generally, price fluctuations are likely to be most extreme in the short run, when supply is most inelastic, and more moderate over the longer run, when supply has had sufficient time to adjust.

Space tourists
The first two "space tourists" each paid US$20 million for a week in space.

In May 2004, Picasso's painting "Boy with a Pipe (The Young Apprentice)" sold at auction for US$104.1 million.

IN THE NEWS

Golf Fees

By 2005, golf courses in the Greater Toronto Area (GTA) were charging as much as $150 to $240 for a round of 18 holes. By contrast, you could golf at courses not far outside the Greater Toronto Area for less than $50. ▪

QUESTIONS

1. Explain what contributed to such high prices at the GTA courses, referring in your answer to factors
   (a) on the demand side of the market, and
   (b) on the supply side of the market.
2. In the future, would you expect that the prices at the GTA courses would be more likely to increase further, or to decrease?

How Markets Adjust: An Example

World oil markets provide a good example of how markets adjust over time to changed circumstances.

The first major increase in oil prices by the Organization of Petroleum Exporting Countries (OPEC) in 1973–74 caught consumers unaware. Because many were unprepared to cut back on their consumption of gasoline, demand was quite inelastic. This inelastic demand made it possible for OPEC to impose a major price increase that generated the greatest international transfer of wealth in the history of the world.

Following the 1973–74 price increases, consumers gradually adjusted to higher prices through energy conservation measures that held down the demand for oil; demand was slowly becoming more elastic. However, after the second major OPEC price increase in 1979 (a further doubling of prices), conditions in world oil markets changed more rapidly on both the demand side and the supply side of the market.

On the *demand side* of the world oil market, demand for oil in the non-communist world decreased by 11 percent from 1979 to 1985. This decrease in demand represented a cut in oil purchases of roughly six million barrels per day, leaving OPEC producing more oil than consumers were willing to buy at the current price. Developments on the *supply side* of the world oil market compounded this situation. High oil prices had attracted into world oil markets a number of new producers, including the United Kingdom, Mexico, and Norway. As a result of these developments, there were considerable surpluses of oil on world markets, and prices fell sharply, from about US$34 per barrel to US$12–20 after 1985.

www.opec.org

These price adjustments reflect the elasticity of both demand and supply. They also show why it is naive to project that because a price *has increased* sharply, it will *continue to increase* rapidly. If anything, it is more likely that it will *not* continue to increase rapidly (and may actually fall) as the higher prices cause more of the product to be supplied and less to be demanded. However, many believed that the oil-price increases of 2004–05 might be different; see the accompanying "In the News" box for the reasons why.

IN THE NEWS

World Oil Prices

In the past, sharp increases in the price of gasoline, such as occurred in 1973, 1980, and 1991, were usually the result of temporary reductions in the supply of crude oil. After a time lag, the supply of crude oil was increased, and prices came back down. In 2004–05, the price of crude oil shot up sharply again, past US$50 per barrel, as the graph below illustrates. The graph shows the actual price each year, and the price adjusted for inflation, or in 2004 dollars. For instance, the 1974 price of US$10 per barrel in 1974 dollars would be the equivalent of US$40 in 2004 dollars, because inflation has made a dollar worth about one-quarter of what it was worth in 1974.

World Price of Crude Oil

Sources: International Energy Agency (**www.iea.org**) and Bureau of Labor Statistics (**www.bls.gov**).

Many observers believed that the price increases of 2004–05 were different—that the price increases were mainly caused by *rising demand* for energy from rapidly growing economies such as China and India. It was also believed that the price of oil was likely to remain high and possibly increase further, because the supply curve was shaped as shown in the following graph. ■

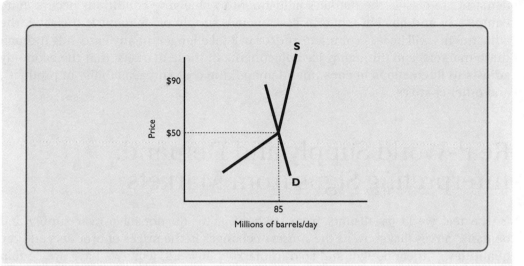

QUESTIONS

1. What does the shape of the supply curve in the graph indicate about the world supply of crude oil?

2. Use the graph to estimate how a 10 percent increase in demand would affect the price of oil. (Tip: Measure the length of the horizontal dotted line, then add 10 percent to it and "draw" the new demand curve through that point.) What is the new price that is projected by this exercise?

3. What developments on the supply side of the oil market could make the price increase by less than the projection in question 2?

4. What developments on the demand side of the oil market could make the price increase by less than the projection in question 2?

5. What has actually happened to the prices of crude oil and gasoline since late 2005, when crude oil was about US$60 per barrel, and in Canada gasoline was around 85–90 cents per litre?

Summary

It can be said that, in many markets, equilibrium prices and quantities are constantly changing in response to changes in supply and demand (see the "In the News" box below for an interesting example). In those cases where supply and

IN THE NEWS

Commercials During the Super Bowl

For the 2005 Super Bowl game, advertisers paid *US$2.4 million (about Cdn$3 million)* for just *30 seconds* of commercial time. ▮

QUESTIONS

1. What factors on the demand side of this market would help to explain such a high price?

2. What factors on the supply side of this market would help to explain such a high price? (Hint: Define exactly what it is that advertisers buy from television networks.)

demand are elastic, the market's adjustment to changing conditions occurs quite completely and quickly, while in cases where supply or demand is inelastic, the adjustments will be less complete and/or will take longer. In any case, it is through these markets, and through price adjustments in these markets, that the economy adjusts to fluctuations in consumer demand, the cost and availability of products, and other changes.

Real-World Supply and Demand: Interpreting Signs from Markets

In the real world (as distinct from textbooks), we do not have neat supply and demand curves that show us the *causes* of changes in the prices of products and the quantities of them bought and sold in markets. Instead, what we have are certain facts concerning changes in prices and quantities bought and sold, together with other information relevant to demand and supply in those markets. From such information, it is usually possible to interpret what *has happened* concerning demand and supply in those markets. More interestingly, it is sometimes possible to use such information to predict *what will happen* concerning demand, supply, prices, and sales volumes. In the following sections, we will consider a few examples of how this can be done.

Rising Sales and Prices

In the late 1980s, both *sales* of houses (the quantity demanded) and the *prices* of houses increased very sharply. What would likely have caused these two trends? It is logical to conclude that *rising demand* was driving both sales and prices up. And, indeed, that is what happened—in the late 1980s, many of the "baby boomers" (the very large group of Canadians born between 1946 and 1966) reached the age at which people tend to buy homes, driving the demand for houses to unprecedented levels.

But what happened next to house prices? Many people assumed that prices would continue to rise, but the information in the previous paragraph could be used to predict that the opposite would happen. Once the baby boomers had bought their homes, the demand for housing would fall considerably. When this happened, housing prices would also fall—as they in fact did. People who understood these market dynamics were able to take advantage of them by selling or buying at the right time. Those who did not understand the market might buy or sell a home at the wrong time—an error which in that market could have cost them $100 000 or more.

Rising Sales and Falling Prices

If the *sales* of an item were higher than usual but its *price* were falling, the logical conclusion would be that the *supply of that product had increased*. For example, large harvests sometimes lead to high inventories of unsold wheat that depress prices.

Does this mean that prices will continue to fall even lower? Not likely—the lower prices will lead farmers to plant less wheat, and they will help to increase sales and reduce inventories. Eventually, it can be expected that this combination of forces will cause prices to recover.

Falling Sales and Prices

If *both* the *sales* of an item and its *price* fall, the logical conclusion is that *falling demand* is pulling both down. This situation happened in the early 1990s in the housing market, when demand fell not only because the baby boomers had purchased their homes but also because of very high interest rates on mortgage loans. In some markets, the prices of homes fell by as much as 40 percent.

Does this mean that housing prices would continue to fall? Again, not likely—such low prices would discourage not only new home construction but also resales of homes, as homeowners would wait for the market to improve before selling. And, as buyers returned to the market (encouraged, in part, by low prices), sales and prices would begin to recover.

Falling Sales and Rising Prices

A combination of *falling sales* and *rising prices* would indicate that the *supply of the item had decreased*. For instance, if weather conditions or crop disease caused a low supply of strawberries, the volume sold would fall and the price would increase. Again, however, it is not likely that the price would continue to increase. The higher price would not only curb demand but also would create an incentive for farmers to increase their production of strawberries.

In summary, from the information available concerning the sales and the price of an item, together with other information concerning the demand for and/or supply of that item, it is possible to determine what has caused the changes in the sales volume and price. More importantly, it is often possible to forecast future trends in the market for that item. And finally, it is often the case that due to changes in demand and/or supply, the probable future trend is the opposite of the past one.

YOU DECIDE

The Internet and Markets

With more and more businesses using the internet, consumers are able to research purchases by visiting the websites of a large number of sellers from the convenience of their home.

A related development is that some people in large urban areas use the internet to post notices that they will be holding garage sales.

QUESTIONS

1. What effect would you expect the internet to have on the average prices paid by buyers who shop online, and why?
2. What effect would you expect their internet postings to have on the prices received by the people holding garage sales, and why?
3. Why is the effect of the internet on prices different in the situations presented in questions 1 and 2?

Government Intervention: Price Supports and Price Ceilings

We have been describing markets in which prices are free to increase or decrease to their equilibrium level in response to changes in demand and supply. However, sometimes markets are not allowed to operate freely in this way; sometimes, governments will intervene in markets in order to keep prices either above or below their equilibrium levels.

For instance, if apartment rents (which are the price of using an apartment) are rising rapidly, tenants may put political pressure on the government to pass laws that hold rents below their market rate. In the case of some farm products, the opposite has happened—prices have been so low that the government has tried to keep them above their equilibrium level, so as to help the farmers. On the surface, this seems like a fairly simple solution to problems of prices that are seen as "too high" or "too low," but as we consider each of these policies in turn, we will see that they are not as simple as they appear.

Price Supports (Price Floors)

price support (floor)
An artificially high price, held above the equilibrium level by the government.

A good example of a government **price support** program designed to hold prices above their equilibrium level is one of the methods used to subsidize farmers. For many years, North American farmers have suffered from a tendency to oversupply the market. Improved technology and farming methods greatly increased the productivity of farmers, oversupplying the market and driving prices down. The problem was aggravated by the inelastic demand for food generally; as prices fell, people would not buy significantly more food, so the increased supply of food drove prices down more. In some cases farm prices and incomes were depressed to the point that they threatened the long-term survival of parts of Canada's agricultural sector.

Unable to solve the problem on their own, some groups of farmers turned to the government, which provided assistance in a number of ways. One such program is *farm price supports*, under which the government would prevent the price of a farm product from falling below a certain level. The government could achieve this by *offering to buy the product* from the farmers at a certain price. Then no farmer would have to sell for a lower price, so all farmers would be guaranteed at least that price for their entire crop.

While such a program would support farm prices and incomes, it would have complicating side effects, which are illustrated in Figure 6-8. As the graph shows, the equilibrium point would have been E, making the equilibrium price of wheat $1.25 per bushel and the equilibrium quantity 50 million bushels. However, if the government supported the price at $2, two adjustments would take place. First, at the higher price, somewhat less wheat would be demanded: on the graph, point A shows that at a price of $2, 45 million bushels would be bought, which represents a decline in sales of 5 million bushels.

This decrease is a fairly small change because the demand for wheat is quite inelastic. The second change, however, could be considerably greater: assured of a price of $2, farmers would *increase their production*. On the graph, point B shows that the quantity supplied would increase from 50 million to 65 million bushels as farmers responded to the incentive of a guaranteed higher price. The combined effect of these two adjustments to the new, higher price (a 15-million-bushel increase in quantity supplied and a reduction of 5 million in the quantity demanded) would be a *surplus* of 20 million bushels—20 million more bushels of wheat will be produced than people would be willing to buy at the $2 price.

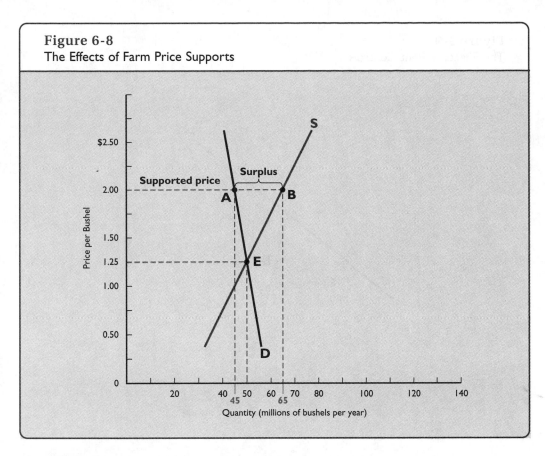

Figure 6-8
The Effects of Farm Price Supports

Where would this surplus go? It would wind up in the possession of the government, which would act as a *reserve buyer* in the wheat market, supporting the price by buying whatever the farmers produced at a price of $2 per bushel. In some cases, such surpluses grew to sizes that they became costly and caused political embarrassment. This situation led governments to try other ways of supporting farm prices and incomes, such as paying farmers *not* to grow certain crops and setting up marketing boards empowered to set maximum production limits for farmers so as to reduce the supply of products. These policies are discussed further in Chapters 9 and 15.

Price Controls (Price Ceilings)

Sometimes, governments want to hold a price *below* its equilibrium level. Controls of this sort are known as **price controls** (or **price ceilings**). *Rent controls* (legal limits on the level of rents and/or on the rent increases charged by landlords) are probably the best illustration of such policies. In response to the complaints of tenants (who constitute a significant political pressure group in some areas), governments have imposed various sorts of rent controls to limit the rents charged by landlords to lower levels than could have been charged under prevailing market conditions. While rent controls benefit tenants who are already in apartments, they can have the unfortunate side effect of creating shortages of rental accommodation, as illustrated in Figure 6-9 on the next page.

While the graph shows an equilibrium rent of $900 per month and a government-controlled rent of $700 per month, this information should not be interpreted as meaning that the government arbitrarily *reduced* rents by $200 per month. Rather, it should be interpreted as meaning that rent controls were imposed some time ago and have held rents to $700 per month, but since then demand has increased to the point where, without the controls, rents *would now be* $900 per month in a free market.

price control (ceiling)
A legal limit on a price or on increases in a price, which holds the price below its equilibrium level.

Figure 6-9
The Effects of Rent Controls

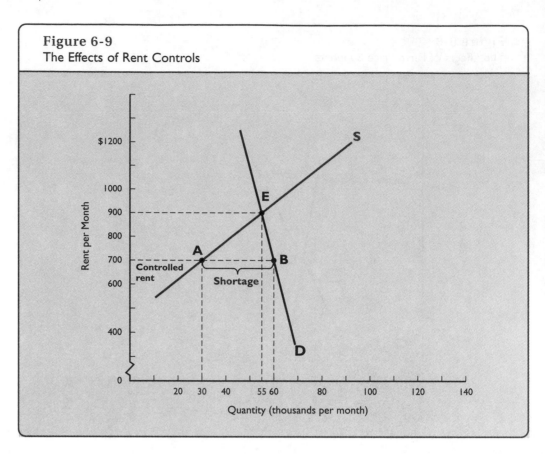

Point E represents *what would have happened* if rents were not controlled—the equilibrium price (rent) would have been $900 and the equilibrium quantity would have been 55 000 rental units on the market.

At the controlled rent of $700 per month, the situation is quite different. As point B shows, the lower rent has caused a small (5000-unit) increase in the quantity demanded, from 55 000 units to 60 000 units. There is a much more important adjustment on the supply side. Here, as point A shows, the quantity supplied at the controlled rent of $700 is only 30 000 units, whereas at the uncontrolled rent of $900 the quantity supplied would have been 55 000 units. In other words, there are 25 000 fewer rental units on the market at the $700 controlled rent than there would have been without the rent controls. When this 25 000-unit reduction in quantity supplied is added to the 5000-unit increase in quantity demanded due to the lower rents, the effect of the rent controls is to create a shortage of apartments to the extent of 30 000 units. The reason for the shortage is not that the landlords of existing buildings refuse to rent their apartments at the controlled rents—they have little choice but to accept the situation (although some landlords may convert their apartments to condominiums, which they can sell as private residences at prices not subject to government controls).

Rather, the shortage will occur mainly because the construction of new apartments will be depressed by the rent controls, which make apartments a less attractive investment. Developers will invest less capital into apartments and more into projects on which their returns are not controlled, such as single-family dwellings, townhouses, condominiums, shopping malls, and offices. Because of this problem, governments often use what are called "soft controls," which exempt new buildings from controls for several years and/or allow rents to rise when landlords' costs increase.

Prices: A Final Perspective

Prices are much more than tags on items telling buyers how much they must pay to get those items. Rather, prices play the role of *a key link in a market system* between the demand side and the supply side of markets. If the demand for an item increases, higher prices will create incentives to produce more of it. Conversely, falling demand will depress prices and discourage production of an item. Another perspective on this process is that, as demand and supply constantly change, changes in prices send *signals to buyers and sellers* that indicate how much of an item they should buy or produce and sell. And if government policies increase the price of an item or decrease it, those policies will interfere with these signals. Once a competitive market has established an equilibrium price, governments cannot change that price without affecting the amounts that buyers are willing to buy and sellers are willing to offer for sale. Programs to support prices above the equilibrium level will have the side effects of generating surpluses of that product, while controls that hold prices below their equilibrium level will create shortages of those products.

Chapter Summary

1. In competitive markets, supply and demand interact freely to determine the equilibrium price and quantity, which will change as supply or demand changes. (L.O. 1)
2. Markets adjust more rapidly to changes in supply when demand is more elastic. (L.O.2)
3. Markets adjust more rapidly to changes in demand when supply is more elastic. (L.O.3)
4. By using information concerning the sales volume and price of an item, together with other information on market developments, you can determine what has caused those changes in price and sales volume and often forecast future changes. (L.O. 4)
5. If the government intervenes in a market to hold the price of a product above its equilibrium level, the result will be a surplus of that product. (L.O. 5)
6. If the government intervenes in a market to hold the price of a product below its equilibrium level, the result will be a shortage of that product. (L.O. 6)

Questions

1. Suppose you hear that the price of new housing has increased by 10 percent over the past year and that sales of new houses have been growing rapidly.
   (a) What is the most logical explanation for these changes?
   (b) Draw a graph that shows these changes in the market for new housing.
   (c) How will elasticity of supply affect how much new housing prices rise?

2. Suppose you hear that the price of tomatoes has increased by 10 percent over the past year and that sales of tomatoes have decreased.
   (a) What is the most logical explanation for these changes?
   (b) Draw a graph that shows these changes in the market for tomatoes.
   (c) How will elasticity of demand affect how much the price of tomatoes rises?

3. The present price of crabapples is $2 per kilogram, and crabapple farmers are insisting that the government set a legal minimum price of $4 in order to cover their costs and let them earn a modest profit.
   (a) With the aid of a graph of the market for crabapples, explain to the government why setting a minimum legal price for crabapples will not be a simple solution to this situation.
   (b) If the government does not assist the farmers in any way, what will be the market's solution to this situation?

4. From 1997 to 2001, the price of coffee on world markets fell from $1.60 U.S. per pound to $0.56 U.S. per pound—a decrease of *65 percent*.
   (a) What is the most logical explanation for such a decrease in price?
   (b) What explains the large size of the price decrease?
   (c) Draw a graph representing the factors in (a) and (b).

5. The graph below shows that, in August, Canadians can buy corn on the cob for about $3.50 per dozen.
   In the winter, packages of five cobs sell for prices that work out to about $11 per dozen.
   (a) Draw a graph that explains this seasonal increase in corn prices.
   (b) Why does the government not attempt to protect consumers against such price increases by placing legal limits on corn prices? On the graph, show the effect that a legal limit on prices in the winter would have on this market.

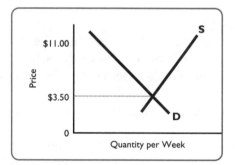

6. For World Series baseball games, ticket prices are approximately triple the prices for the same seats during the regular season. These price increases are decided by Major League Baseball (the Commissioner's Office), in consultation with the players' association (MLBPA).
   (a) Why do ticket prices increase so much for World Series games? Consider not only changes on the demand side of this market but also the nature of the supply side. On graph paper, draw a graph of the market, showing the demand and the supply for regular-season games, and how the market changes during the World Series.
   (b) Do you agree with those who say that it is "highway robbery" to increase prices for these games? If prices were *not* increased by the clubs, what would happen?
   (c) What could prevent prices from increasing so much?

7. One of the key prices Statistics Canada monitors is the price of new housing. The statistics do not show the actual price of housing in dollars, but rather an "index" of prices that is set at 100.0 in 1997, with the index in each year after 1997 showing how much prices have increased since 1997. To see how the price of new housing has changed over the past 5 years, visit the Statistics Canada website at **www.statcan.ca**, and click on, in sequence, *Canadian Statistics > Tables by subject >*

Construction > Construction industry > New housing price index. Calculate the percentage increase in new housing prices each year over the past five years. What trends do you see in new housing prices, and what demand side or supply side factors might explain these?

8. To see the most recent developments in new housing prices, visit Statistics Canada's website and search *The Daily* for "new housing prices." What has been the most recent trend in new housing prices? Does *The Daily* indicate whether the main reason for the recent trend lies on the demand side of the housing market or on the demand side?

Study Guide

Review Questions   (Answers to these Review Questions appear in Appendix B.)

In answering questions 1–4, you may find it helpful to refer to the above diagram.

1. If the demand for the product increased (and the supply remained unchanged), the equilibrium price would _____ and the equilibrium quantity would _____.

2. If the demand for the product decreased (and the supply remained unchanged), the equilibrium price would _____ and the equilibrium quantity would _____.

3. If the supply of the product increased (and the demand remained unchanged), the equilibrium price would _____ and the equilibrium quantity would _____.

4. If the supply of the product decreased (and the demand remained unchanged), the equilibrium price would _____ and the equilibrium quantity would _____.

5. When the supply of a product changes, the resultant change in its price will be greater,
    (a) the more elastic the demand for the product is.
    (b) the more inelastic the demand for the product is.
    (c) the larger the demand for the product is.
    (d) the smaller the demand for the product is.
    (e) None of the above.

6. When the demand for a product changes, the resultant change in its price will be greater,
    (a) the more inelastic the supply of the product is.
    (b) the more elastic the supply of the product is.
    (c) the larger the supply of the product is.

(d) the smaller the supply of the product is.

(e) None of the above.

Answer questions 7–11 on the basis of the following graph.

7. The equilibrium for this market is a price of $ ____ per unit and a quantity of _____ units per week.

8. If the government supported the price of this product above the equilibrium price, at a price of $5, the result would be

(a) a surplus of 20 units.

(b) a surplus of 30 units.

(c) a surplus of 60 units.

(d) a shortage of 60 units.

(e) reduced profits for producers of this product.

9. The two reasons for the situation described in question 8 are

(a) _____ and

(b) _____ .

10. If the government placed controls on the price of this product to hold it below the equilibrium price, at a price of $2, the result would be

(a) a shortage of 20 units.

(b) a shortage of 40 units.

(c) a surplus of 40 units.

(d) a surplus of 20 units.

(e) increased production of the product.

11. The two reasons for the situation described in question 10 are

(a) _____ and

(b) _____ .

12. The price of movie tickets is 5 percent lower than last year, and sales of movie tickets are also lower than last year. The most likely cause of these changes is

(a) an increase in demand.

(b) a decrease in demand.

(c) an increase in supply.

(d) a decrease in supply.

(e) None of the above.

13. The price of strawberries is 5 percent lower than last year, and sales of strawberries are higher than last year. The most likely cause of these changes is

(a) an increase in demand.

(b) a decrease in demand.

  (c) an increase in supply.
  (d) a decrease in supply.
  (e) None of the above.

14. The price of lobsters is 20 percent higher than last year, and sales of lobsters are lower than last year. The most likely cause of these changes is
   (a) an increase in demand.
   (b) a decrease in demand.
   (c) an increase in supply.
   (d) a decrease in supply.
   (e) None of the above.

15. The price of tickets to a new theme park is higher than last year, and so are ticket sales. The most likely cause of these changes is
   (a) an increase in demand.
   (b) a decrease in demand.
   (c) an increase in supply.
   (d) a decrease in supply.
   (e) None of the above.

Critical Thinking Questions

(Asterisked questions 1 to 5 are answered in Appendix B; the answers to questions 6 to 9 are in the Instructor's Manual that accompanies this text.)

*1. Using the above graph as a starting point,
   (a) draw a graph showing the new demand and/or supply curve(s) associated with each of the following events, and
   (b) explain the changes that occur in the market as a result of that event.

   Events:
   (i)   The prices of substitutes for the product increase.
   (ii)   A technological advance enables producers to make the product more efficiently, at a significantly lower production cost per unit.
   (iii) New substitutes for this product come onto the market.
   (iv)   The cost of producing this product increases considerably.
   (v)   The government puts price controls on this product, making it illegal to charge more than $5 per unit for it.
   (vi)   A severe recession occurs, reducing the consumer income available for purchasing this product.
   (vii) The government imposes a $2 per item tax on this product.
   (viii) A strike at several producers limits the production of this product (temporarily). No more than 70 units per week can be produced.

(ix) The government supports the price of this product at $15 per unit by standing ready to purchase it at that price.

(x) This item becomes much more popular with consumers *and* many new producers enter the industry.

*2. Following are four descriptions of changes occurring in markets. For each of these, explain what would be the most likely cause the changes, and draw a graph showing the changes in that market.

(a) Compared to a year ago, sales of corn are up 8 percent and corn prices are 6 percent lower.

(b) Over the past three months, sales of natural gas (used for heating homes) have risen by 12 percent and the price of natural gas has increased by 6 percent.

(c) Compared to the same period last year, the number of boats being rented has decreased by 15 percent and boat rental rates have fallen by 10 percent.

(d) Compared to last year, strawberry sales are down 20 percent and prices are 25 percent higher.

*3. Suppose that after a large employer locates near a town, an influx of people causes apartment rents to increase sharply. In turn, residents of the town press the town council to pass a law limiting how high rents can be.

(a) Draw a graph that shows the market for apartments and the reason for the increase in rents.

(b) Explain to the town council why limiting apartment rents will not be the simple matter that it may seem to be. Use your graph to show why this is true.

*4. Gasoline prices are sometimes highest early in the morning, then come down later in the day. What could explain this pattern?

*5. Draw a graph showing the market for houses with an equilibrium price of $300 000. Now suppose that housing prices are currently $300 000 and that media reports of soaring house prices make people expect that prices will increase considerably next year because no more land is available for construction. Show on the graph how this expectation would affect the demand curve for housing, the supply curve for housing, and the price of housing *over the next few months*.

6. For several years, the prices of personal computers decreased sharply, and sales of computers grew rapidly.

(a) What is the most logical reason for these changes in the market for personal computers?

(b) Draw a graph of the market for personal computers that shows these changes.

(c) Why was the increase in sales so large? Does your graph make this clear?

7. Ticket "scalping" is buying tickets to an event with the intention of reselling them at higher prices, usually at the scene of the event. At the 2005 Super Bowl, some scalpers were selling tickets for more than $5000.

(a) Explain, with the aid of a graph, why scalpers could charge such high prices.

(b) The popular view of scalpers is that they are getting away with "highway robbery," by selling tickets for far more than they are worth. Is this necessarily correct?

(c) Can you make an argument that scalpers actually *increase* the total benefits enjoyed by fans at the game?

(d) What could the government do to prevent ticket scalping?

8. One example of unusual market behaviour is the so-called "Monday effect" that occurs in the stock market. Typically, share prices fall somewhat on Mondays, whereas they rise during the rest of the week. Also, over a 25-year period, seven of the fifteen worst one-day declines in stock prices occurred on Mondays. Two additional facts are that four of every five share-price declines on Mondays happened after a fall on the previous Friday, and the "Monday effect" is really a Monday-*morning* effect: after 1:00 p.m., share prices tended to edge up. Finally, most of the selling on Mondays that caused stock prices to decline was by small shareholders.

(a) Why would stock prices have a greater tendency to fall on Mondays?

(b) Why would a decline in stock prices on Monday apparently often be related to a decrease on the previous Friday?

(c) After falling on Monday morning, why would stock prices tend to recover after 1:00 p.m.?

9. China is suffering from severe water shortages, with over 100 big cities short of water and half of these "seriously threatened." Prices in China are set by the government, and until 1985, most users paid nothing for water. Today, water is still heavily subsidized by the government, and most users pay only about 60 percent of the cost of the water that they use.

(a) Explain to the Chinese government the connection between its water shortages and the government's own pricing policies.

(b) Why do you think the Chinese government continues to subsidize water prices under these circumstances?

(c) How could the market help to avoid a future water crisis in China?

Use the Web   (Hints for this Use the Web exercise appear in Appendix B.)

1. Statistics Canada keeps track of the average prices of various *categories* of goods and services (e.g., food, transportation, etc.) in its *Consumer Price Index*. To see how the average prices of items in various categories have changed over the past five years, visit the Statistics Canada website at **www.statcan.ca**, and click on, in sequence, *Canadian Statistics > Tables by subject > Prices and price indexes > Consumer Price Index > Consumer Price Index, by province*.

(a) Calculate the percentage price increase in each category over the past five years.

(b) Which category has increased in price the most rapidly? What do you think might explain why the prices of items in this category increased so rapidly?

(c) Which category has increased in price the least rapidly? What do you think might explain why the prices of items in this category increased so slowly?

7

Market Structures

After studying this chapter, you should be able to

1. State the three characteristics of a perfectly competitive industry, sketch the demand curve for an individual firm in that industry, and explain the strategies that such firms will tend to pursue.

2. State the three characteristics of a monopolistically competitive industry, sketch the demand curve for an individual firm, and explain the strategies that such firms will tend to pursue.

3. Define *market power*, and identify the three things that a group of firms must achieve in order to exercise market power.

4. Define *oligopoly*, sketch the demand curve for an oligopolist, and explain the types of competitive strategies that oligopolists tend to favour and those that they tend to avoid.

5. Identify five barriers to entry into industries, and explain the relationship of such barriers to oligopolistic market power.

6. List four factors that could prevent oligopolists from raising prices as much as they might like.

7. Define *monopoly*, and explain how a monopolist maximizes profits.

8. Explain why some industries are considered to be natural monopolies.

9. Identify industries as examples of perfect competition, monopolistic competition, oligopoly, or monopoly.

10. Apply the concepts of market structure to various real-world situations.

We have seen how prices are determined through the interaction between the demand side (buyers) and the supply side (sellers) of markets. In this chapter, we will examine in more detail the supply side of markets—that is, the industries that produce goods and services. The supply side of markets varies widely: in some industries such as restaurants and farming, the supply side consists of large numbers of small producers, while in other industries such as cable television, there is only one seller (in any given market). Also in this chapter, we will organize industries according to how much competition there is between producers/sellers, as shown in Figure 7-1. The most competitive industries are at the left end of the spectrum in Figure 7-1, while the least competitive are at the right end.

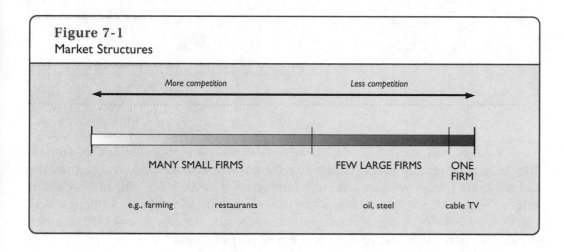

Figure 7-1
Market Structures

More competition   Less competition

MANY SMALL FIRMS   FEW LARGE FIRMS   ONE FIRM

e.g., farming   restaurants   oil, steel   cable TV

The left side of Figure 7-1 represents industries in which there is strong competition among large numbers of producers/sellers. Such competitive industries comprise a large and important part of the Canadian economy—the small business sector as described in Chapter 3. To the right are industries that are dominated by a few large firms, and at the far right are monopolies, in which there is only one seller. Together, these last two types of industries comprise the big business sector of the economy, as was also discussed in Chapter 3.

In this chapter, we will see how these different supply-side conditions (market structures) can affect the decision making of producers/sellers about pricing, output levels, marketing, and product design. In addition, we will see how different market structures can result in quite different results for consumers. First, we will consider the "competitive" industries on the left side of Figure 7-1.

Part A: Competitive Industries

In Chapters 5 and 6, we saw how, in competitive markets, supply and demand interact to determine the prices of goods, services, and labour. In such markets, there are large numbers of both buyers and sellers, and neither buyers nor sellers are organized in such a way as to influence the price. As a result, the price will be determined impersonally and automatically by the *total supply* of all sellers and the *total demand* of all buyers in the marketplace, as illustrated in Figure 7-2. Once the market price for the product has been determined in the marketplace, all producers and sellers will have to keep their prices at or very near the market price. If a firm's price is too high, there are many competitors to whom the firm's customers can readily switch.

Figure 7-2
Determination of the Equilibrium Price in a Competitive Market

This, then, is the essence of what we have called *competitive* industries—industries in which there are so many small firms and it is so easy for new firms to enter the industry that producers have little or no influence over the price. The market determines the price, and each individual producer is a *price-taker*, that is, each producer has no choice but to charge a price equal to or very near the market price. Economists divide competitive industries into two types: *perfect competition* and *monopolistic competition*.

Perfect Competition

perfect competition
A term describing industries that consist of a large number of small firms, where entry to the industry by new firms is easy, and where all firms in the industry sell identical products.

Perfect competition is the most competitive situation imaginable. It is considered to exist only if the following three conditions are met:
 (a) there are *many small firms* in the industry,
 (b) it is *easy for new firms to enter* (and exit) the industry, and
 (c) all firms in the industry sell *identical products*.

It is the last condition that makes perfect competition so extremely competitive and quite rare. If each producer's product is *identical* to those sold by the other producers, each producer will be forced to charge *exactly the same price* as the others; in Figure 7-2, all producers will have to charge the market price of $1 per kilogram. If any producer charges more than $1, that producer's sales will *fall to zero*, as buyers will buy instead from the numerous competitors who would be charging less for an identical product.

For example, suppose the product is carrots, the buyers are wholesalers, canners, and processors, and the sellers consist of a large number of very small farmers, each selling identical products—carrots. If the going price for carrots is $1 per kilogram, each farmer will be able to sell his or her entire output of carrots at $1 per kilogram, but only at a price of $1. If any one farmer were to try to charge more than $1 per kilogram, that farmer's sales would be zero. The buyers will be able to get all the carrots they need from the other farmers, and will simply not find it necessary to buy that farmer's output.

A Canadian farm that produces 35 000 bushels of wheat might seem large. Total world wheat production would be about *600 000 times* that farm's output.

Figure 7-3 illustrates the position of one producer in this market—Vera's Vegetable Farm. Vera operates one of many small farms in the industry, with a maximum

Figure 7-3
Market Demand, Market Supply, and the Demand Curve for the Individual Producer's Product in a Perfectly Competitive Market

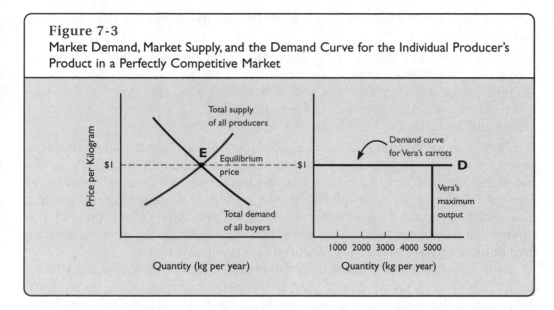

("capacity") production of 5000 kg of carrots per year. If Vera produces 1000 kg, she will get a price of $1 for each kilogram; if she produces 2000 kg, the price would be the same; and if she produces all she can (5000 kg), the price she receives will still be the same. The price remains the same because Vera is such a small part of the overall supply that variations in her output will have no effect on the total market supply and therefore on the price. By contrast, if General Motors boosted its production to its maximum possible level, there would be so many new cars on the market that prices would have to fall in order to sell them all.

As a result, the demand curve for Vera's carrots will consist of a *perfectly horizontal line* at a price of $1, as in Figure 7-3. This unusual demand curve illustrates an unusual situation. At the market price of $1, Vera can sell all the carrots that she can produce. However, if Vera tries to charge more than $1, her sales will fall to zero. This demand curve illustrates **perfectly elastic demand**, reflecting the fact that *any* increase in price will cause *all* sales to be lost. Obviously, the case of perfect competition is the most competitive situation imaginable, where the seller has no *control over the price* of the product, because there are so many sellers competing to sell identical products.

Because perfect competition is restricted to situations involving industries with many small firms, easy entry into the industry, and identical products, this type of extreme competition is rare. It is, for the most part, restricted to markets for certain agricultural products and natural resource products, and to markets in which the buyers are mostly processors or wholesalers buying food items, or manufacturers buying parts for their products.

perfectly elastic demand

A situation in which any price increase above the market price will cause a firm's sales to fall to zero; represented by a horizontal demand curve.

Incentives and Strategies for Producers

What types of business strategies can Vera utilize so as to make as much profit as possible? As we have seen, she cannot *increase her price* because her sales would collapse. And a *price reduction* would serve no purpose—she can already sell all that she can produce, so why reduce her price? A strategy of *product differentiation* (making her product different from her competitors') is out of the question—a carrot is, after all, a carrot. For the same reason, *advertising* would be futile—Vera's carrots are identical to everyone else's carrots, and the buyers know this. All that Vera (and all of her many competitors) can do is

(a) reduce production costs per unit of output to the lowest possible level; that is, produce as efficiently as possible;

(b) produce as much output as is profitable at these low unit-cost levels (which usually means as much output as she can); and

(c) sell the product for whatever price the market determines.

This is essentially what producers in such industries actually do—small vegetable farmers cultivate as large a crop as they can afford, as efficiently as possible (at the lowest possible cost per unit), harvest it, and, together with all the other farmers, sell it on the market for whatever price they can get for it. In seeking to maximize their own profits in this way, these competitive producers contribute to the welfare of consumers, not only by producing what consumers want to buy, but also by maximizing their output of it, and minimizing production costs and prices.

While such behaviour is beneficial to the consumer, it makes matters quite difficult for the producers. Generally, the intensity of competition in such industries will force the profits of the average firm to very low levels, and there will be many marginal producers who are barely able to stay in business. Unable to develop a product that is different from its competitors' and unable to charge a higher price, the only way a producer in such industries can earn an above-average profit is to increase productive efficiency so as to reduce production costs per unit and thereby increase profits per unit of output. Those producers who are able to achieve these goals will be able to earn profits above the average for the industry, representing a reasonable rate of return on their capital. However, if the rest of the producers in the industry imitate these improvements in efficiency, production costs will fall across the industry, and competition will drive prices still lower, and profits back down to minimal levels.

As noted above, perfect competition is a rare situation. Much more common (but still very competitive) is the case of monopolistic competition, which is discussed in the next section.

Monopolistic Competition

monopolistic competition

A term describing industries that consist of many small firms, where entry to the industry by new firms is easy, and where the products or services of individual firms, while basically similar, are differentiated from each other to a degree.

Typically, even in competitive industries, each producer is not selling an identical product or service. While there may be large numbers of sellers selling products that are very similar, each seller's product is usually at least a little different from the rest, particularly in industries that cater to the consumer. We will use the term **monopolistic competition**[1] to describe such industries. Monopolistic competition has three characteristics:

(a) there are many small firms in the industry,

(b) it is easy for new firms to enter the industry, and

(c) all firms' products are not identical—each firm's product or service is in some way different from those of its competitors.

The facts that there are many small firms and that it is easy to enter the industry ensure that there will be strong competition and that prices and profits will be held down to low levels. However, the fact that each firm sells a product that is in some way

---

[1] This is a very confusing name for describing this type of industry. The term *monopolistic competition* is meant to convey the impression that, while the industry is highly *competitive* (due to the large number of firms), each producer's position can be regarded (to a *slight* degree only) as similar in a small way to that of a monopoly, because its product is different from those of other firms. However, the basic nature of the industry is very competitive. It is essential to avoid confusing this with the position of a real monopoly, such as Canada Post, which is the *only* firm in the market for first-class mail.

different from the other firms' products adds a new dimension to the situation: because the products of different firms are not identical, their prices do not need to be identical. So a firm in a monopolistically competitive industry has some (small) opportunity to increase the price of its product—although not by much, because with so many competitors selling similar products, a firm would lose many sales if it increased its price by much.

Product Differentiation

To the extent that a firm can make its product or service *more different* from those of its competitors—that is, practise **product differentiation**—it can increase its ability to raise prices (within limits) without losing too many sales.

For instance, Harry's Hamburg Haven is a firm in a monopolistically competitive industry (fast foods) comprised of a large number of small outlets, each with its own characteristics such as product, service, and location. Harry's Hamburg Haven is differentiated by its location (between the beer store and the drive-in theatre), its product (Harry's hamburgers are not prepackaged, but charbroiled and dressed to the customer's taste), its service (Harry's employees are carefully selected), and its ambience (Harry's is somewhat of a sports bar/hamburger place, and Harry has a personal following in town because he was the highly popular penalty minutes leader for the local minor-pro hockey team for several years). At a price of $5 per meal (the average price in the area), Harry sells 2000 meals per week, as indicated by the dot on the diagram in Figure 7-4.

The demand curve in Figure 7-4 is generally quite elastic, due to the competitiveness of the industry. However, around the market price of $5, it is *less elastic*, due to the fact that Harry's product is differentiated from his competitors' products. This differentiation would allow Harry to raise his price *a little* (say, to $5.50) without losing many sales. While some of his customers would abandon him, the vast majority would stay with him. Although perhaps not delighted about paying the premium price, they would feel that the combination of location, product, service, and atmosphere made eating at Harry's worth a little more. So for a small price increase, the demand for Harry's meals could be *inelastic*, making it profitable for Harry to raise his price a little. However, if Harry were to raise his price *a lot* (say, to $6.50), he would likely find that the demand for his burgers becomes elastic, as numerous customers decide that

product differentiation
Attempts by individual firms to distinguish their products or services from those of their competitors.

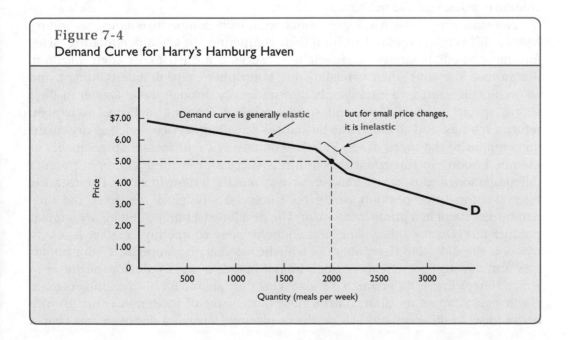

Figure 7-4
Demand Curve for Harry's Hamburg Haven

Harry's burgers are not worth the extra $1.50 each to them, and switch to other eating places, causing Harry's sales (and probably his profits) to fall. At prices above $7.00, not even his mother will eat at Harry's. So, in monopolistic competition, the fact that each firm's product is somewhat different from its competitors' can give it an opportunity to raise its price, but only by quite a limited amount.

A similar effect occurs with price reductions—a *small* price cut by Harry will not likely attract many more customers from his competitors. These people are patronizing Harry's competitors because they prefer their product, location, or other features, and will not likely be lured away by the prospect of saving a few cents per burger at Harry's. A *large* price cut is out of the question in an industry as competitive as this— while it would increase Harry's sales greatly, he would lose money on every burger sold, and go bankrupt.

In summary, then, the demand curve for the differentiated product of a firm in monopolistic competition is basically very elastic, but for small changes around the market price, it will probably be inelastic. As a result, the firm might have the opportunity to increase its price by a small amount. Whether or not it actually decides to *do* so is a matter of business strategy.

Incentives and Strategies for Producers

What business strategies are available to Harry for increasing his profits? Like Vera's situation of perfect competition, the highly competitive nature of Harry's industry limits his ability to raise prices. This restriction creates a strong incentive for producers in monopolistic competition to *increase productive efficiency*, so as to produce at the lowest possible cost per unit.

However, Harry can adopt some strategies that Vera could not. A firm in monopolistic competition can practise *product differentiation* in order to widen the difference between its product and its competitors', and so gain an advantage in the marketplace. Also, it can use *advertising*, to stress to consumers the advantages of its products or services.

If Harry's customers prefer his place, he may have an opportunity to *raise his prices*, at least a little. So Harry can choose between making a smaller profit per unit on a larger volume of units sold, or making a higher profit per unit with a lower volume of sales. Vera did not have this choice.

Not surprisingly, many sellers in monopolistically competitive industries will try hard to differentiate themselves from their competitors. A key differentiating factor for many small businesses, especially in service industries, is their *location*. Restaurants also stress their special menus, atmosphere, type of entertainment, and so on. Retailers strive to establish their own identity through the character of their shops, special product lines, and special services (parking, delivery, exchanges, returns, refunds, and so on). Some businesses providing services (such as dry cleaning) emphasize the speed of service, while other service businesses stress quality or extended hours. To the extent that a firm is successful in these efforts at product differentiation, it can alter its demand curve by making it more inelastic. For instance, Harry's competitive position would be enhanced strongly if his were the only hamburger stand in a prime location, or if he developed a unique and highly popular product line. On the other hand, a monopolistically competitive market is a very dynamic situation, and Harry must live with the risk that his competitors—or a brand-new firm starting up—may successfully imitate his advantages, reducing the degree to which Harry's firm is differentiated and making the demand for his hamburgers more elastic again. Worse yet (from Harry's viewpoint), some of them may come up with better ideas to differentiate their products, placing Harry at a disadvantage. People

The Big "IF": Suppose that Harry earns $10 of profit on $100 of sales. If he increased his prices by 1 percent, his profits would grow by $1 (10 percent), IF the price increase did not reduce the number of meals people would buy.

who have operated small businesses successfully for years tend to downplay flashy promotional stunts as short-term tactics, and stress instead the importance of establishing a reputation as an honest, reliable firm, if long-term success is to be achieved. They claim that providing "value" in this way is the best type of product differentiation that a firm can establish.

In conclusion, product differentiation, however achieved, can benefit the firm in two ways. First, it can build *consumer loyalty* to the firm and its products, and thus protect the firm against competition; and second, it can provide an opportunity for the firm to *charge higher prices* for its products, to the extent that consumers believe the product differentiation to be worth a higher price. All firms welcome the advantages of consumer loyalty; some will also charge a higher price.

Product differentiation can introduce a slight degree of monopoly power into a very competitive situation, in the sense that each firm's product or service is, in a small way, unique. Obviously, the degree to which this occurs will vary from situation to situation: it is one thing to be the only one of eight hamburger stands in town with a particular location, and quite another to be the only Chinese restaurant or the only restaurant in the town's indoor mall that has a liquor licence and entertainment. Nonetheless, new restaurants can easily open, emphasizing the fact that, while monopolistic competition is less competitive than perfect competition, it still represents a highly competitive situation. As a result, profits in monopolistically competitive industries generally tend to be relatively low, with many firms earning only marginal profits. However, firms that enjoy cost advantages, or that have succeeded in practising product differentiation to their advantage, will earn above-average profits, and some can be very profitable indeed.

Competitive Industries in Review

Let's review and compare the two types of competitive industries that we have discussed. While the large number of firms and ease of entry into the industry make both perfect competition and monopolistic competition highly competitive, product differentiation gives firms in monopolistic competition somewhat more room to manoeuvre. Harry can at least try to make his Hamburg Haven more different from his competitors and possibly charge a slightly higher price, whereas Vera has no such opportunity—the only strategy open to her is to produce as much as she can and sell it on the market for whatever she can get for it.

Economists' descriptions of competitive industries sometimes place such emphasis on *prices* that students get the impression that an industry cannot be classified as competitive unless producers practise aggressive price-cutting tactics against each other on a day-to-day basis, to the point of nearly driving each other out of business. Since few industries fit this description, the concept of competitive industries can seem more theoretical than realistic.

However, the economics of competitive industries are more subtle. Because it is so easy for new producers to enter competitive industries, such industries tend to become crowded with large numbers of producers. And because producers as a group are unable to control supply (partly because there are so many of them and partly because it is easy to enter the industry), the incentive for each is to produce as much as possible. When all producers do so, the result is a *high supply*, which generates downward pressure on prices and profits.

The result—low prices and profits—is the same. However, the origin of this situation lies in the inability of producers to control supply rather than in any extraordinary tendency on their part to wake up in the morning determined to slash prices viciously.

IN THE NEWS

VoIP Price Wars

In 2002, about 95 percent of the $10 billion per year local residential and business telephone markets was controlled by former monopolies such as Bell and Telus. Two years later, the development of VoIP (Voice over Internet Protocol, which lets people save 25 to 40 percent by making telephone calls using a broadband internet connection instead of a regular analog phone line) had created a competitive free-for-all in the telephone market, with more than 1100 VoIP providers.

The largest competitor was Skype, the cheapest VoIP provider, which was promoted by Kazaa inventor Niklas Zennstrom. Other early players included Primus, Verizon (VoiceWing), AT&T (CallVantage), Vonage, Packet8, Lingo, Sunrocket, Speakeasy, and NetFone. As of mid-2005, communications giants such as Rogers Cable, Shaw Communications, and Telus were planning to enter the VoIP market, and Bell Canada, the industry's largest player, was planning to channel all of its phone traffic through the internet by 2007. ■

QUESTIONS

1. Why would it be logical to expect that after a few years, there would be only a few VoIP providers in the marketplace?
2. Have all of the various VoIP providers named above survived the competitive struggle in this industry? (Search the internet for their names.)
3. Why were some observers expressing concern that such a highly competitive industry might eventually become a monopoly?
4. What has actually happened to the number of competitors in the telephone/VoIP market since 2005?

The Extent of Competitive Industries

Determining the actual number and extent of competitive industries is not a simple matter, because of the difficulties in defining *small business* and deciding whether a particular firm is in a competitive industry or not. As we have said, perfect competition is a rare situation because of the requirement that products be identical; however, monopolistic competition is a very common form of market structure that includes most of the small business sector of the economy discussed in Chapter 3. Taken together, competitive industries probably account for more than half of the economy's output, concentrated for the most part in some sectors of agriculture and fishing, retail trade, small-scale manufacturing, and especially the large number of service industries (restaurants, fast-food outlets, retail shops, travel agencies, and so on) that have expanded rapidly in recent years.

Part B: Concentrated Industries

In Part A of this chapter, we examined competitive industries in which strong competition constantly pushes downward on prices and profits. In this section, we will examine industries of a different nature—industries where there is often less competition and where producers can influence the supply and the price of their product.

These industries are described as *concentrated industries* because the supply side of such industries is concentrated in a small number of firms.

The Concept of Market Power

In Chapter 2, we introduced the concept of market power, which was described as the ability of producers or sellers to increase prices. In this chapter, we will examine more closely the concept of market power and how producers obtain it and exercise it. In order for the firms in an industry to exercise market power, the following conditions are necessary:

(a) the producers make an agreement concerning price and output;
(b) the producers maintain that agreement;
(c) newcomers and foreign competition are kept out of the industry; and
(d) the demand for the product is inelastic.

An Agreement Concerning Price and Output

The producers need to agree on the price to be charged, and not to undercut each other on price. Because less output can be sold at this higher price, the agreement must apply to *output* as well as to *price.* That is, each producer must agree to limit its production so as to avoid over-supplying the market. If output were not restricted, inventories of unsold product would accumulate, which could lead to an outbreak of price-cutting and the collapse of their agreement. (It should be noted that such agreements to restrict competition are illegal; however, at this point the focus is on the economics of this matter. The legalities will be considered in Chapter 9.)

Maintaining the Agreement

The producers must stick to their agreement. While this condition may sound obvious, there is considerable temptation for producers to enter into such an agreement and then break it, especially if it would be difficult for the other producers to know that this has been done. For instance, in the case of products sold by private contract to industrial buyers, one of the firms selling the product might be able to cut its price without its competitors knowing that it was breaking their price agreement.

Keeping Out Newcomers and Foreign Competition

An agreement among oligopolists could collapse if new competitors entered the market, either from new firms starting up or from foreign producers who were not party to the agreement. As we will see shortly, there are various obstacles that can prevent new domestic firms from starting up in many industries. Fending off foreign competition is more difficult and usually requires government assistance in the form of tariffs and other barriers to imports.

Because concentrated industries often have high prices and profits, they do tend to attract new competition from outside. For instance, many major North American industries that in the past had experienced relatively little competition have been more recently subject to considerable foreign competition, especially in the manufacturing sector.

Inelastic Demand

A final key to market power—and one over which the producers do not have much influence—is that the demand for the industry's product must be *inelastic.* With an inelastic demand, price increases will not reduce sales by too much, so that the industry's income will be increased if prices are raised. Generally, if demand is to be inelastic, there must be no close substitutes available.

oligopoly
A situation in which four or fewer firms account for at least half of the sales of an industry.

monopoly
A situation in which there is only one seller of a particular good or service.

As the conditions outlined above indicate, it is not an easy task for a group of firms to develop—and maintain—market power. What can be said, however, is that the fewer firms there are in an industry (or the more concentrated the industry is), the more likely they will be able to exercise market power. In this part of Chapter 7, we will consider two types of concentrated industries—**oligopoly**, in which an industry is dominated by a few large firms, and **monopoly**, in which there is only one firm. We will begin by examining the larger and more important of these—oligopoly.

Oligopoly

Oligopoly refers to a situation in which a few sellers (or producers) dominate a market (or industry). More specifically, an industry is called oligopolistic if four (or fewer) producers account for 50 percent or more of the industry's sales.

Behind this dry and quantitative definition lie certain economic realities that are important to understand. When only a few firms dominate an industry, it's possible that they will band together to increase their prices and profits. For such oligopolistic power to exist, it is not necessary that the industry consist of *only* four or fewer firms. As long as the dominant four firms account for half the industry's sales, the rest of the sales could be split up among a considerable number of small firms. In these circumstances, the dominant firms would probably decide the price and the smaller firms would very likely follow along, making the industry oligopolistic, despite the presence of considerably more than four firms. Similarly, there could be dozens of firms in an industry *across Canada*, but if they are fragmented into relatively small local markets with *only a few firms selling in each local market*, each of these markets will be oligopolistic. There are probably dozens of road-paving firms in Canada, but all do not serve a national market: if a municipality offers a contract for road paving, bids may be received from only four or five local firms, a situation that certainly looks oligopolistic. In deciding whether an industry is oligopolistic, then, the total number of producers is less important than the number that buyers actually have to choose from.

This is the key aspect of oligopoly: unlike the competitive situations we looked at earlier, in an oligopoly the market is dominated by a few firms that together have a strong grip on a large share of the market. This limitation on buyers' choices increases the potential market power of the producers.

The Extent of Oligopoly

Oligopolistic industries have historically comprised an important part of the Canadian economy. We can get an indication of their importance by listing some of them: steel, automobile manufacturing, banking, airlines, heavy machinery, farm implements, pulp and paper, tobacco, beer, liquor, soft drinks, electrical apparatus, aircraft, transportation equipment, explosives and ammunition, sugar, petroleum refining, cement, meat packing, and soap. As these examples show, a substantial proportion of the goods and services produced and consumed in the Canadian economy comes from industries that are quite different from the small businesses discussed in the first part of this chapter.

Barriers to Entry

Because they have more market power, oligopolistic industries will generally enjoy higher rates of profit than competitive industries. In competitive industries, such above-average rates of profit would attract new producers into the industry, causing output (supply) to rise and putting downward pressure on prices and profits. This does not happen so readily in oligopolistic industries because of the *barriers to entry* into these industries—factors that make it difficult for new competitors to start up.

A major barrier to entry into many oligopolistic industries, such as steel mills and automobile manufacturing, is the vast amount of *capital* required to start business on a large enough scale to be efficient and competitive. A related problem for newcomers is in winning a sufficient *volume of sales* to support an efficient level of production. A very high sales/production volume and *extensive advertising* are often required to compete with industry leaders in many manufacturing industries. Another problem facing a newcomer is *consumer acceptance*. Consumers have become familiar with the products of the established firms over the years, and this familiarity is strongly reinforced by the heavy advertising that oligopolists usually do. It can be quite difficult for a newcomer to break down these attitudes.

Another problem that prevents newcomers from imitating an established producer's product can be *patents*, through which a firm gains a legal monopoly over a product or process for a period of time. While patents are intended to provide incentives for the development of new products and processes, another effect is to give monopolies to those firms that hold patents. The drug industry is probably the most notable for using patents to protect firms against imitators.

Another obstacle facing new entrants to some industries is *government licensing*; for example, the need to obtain a taxi licence, a commercial airline licence, or a farm product quota poses major barriers to entry into these fields. While government licensing is intended to protect the consumer against unqualified businesses, it can also have the effect of reducing competition and supporting higher prices.

In the past, it was quite common for the established firms to engage in *predatory pricing*, or price wars, to drive newcomers out of business. Today, such tactics are illegal, and it is much more common for the established firms to buy out new competitors, through *mergers*. Some mergers are "friendly," in that the owners/managers of the firm are offered generous terms for surrendering control of their firm. Alternatively, there may be a *hostile takeover*, in which one firm buys enough of another's shares to give it a controlling interest, after which it elects its own board of directors and replaces the management of the firm.

The problem of foreign competition is more difficult, because foreign competition is beyond the direct control of oligopolists. Traditionally, industries hold off foreign competition by enlisting the assistance of their government in the form of *tariffs or other barriers to imports*. However, in recent years this tariff protection has been decreasing, exposing Canadian producers to considerably stronger foreign competition. This trend has been the result of a worldwide trend toward freer trade and increased international competition, and, of course, the North American Free Trade Agreement between Canada, the United States, and Mexico. This trend is extremely important, as it means that some industries that formerly enjoyed powerful tariff-protected oligopolistic positions within the Canadian market are now being faced with strong import competition that can reduce or even eliminate their market power.

The barriers to entry described above provide formidable obstacles to the entry of new firms into some industries, and are less formidable in other cases. Generally, their effect is to limit competition and increase profits. Studies have shown that, as a general rule, the higher the barriers to entry into an industry are, the higher the profits (expressed in terms of rate of return on investment) of the firms in that industry tend to be.

In Toronto in the late 1990s, people who owned a government-issued taxi licence could sell it for about $90 000.

Small regional airlines attempting to start up in competition with Air Canada have frequently complained that Air Canada cuts its fares in a deliberate attempt to drive them out of business.

Price-Fixing

When an industry is dominated by a few producers and is not subject to foreign competition, these producers will have an opportunity to reach an agreement among themselves for avoiding price competition, so that all of them can earn higher profits than otherwise would have been possible. As a result, the pricing policies of oligopolists

price-fixing

Agreements among oligopolists to raise their prices above levels that would prevail in a competitive situation.

administered prices

A term used to describe prices that have been fixed by sellers. See *price-fixing*.

sometimes reflect a "live-and-let-live" approach to competitors, rather than the strong competition that often characterizes competitive industries.

The control of prices by producers is sometimes referred to as **price-fixing**, or administered prices. In order to control prices successfully, oligopolists must *control the supply* of their product. Therefore, price-fixing agreements must include an agreement concerning how much of the product should be produced by the oligopolists.

Typically, then, once the oligopolists have set the price of the product for a given period (say, one year, as with automobiles), they make every effort to maintain that price for the entire period. Such **administered prices** tend to be particularly resistant to downward movements. Should the demand for their product prove weaker than expected, the oligopolists will usually cut back their production rather than reduce their prices and risk an outbreak of price-cutting.

Price Stickiness

The reason why oligopolistic prices, once set by the industry, tend to remain unchanged for considerable periods is shown in Figure 7-5. The demand curve in Figure 7-5 represents the demand for the product of one firm in an oligopolistic industry in which it and three other companies are all pricing their product at $100.

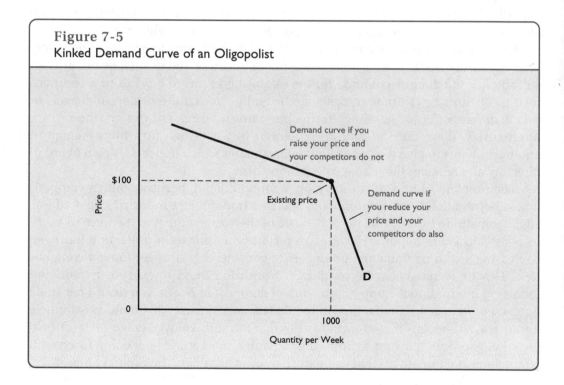

Figure 7-5
Kinked Demand Curve of an Oligopolist

The unusual "kink" in the oligopolist's demand curve is the result of the following two situations.

First, if this one oligopolist *increases* its price, and the others do not, the oligopolist that raised its price will lose a considerable volume of sales. That is, for each firm, demand will be *elastic* for price increases, making a unilateral price increase an unattractive strategy.

Then what about a unilateral *price reduction* by one of the oligopolists? We must assume that any price cut by one oligopolist (in violation of their agreement, of course) would be matched by the other oligopolists, so that our oligopolist's strategy would not gain many sales. That is, for price reductions, demand will be *inelastic*.

With the demand for a product elastic for price increases and inelastic for price reductions, the oligopolist finds that *neither* price increases *nor* price reductions are profitable.

Rather, the most profitable—and safest—strategy is to let the price remain at the present level of $100, until the producers *as a group* decide to change it. Thus, once set by the producers, oligopolistic prices tend to be quite *sticky*, or resistant to change. This price behaviour is quite different from the behaviour of prices in competitive markets, which fluctuate frequently as supply and demand change.

Oligopolistic Versus Competitive Price Behaviour

Generally, the prices of the products in highly competitive industries tend to fluctuate considerably more than oligopolistic prices. In competitive markets prices vary as supply and demand fluctuate; a good example is seasonal vegetable prices. By contrast, the administered prices of oligopolists tend to remain at the level set by the producers until the oligopolists decide to change them, which generally happens only periodically.

Also, competitive and oligopolistic industries respond quite differently to recessions during which demand decreases. In competitive industries, producers cannot control supply, so *prices* tend to decrease during a recession. In oligopolistic industries, on the other hand, producers often cut back on *output* (and lay off workers) in order to maintain prices during periods of weak demand.

Price-Fixing Techniques

There are various ways in which oligopolists can actually go about fixing prices, including the following:

(a) **Price leadership** is probably the most common technique for fixing prices. Under price leadership, the price leader in the industry (usually the largest firm) announces an increase in prices, and all the other firms follow suit in short order. The technique is especially well-suited to situations in which all firms are selling undifferentiated products, such as gasoline or steel, whose prices need to be identical because the products are identical.

> **price leadership**
> A technique of price-fixing in which one firm (the price leader) sets its price and the rest of the firms in the industry follow suit.

(b) *Formal agreements* are sometimes worked out by oligopolists to avoid competition. Such agreements generally cover matters such as prices, product quality, the division of the market into territories to be reserved for each firm, and techniques for fixing bids on government contracts. These agreements are sometimes quite complex, requiring meetings between executives of the firms and/or written communications and agreements. Because price-fixing is illegal, and such agreements increase the risk of detection, they tend to be used less frequently than price leadership. A group of oligopolists bound by a formal agreement is also known as a **cartel**.

> **cartel**
> A formal agreement among producers to coordinate their price and output decisions for the purpose of earning monopoly profits.

(c) *Informal understandings* about prices are sometimes reached between oligopolists. In these situations, there is no apparent communication among the oligopolists and no clear indication of price leadership, yet the firms' prices come out remarkably close to each other. The automobile industry is believed to be an example of such a situation: knowing each other's costs reasonably well, knowing the general economic situation, knowing how each other calculates prices and each other's plans for model changes, each firm could work out its own prices in reasonable confidence that they would be quite close to the prices of the other firms. This process will not yield identical prices in the way that price leadership does, but automobiles themselves are a quite differentiated product, so identical prices are not necessary.

Non-Price Competition Among Oligopolists

As a means of competing, price-cutting has major disadvantages for the firms involved. First, price cuts are easily imitated; if one firm cuts its price, its competitors can quickly match its price cut, removing any competitive advantage that the firm might have gained. Second, price-cutting can escalate into costly price wars, in which all the companies lose. And third, the costs of price-cutting fall on the producers through lower profit margins. With other forms of competition, known as **non-price competition**, these disadvantages are less of a problem.

While oligopolists may tend to avoid price competition, they certainly do not refrain from other types of competition. In fact, the marketing rivalry between firms in oligopolistic industries such as soft drinks, automobiles, soaps, detergents, beer, and so on is a well-known and highly visible feature of our economy. This rivalry, which uses a variety of methods other than price competition, is directed toward *increasing sales and market share*. One measure of the success of an oligopoly is its market share, which means its percentage of the total sales of the industry. Oligopolistic firms tend to be quite concerned with the size of their market share and whether it is growing or falling.

To increase their sales and market share, oligopolists extensively use non-price competition, such as *product differentiation*, *advertising*, and *sales promotion*. Product differentiation makes a product distinctive from the products of competitors, while advertising is used to persuade consumers that these differences are important. Sales promotion is a short-term tactic for boosting sales and market share.

Some efforts at product differentiation, such as more fuel-efficient cars, will serve real consumer needs; others, such as minor styling changes, will be trivial; and others, such as the "feeling" one supposedly gets from using a product, will be contrivances of advertising imagery. Many of them will be costly, as will the advertising and promotion campaigns associated with them. Generally, oligopolists are heavy spenders in the areas of market research, product design/differentiation, and advertising. Non-price competition is not cheap competition, but for oligopolists it is preferable to price competition for a few reasons.

First, an advantage gained through effective non-price competition, such as a new product or a unique advertising appeal, cannot be quickly offset by your competitors' simply imitating it, as they can with price reductions. Second, there is much less of a risk of non-price competition escalating in a costly manner, as can happen with price wars. The costs of non-price competition are more readily kept within limits; for instance, many oligopolists set their advertising budgets as a certain percentage of their sales. And third, assuming that the industry has a price-fixing arrangement, at least part of the cost of advertising and product differentiation can be passed on to the consumer through higher prices. As a result, oligopolists prefer, when possible, to practise non-price competition rather than price competition.

Predicting Behaviour

Earlier, we noted that once oligopolists have set the price of their product, the price tends to be "sticky," or resistant to change. However, we have not yet considered how oligopolists *actually decide* what price to charge and what output to produce in the first place. Considering the importance of oligopolistic industries in the economy, this is an important question.

Unfortunately, it is quite difficult to generalize about, or predict, the pricing behaviour of most oligopolistic industries. In competitive industries, we can predict that prices will be driven downward toward a minimum level. But oligopolists often have considerably more discretion over the prices of their products, which makes it much more difficult to analyze and predict their pricing decisions.

non-price competition Competition between sellers based not on price but rather on factors such as product differentiation and advertising.

Research has shown that the widely held belief that oil companies regularly raise gasoline prices as long weekends commence is untrue.

While the domination of an industry by a few firms creates the *potential* for price-fixing, several factors will influence the *actual* pricing decisions of these firms and industries. The possible range of oligopolists' power over prices is quite wide. At one extreme, a tightly organized group of oligopolists without any foreign competition and facing an inelastic demand for its product is in an excellent position to raise prices to very high levels. At the other extreme, oligopolists facing strong foreign competition may find themselves without any real power over prices at all. In the following section, we will consider some of the factors that limit the power of oligopolists to raise prices.

YOU DECIDE

Coffee Crop Control

At times in the past, the world's major coffee producers have agreed to burn a considerable portion (as much as 20 percent) of their harvests. ■

QUESTIONS
1. What would be the purpose of destroying so much coffee?
2. What would be required in order for such a plan to achieve its objective?
3. What could prevent the plan from being successful?

Limits on Prices

Foreign competition has in recent years become the most important factor limiting the market power of many oligopolists, especially in the manufacturing sector of the economy. As international trade agreements have reduced tariffs both in North America and globally, many Canadian manufacturers have found themselves facing increasingly strong competition from imports. In many major industries, such as automobiles, steel, electronic equipment, and textiles, the market power of Canadian (and American) industries has been sharply reduced or even eliminated by competition from imports.

Lack of cooperation among oligopolists can also limit their control over prices. If any of the firms in the industry has a tendency to use price competition, either openly or by cheating on the agreement, the other firms will have to respond in kind, or face a decrease in their market share. Price-cutting is more likely during recessions, when sales are slow.

Elasticity of demand for the product is another factor that can limit the ability of oligopolists to raise prices. If substitutes for the product make the demand for it elastic, sales will fall by so much that it will be futile for the oligopolists to raise prices. Usually there are few if any substitutes, since the oligopolists control the entire market for a given product; however, this is not always the case. For instance, in some uses, steel has to contend with competition from aluminum, plastics, and even glass, and the airline industry is to some extent in competition with other vacation packages. And, as technology generates new materials, processes, and products, this kind of inter-product and inter-industry competition has been presenting some previously secure industries with competition from new and unexpected quarters. This trend has been particularly evident in the communications field recently.

Fear of prosecution for price-fixing may also act as a deterrent to oligopolists. As we will see in Chapter 9, price-fixing is illegal under Canadian law, so companies that fix prices face a risk of being prosecuted and fined. While the law has not stopped price-fixing, it seems likely that it has acted as a deterrent.

"All players are competitors on the market, but before that they are partners within OPEC."

— HOSSEIN KAZEMPOUR ARDEBILI, IRANIAN OPEC REPRESENTATIVE

IN THE NEWS

OPEC

The Organization of Petroleum Exporting Countries (OPEC) is an organization of 11 countries that produce and export oil. OPEC countries produce roughly 40 percent of the world's oil. Periodically, the media report that OPEC is considering reducing production by its member countries in order to increase world oil prices. These media reports often include two other interesting comments. The first is that a seemingly small reduction in OPEC's production (for example, 4 percent, which would represent roughly 1.6 percent of total world output) is expected to lead to price increases of 10–20 percent. The second is that in the opinion of oil industry experts, OPEC will have great difficulty in achieving its objectives. ■

QUESTIONS

1. What does this information tell us about the elasticity of the demand for oil?
2. Why do you think that OPEC has often failed to achieve the increases in the price of oil that oil-consuming nations had feared?

How Much Market Power?

There is no simple answer to the question of how much market power oligopolists possess—it varies widely from industry to industry and from time to time, so it is impossible to generalize. In some situations, in which the oligopolists are well-organized and face no foreign competition, they can have considerable market power. In other cases, one or more of the factors outlined in the previous section can take away most or even all of their ability to charge high prices.

Furthermore, the effectiveness of these limits on prices can vary from time to time, as conditions change. For instance, the automobile industry was for many years considered a classic example of a powerful oligopoly as a few dominant firms kept competition within bounds and both workers' wages and companies' profits were well above average levels. However, over the past 35 years, import competition has limited the market power of both the companies and their unions.

Regardless of the factors that may—or may not—restrain the market power of oligopolists, the fact remains that some large corporations do possess considerable power over prices, particularly when economic conditions are favourable. These large corporations, and the market power that some of them possess, are a long way from the competitive industries described in the first part of this chapter. This difference is reflected in the fact that, on average, the profits of larger corporations represent a significantly higher rate of return on the owners' investment than do the profits of smaller businesses.

Monopoly

Suppose that as the result of a patent,[2] Global Gadgets, Inc., is the only producer of a particular component used in snowmobiles. Since Global Gadgets is the only producer of this product, the total market demand for the product and the demand for Global Gadgets' product are the same thing. This demand is illustrated in Figure 7-6, in both schedule and graph form.

---

[2] A patent gives the inventor of a product a legal monopoly over the production of it for a certain period.

Figure 7-6
Demand for Global Gadgets' Product

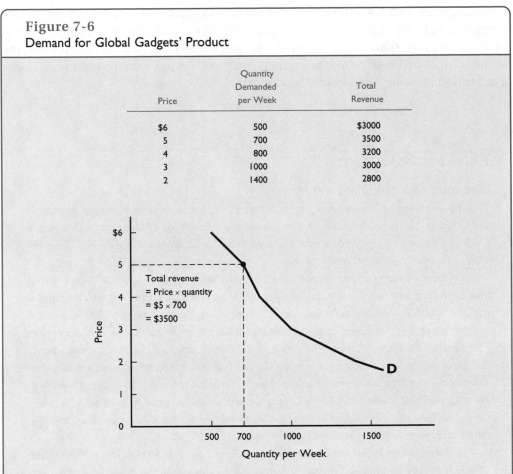

Price	Quantity Demanded per Week	Total Revenue
$6	500	$3000
5	700	3500
4	800	3200
3	1000	3000
2	1400	2800

Total revenue
= Price × quantity
= $5 × 700
= $3500

Total revenue (the area of the rectangle under the demand curve) is maximized at a price of $5.

What price will the monopoly charge for its product? While our initial response may be that the monopoly will select the highest price, Figure 7-6 shows that the *highest* price may not be the *most profitable*. By charging a price of $5 and producing 700 units per week, the monopoly can make a higher total revenue than if, for instance, the price were raised to $6, and sales dropped to 500 units per week. (Note that we are looking at only the *revenue* side of the picture, and are ignoring the *costs*. In effect, we are assuming that if the monopoly maximizes total revenue, it is also maximizing profits. In Chapter 8, we will consider costs.)

Under these assumptions, the monopoly will raise its price as long as the demand is inelastic. At prices above $5, the demand becomes elastic as buyer resistance to such high prices cuts sales and revenues.

At a price of $5, only 700 products can be sold per week. If more were produced, they could not be sold without lowering the price. So the key to the monopolist's ability to raise the price to $5 lies in the fact that the monopolist *controls the supply* of the product, and can restrict the supply to 700 per week.

Monopoly Compared to Competition

By making *prices higher* and *output lower* than they would otherwise be, monopoly imposes a twofold burden on society economically. In Figure 7-6, suppose that the minimum price for which the product could be sold profitably were $3. If there were strong competition in the industry, the price would fall to $3 (instead of $5) and production would be 1000 units (instead of 700). But with a monopoly in the industry, the public is burdened with *both* higher prices *and* lower output than would exist under competition (see the "You Decide" box below).

YOU DECIDE

The International Diamond Monopoly

One of the most famous monopolies of all time is the international diamond monopoly organized by De Beers, a South African corporation. For most of the twentieth century, De Beers owned or controlled all the diamond mines in South Africa and owned diamond-trading companies in various countries.

De Beers' success stemmed not only from its control of the *supply* of diamonds, but also from its ability to influence the *demand* for them. Starting in 1938 (at which time diamond prices had declined badly due to the Depression), the demand for diamonds in the United States was promoted by a sophisticated advertising campaign that virtually *created* a "tradition": the diamond engagement ring, and the association of diamonds with romance and permanence—"A Diamond Is Forever." By the late 1950s a diamond was generally considered essential to an engagement in North America, and in 1967 this 29-year-old American tradition was successfully "exported" to Japan with the help of an advertising campaign. By 1980, 60 percent of engaged Japanese women received diamonds, and diamond sales in Japan had reached $1 billion per year.

However, even a monopoly as powerful as De Beers was not without its problems, most of which related to keeping control of the supply. In the 1960s the diamond market was threatened by a large inflow of Russian diamonds, which were considerably smaller than De Beers' traditional South African gems. To avoid a depressed market, De Beers undertook to market these diamonds for the Soviets, and an advertising campaign was mounted to shift demand toward smaller diamonds sold in new "eternity rings" for older married women. This campaign was remarkably successful; however, it had the side-effect of undercutting the market for De Beers' traditional larger diamonds. By the late 1970s, these were being discounted by as much as 20 percent—a sign that De Beers was losing control of the supply.

www.debeers.ca

Meanwhile, other developments threatened De Beers' control of the diamond market. In the late 1970s the discovery of vast diamond deposits in Western Australia made it even more difficult for De Beers to control the supply. In addition, political instability in South Africa made it uncertain whether De Beers would be able to hold together the key suppliers in that region.

When De Beers had controlled 80 percent of the world supply of diamonds, it could control the price simply by cutting back on the volume of diamonds that it allotted each year to about 300 hand-picked dealers. However, as other suppliers came into play, De Beers found it increasingly necessary to keep their diamonds off the market, by buying diamonds and storing them. Over time, De Beers accumulated an inventory of diamonds worth over $4 billion, and was finding itself short of cash to buy up additional diamonds in order to support the price.

And support of the price of diamonds was crucial to De Beers' strategy. It is estimated that the public holds more than 500 million carats of gem diamonds. It is essential that this half-billion carat stock of diamonds be retained by its owners, and not placed on the market. If only a small proportion of this stock were sold in any one year, the price could collapse. While it is unlikely that people would sell their engagement rings (a diamond is, after all, forever), there was an increasingly large stock of "investment diamonds" in the hands of both wealthy individuals and financial institutions. In the event of price decreases, these investment diamonds might be dumped onto the market, depressing prices further.

Ironically, only by maintaining the price of diamonds (described by some observers as the "diamond illusion") could De Beers prevent such a sell-off of diamonds, and the risk of a price collapse that this could bring. Yet, as additional suppliers came onto the diamond market, it became more difficult to preserve that price by controlling the supply.

Finally, with its market share down to 63 percent, De Beers decided that it could no longer control the supply of diamonds. Instead, De Beers repositioned itself in 2000 as a seller of high-quality diamonds *and* luxury products, using advertising to influence consumer demand for its own products. ■

QUESTIONS
1. Why might diamonds be considered a risky long-term investment?
2. According to some economists, monopoly can never be more than a temporary market condition. Explain the reasoning behind this theory, and why you agree or disagree with it.

The Extent of Monopoly

Monopoly is a relatively rare form of market structure. Most monopolies in the Canadian economy are in public utilities or public services such as electricity, water, postal service, natural gas, and cable television. Such industries are called **natural monopolies** because by having only one producer, the high costs of the capital equipment that is required can be spread over the maximum number of users, reducing the cost of these services to each user. In order to protect the public against the market power of such monopolies, the government has usually either regulated the rates that they charge or taken over ownership and operation of them. In Chapter 9, we will examine in more detail the issues and the arguments concerning the question of government policy regarding these natural monopolies.

natural monopoly
An industry, such as public utilities, that by its nature lends itself to a monopolistic form of organization.

In Conclusion

Figure 7-7 on page 148 summarizes and compares the four basic types of market structures, ranging from perfect competition to monopoly.

It should be noted that these four market structures represent only *types* of market structures, and that any particular real-life industry may consist of some combination of these types. For instance, an industry with three major Canadian firms that have 50 percent of the market, several smaller Canadian firms, and imports from several large foreign firms would look something like Figure 7-8 on page 149.

The industry in Figure 7-8 would fall very near the middle of the spectrum of industries shown in Figure 7-1 at the start of this chapter. While it might fall under the strict definition of *oligopoly* (four firms or less having 50 percent of the market), there would be considerably more competition and less opportunity for price-fixing in it than in a classic oligopoly. Indeed, it might well be sufficiently competitive that firms in it would have to behave more like firms in a competitive industry than like oligopolists.

In addition, it should be noted that the market structure of an industry can *change* over time, especially when larger size (economies of scale) allow larger firms to enjoy lower production costs. In the 1920s, there were 241 automobile manufacturing firms in North America. Over the years, competition reduced this to three giant companies that enjoyed economies of scale that smaller firms could not achieve.

Figure 7-7
Summary of the Four Types of Market Structures

	Perfect Competition	Monopolistic Competition	Oligopoly	Monopoly
Characteristics	(a) many firms (b) easy to enter (c) identical products	(a) many firms (b) easy to enter (c) differentiated products	(a) few firms (b) difficult to enter	(a) one firm (b) difficult to enter
Demand Curve				
Economic Incentives / Business Strategies	Each producer gains by (a) maximizing efficiency, (b) producing as much output as is economical, and (c) selling output for the market price.	Each producer gains by (a) maximizing efficiency, and (b) using product differentiation, and (c) advertising, and (d) possibly increasing prices slightly.	All producers can gain by acting together to restrict competition, restrict supply, and raise prices; competition is restricted to non-price areas such as product differentiation and advertising.	The monopolist controls the entire supply and gains by restricting it so as to maximize profits.
Results / Market Power	Downward pressure on prices and profits: each firm has *no* control over the price of its product.	Downward pressure on prices and profits: each firm has a *potential slight degree of control* over the price of its product.	Producers may (or may not) be able to exercise *considerable control* over the prices of their products and to earn profits above competitive levels.	Monopolists can maximize their profits by exercising the *maximum degree of control* over the prices of their products.
Extent	Rare, some agricultural products and resource products.	Common, mostly in service industries, retail trade, and small-scale manufacturing.	Common, concentrated in the manufacturing and resource sectors.	Rare, mostly restricted to public utilities such as electricity, water, etc.

Figure 7-8
Industry Combining Market Structures

Competition in the Canadian Economy

Historically, there has been less competition in Canada's economy than in many other countries. In part, this has been the natural result of Canada's small market, since in some industries there was only room in the market for a few firms. However, government policies have also played a role in limiting competition. Many manufacturing industries were protected from foreign competition by tariffs, and government regulation of some sectors of the economy, such as communications and transportation, prevented competition.

In recent years, however, the situation has been changing as the intensity of competition in the Canadian economy has increased since the 1980s. In part, this change has been due to changing government policies. As tariffs on imports have come down under *trade agreements* such as the North American Free Trade Agreement and the WTO (World Trade Organization) agreements, some industries that were dominated by a few Canadian oligopolists have become much more like competitive industries. In addition, the *deregulation by governments* of some industries such as communications and transportation has allowed more competition in sectors previously dominated by monopolies. In part, the trend toward increasing competition has been the result of changes in the economy itself. Another important trend has been the *growth of the service sector* of the economy. Service industries tend to consist of large numbers of smaller businesses, creating a highly competitive environment. As a result of these factors, there is more competition in the Canadian economy today than in the past.

Finally, the internet is increasing competition in the Canadian economy, by allowing buyers to compare both products and sellers much more readily. In 2005, Ford found that before even entering a showroom, eight out of ten of its customers had already used the internet to decide what car they wanted to buy, and how much they were willing to pay. For an insight into how the internet boosts competition, do question 9 on page 151 in the "Questions" section.

PayPal now has more than 60 million account-holders worldwide.

Chapter Summary

1. In perfect competition, the most competitive situation possible, many small firms sell identical products, and no individual firm has any influence over the price of its product since it faces a perfectly elastic demand curve. Prices and profits tend to be low. (L.O. 1)

2. The incentives for a firm in perfect competition are to minimize production costs per unit (maximize efficiency), produce as much output as it can afford to, and sell its output for whatever price the market determines. (L.O. 1)

3. Monopolistically competitive industries are also very competitive but differ from perfect competition in that these firms have an opportunity to practise product differentiation, thereby making demand somewhat less elastic and (possibly) enabling the firms to increase prices a little. (L.O. 2)

4. To exercise market power, firms have to make and keep an agreement concerning both price and supply and have to keep out new competitors and foreign competition. Also, demand for their product must be inelastic. (L.O. 3)

5. Oligopolies consist of sufficiently few firms that they are often able to act together so as to fix prices, using various techniques. However, they often do compete strongly in non-price areas. (L.O. 4)

6. The high profits of some oligopolistic industries are protected by various barriers to entry that keep new entrants out of these industries. (L.O. 5)

7. Under some circumstances, oligopolists can possess considerable power over their prices. However, various factors, especially foreign competition, can restrict their market power. (L.O. 6)

8. A monopoly is able to restrict the supply and thus raise the price of its product so as to maximize its profits. (L.O. 7)

9. Monopolies are quite rare, being restricted mainly to public utilities, which tend to be natural monopolies that are regulated or owned by the government. (L.O. 8)

Questions

1. Pat is one of many small farmers in the potato farming industry, which is perfectly competitive.
   (a) Why is this industry described as perfectly competitive?
   (b) If Pat increases his price by a small amount, what will happen to Pat's sales, and why?
   (c) On graph paper, draw a graph showing the demand curve for Pat's potatoes.

2. Pierre is one small operator in the barbershop industry.
   (a) How is Pierre's industry different from Pat's in question 1, and what name would economists use to describe the barbershop industry?
   (b) If Pierre increases the price of his haircuts by a small amount, what will happen to Pierre's sales, and why?
   (c) On graph paper, draw a graph showing the demand curve for Pierre's haircuts.

3. (a) What does the term *market power* mean?
   (b) What are the conditions required in order for a group of producers to be able to exercise market power?
   (c) Is it necessary for *all* of the conditions in part (b) to exist in order for the producers to possess market power? Why or why not?
   (d) How much market power does Pat (in question 2) possess? Why?
   (e) How does the market power of Pierre (in question 3) compare to Pat's? Why?

4. Suppose that three companies control 80 percent of the sales in the Canadian fertilizer industry.
   (a) What concerns would this situation raise?
   (b) Explain four factors that could prevent the concerns in part (a) from becoming a reality.

5. Classify each of the following as an example of *perfect competition, monopolistic competition, oligopoly,* or *monopoly.*
   (a) cable television _____
   (b) home repair contractors _____
   (c) steel mills _____
   (d) small farmers selling turnips _____
   (e) pizzerias _____

6. Generally speaking, convenience stores carry the same merchandise as each other. Would you therefore consider the convenience stores in your community to be in "perfect competition" with each other? Why or why not?

7. (a) How do the prices charged by a gas station in a large urban area compare to prices at a gas station located on a limited-access superhighway?
   (b) What explains the difference in their prices?

8. The text notes that over about 50 years, the automobile manufacturing industry evolved from 241 firms to 3 vast companies.
   (a) How did the evolution of the barbershop industry over the same period differ from that of the auto industry?
   (b) What explains the difference between the histories of these two industries?

9. For an indication of how the internet increases competition, visit **www.bizrate.com** and "shop" for a digital camera (or any other product of your choice). First, compare the various *products* available, and make your choice of product. Then, check out all the *sellers of that product*, and compare not only their prices, but also their ratings. If *you* were one of those sellers, how could you use Bizrate, and how would this affect the competitiveness of the marketplace?

Study Guide

Review Questions (Answers to these Review Questions appear in Appendix B.)

1. Name the three characteristics of *perfect competition.*
   (a) _____
   (b) _____
   (c) _____

2. As a result of the situation described in question 1, if an individual seller in a perfectly competitive industry increases the price of its product,
   (a) its sales will fall to zero.
   (b) other sellers will increase their prices, too.
   (c) its profits will increase.
   (d) some buyers will switch to other sellers.
   (e) None of the above.

3. Which of the following industries most closely approximates perfect competition?
   (a) railroads
   (b) steel manufacturing

    (c) vegetable farming

    (d) clothing

    (e) automobile manufacturing

4. *Monopolistic competition* and perfect competition are similar in that
   (a) profits are higher than in other types of industries.
   (b) if producers raise their prices, their sales will fall to zero.
   (c) producers restrict the supply of their product in order to raise prices.
   (d) there are many sellers and it is easy for new firms to enter the industry.
   (e) None of the above.

5. In what way is monopolistic competition different from perfect competition? In monopolistic competition,
   (a) profits are lower than in perfect competition.
   (b) there are fewer sellers than in perfect competition.
   (c) it is more difficult for new firms to enter the industry.
   (d) there is only one seller.
   (e) the product of each producer is not identical to the products of its competitors.

6. Which of the following industries would be classed as monopolistic competition?
   (a) railroads
   (b) aircraft manufacturing
   (c) wheat farming
   (d) restaurants
   (e) cable television

7. In monopolistic competition,
   (a) each seller has a great deal of control over the price of its product.
   (b) while profits are still quite low on average, individual sellers may be able to raise their price by a small amount without losing many sales.
   (c) the demand for each seller's product is more elastic than in perfect competition.
   (d) producers usually make agreements not to compete on prices.
   (e) the one seller has total control of the market.

8. If a producer in a monopolistically competitive industry succeeds in differentiating its product from those of its competitors, the demand for its product will tend to
   (a) become more inelastic.
   (b) become more elastic.
   (c) become neither more nor less elastic.
   (d) None of the above.

9. *Market power* refers to the ability of producers/sellers to _____.

10. The conditions necessary for a group of producers to exercise market power are
    (a) _____
    (b) _____
    (c) _____
    (d) _____

11. *Oligopoly* refers to a situation in which
    (a) an industry is dominated by a few large firms.
    (b) prices and profits are above competitive levels.
    (c) two or three firms do all of the business in a particular market.

(d) one very large corporation is the largest (but not the only) firm in a particular market.

(e) None of the above.

12. According to the text, the demand curve faced by oligopolists often creates an incentive for each individual oligopolist to

(a) increase its price.

(b) leave its price at the present level.

(c) change its price only if the other firms in the industry do so.

(d) reduce its price.

(e) (b) and (c) are both correct.

13. Which statement best describes the competitive behaviour of most oligopolists?

(a) They engage in vigorous competition of all sorts: advertising, price cutting, etc.

(b) They focus mostly on price competition, using relatively little advertising and other non-price methods.

(c) They use extensive advertising, in order to save money and increase profits.

(d) They generally avoid all forms of competition of any sort: advertising, price cutting, etc.

(e) They often seek to avoid price competition so as to protect prices and profits, and instead use other forms of competition, such as advertising and product differentiation, to compete for sales and market share.

14. *Monopoly* is a situation in which _____.

15. Generally, a monopolistic producer will

(a) charge a lower price and produce a higher output than a competitive industry.

(b) charge a lower price and produce a lower output than a competitive industry.

(c) charge a higher price and produce a lower output than a competitive industry.

(d) charge a higher price and produce a higher output than a competitive industry.

(e) charge a higher price and produce the same output as a competitive industry.

16. The most basic reason why a monopoly has the greatest amount of market power is that it is able to _____.

Critical Thinking Questions

(Asterisked questions 1 to 5 are answered in Appendix B; the answers to questions 6 to 10 are in the Instructor's Manual that accompanies this text.)

*1. Ed Harasymchuk is one of thousands of grain farmers who produces only #1 grade Northern wheat. His farm can grow up to 40 000 bushels of wheat per year. Last year he harvested and sold 40 000 bushels for a price of $4 per bushel. Total world production of wheat last year was 21 000 000 000 bushels.

(a) Would you describe this industry as an example of

(i)   monopoly?

(ii) monopolistic competition?

(iii) perfect competition?

(iv) oligopoly?

(b) Why did you make the choice that you made in part (a)?

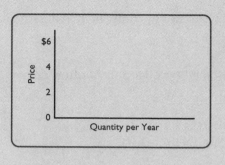

(c) On paper, draw the demand curve facing Mr. Harasymchuk.

(d) How much wheat should Mr. Harasymchuk produce?

(e) What would happen if he were to increase his price slightly above the market price of $4 per bushel?

(f) Should he lower his price below $4 in order to capture more of the wheat market? Why or why not?

(g) Should he spend money on advertising in order to boost his sales?

(h) If you could make *only one* suggestion to Mr. Harasymchuk that would increase his profits, what would that suggestion be?

*2. Pietro's Pizzeria operates in a city in which there are dozens of pizzerias. In this market, Pietro's combination of good pizzas, special toppings, and entertainment have given him a base of loyal customers. In an average week, Pietro sells 2000 pizzas for an average price of $15.

(a) Would you describe this industry as an example of
   (i)   monopoly?
   (ii) monopolistic competition?
   (iii) perfect competition?
   (iv) oligopoly?

(b) Why did you make the choice that you made in part (a)?

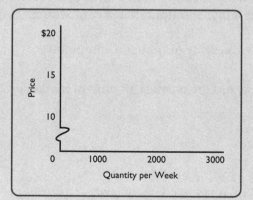

(c) On the above graph, draw the demand curve faced by Pietro's Pizzeria.

(d) To increase his profits, what should Pietro do regarding
   (i)   his product design?
   (ii) his production methods?
   (iii) his advertising?
   (iv) his pricing?

*3. What is the *most basic reason* why competitive industries (both perfect competition and monopolistic competition) generally have low prices and low profits?

*4. (a) What are barriers to entry to an industry? Provide examples.
   (b) Why are barriers to entry a key to the market power of oligopolists?

*5. (a) On the graph below, draw the general shape of the demand curve for a single firm in an oligopolistic industry in which the market price is currently $50. The firm is currently selling 100 units per week.

  (b) If the firm increases its price, what will happen to its sales and sales revenue?

  (c) If the firm decreases its price, what will happen to its sales and sales revenue?

  (d) What incentives do the situations in parts (a) and (b) create for firms in this industry regarding their pricing strategies?

6. The text notes that service industries are generally very competitive.

  (a) Why is this generally the case?

  (b) Can you think of some exceptions to this generality?

  (c) What explains why some service industries are concentrated?

7. In Toronto in recent years, a taxi licence (by which the government gives its owner the legal right to operate a cab) has sold for about $90 000. What would explain such a high price?

8. Over a period of several weeks, monitor the prices in your local supermarket of a popular breakfast cereal and fresh lettuce. What differences do you observe in the behaviour of the price of these products? How do you explain these differences?

9. Two of the most fundamental forces driving change in recent years have been free trade agreements (such as the North American Free Trade Agreement and the World Trade Organization) and communications technology (such as telecommunications and the internet). What are the implications of these changes for market structure and the degree of competitiveness in the Canadian economy?

10. When the price of gasoline increases considerably, some angry consumers sometimes try to organize a boycott of the products of one or more of the big oil companies.

  (a) What would be the objective of such a boycott?

  (b) How successful would you expect such a tactic to be?

Use the Web (Hints for this Use the Web exercise appear in Appendix B.)

1. Let's look into how much competition there is in various markets for used cars. Visit AutoTrader at **www.trader.ca** and click on *AutoTrader*, then *Search for a Car*. Select a region that interests you, and under *Ad Type*, select *Dealer Listing*, so that you will see the firms in the industry and not private sellers.

  (a) Now select a very common make and year of used car (Honda Civic is an excellent example; leave the model and price range unspecified). Click on

Submit. How many dealers were offering this particular used car? How many of these cars were for sale?

(b) Now select a very unusual make of used car (Bentley, Ferrari, and Lamborghini are good examples, but Alfa Romeo and Aston Martin are good too; after all, this is a matter of taste!); again, leave the model and price range unspecified. Click on *Submit.* How many dealers were offering this used car? How many of these cars were for sale?

(c) What do you conclude about the degree of competition in these different markets for used cars?

8

The Costs and Revenues of the Firm

LEARNING OBJECTIVES

After studying this chapter, you should be able to

1. Identify a firm's costs as either fixed costs or variable costs, and describe how fixed cost per unit and variable cost per unit change as output is increased.

2. Explain the *Law of Diminishing Returns*.

3. Using sales revenue data for a firm, calculate and graph the average revenue per unit and marginal revenue per unit over a range of output and sales.

4. Using cost data for a firm, calculate and graph the average fixed, variable, and total cost per unit and the marginal cost per unit over a range of output and sales.

5. Using revenue and cost data for a firm, identify the level of output at which profits will be maximized, and calculate this maximum level of profits.

6. Using revenue and cost data, calculate the output/sales level above which a firm will make profits (its break-even point).

7. Using revenue and cost data, calculate the output/sales level below which a firm should shut down.

8. Apply the cost and revenue concepts used in this chapter to a variety of situations.

In Chapter 7, we examined the behaviour of the individual business firm under the four basic types of market structures: perfect competition, monopolistic competition, oligopoly, and monopoly. While we discussed various strategies whereby firms could increase their profits under various conditions, we focused our attention on the total (sales) *revenue* of the firm more than its *profits*; indeed, in some cases, we treated total revenue as if it were the same as profits, speaking in terms of the firm maximizing its total revenue rather than its profits. While this approach allowed us to discuss the limitations facing the business firm and its behaviour under various conditions, it is not really accurate to consider total revenue to be the same as profits. Total revenue is the result of the firm's sales, while profits are the net result of the firm's sales revenues *and* its production costs. In this chapter, we will examine the nature and behaviour of production costs and how they interact with sales revenues to determine not only the business firm's profits but also its decisions regarding prices and output.

As we saw in Chapter 1, the more effectively and efficiently a society's economic resources are used, the more economically prosperous its people will be. In a market economy, business firms make many of the key decisions about the use of economic resources. In seeking to increase their sales and sales income, business firms are trying to use economic resources *effectively*, by producing what buyers want. And in seeking to minimize their costs, business firms are trying to use economic resources *efficiently*, by getting the maximum output from the resources employed. So the more effectively and efficiently business firms use their resources, the higher their profits will be.

In this chapter, we will examine these decisions by business firms seeking to maximize their profits. First, we will consider production costs and then sales revenue, and how costs and revenue interact to determine profits.

Production Costs

To illustrate the nature and behaviour of the production costs of the firm, we will use the example of Barry's Bolts Ltd., one of many small manufacturing firms selling an undifferentiated product (bolts) to industrial buyers in a highly competitive market. Since competition limits Barry's price to $3 per 100 bolts, his success is mainly dependent upon his ability to keep his production cost per 100 bolts as low as possible, by producing bolts as efficiently as possible. From Barry's business, we can learn some of the basic facts related to the production costs of a firm.

Fixed Costs

fixed costs
Production costs that remain constant, regardless of the level of output (for example, rent).

We will suppose that Barry has leased a building and equipment for his business, and that the cost of these, plus other overhead items such as light and heat, amounts to $120 per day. These are called Barry's **fixed costs**, meaning that they will remain at $120 per day regardless of how much he produces. Whether he produces only a few bolts per day or a large number of bolts per day, his fixed costs will be $120. This fact makes it essential that Barry produce and sell a certain number of bolts per day because if his production is too low, the fixed costs per unit (a unit is a box of 100 bolts) produced will be so high that he will be unable to make a profit. Barry's research into this matter is shown in Figure 8-1, which shows that fixed costs per 100 bolts are extremely high at low volumes of output. Considering that the market price of 100 bolts is $3, it is apparent that Barry can succeed only if he attains a sufficiently high volume of sales and production to spread his fixed costs over a large number of units.

And by doing so, he will keep the fixed costs per 100 bolts low. Generally, then, fixed costs per unit of output are very high at low volumes of output, and decrease as output is increased.

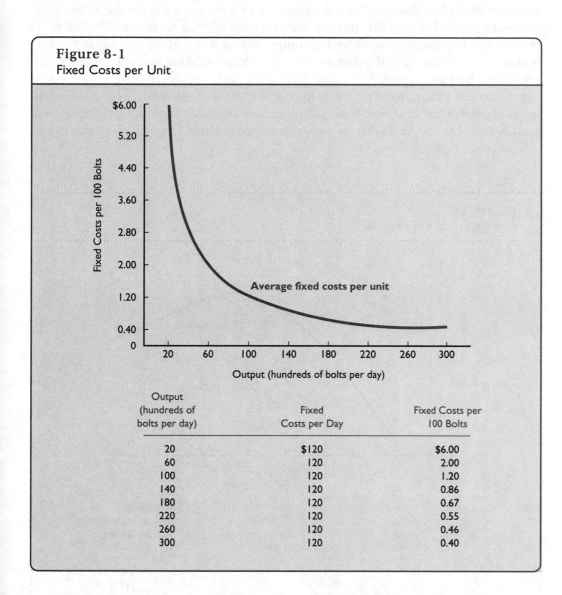

Figure 8-1
Fixed Costs per Unit

Average fixed costs per unit

Fixed Costs per 100 Bolts

Output (hundreds of bolts per day)

Output (hundreds of bolts per day)	Fixed Costs per Day	Fixed Costs per 100 Bolts
20	$120	$6.00
60	120	2.00
100	120	1.20
140	120	0.86
180	120	0.67
220	120	0.55
260	120	0.46
300	120	0.40

Variable Costs

In addition to his fixed costs, Barry will have **variable costs**. These are costs, such as direct labour and materials, that will increase as Barry's output of bolts increases.[1] To simplify our illustration, we will assume that there are no material costs, so that the only variable cost with which we will be concerned is direct labour.

The labour cost per unit (100 bolts) will depend on two factors: how much the average worker is *paid* per day, and how many bolts he or she *produces* per day. At first glance, we might expect both of these factors to be constant regardless of how many bolts the plant produces. That is, hiring additional workers should not affect either the daily wages

variable costs
Production costs that vary with the level of output (for example, direct labour and materials).

---

[1] *Direct* merely specifies that such labour is directly used for producing the product, as distinct from office labour, which is more like fixed or overhead costs.

or the average daily output of the workers. However, the average daily output of each worker will, in fact, change as additional workers are added to Barry's plant.

The reason for this change is that the plant is of a certain size and is best suited to a certain level of production. If production is too far below or too far above this level, efficiency will suffer, and the average daily product of each worker will be below its peak. This relationship between average output per worker and the number of workers is illustrated in Figure 8-2. If only one or two people are working in the plant, the workers will not be able to specialize at particular tasks. Each worker will have to perform so many different tasks as to be unable to do any of them very efficiently. As a result, at low levels of production and with few workers employed, average output per worker will be very low (4 units per day if one person is employed and 14 units per day with two workers on the job).

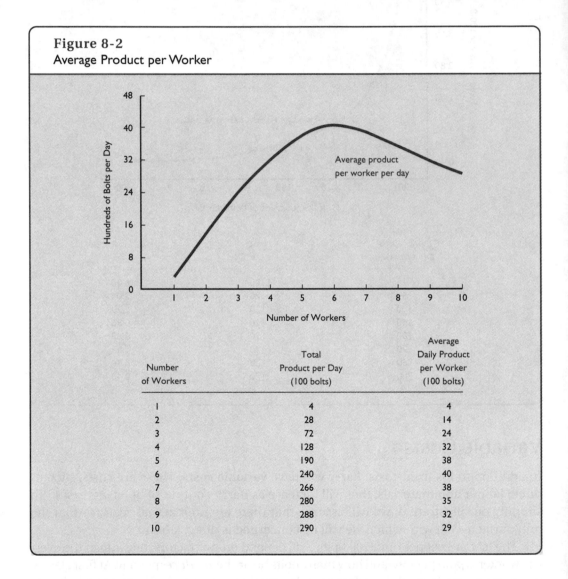

Figure 8-2
Average Product per Worker

Number of Workers	Total Product per Day (100 bolts)	Average Daily Product per Worker (100 bolts)
1	4	4
2	28	14
3	72	24
4	128	32
5	190	38
6	240	40
7	266	38
8	280	35
9	288	32
10	290	29

Barry will find, however, that as he increases production and hires additional workers, average output per worker improves significantly. With more workers in the plant, each can become more specialized. Some can prepare materials for production, some can operate the bolt-making machinery, some can finish and paint the bolts, while others can package them for shipping. As each worker becomes more specialized, efficiency increases and average output per worker rises considerably, reaching 40 units per day when six workers are employed.

However, Barry will find that hiring additional workers improves output per worker only up to a certain point. As Figure 8-2 shows, once Barry hires additional workers beyond the sixth, average output per worker decreases, because Barry's plant is only so large, and we have moved beyond the point at which it operates at *peak efficiency*. The addition of more workers does not increase the opportunities for specialization as it did earlier; in effect, the additional workers are crowding the fixed amount of equipment in the plant, and therefore are actually reducing the efficiency of the workforce, or average output per worker. As Figure 8-2 shows, the addition of the seventh through tenth workers causes the plant's *total* output to rise, but *average output per worker* decreases once production is past the level of peak efficiency for that plant.

This phenomenon is known as the **Law of Diminishing Returns**, which can be stated in general terms as follows: "If additional units of one productive input (here, labour) are combined with a fixed quantity of another productive input (here, capital equipment), the average output per unit of the variable input (labour) will increase at first, and then decrease."

The Law of Diminishing Returns places an important limitation on Barry's production decisions. While Barry *physically can* increase output to certain levels, doing so may reduce efficiency to such an extent that it becomes *unprofitable* to increase output.

Marginal Productivity

We can analyze the data in Figure 8-2 in another useful way: rather than looking at total output, or average output per worker, we can examine the *increase* in production resulting from the hiring of *one additional worker*, or the **marginal productivity** (marginal output) per worker. This information is presented on the next page in Figure 8-3, which shows that the hiring of the fifth worker increases production by 62 units, and the sixth worker adds 50 units to total output. After that, additional workers add much less. The seventh worker only increases production by 26 units, the eighth and ninth only add 14 units and 8 units, respectively, while the tenth worker barely adds to total output at all—his marginal output is only 2 units. It is important to remember that this does not mean that the quality of the workers is declining. The reason for the decrease in marginal output per worker is the Law of Diminishing Returns: once production in Barry's plant moves past the point of peak efficiency, average output per worker will decrease because each additional worker will not add as much to output as previous workers did. This diminishing return will have an important impact on production costs because the cost of the extra units (marginal output) produced by additional workers will rise very rapidly beyond a certain point, making it uneconomical to hire workers and increase output beyond that point. For instance, it is very doubtful that the marginal output of the ninth and tenth workers (8 units and 2 units, respectively) warrants hiring them. Or, viewed differently, the cost per unit of increasing output from 280 units to 290 units would be so high as to be uneconomical.

The cost and productivity factors that we have been discussing restrict Barry's production decisions. Because fixed costs per unit are very high at low levels of output, he must achieve a certain level of production (and sales) in order to operate economically. However, due to the Law of Diminishing Returns, it will not prove economical to increase his output beyond a certain point, since the variable costs per unit (labour costs) will rise to higher levels, as Figure 8-4 shows.

Law of Diminishing Returns
A physical law stating that, if additional units of one productive input (such as labour) are combined with a fixed quantity of another productive input (such as capital), the average product per unit of the variable input (labour) will increase at first and then decrease.

marginal productivity (per worker)
The increase in production resulting from the hiring of one additional worker.

Figure 8-3
Average and Marginal Productivity per Worker

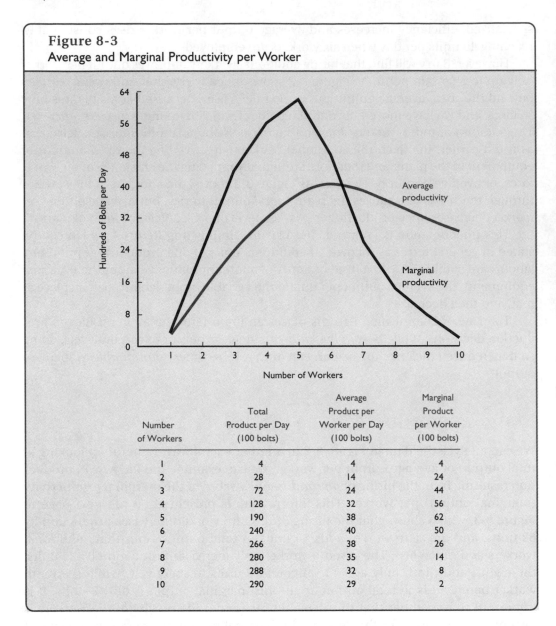

Number of Workers	Total Product per Day (100 bolts)	Average Product per Worker per Day (100 bolts)	Marginal Product per Worker (100 bolts)
1	4	4	4
2	28	14	24
3	72	24	44
4	128	32	56
5	190	38	62
6	240	40	50
7	266	38	26
8	280	35	14
9	288	32	8
10	290	29	2

In general terms, then, we have outlined the situation Barry's firm faces with respect to production costs, and how this will affect its operations. On the basis of these two figures, Barry can make two more calculations that will help to decide exactly what volume of output to produce. These are the average cost per unit and the marginal cost per unit.

Average Cost per Unit

Table 8-1 summarizes the production costs of Barry's bolt plant. The information in the table is based on the production information discussed earlier: *fixed costs* of $120 per day regardless of the level of output, and *variable costs* consisting only of wages of $60 per day for each worker. *Total costs* are fixed costs plus variable costs, and *average cost per unit* is total costs divided by total output. As we saw earlier, at low levels of output, average cost per unit is high, because of high fixed costs per unit. As output increases, the plant operates more efficiently, reaching a minimum average cost per

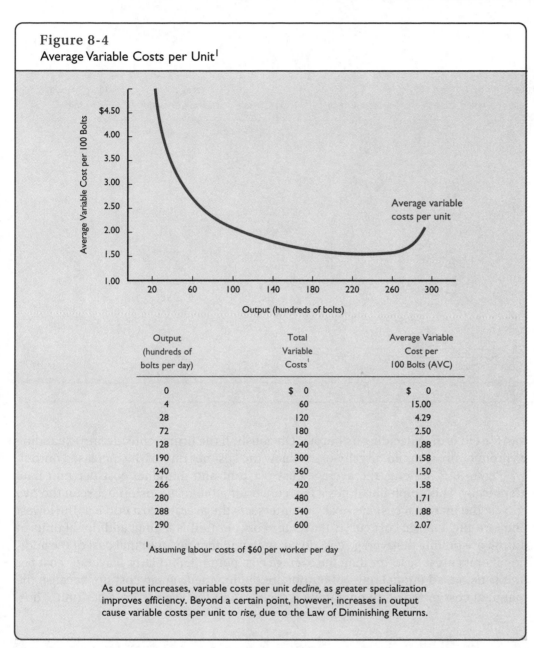

Figure 8-4
Average Variable Costs per Unit[1]

Output (hundreds of bolts per day)	Total Variable Costs[1]	Average Variable Cost per 100 Bolts (AVC)
0	$ 0	$ 0
4	60	15.00
28	120	4.29
72	180	2.50
128	240	1.88
190	300	1.58
240	360	1.50
266	420	1.58
280	480	1.71
288	540	1.88
290	600	2.07

[1] Assuming labour costs of $60 per worker per day

As output increases, variable costs per unit *decline*, as greater specialization improves efficiency. Beyond a certain point, however, increases in output cause variable costs per unit to *rise*, due to the Law of Diminishing Returns.

unit of $2 at a daily output level of 240 units. Further increases in output cause the plant to operate beyond its most efficient level, so that the Law of Diminishing Returns pushes variable costs per unit up again. As a result, average cost per unit increases still further, rising to $2.48 at an output level of 290 units per day.

Marginal Cost per Unit

The last column in Table 8-1 on the next page—marginal cost per unit—requires some explanation. **Marginal cost per unit** is the addition to total costs resulting from the production of one additional unit of output. For instance, when output is increased from 4 units to 28 units, total costs rise from $180 to $240. In other words, it costs $60 more to increase output by 24 units, making the cost of each additional unit (the marginal cost per unit) $2.50 ($60 ÷ 24). These calculations, together with other examples, are shown in Table 8-2 on the next page. Marginal cost per unit can be an important

marginal cost per unit
The addition to total costs resulting from the production of one more additional unit of output.

Table 8-1
The Costs of the Firm

Number of Workers	Total Output per Day[a]	Fixed Costs	Variable Costs	Total Costs	Average Cost per Unit[b]	Marginal Cost per Unit[c]
0	0	$120	$ 0	$120	—	—
1	4	120	60	180	$45.00	$15.00
2	28	120	120	240	8.57	2.50
3	72	120	180	300	4.17	1.36
4	128	120	240	360	2.81	1.07
5	190	120	300	420	2.21	0.97
6	240	120	360	480	2.00	1.20
7	266	120	420	540	2.03	2.31
8	280	120	480	600	2.14	4.29
9	288	120	540	660	2.29	7.50
10	290	120	600	720	2.48	30.00

[a] Output measured in units of 100 bolts

[b] $\dfrac{\text{Total costs}}{\text{Total output}}$ [c] $\dfrac{\text{Change in total costs}}{\text{Change in total output}}$

tool for the firm in deciding its output. Obviously, if the firm is considering expanding its production, it would be valuable to know the cost per unit of the increased output.

Figure 8-5 presents the average cost per unit and marginal cost per unit data graphically. This graph illustrates a fact concerning the relationship between the two curves: the marginal cost curve always intersects the average cost curve at the lowest point on the average cost curve. If average cost per unit is falling, additional units of output are pulling the average cost down, meaning that the marginal cost of the additional units must be lower than the average cost per unit. Similarly, if average cost per unit is rising, additional units of output are pulling the average cost up, because the marginal cost of the additional units is higher than the average cost per unit. Thus,

Table 8-2
Calculation of Marginal Cost per Unit

Total Output per Day	Total Costs	Marginal Cost per Unit of 100 Bolts	=	$\dfrac{\text{Increase in Total Costs}}{\text{Increase in Total Output}}$
0	$120			
4	180	$15.00	=	$\dfrac{\$180 - 120}{4 - 0}$
28	240	2.50	=	$\dfrac{\$240 - 180}{28 - 4}$
72	300	1.36	=	$\dfrac{\$300 - 240}{72 - 28}$

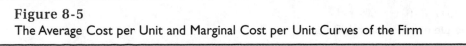

Figure 8-5
The Average Cost per Unit and Marginal Cost per Unit Curves of the Firm

when average cost is falling, marginal cost is below the average, and when average cost is rising, marginal cost is above the average—it is only at that point where average cost is at its minimum (neither falling nor rising) that average cost per unit and marginal cost per unit are exactly the same, and the curves intersect. Beyond this output level, as Figure 8-5 shows, marginal cost per unit rises very quickly, as the Law of Diminishing Returns makes it increasingly difficult to increase output by simply adding more workers to the plant.

To summarize information about Barry's production costs, increasing output causes average cost per unit to decrease until it reaches a minimum at an output level around 240 units per day. At output levels beyond these outputs, average cost per unit increases again, and rapidly rising marginal cost per unit makes increasing output beyond a certain point uneconomical. What this "certain point" is—and at what level of output Barry will actually decide to produce—will depend not only on how much additional units *cost* to produce but also on how much additional *revenue* they bring in. To complete our analysis of Barry's bolt firm, we must now consider the revenues, or *sales* of the business.

The Revenue Side

Average Revenue per Unit

We will assume that Barry's is one of many small firms in the highly competitive bolt industry, and that the market price of bolts is $3 per unit (box) of 100 bolts. At this price, the firm can sell as many bolts as it can produce, up to its maximum possible output of 290 units per day. In other words, the demand for Barry's product is perfectly elastic, as shown by the demand schedule and demand curve in Figure 8-6. Figure 8-6 also shows that the *price* of the product can be viewed as the *average revenue per unit*; since the firm can sell as many as it produces for $3 per unit of 100 bolts, the *demand curve* can be viewed as the *average revenue per unit sold.*

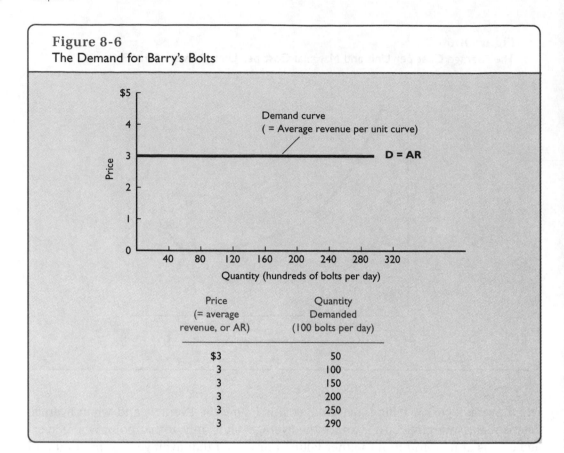

Figure 8-6
The Demand for Barry's Bolts

Price (= average revenue, or AR)	Quantity Demanded (100 bolts per day)
$3	50
3	100
3	150
3	200
3	250
3	290

Marginal Revenue per Unit

marginal revenue per unit
The addition to total revenue resulting from the sale of one additional unit of output.

From the demand for Barry's bolts, we can develop a table of information concerning the firm's sales revenues, as shown in Table 8-3. Since the firm can only charge $3 per unit, the average revenue per unit is always $3. *Total revenue*, which is simply price (or average revenue) times quantity demanded, rises in proportion to sales. **Marginal revenue per unit** is the addition to total revenue gained from the sale of one more unit. It can be calculated in the same way as we calculate marginal cost per unit, by dividing the increase in total revenue by the increase in units sold; in each case, total revenue

Table 8-3
The Revenue Side of Barry's Bolts

Price (= Average Revenue)	×	Quantity Demanded per day	=	Total Revenue per day	Marginal Revenue per Unit[a]
$3		50		$150	
3		100		300	$3
3		150		450	3
3		200		600	3
3		250		750	3
3		290		870	3

[a] $\dfrac{\text{Increase in total revenue}}{\text{Increase in quantity demanded}}$

rises by $150 and the number of units sold rises by 50, making the marginal revenue per unit $3 at all levels of sales. With the price always $3 per unit, each additional unit sold must bring in marginal revenue of $3, making the marginal revenue curve identical to the demand curve and the average revenue curve, as Figure 8-7 shows.

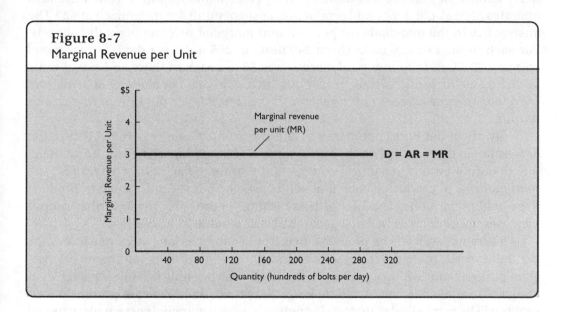

Figure 8-7
Marginal Revenue per Unit

The Most Profitable Output

We now have all of the information about Barry's costs and revenues that the firm needs in order to decide what level of output to produce. Table 8-4 summarizes all of the information we have developed about Barry's costs and revenues and adds a column for total profits, which are total revenue minus total costs. The table shows that low levels of output are unprofitable due to fixed costs, and that profits are maximized at $258 per day by producing 266 units of 100 bolts per day, using 7 workers.

Table 8-4
The Costs and Revenues of Barry's Bolts

Number of Workers	Total Output per day	Fixed Costs	Variable Costs	Total Costs	Total Revenue	Total Profit (+) or Loss (–)Cost	Average Cost per Unit	Marginal Cost per Unit	Marginal Revenue per Unit
0	0	$120	$ 0	$120	$ 0	–$120	—	—	—
1	4	120	60	180	12	– 168	$45.00	$15.00	$3.00
2	28	120	120	240	84	– 156	8.57	2.50	3.00
3	72	120	180	300	216	– 84	4.17	1.36	3.00
4	128	120	240	360	384	+ 24	2.81	1.07	3.00
5	190	120	300	420	570	+ 150	2.21	0.97	3.00
6	240	120	360	480	720	+ 240	2.00	1.20	3.00
7	266	120	420	540	798	+ 258	2.03	2.31	3.00
8	280	120	480	600	840	+ 240	2.14	4.29	3.00
9	288	120	540	660	864	+ 204	2.29	7.50	3.00
10	290	120	600	720	870	+ 150	2.48	30.00	3.00

Tools of Analysis

While it is easy to see why Barry would choose to produce 266 units per day, we can use this simple example to develop other, more sophisticated concepts. Why didn't Barry choose to produce 240 units per day? (This is the output at which the firm operates at peak efficiency and production costs per unit are minimized at $2.) The answer lies in the marginal cost per unit and marginal revenue per unit columns. For each of the extra 26 units (from 240 units to 266 units per day), the *marginal cost* was $2.31 and the *marginal revenue* was $3. So each of these additional units *added* $0.69 of profit to the firm. From this, we can conclude that *whenever marginal revenue exceeds marginal cost, it is profitable for the firm to increase its output.*

Why, then, did Barry not increase output *beyond* 266 units per day? Again, the answer lies in the marginal revenue and marginal cost columns. While each additional unit of output beyond 266 units per day will still bring in *marginal revenue* of $3, the *marginal cost* of producing each unit will be $4.29. So it is unprofitable to produce these additional units. The Law of Diminishing Returns has made further output increases uneconomical by forcing marginal cost per unit to high levels.

To summarize, it will be profitable to increase output as long as marginal revenue per unit exceeds marginal cost per unit. However, as diminishing returns set in, marginal cost per unit will rise, and once marginal cost per unit becomes greater than marginal revenue per unit, it will no longer be profitable to increase production. So profits will be maximized at that level of output at which marginal cost equals marginal revenue—that is, where the marginal cost curve intersects the marginal revenue curve. This principle is illustrated in Figure 8-8, which shows that profits are maximized by

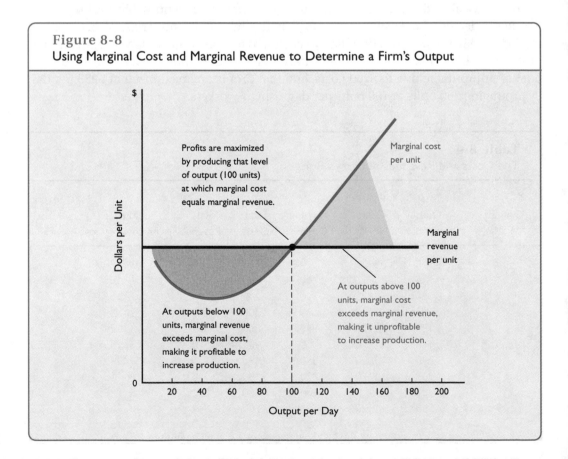

Figure 8-8
Using Marginal Cost and Marginal Revenue to Determine a Firm's Output

producing 100 units of output. In the remainder of this chapter, we will use this approach to analyze the price and output decisions of business firms under different market structures, starting with perfect competition as discussed in Chapter 7.

YOU DECIDE

Ebusiness Costs

Some ebusinesses produce and sell only electronic products, such as software and games. Such businesses often have high fixed costs for hardware and software, but once the "original" product has been created on their server, buyers can simply download additional copies of it from the firm's website, without any of the costs associated with physical products, which must be produced and delivered. ▩

QUESTIONS

1. How does this technology affect the marginal cost per unit of these electronic products?
2. How would the situation concerning their fixed costs and marginal costs affect the pricing strategies of business firms producing such products?

Different Market Structures

Perfect Competition

As we saw in Chapter 7, perfect competition is a rare situation in which there are many small firms in an industry, it is easy for new firms to enter the industry, and all firms are selling identical products. The result is the most competitive situation imaginable, in which producers have no control over the price of their products and there is constant downward pressure on profits. Using analysis based on costs and revenues as developed earlier in this chapter, we can now examine the case of perfect competition more closely.

The costs and revenues of the firm in perfect competition will be like those of Barry's Bolts Ltd., which we described as a small firm in a highly competitive industry. The cost curves will have the usual shapes as were described earlier in this chapter, with average cost per unit decreasing as output increases up to a point, then increasing again.[2] The marginal cost per unit curve rises quite sharply beyond a certain output level and intersects the average cost per unit curve at that curve's minimum point, as shown in Figure 8-9. In perfect competition, the existence of many small firms selling identical products ensures that the demand for any one firm's product will be perfectly elastic. So, if the market price of the product is $3 per unit, the demand curve of the individual firm will consist of a horizontal line at a price of $3, as in Figure 8-9. This line will also represent the *average revenue* from each sale (AR) and the *marginal revenue* (MR) for each additional sale, as indicated on the graph.

Figure 8-9 on the next page shows a profitable individual firm in a perfectly competitive industry. *Profits* are maximized by producing the output at which marginal

---

[2] The shapes of the cost curves are determined by physical factors such as the Law of Diminishing Returns; as a result, cost curves have the same general shape regardless of whether the firm is small or large, or in an industry that is highly competitive, oligopolistic, or monopolistic.

Figure 8-9
The Firm in Perfect Competition with Profits

cost equals marginal revenue (or price), which is 275 units per day, as point E indicates. Total revenue will be $825 per day ($3 × 275 units). Point F indicates that, at an output level of 275 units, average cost per unit is $2.05, and total costs are $564 ($2.05 × 275 units). So total daily profit will be maximized at $261 ($825 – $564), at an output level of 275 units. The shaded area on the graph represents the total profit (275 × $0.95) earned by the firm in this situation.

Dynamics of Perfect Competition

If the firm we have been discussing is a typical firm in the industry, the situation cannot remain as it is shown in Figure 8-9. The profitability of firms in this industry will attract new competitors into the industry, increasing the supply of the product and *reducing its price.* When this happens, the demand curve (labelled AR = MR in Figure 8-9) will move downward as the price declines, reducing the profits of a typical firm. How far can the price fall? Figure 8-10 shows what would happen if the price fell to $1.50: at *every* level of output, average cost per unit exceeds average revenue per unit. As a result, it would be impossible to make a profit at a price of $1.50. By producing 250 units, where marginal cost equals marginal revenue, the firm could minimize its losses, but it would still be losing money.

If the typical firm in the industry were losing money, it is obvious that some firms would have to leave the industry—a polite way of saying that they would go bankrupt. As they left, the supply of the product would decrease, and the price would increase again. How high will the price rise, and at what level will it settle? Figure 8-11 provides the answer: the price will rise to (and settle at) just under $2 per unit, at which point output will be 260 units. At this price, two conditions exist:

(a) marginal cost equals marginal revenue, so that the firm's profits are maximized, and the firm has no incentive to increase or decrease its output, and

(b) average cost equals average revenue, so that profits are zero, providing no incentive for anyone to enter or leave the industry.

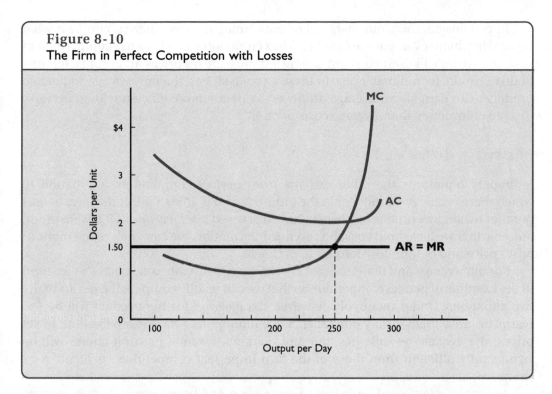

Figure 8-10
The Firm in Perfect Competition with Losses

Since one might wonder why anyone would even stay in a business with no profits, we should define profits more precisely. By *profits* we mean business income *over and above the owner-manager's salary,* which represents the opportunity cost of the owner's time and capital. Viewed differently, we assume that the owner–manager will only continue in business if a certain minimum income level is earned, and include that person's salary in the production costs of the business, as a fixed cost.

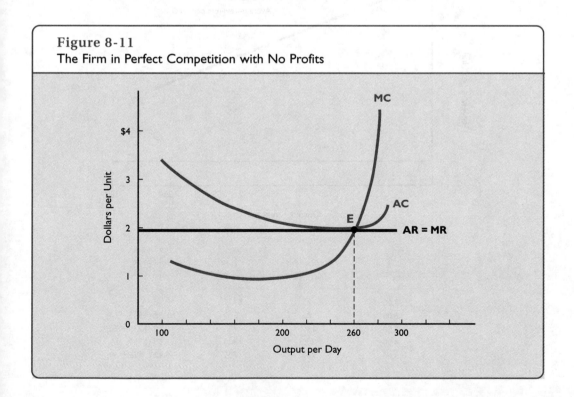

Figure 8-11
The Firm in Perfect Competition with No Profits

In conclusion, then, our marginal revenue/marginal cost analysis confirms what we said in Chapter 7 about the firm in perfect competition: the intense competition in such industries will exert constant downward pressure on prices and profits, tending to drive profits to minimal levels. In these circumstances, the only way an individual producer can earn above-average profits is to operate more efficiently than average, so as to enjoy lower-than-average costs per unit.

Monopoly

Monopoly represents the other extreme from perfect competition: a situation in which there is only *one* producer in the industry, who is able to select the level of output that maximizes profits. In Chapter 7, we discussed *total revenue* as if it were profit, but now that we have both cost and revenue information, we can analyze the monopolist's price and output decisions more precisely.

For our average and marginal cost curves, we will use the same curves as we used in the example of perfect competition so that we can readily compare the results of the two situations. Under monopoly, however, the *demand* for the product will be *less elastic* because there is only one seller. Since monopolists have more freedom to set prices, the average revenue per unit and marginal revenue per unit curves will be significantly different from those of the firm in perfect competition, as Figure 8-12 shows.

As output is increased, marginal revenue per unit falls more rapidly than average revenue per unit, or the demand curve. The reason why marginal revenue per unit

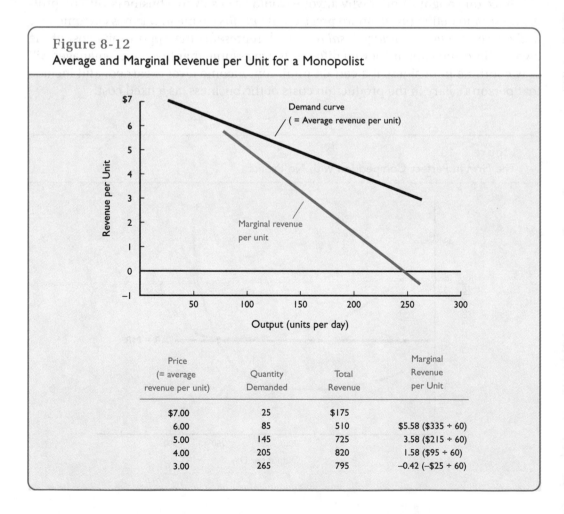

Figure 8-12
Average and Marginal Revenue per Unit for a Monopolist

Price (= average revenue per unit)	Quantity Demanded	Total Revenue	Marginal Revenue per Unit
$7.00	25	$175	
6.00	85	510	$5.58 ($335 ÷ 60)
5.00	145	725	3.58 ($215 ÷ 60)
4.00	205	820	1.58 ($95 ÷ 60)
3.00	265	795	−0.42 (−$25 ÷ 60)

falls so rapidly is that, in order to *sell more units*, the monopolist must *reduce the price*, not only on the additional units sold but also *on all units sold*. For instance, when sales are increased from 85 units to 145 units by reducing prices from $6 to $5, the additional 60 units sold bring in $300 ($5 × 60), but there is $85 less total revenue on the 85 units, because they are selling for $1 less per unit. Thus, the net marginal revenue on the 60 additional units is $215 ($300 – $85), or $3.85 per unit, as shown in Figure 8-12. As sales increase, the monopolist's marginal revenue curve will fall, and will fall more steeply than the demand curve does—a fact that will have an important bearing on the monopolist's price and output decisions.

Price and Output Decisions

To maximize profits, the monopolist will follow our rule of producing that output at which marginal revenue equals marginal costs. Figure 8-13 shows that doing this will result in a decision to produce 220 units of output per day. Point P on the demand curve shows that, to sell 220 units per day, a price of $3.75 per unit must be charged. Thus, the monopolist will maximize profits by charging a price of $3.75 and producing 220 units per day. At this level of output, the monopolist's average revenue per unit will be $3.75 (the price), and average cost per unit will be $2.10 (from point C on the average cost curve). The average profit per unit will then be $1.65 ($3.75 – $2.10), and the monopolist's total profits will be $363 per day ($1.65 × 220). The shaded area on the graph in Figure 8-13 represents these profits.

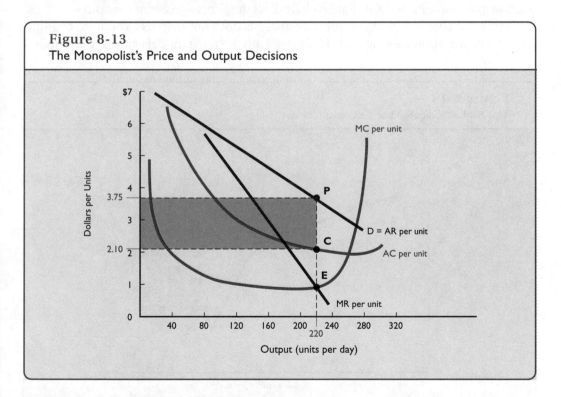

Figure 8-13
The Monopolist's Price and Output Decisions

Monopoly and Competition Compared

In a perfectly competitive industry, we saw that the price of each firm's product would be $1.95, the output of a typical firm would be 260 units per day (Figure 8-11), and that competition would push profits downward toward the "normal" level, or the minimum required to keep firms in business. Under monopoly, and using the same cost curves, the price would be $3.75, output would be 220 units (Figure 8-13), and there would be substantial profits.[3] Furthermore, because new firms cannot enter the industry, these profits are secure from competition.

Oligopoly

In Chapter 7, we saw that, while the price and output decisions of oligopolistic industries were of great importance, we could not develop a theoretical basis for analyzing and predicting those decisions. In this chapter, we have developed considerably more sophisticated techniques for analyzing the costs, revenues, and price and output decisions of the firm. However, we are still unable to analyze and predict the decisions of oligopolists precisely, even using these techniques. The problem lies in the nature of the oligopolist's demand curve.

Figure 8-14 shows the demand curve for one firm in an oligopolistic industry in which the firms have agreed upon a price of $6. If this one firm increases its price and the other firms leave their prices at the agreed level of $6, the firm that increases its price will suffer a considerable loss of sales and profits. And if one firm reduces its price, it is reasonable to assume that the other firms will match its price reduction. In that case, the firm that reduces its price will not gain in terms of its market share, and will very likely lose financially. So the demand curve for an oligopolistic firm tends to be "kinked," as Figure 8-14 shows. For price increases, demand is elastic, while for price reductions, it is inelastic. Therefore, a single firm cannot gain by either increasing or decreasing its price. So once the price has been established, there is an incentive for each firm to leave its price at that level, until all the firms agree to a new price.

Marginal cost and marginal revenue analysis does not help us to analyze oligopolists' decisions further. As Figure 8-15 shows, even the most modest kink in the demand

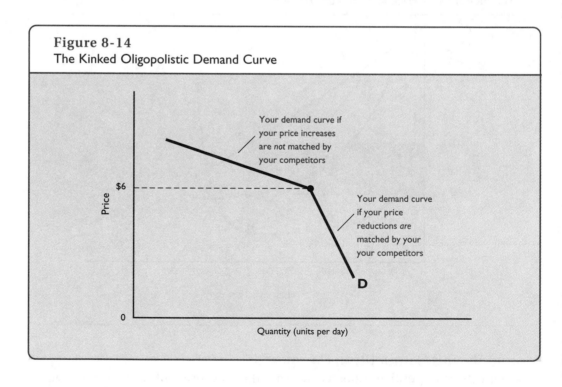

Figure 8-14
The Kinked Oligopolistic Demand Curve

---

[3] For comparative purposes, we have used the same cost curves for the small firm in perfect competition and for the monopolist. This ignores the possibility that the monopolist's costs per unit may in fact be *lower* than the small firm's, due to improved technology and mass-production techniques. We will consider this possibility further in Chapter 9.

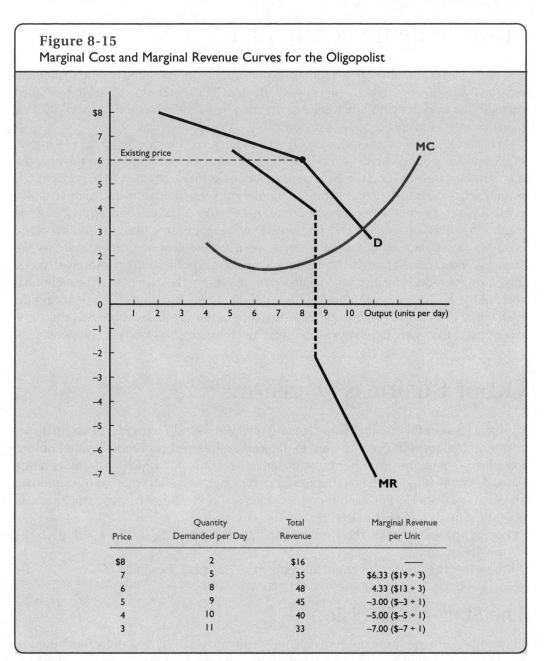

Figure 8-15
Marginal Cost and Marginal Revenue Curves for the Oligopolist

Price	Quantity Demanded per Day	Total Revenue	Marginal Revenue per Unit
$8	2	$16	——
7	5	35	$6.33 ($19 ÷ 3)
6	8	48	4.33 ($13 ÷ 3)
5	9	45	−3.00 ($−3 ÷ 1)
4	10	40	−5.00 ($−5 ÷ 1)
3	11	33	−7.00 ($−7 ÷ 1)

curve causes strange changes in the marginal revenue curve. At the level of output where the demand curve is kinked, the marginal revenue curve becomes *discontinuous* (see the dotted line in Figure 8-15), leaving us with no clear intersection point for the marginal cost and marginal revenue curves. As a result of this, marginal cost and marginal revenue analysis cannot help to pinpoint oligopolists' price and output decisions. All we can say is that the existence of a kinked demand curve provides a strong incentive for individual oligopolists to leave their price and output unchanged. As Figure 8-15 shows, it would take a major increase in production costs (upward shift of the marginal cost curve) to cause our oligopolist to reduce output and increase prices, while no reduction in costs would induce a price reduction. So all that we can conclude concerning oligopolistic prices through marginal cost and marginal revenue analysis is what we concluded in Chapter 7—that, once set by the industry, oligopolistic prices tend to be quite sticky and especially resistant to downward movements.

How Realistic Is All This?

A student can reasonably ask the following question about marginal revenue/marginal cost analysis: "Does anybody actually *do* all this?" In the sense of making detailed calculations and drawing exact graphs, the answer to this question is certainly "not many people—mostly economics students."

However, this does not mean that marginal analysis is irrelevant in the real world. While few if any businesspeople make the kinds of calculations referred to in this chapter, it is certainly arguable that the *basic approach* of marginal analysis is used implicitly by businesses. A decision whether to hire additional workers, whether to add more machinery to a plant, or whether to increase output necessarily involves some *estimates* of the impact that decision would have on the costs and revenues (and thus the profits) of the business. Some large companies that have sophisticated cost accounting systems use marginal cost calculations and make pricing decisions based on marginal costs. Implicitly, *every* decision involves marginal considerations; that is, whether the additional costs of the decision are warranted by the additional benefits. While it is not always (or even often) possible to reduce these considerations to numbers as we have done here, the fact remains that marginal analysis is a useful tool for making all kinds of decisions.

Other Business Decisions

We have seen in this chapter how cost and revenue data (in particular, marginal cost and marginal revenue) can be used to determine the most profitable level of output for a firm. There are two other basic business decisions for which cost and revenue data are vitally important: whether to start a new business and whether to shut down an existing business. For example, the owner of Barry's Bolts can use the cost and revenue data in Table 8-1 to decide:

(a) what volume of sales the firm must achieve in order to justify *starting up* the business, and
(b) how low the firm's sales could fall before the business should be *closed*.

The Start-Up Decision

In deciding whether to start up his business, the owner of Barry's Bolts faces the key question of whether he can sell enough bolts to cover the firm's costs. Because high fixed costs per unit cause the average cost per unit to be high at low levels of output, the firm must achieve a certain volume of sales in order to cover its costs, or break even. To make this decision, the owner will use average cost and average revenue data rather than the marginal cost and revenue data that we used for determining the most profitable level of output.

Figure 8-16 shows the relationship between average cost and average revenue in this way: if the price per 100 bolts (average revenue per unit) is $3, Barry must sell more than 118 units of 100 bolts per day in order to make a profit. At point A, with an output of 118 units, average cost and average revenue per unit are equal, making Barry's profit zero—the firm is breaking even.

At output levels below 118 units, average cost exceeds average revenue per unit, and Barry loses money, while at output levels above 118 units, average revenue exceeds average cost per unit, and Barry earns a profit. Unless the firm's owner can realistically plan on sales in excess of 118 units per day, he should not start up in business.

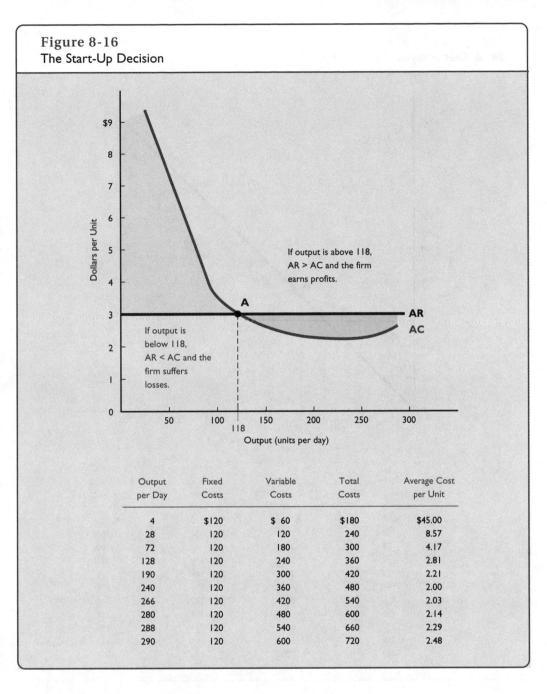

Figure 8-16
The Start-Up Decision

If output is above 118, AR > AC and the firm earns profits.

A

If output is below 118, AR < AC and the firm suffers losses.

AR

AC

118

Output (units per day)

Dollars per Unit

Output per Day	Fixed Costs	Variable Costs	Total Costs	Average Cost per Unit
4	$120	$ 60	$180	$45.00
28	120	120	240	8.57
72	120	180	300	4.17
128	120	240	360	2.81
190	120	300	420	2.21
240	120	360	480	2.00
266	120	420	540	2.03
280	120	480	600	2.14
288	120	540	660	2.29
290	120	600	720	2.48

In business terminology, 118 units per day is said to be Barry's *break-even point*, because at this level of output the firm just barely covers its costs, or breaks even. Break-even analysis similar to that shown in Figure 8-16 is useful when considering whether to start a business; however, it is usually done with *total cost* and *total revenue* data, as shown in Figure 8-17 on the next page, rather than with average cost and revenue data.

The total cost and total revenue data in Figure 8-17 lead Barry to the same conclusion reached earlier: the firm must sell more than 118 units per day in order to make a profit. At sales of 118 per day (point A), it breaks even, with total revenue equal to total costs. At lower levels of output, total costs exceed total revenue, causing the firm to lose money. Only by selling more than 118 units per day can Barry earn a profit.

Figure 8-17
Break-Even Analysis

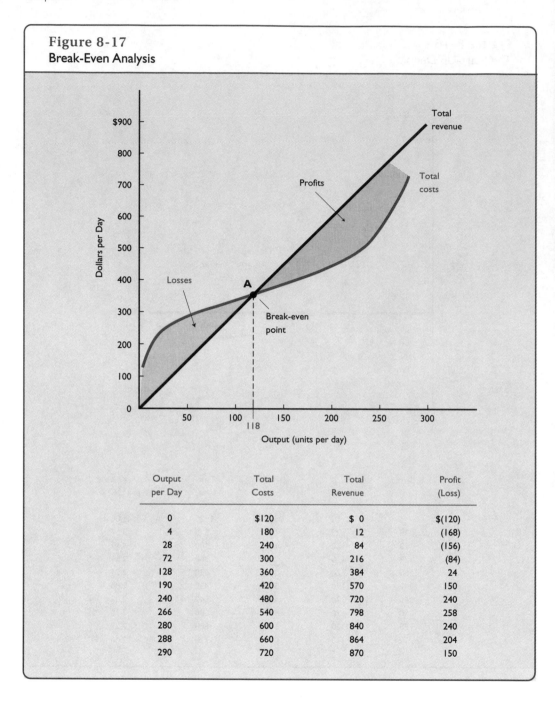

Output per Day	Total Costs	Total Revenue	Profit (Loss)
0	$120	$ 0	$(120)
4	180	12	(168)
28	240	84	(156)
72	300	216	(84)
128	360	384	24
190	420	570	150
240	480	720	240
266	540	798	258
280	600	840	240
288	660	864	204
290	720	870	150

Figure 8-17 illustrates another point seen earlier in this chapter: the firm will not maximize profits by producing as much output as is physically possible. If output is increased beyond a certain point, the Law of Diminishing Returns causes costs to increase rapidly, making it unprofitable to increase output further. Rather, profits are maximized at an output level of 266 units per day, as we saw earlier.

The Shut-Down Decision

Suppose that, some time after Barry's Bolts was established, the firm's sales begin to decrease. How low can sales fall before the owner should decide to go out of business?

The key factor in this situation is that, even if Barry stops production, he must still pay his fixed costs, such as rent, interest on debt, and so on.[4] To stop production means incurring fixed costs (losses) of $120 per day. Consequently, it would be better for Barry's Bolts to remain in business (at least in the short run), as long as its losses are *less* than $120 per day. For instance, the table in Figure 8-18 shows that if sales fall to 72 units per day, the firm will lose $84 per day—$36 *less* than the $120 it would lose by stopping production altogether. Why is this so? Because while the firm *is* incurring losses, its total revenue of $216 exceeds its variable costs of $180 by $36. As a result, by

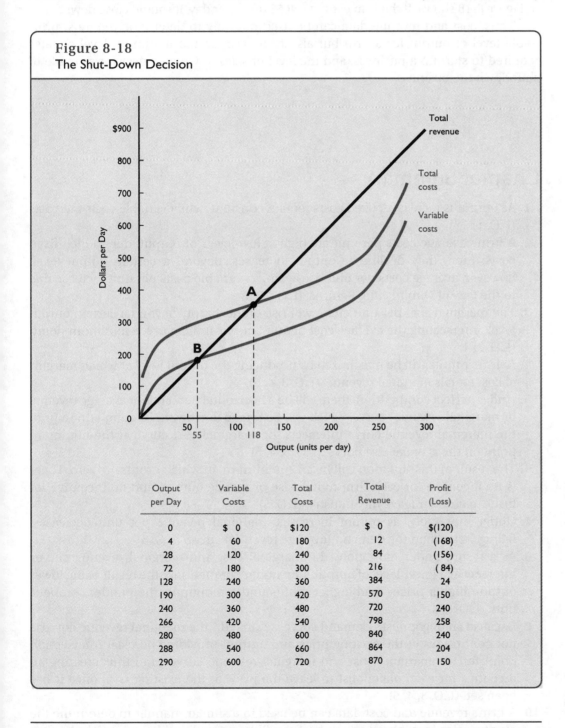

Figure 8-18
The Shut-Down Decision

Output per Day	Variable Costs	Total Costs	Total Revenue	Profit (Loss)
0	$ 0	$120	$ 0	$(120)
4	60	180	12	(168)
28	120	240	84	(156)
72	180	300	216	(84)
128	240	360	384	24
190	300	420	570	150
240	360	480	720	240
266	420	540	798	258
280	480	600	840	240
288	540	660	864	204
290	600	720	870	150

---

[4] These fixed costs must still be paid in the short run; for instance, rent must be paid until his lease expires. Over a longer period of time, *all* costs can be viewed as variable (particularly if the firm goes out of business!).

continuing production, it can use this $36 to offset some of the fixed costs, so that it loses $84 rather than the $120 it would lose by stopping production completely. The firm is therefore $36 better off (or less badly off) to remain in business producing 72 units per day, than to stop altogether.

As a general rule, we can conclude that as long as total revenue exceeds variable costs, the firm should remain in business rather than close down, because its losses will be smaller. Put differently, only when variable costs exceed total revenue should the firm close. For Barry's Bolts, this occurs when sales fall below 55 units per day, as the graph in Figure 8-18 shows. If the firm cannot sell 55 units per day, it should close down.

Thus, cost and revenue data can be used not only to determine the most profitable level of output for a firm but also to determine the minimum level of sales required to start up a business, and the level of sales at which a decision is made to shut down the business.

Chapter Summary

1. As output is increased, fixed costs remain constant, while variable costs increase. (L.O. 1)
2. A firm's average costs per unit are high at low levels of output, due to high fixed costs; then, they decline as output increases. Beyond a certain output level, however, average costs per unit rise again, as variable costs per unit increase due to the Law of Diminishing Returns. (L.O. 2)
3. The marginal cost per unit curve will rise quite sharply beyond a certain output level, intersecting the average cost per unit curve at that curve's minimum point. (L.O. 2, 4)
4. A firm's profits will be maximized by producing the output level at which marginal cost equals marginal revenue. (L.O. 3, 4, 5)
5. Under perfect competition, there will be a horizontal demand (or average revenue or marginal revenue) curve, which will be forced downward by competition until the marginal revenue curve intersects the marginal cost curve at the minimum point on the average cost curve. (L.O. 3, 4, 5)
6. The result of this situation will be an equilibrium, in which profits are zero. There is no incentive for each firm to increase or reduce output, and no incentive for firms to enter or leave the industry. (L.O. 5)
7. Under monopoly, as output increases, marginal revenue per unit decreases, falling faster than the demand (average revenue) curve. (L.O. 3)
8. As a result, under monopoly, the marginal cost and marginal revenue curves intersect at a lower level of output than under competition, the result being lower output, higher prices, and higher profits under monopoly than under competition. (L.O. 3, 4, 5)
9. Because an oligopolist's demand curve is "kinked," the marginal revenue curve is not continuous at the existing price and output, providing no clear intersection point for the marginal cost and marginal revenue curves and thus creating an incentive for each oligopolist to leave the price at the existing level once it has been set. (L.O. 3, 4, 5)
10. A firm's revenue and cost data can be used in a similar manner to determine the output/sales level above which profits will be earned and below which the firm should be shut down. (L.O. 6, 7)

Questions

1. You are paying a student $10 per hour to pick strawberries on your farm.
   (a) Explain how the Law of Diminishing Returns will limit the number of hours for which you decide to employ this student.
   (b) Explain your decision using the terms *marginal revenue per box of berries* and *marginal cost per box*.

2. Raj's Raspberry Ranch sells berries at a price of $15 per box. Raj's fixed and variable production costs are indicated in the following table.

Boxes per Day	Fixed Costs	Variable Costs	Total Costs	Average Total Cost per Box	Marginal Cost per Box	Average Revenue per Box	Total Revenue	Marginal Revenue per Box	Profit
0	$20	$ 0	—	—	—	—	—	—	—
10	20	130	—	—	—	—	—	—	—
20	20	250	—	—	—	—	—	—	—
30	20	370	—	—	—	—	—	—	—
40	20	519	—	—	—	—	—	—	—
50	20	680	—	—	—	—	—	—	—
60	20	860	—	—	—	—	—	—	—

   (a) Complete the seven remaining columns in the table.
   (b) The level of output at which profits will be maximized is _____ boxes per day.
   (c) At this level of output, the level of profits will be $_____ per day.
   (d) On graph paper, draw the average cost per box, marginal cost per box, average revenue per box, and marginal revenue per box curves.
   (e) Use the graph that you drew for your answer to part (d) to show the most profitable level of output and sales.
   (f) Using the concepts of marginal revenue and marginal cost, explain why your answer to part (e) is the most profitable level of sales and output. Why would it *not* be more profitable to increase output and sales beyond this point?
   (g) From the information available, does this appear to be a perfectly competitive industry or not? Why?

3. Petra's Pet Treats sells bags of special pet food to retail stores for a wholesale price of $8 per bag. Following is a table showing Petra's weekly costs and revenues. Complete the remaining columns in the table.

Output (bags per week)	Fixed Costs	Variable Costs	Total Costs	Total Revenue	Profit
0	$800	$ 0	—	—	—
100	800	400	—	—	—
200	800	800	—	—	—
300	800	1200	—	—	—
400	800	1600	—	—	—

   (a) In order to break even, Petra must sell _____ bags per week.
   (b) Assuming that 400 bags per week is her maximum output, the maximum profit that Petra can earn is $ _____ per week.

4. Petra is considering a different business model, in which, instead of selling to retailers at the wholesale price of $8 per bag, she establishes a website, becomes an ebusiness, and sells directly to consumers (who order over the

internet) at a retail price of $15 per bag. However, this ebusiness model will also involve higher costs:

- Due to the cost of the website and other assets she will need, her fixed costs will double from $800 to $1600 per week, and
- Due to higher costs of delivery and customer service, her variable costs will double from $4 to $8 per bag

(a) Complete the following table, showing Petra's costs, revenue and profits.

Output (bags per week)	Fixed Costs	Variable Costs	Total Costs	Total Revenue	Profit
0	—	—	—	—	—
100	—	—	—	—	—
200	—	—	—	—	—
300	—	—	—	—	—
400	—	—	—	—	—

Compare the profits of the conventional business model in question 3 to the ebusiness model in this question, at each level of output and sales shown:

(b) What is less attractive about the ebusiness model? Why does this risk exist?

(c) What is more attractive about the ebusiness model? Why does this opportunity exist?

(d) What will Petra have to achieve in order to avoid the risks and secure the opportunities of the ebusiness model, so that it is more profitable than the conventional model?

(e) What obstacles will she have to overcome in order to achieve the goals outlined in part (d)?

5. Some ebusinesses produce and sell only electronic products, such as software and games. Once the original product has been produced, buyers can simply download additional copies of it from the firm's website, without any of the costs associated with physical products, which must be produced and delivered. As a result, the marginal cost per unit of these electronic products is extremely low, and stays very low as sales and output are increased. What are the implications of this situation for the pricing and output strategies of business firms producing such products?

6. Using the terms *marginal revenue* and *marginal cost*, explain why airlines sell tickets at very low prices to people who book a flight at the very last minute (if a seat is available).

7. Visit **http://hadm.sph.sc.edu/COURSES/ECON/MCost/MCost.html** and do the interactive tutorial on Marginal Cost and the Output Rate Under Competition.

Study Guide

Review Questions (Answers to these Review Questions appear in Appendix B.)

1. Identify each of the following as a *fixed cost* or a *variable cost*.
   (a) the monthly rent paid for a firm's office _____
   (b) the paint used to finish a firm's product _____
   (c) the cost of delivering product to buyers _____
   (d) the $100 000 per year paid for leasing of equipment _____

(e) the salary of the president _____

(f) the wages paid to production workers _____

2. As a firm's output increases, its total fixed costs
   (a) increase.
   (b) remain constant (do not change).
   (c) decrease.

3. As a firm's output increases, its fixed costs *per unit*
   (a) increase.
   (b) remain constant (do not change).
   (c) decrease.

4. If a firm's sales and output are low, it tends to have losses (or very low profits), in large part because at low levels of sales and output
   (a) its labour costs per unit will be high.
   (b) its variable costs per unit will be lower.
   (c) its prices will be lower.
   (d) its fixed costs per unit will be very high.
   (e) None of the above.

5. As successive units of one production input (e.g., labour) are added to fixed amounts of other inputs (e.g., capital equipment), the average output of the variable input will
   (a) increase at first, then decrease.
   (b) remain unchanged.
   (c) increase at a constant rate.
   (d) decrease gradually.
   (e) None of the above.

6. The phenomenon described in question 5 is known as the _____.

7. As output is increased, average variable cost *per unit*
   (a) falls at first, then rises.
   (b) rises at first, then falls.
   (c) falls continually.
   (d) rises continually.
   (e) None of the above.

8. Marginal cost per unit is
   (a) the net effect of declining fixed costs per unit and rising variable costs per unit as output is increased.
   (b) the total costs divided by the total number of units produced.
   (c) the total variable costs divided by the number of units produced.
   (d) the addition to total costs arising from the production of one more unit.
   (e) None of the above.

9. If output is increased from 25 units to 26 units per day, and total costs increase from $615 to $638 per day, the marginal cost per unit is
   (a) $24.60
   (b) $24.54
   (c) $23.00
   (d) $638.00
   (e) None of the above.

10. Suppose the firm in question 9 can sell the 26th product for $24.
    (a) Its marginal revenue per unit is $_____.
    (b) Should it produce the 26th unit? Why or why not?

11. Complete the last five columns of the following table.

Units of Output per Day	Fixed Costs	Variable Costs	Total Costs	Average Fixed Cost per Unit	Average Variable Cost per Unit	Average Total Cost per Unit	Marginal Cost per Unit
0	$600	$ 0	——	——	——	——	——
5	600	150	——	——	——	——	——
10	600	200	——	——	——	——	——
15	600	225	——	——	——	——	——
20	600	300	——	——	——	——	——
25	600	550	——	——	——	——	——

  (a) As output increases, why do the following cost factors change as they do?
    (i) average fixed cost per unit
    (ii) average variable cost per unit
    (iii) average total cost per unit
  (b) What does *marginal cost per unit* mean? Why does it change in the way it does as output increases?

Critical Thinking Questions

(Asterisked questions 1 to 4 are answered in Appendix B; the answers to questions 5 to 8 are in the Instructor's Manual that accompanies this text.)

*1. Following are recent prices for "cool white" fluorescent lighting tubes of various sizes:
- 15": $8.99
- 48": $1.79

Why do you suppose the *larger* tube has the *lower* price?

*2. What explains the fact that the classic 939-page *Dr. Spock's Baby and Child Care* sells for the same price as an unremarkable novel of half its length by an unknown author?

*3. Suppose you have the following plans for a new business:
Fixed costs: $500 per week
Variable costs: $5 per product
Price: $10 per product

Output (Units per Week)	Fixed Costs	Variable Costs	Total Costs	Total Revenue	Profit
0	——	——	——	——	——
100	——	——	——	——	——
200	——	——	——	——	——
300	——	——	——	——	——
400	——	——	——	——	——
500	——	——	——	——	——

  (a) Complete the table. If you are expecting to sell 400 products per week, what will your weekly profit be?
  (b) Suppose that you had been overly optimistic in your planning of your business, and the actual situation turns out to be as follows: fixed costs are $800 per week rather than $500, variable costs are $6 per product instead of $5, and competition limits your price to $8 (instead of $10) and your weekly sales to 300 products (rather than 400). What will your profit be now?

*4. Sally's Shirts Ltd. sells shirts at a price of $22 each. Sally's fixed and variable production costs are indicated in the following table.

Units of Output per Day	Fixed Costs	Variable Costs	Total Costs	Average Cost per Unit	Average Revenue per Unit	Marginal Cost per Unit	Marginal Revenue per Unit
0	$200	$ 0	——	——	——	——	——
10	200	170	——	——	——	——	——
20	200	320	——	——	——	——	——
30	200	440	——	——	——	——	——
40	200	580	——	——	——	——	——
50	200	800	——	——	——	——	——
60	200	1100	——	——	——	——	——

(a) Complete the five remaining columns in the table.
(b) On graph paper, draw the curves for the average cost per unit, marginal cost per unit, average revenue per unit, and marginal revenue per unit.
(c) Use the graph that you drew for your answer to part (b) to determine the following:
   (i) The level of output at which profits will be maximized is _____ units per day.
   (ii) At this level of output, the level of profits will be $_____ per day. (Show your calculation of the level of profits.)
(d) Is Sally's Shirts Ltd. operating in a perfectly competitive market?
(e) If this firm is in a perfectly competitive industry and is a typical firm that is making profits, what adjustment will occur in the price of the product, and how will this affect the profits of this typical firm?

5. For the firm whose costs and revenues are shown in the graph below,
   (a) profits will be maximized at a level of output of ___ units per week, and
   (b) at this level of output, profits will be $___ per week. (Show your calculations.)
   (c) Is this firm operating in a perfectly competitive market?
   (d) If this firm is in a perfectly competitive industry and is a typical firm that is making profits, what adjustment will occur in the price of the product, and how will this affect the profits of this typical firm?

6. Following are the cost and revenue data for tables produced by Peter's Patios Ltd.

If the company charges this price per table:	It will sell this many tables per week:
$38.00	0
33.50	20
29.00	40
24.50	60
20.00	80
15.50	100
11.00	120

The company's fixed costs and variable costs are shown in the following table.

Units of Output per Week	Fixed Costs	Variable Costs	Total Costs	Average Cost per Unit	Average Revenue per Unit	Marginal Cost per Unit	Marginal Revenue per Unit
0	$400	$0	___	___	___	___	___
20	400	180	___	___	___	___	___
40	400	330	___	___	___	___	___
60	400	430	___	___	___	___	___
80	400	560	___	___	___	___	___
100	400	780	___	___	___	___	___
120	400	1080	___	___	___	___	___

(a) Complete the five remaining columns in the table.
(b) On graph paper, draw the curves for the average cost per unit, marginal cost per unit, average revenue per unit, and marginal revenue per unit.
(c) Use the graph that you drew for your answer to part (b) to determine the following:
 (i) The level of output at which profits will be maximized is ___ units per week.
 (ii) At this level of output, the level of profits will be $___ per week. (Show your calculation of the level of profits.)
(d) Is Peter's Patios Ltd. operating in a perfectly competitive market?

7. For the firm whose costs and revenues are shown in the graph below,

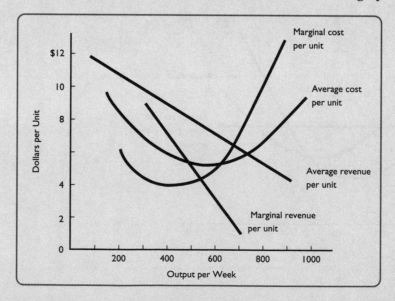

(a) profits will be maximized at a level of output of _____ units per week, and

(b) at this level of output, weekly profits will be $_____. (Show your calculations.)

(c) Is this firm operating in a perfectly competitive market?

8. Kermit's Kandles Ltd. sells candles at a price of $8 each. The following table shows Kermit's fixed and variable production costs.

Units of Output per Day	Fixed Costs	Variable Costs	Total Costs	Total Revenue
0	$400	$0	——	——
100	400	1000	——	——
200	400	1700	——	——
300	400	2200	——	——
400	400	2500	——	——
500	400	3200	——	——
600	400	4400	——	——

(a) Complete the remaining two columns in the table.

(b) On graph paper, draw the total revenue, total costs, and variable costs curves.

(c) The graph indicates that the minimum level of output (sales) required for this firm to start up in business (its break-even point) is _____ units per day.

(d) The graph indicates that, before this firm should go out of business, its sales should fall below a level of _____ units per day.

(e) Explain the reasons for your answers to (c) and (d).

Use the Web   (Hints for this Use the Web exercise appear in Appendix B.)

1. Visit **http://economics.about.com/od/coststructure/ss/revenue_costs.htm** and do the five-step practice question on marginal revenue and marginal cost.

9

Government Policy Toward Business

LEARNING OBJECTIVES

After studying this chapter, you should be able to

1. Explain the doctrine of *laissez-faire*, and why government policy toward business in Canada is not based on laissez-faire.

2. State two ways in which government policies support the incomes of farmers.

3. Describe three ways in which government policies assist small businesses, and two types of government actions that have negative effects upon small businesses.

4. Explain why industrial concentration is of concern to governments, and state four reasons for the high degree of industrial concentration in the Canadian economy.

5. State the basic purpose of Canada's Competition Act, and its provision concerning price-fixing.

6. Summarize the arguments in favour of and against governments restricting mergers of large Canadian corporations, and explain how Canada's Competition Act attempts to address both of these arguments.

7. Describe two traditional government methods for protecting consumers against the market power of natural monopolies.

8. Explain why governments have recently opened up some natural monopolies to competition and have privatized some government enterprises.

9. Apply the concepts and facts of this chapter to various situations.

Sometimes, we see reports of corporations being fined millions of dollars for conspiring to increase prices. At other times, we see governments announcing programs to use tax resources to provide various sorts of assistance to business. In this chapter, we will examine these seemingly contradictory government policies toward business. But first, let's start by returning to some of the basics covered earlier.

The Ideal of Competition

Chapter 1 stressed the importance of producers being *effective* (by producing things that are useful and wanted) and *efficient* (by producing those items without wasting scarce economic resources). Generally, economists and government policy-makers have tended to prefer competitive industries to concentrated ones, on the grounds that competition serves the consumer best, by promoting both effectiveness and efficiency. In competitive industries, consumer demand pushes businesses to produce whatever consumers will buy, and competition pushes businesses to produce it efficiently. Strong competition among businesses also ensures that consumers will not pay excessively high prices and that producers' profits will be reasonable.

The Theory of Laissez-Faire . . .

If the entire economy consisted of industries that were competitive in this way, it would comprise a self-regulating system for determining the answers to basic economic questions such as what to produce and how to produce it. The marketplace would do such a good job of promoting effectiveness and efficiency that there would be no need for government intervention to improve the operation of the economy.

This theory of a competitive economy that serves the consumer so well that there is little or no need for government regulation or intervention is known as **laissez-faire**. The concept of laissez-faire originated in France at the time of Louis XIV, as a reaction to a web of government regulations of business that had grown so complex and restrictive that it stifled incentives and was actually causing the economy to stagnate. By comparison, a free competitive economy would be much more effective at promoting prosperity.

laissez-faire
The doctrine or philosophy that from the viewpoint of the public interest, it is neither necessary nor beneficial for governments to intervene in the operation of the economy.

. . . Versus Economic Reality

But our modern economy is not as simple as that of the theory of laissez-faire. Vigorous competition in an industry is not a stable condition; rather, a combination of competition and economies of scale can eliminate so many firms that only a few are left. And as we saw in Chapter 7, in some industries such as petroleum and communications, the competitive marketplace has evolved to the point where there are only a few corporations left, raising concerns that in those industries there is *too little* competition, and not much chance of new competitors starting up. At the other extreme, in parts of the agricultural sector, there are so many small producers with low incomes that there are concerns that *excessive* competition will force too many farmers out of business and undermine this important industry.

In pursuing the ideal of vigorous competition, then, governments have found themselves in some cases introducing policies that seek to *restrict and regulate* the market power of large firms with little competition, while in other cases government policies seek to *support and assist* small firms in highly competitive environments.

Government Policies Toward Business

In Chapter 7, we examined the four basic types of market structure:
- perfect competition, the most competitive possible situation,
- monopolistic competition, which describes most of the small business sector of the economy,
- oligopoly, in which industries are dominated by a few large firms, and
- monopoly, in which there is only one seller.

The market power of firms operating under these market structures ranges from none whatsoever (in the case of perfect competition) to very great (in the case of a monopoly). Accordingly, government policy toward businesses tends to differ from one type of market structure or industry to another. In general, we will find that the more competitive an industry is, the more *supportive* government policy will be, and the less competitive it is, the more *restrictive* government policy is likely to be. In this chapter, we will consider some of the highlights of government policies toward business in Canada, the reasons for the variations in these policies, and some of the problems concerning them. To organize the discussion, we will use the four types of market structure described above.

Government Policies Concerning Competitive Industries

Perfect Competition

The sector of the Canadian economy that most closely resembles perfect competition is *agriculture*. In agriculture, there are large numbers of producers selling products that are more or less identical to those of other farms. Technological advances have increased farm productivity to the point where there is a general tendency to over-supply markets, with the result being low farm prices and incomes. To make matters worse, fluctuations in weather and crop size cause farm prices and incomes to be unstable, as well as generally low.

Because of the extreme competitiveness of agricultural markets and the problems that this creates for farmers, the general thrust of government policy has been to *support farm prices and/or incomes* through a variety of programs.

As we saw in Chapter 6, governments have sometimes employed *price supports* for some farm products. Under this method, the government establishes the price of the farm produce and undertakes to purchase from the farmers at that price any produce that is unsold. As we also saw in Chapter 6, the result of farm price supports will be surpluses of farm produce. To avoid the problem of crop surpluses, governments have sometimes employed *acreage restrictions*. Under such a program, farmers are paid *not* to grow crops on part of their land in order to reduce the supply of farm products and increase their prices.

Canadian governments have several programs under which *direct payments* are made to farmers if crop prices or yields fall below the long-term average. These insurance-like programs are partly funded by farmers themselves, and partly financed by the government. These programs are very important to farmers—in bad years, as much as 75 percent of farmers' net income can come from such government programs.

In addition to this assistance, governments help to increase some farmers' incomes through marketing boards. These are government-sponsored organizations of farmers that are intended to restrict how much farmers produce, so as to keep prices higher. As such, a marketing board is a form of price-and-production agreement that is similar to the oligopolistic agreements discussed in Chapter 7, but one that is created by government policy. To protect the high prices charged by **marketing boards**, the government must provide further assistance by *restricting imports* of cheaper products to prevent these from competing with Canadian products. We cover government agricultural policy in much more detail in Chapter 14.

Monopolistic Competition

In monopolistic competition, there are many small firms producing and selling differentiated products or services in a highly competitive environment. This is a reasonable description of the small business sector of the Canadian economy, which, as we saw in Chapter 3, has played a vital role in the creation of jobs.

Because small businesses operate in such a highly competitive environment and face many difficulties as described in Chapter 3, various government programs are available to assist them. Both the federal and provincial governments offer loan guarantees or lower-cost, longer-term financing for small businesses. At the federal level, the Business Development Bank of Canada makes term loans to new or existing businesses that are unable to obtain the required funds from other lenders on reasonable terms and conditions, and offers an extensive management training program. Most provincial governments offer financial help through similar agencies, with loan guarantees arranged through regular financial institutions and screening processes to minimize failure rates.

The Canada Small Business Financing (CSBF) program helps small businesses to obtain financing by providing government guarantees of 85 percent of losses to lenders (mostly banks) for certain types of loans to small businesses. Counselling programs are also available from the federal government and most provinces to assist small business owners with their management problems. Such programs help small businesses that are unable to afford expert counselling, utilizing various people, including Masters of Business Administration students, retired executives, and professional counsellors. Also, marketing programs are offered by all provincial governments. These programs are intended to assist small businesses in the opening up of new markets, both in Canada and abroad, and some are designed to complement programs offered through the federal Export Development Corporation. Some provinces also offer personnel assistance programs to help small businesses find skilled employees, and in some cases, the wages of employees are subsidized by the government in order to aid small businesses in recruiting. Finally, government programs provide research and development assistance in the form of subsidies and by helping small businesses apply new technology in various ways.

In total, there is a bewildering array of hundreds of programs for small business offered by the federal, provincial, and municipal governments. According to some observers, a major problem facing many small business owners is finding the time to evaluate the wide variety of programs that could be of value, and to work through the extensive paperwork that many of them require. To aid in these matters, some governments have set up information centres to help small businesses determine where to look for aid, and have undertaken to reduce the amount of paperwork involved.

However, not all government policies and programs are helpful to small business. According to the Canadian Federation of Independent Business (CFIB), *taxation* and *government regulation* are the two major impediments to the operations and growth of small and medium-sized businesses in Canada.

marketing boards
Government-sponsored organizations of farmers that support farm incomes by restricting the supply of produce, usually through a system of quotas on individual farmers.

www.bdc.ca

In 2002–03, the CSBF program made 11 252 loans totalling $956 million, creating some 31 000 new jobs.

www.edc.ca

Small businesses benefit from a lower tax rate of 12 percent on the first $300 000 of their profits.

www.cfib.ca

CFIB research has shown that labour-intensive small businesses actually pay a higher proportion of their profits to taxes than many larger businesses do. The main reason for this anomaly is that the burden of payroll taxes, such as Employment Insurance, workers' compensation premiums, and taxes for health care, falls most heavily on smaller, more labour-intensive businesses, whose labour costs are a higher proportion of their total costs.

Government red tape and paper burden was the second most frequently identified problem by CFIB members. Small business owners cannot afford the considerable amount of time they are required to divert from managing their operation to filling out government forms relating to statistical information and tax collection—for many, this amounts to 5 to 10 hours per week.

Finally, there is the question of how much assistance should actually be given to small businesses. Sometimes, businesses should be allowed to fail because they are not viable, or the people involved do not have the abilities required to operate a successful business. But neither the government, nor anyone else, knows how to recognize the potential of a new, small business or how much assistance is appropriate. Nonetheless, the importance of small business to the Canadian economy has led to a variety of government programs intended to help small businesses, particularly in starting up.

Government Policies Regarding Concentrated Industries

Oligopoly

In Chapter 7, we saw that when an industry is dominated by a few large firms, or oligopolists, it is possible that these firms will agree among themselves to fix prices. It was also mentioned in Chapter 7 that this practice is illegal in Canada, as it is in most countries. However, as we will see, the question of Canadian government policy toward large corporations is considerably more complex than simply outlawing price-fixing.

Industrial Concentration in the Canadian Economy

industrial concentration
The degree to which an industry is dominated by a few firms.

To the extent that a particular industry or market is dominated by a few firms, it is said to be *concentrated*. Studies have repeatedly shown that **industrial concentration** in the Canadian economy is not only high, but also considerably higher than in the U.S. economy.

This domination of much of Canada's economy by large corporations is viewed with concern by some, especially consumer groups. In the corporate concentration in certain sectors of the economy, they see a dangerous extent of oligopolistic power. On the other hand, defenders of big business argue that large corporations increase the prosperity of Canadians, by making their industry more efficient and better able to compete internationally, a consideration made more important by the trend toward freer trade in recent years.

The debate between critics and supporters of big business becomes more heated whenever there are *mergers* of major corporations, such as those that have occurred in recent years in key industries such as brewing, oil, airlines, steel, retailing, forest products, and bookstores. Critics oppose such mergers on the grounds that they only increase the domination of Canadian markets by fewer and larger corporations. But defenders of the mergers argue that Canadian firms can only succeed in highly competitive international markets if they merge in order to grow larger and more efficient.

In this section, we will consider the reasons for the high degree of industrial concentration in Canada, the debate over whether large corporations are a threat or an advantage to Canadians, and the important question of what government policy toward industrial concentration and mergers should be.

Reasons for Concentration

There are various reasons why some industries come to be dominated by a few large firms. One basic reason is the *elimination of firms by competition*: in a competitive market economy, successful firms will expand, and unsuccessful ones will not survive. A major contributing factor to this tendency is **economies of scale**—as successful firms expand, they use mass-production technology that gives them additional production-cost advantages over their competitors.

The *small size of the Canadian market* is also a significant factor in Canada's high degree of industrial concentration. With a total market size about one-tenth that of the United States, there is often simply not enough room in Canada for more than a few firms that are large enough to capture the economies of scale that exist in much of modern business.

Finally, *mergers of corporations* also increase corporate concentration. During the 1990s, merger activity in Canada was spurred by the need for Canadian firms to become more efficient and internationally competitive. Since the early 1980s, there has been a trend toward increased international competition, or the **globalization** of many markets. This trend, together with the Canada–U.S. Free Trade Agreement (1989) and the North American Free Trade Agreement (1994), not only created more intense foreign competition for many Canadian industries in Canadian markets but also increased export opportunities for Canadian firms. To improve their ability to compete with their larger foreign counterparts in the United States and Europe, some Canadian firms merged with others, so as to gain economies of scale, more complete product lines, stronger marketing networks, better access to financial resources, and so on. For instance, the Molson–Carling O'Keefe merger was intended to increase the efficiency and capacity of the company's Canadian brewing operations while giving it access to the worldwide distribution network of Elders IXL Ltd., Carling's Australian parent company. Similarly, Dofasco's merger with Algoma Steel made it the fourth-largest steel-maker in North America while giving it an expanded and balanced product line that was expected to position the company well for competing in the U.S. market. And the takeover of Canada's MacMillan Bloedel by U.S. giant Weyerhaeuser made the Canadian company a key part of the world's third-largest forest products company.

During the 1990s, merger activity increased sharply in many countries, driven in large part by firms' desire to achieve the scale needed for global competition. This trend was assisted by rising stock prices in the 1990s, since in many mergers one firm uses its own shares as payment to shareholders of the firm being acquired. The lower interest rates of the 1990s also helped firms to finance their purchases of other companies. Another factor was conglomerates' sale of companies as part of the trend toward focusing on their core business. Examples of such sales included Imasco's sale of Canada Trust to the Toronto-Dominion Bank and Molson's sale of Beaver Lumber to Home Hardware.

In Canada, there have often been as many as 1000 mergers per year in recent years, as firms reposition themselves to deal with international competition both in foreign markets and in Canada. This merger activity has been unprecedented in terms

economies of scale
Lower production costs per unit made possible by higher volumes of production that permit the achievement of increased efficiencies.

globalization
The growing internationalization of business, trade, and finance that has characterized the period since the early 1980s.

of both the numbers of mergers and the size of many of the enterprises that resulted from these mergers.

The Debate Over Bigness in Business

Critics of big business argue that since the Canadian economy has a high degree of industrial concentration, Canadian consumers are exposed to a high risk of price-fixing by oligopolists. They point to the fact that Labatt and Molson hold a combined market share of about 90 percent of the Canadian beer market as a prime example of unhealthy corporate concentration. In the retail sector, they see evidence of decreasing competition in Hudson's Bay Co.'s purchase of Kmart and its merger of Kmart with its Zellers division, Home Hardware's purchase of Beaver Lumber, the bookstore merger of Indigo and Chapters, and the merger between Superior Propane and ICG Propane. They also point to periodic convictions of corporations for price-fixing and note that the profits of many oligopolists represent a considerably higher rate of return on investment than that earned by an average business.

According to this view, if competition cannot be relied upon to keep prices and profits in check, the government must set down rules for oligopolists to follow and must police their behaviour. In particular, governments must not only prevent price-fixing and other measures that reduce competition but also prevent mergers of companies where these would reduce competition, and possibly even break up excessively dominant corporations into smaller firms if necessary.

Defenders of large corporations argue that these big firms actually contribute to the economic prosperity of Canadians. They emphasize the reinvestment of the profits of big business into capital equipment and improved technology that improve productivity in the Canadian economy.

They argue that this higher productivity benefits Canadians in two ways. First, as we have seen, higher output per worker is the basis for *higher living standards*. By using mass-production technology, large producers can reduce production costs so much that even after their above-average profits are added, the price to the consumer is still lower. If productivity is high enough, it is possible for workers to have high wages, companies to have high profits, *and* consumer prices to be low. And, as supporters of big business point out, if you wanted to show someone a showpiece of Canadian technology, you would probably go to one of the country's vast automobile assembly plants that uses computerized industrial robots and turns out as many as 75 cars per hour.

Second, there is the question of the *international competitiveness* of Canadian producers. Much of Canada's manufacturing industry has historically been small-scale by world standards and, therefore, not very efficient or competitive internationally. So it can be argued that mergers of Canadian firms into fewer but larger and more efficient operations contribute to Canada's international competitiveness. This point is particularly important because so much of the output of the Canadian economy is exported, and so many jobs rely upon the success of Canadian firms in export markets.

The Policy Dilemma

The arguments for and against bigness in business present government authorities with a very real dilemma in deciding government policy toward industrial concentration. To leave the power of big business unchecked would risk exposing consumers to price-fixing. On the other hand, strong restrictions on big business could limit the growth and efficiency of Canadian firms and their ability to compete internationally.

"People of the same trade seldom meet together, even for merriment and diversion, but the conversation ends in a conspiracy against the public, or in some contrivance to raise prices."
— ADAM SMITH, *THE WEALTH OF NATIONS* (1776).

"[Mergers] reduce Canadian competition, raise prices for consumers and cause job losses. I can't see how any of those things in any way benefit Canadians or the economy."
— DAVID McKENDRY, CONSUMERS ASSOCIATION OF CANADA.

This dilemma is especially troublesome in Canada, where the situation can be summarized as follows:

(a) industrial concentration in Canada is *substantially higher* than in comparable industries in the United States;

(b) however, the average size of Canada's 100 largest industrial corporations and Canada's 25 largest financial corporations is *much smaller* than the average size of their counterparts in the United States and other developed countries.

This awkwardly contradictory state of affairs is illustrated in Figure 9-1. It shows that many corporations that are sufficiently large to dominate markets and raise concerns about threats to consumers *within Canada* may be relatively small and not competitive by *international standards*. And, in order to become internationally competitive, these firms would have to grow larger, and thus *more* dominant within the Canadian market. These facts make the policy dilemma referred to earlier particularly severe for Canadian policy-makers—while industrial concentration in Canada is presently high enough to support the argument for strong laws restricting further growth and concentration, policies that do so could prevent Canadian corporations from growing to the size needed to be internationally competitive.

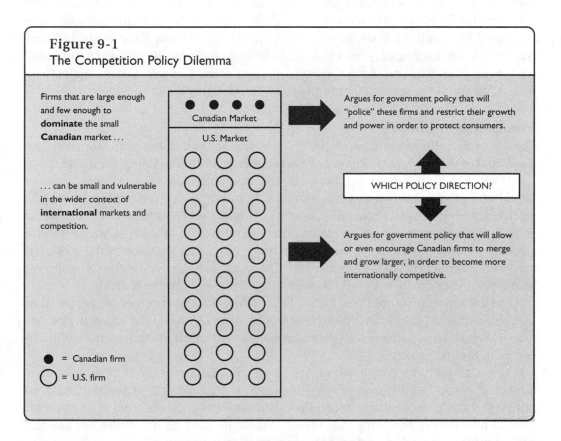

Figure 9-1
The Competition Policy Dilemma

The Changing Economic Environment: Globalization

Historically, Canadian government *trade policy* and *competition policy* were geared to *national markets*. Through its *trade policy*, the government imposed tariffs on imported goods in order to foster the development of Canadian manufacturing industries by protecting them against foreign competition. On the other hand, the government's *competition policy* sought to protect Canadian consumers from price-fixing and other anticompetitive practices by oligopolistic industries (many of which were, themselves, protected by the same government's tariffs against foreign competition). So the government was in the position of trying to *promote competition* among Canadian producers within the Canadian market, while at the same time *restricting competition* from foreign firms in that same market.

The more recent trend toward freer trade has made the concept of gearing policies to national markets less relevant. As nations cut tariffs, international competition became more intense and markets became more international—the process known as *globalization*. As new trade agreements were signed (the Canada–U.S. Free Trade Agreement of 1989, NAFTA in 1994, and the 1995 World Trade Organization agreement), Canadian industry was faced with the prospect of stronger foreign competition. Also, the economic integration of Europe into a single market of 340 million made it likely that North American producers would soon face stronger competition from larger and more efficient European firms. These trends toward the globalization of markets pushed policy-makers toward thinking more about *international* concerns, especially the ability of their nation to compete in global markets. In this context, big business came to be seen in a less unfavourable light than in the past.

The trend toward freer trade had some major implications for the debate on industrial concentration in Canada. First, freer trade made it more important than ever that in framing its policy regarding big business, the Canadian government take into account the ability of Canadian corporations to compete internationally. Also, the increased competition from imports that would come with freer trade reduced concerns about the market power of large Canadian corporations. In the view of many observers, *freer trade* would do more to protect Canadian consumers against the market power of oligopolists than *Canadian laws* possibly could.

The Competition Act

> "The core of the policy is the likely effect of a proposed merger on competition, whether domestic or foreign."
> — WILLIAM STANBURY, UBC FACULTY OF COMMERCE AND BUSINESS ADMINISTRATION.

Canada's competition legislation is the Competition Act, which was passed in 1986. The basic goal of the law is to promote and preserve competition in Canadian markets.

Under the Competition Act, the basic test is whether the effect of firms' actions would be (or had been) to *lessen competition substantially* in a given market. Obviously, a price-fixing agreement between competitors would have this effect and therefore be illegal. With respect to mergers, the situation is less clear-cut—the key is not simply the size of the companies or their share of the market, but rather the effect of the proposed merger on competition in the marketplace. The test of a merger under the Competition Act is whether competition would be substantially lessened by the merger.

In addition, the Competition Act explicitly allows for the approval of mergers that would likely result in *efficiency gains* that would offset any likely reduction in competition. This allows companies to defend mergers that would increase their ability to compete internationally.

www.cb-bc.gc.ca

The Competition Act is administered by the Competition Bureau, which is attached to the Department of Industry (Industry Canada). The Bureau must be notified of any plan to merge or acquire businesses in which the total assets or total annual revenues of the firms exceeds $400 million. After notifying the Bureau, the parties must wait for 7 to 21 days before completing the merger.

The Bureau then reviews the proposed merger or acquisition, considering whether
(a) it is likely to lessen competition substantially.
(b) there are likely to be real gains in efficiency that will exceed, and offset, the lessening of competition.
(c) such gains in efficiency will improve the ability of the merged firms to compete internationally. (Section 96[2])

The second and third considerations here (b and c)—known as the "efficiency exception"—are the Competition Act's attempt to deal with the policy dilemma described earlier, by allowing mergers that increase efficiency, particularly if they improve the firm's ability to compete internationally. The Act recognizes that a merger could present trade-offs in which both negative effects on consumers and positive effects on efficiencies existed, and it empowers the Bureau to weigh these trade-offs when deciding whether to allow a merger.

Other factors to be considered include barriers to entry to the particular market (which would affect future competition), the extent of foreign competition, the effectiveness of the competition that would remain after the proposed merger, and the availability of alternatives (such as selling all or part of a firm involved in a merger to other firms).

If the Bureau has concerns about the effect of the proposal on competition, it will seek to negotiate amendments to the proposal with the companies involved. The result is usually a negotiated agreement. However, if the Bureau has doubts, it can also grant conditional approval for a merger and then monitor the competitive conditions in the market following the merger.

If the Bureau and the companies are unable to agree, the matter is taken to the Competition Tribunal for a decision. The Competition Tribunal is chaired by a judge of the Federal Court of Canada, and consists of 12 members, including business and consumer authorities as well as judges. The Tribunal operates under the same procedural rules as a civil court, and its decisions may be appealed to the Federal Court of Canada.

For instance, in 1996, the Competition Tribunal issued an order that required Interac Inc. and the nine banks and other financial institutions that comprised the charter members of Interac to open up its network to potential participants on a nondiscriminatory basis, and to cease levying new member entry fees that had deterred entry into Interac. The order was issued in response to an application from the Competition Bureau that alleged that the charter members of Interac substantially or completely controlled the market for the supply of shared electronic-network banking services in Canada.

Experience with the Competition Act

With respect to mergers, since the Competition Act was passed in 1986, the Competition Bureau has examined on average some 150 merger proposals each year. Most of these have been accepted without challenge; however, in a few cases, the Bureau asked for changes to proposed mergers or challenged them. In several other cases, the merger plans were voluntarily abandoned by the parties following objections by the Bureau. While the names of the companies involved were not revealed, it is reported that several of these plans involved large and well-known firms. Almost all of the Bureau's concerns were resolved through negotiations; only a small number of cases were forwarded to the Tribunal for adjudication.

The most common type of negotiated settlement between the Bureau and the companies involved restructuring proposed mergers through the sale of some assets to competitors. For instance, in order to gain the approval of the Bureau for their merger, Indigo and Chapters agreed to sell 13 superstores and 10 of Chapters' smaller mall-based stores. And when Cineplex Galaxy acquired Famous Players in 2005, it had to sell off 35 theatres in 17 cities in 6 provinces. In such cases, the Bureau examines the impact of the proposed merger on competition in various local markets, and if appears that the merger would substantially lessen competition in a market area, it requires that assets be sold to competitors.

With respect to price-fixing, there was general agreement that the new law was more effective than the previous law in that convictions were easier to obtain

The Competition Bureau generally will review a merger if the market share of the merged firms would exceed 35 percent.

The 2005 purchase of A&P Canada by Metro Inc. gave Metro a market share of 25 percent in Ontario and 30 percent in the Greater Toronto Area.

and penalties were more severe, including a maximum fine of $10 million. Following the passage of the new law, there were several noteworthy cases involving heavy fines.

www.admworld.com

The largest total of fines in one inquiry occurred in 1999, when several international pharmaceutical companies were fined over $91 million for fixing the prices of various vitamins. In another widely-reported case, Archer Daniels Midland Co., a huge American food company, was fined $16 million for conspiring with seven other companies to fix the prices of a feed additive and a flavour enhancer.

A visit to the Competition Bureau's website (**www.cb-cb.gc.ca**; click on "Law and Litigation," then "Penalties Imposed") shows that most of the offences listed did not involve consumer products that are household names, but rather industrial products sold to other businesses, the cost of which becomes part of the prices that final consumers pay. The list of firms that were fined also shows the international nature of the offences, raising the question the question of whether some sort of international competition legislation is required for the new era of globalized markets and multinational corporations.

Problems with the Efficiency Exception: The Superior Propane Case

In 2000, the Competition Tribunal made an unexpected decision involving a proposed merger between Superior Propane and ICG Propane. Despite the fact that the merger would substantially lessen competition in 66 of 74 local markets for propane, would create a monopoly or near monopoly in 16 other local markets, and would increase the price of propane by an estimated 8 percent at an annual cost of $40.5 million to consumers, the Competition Tribunal *upheld the merger*. The Tribunal gave as its reason the "efficiency exception," arguing that the efficiency gains of the merger were substantial, and that only the estimated $2.6 million cost to *lower-income consumers* should be weighed against those efficiencies. Asserting the need for the Act to protect consumers, the Competition *Bureau* took the unusual step of appealing the decision of the Competition *Tribunal* in the Federal Court of Appeal, but its final appeal was unsuccessful.

This was considered to be a fundamentally important case, as it struck at the very purpose of the Competition Act, and was regarded as unacceptable by the Competition Bureau. In preparation for rewriting the efficiencies provisions of the Act, the Bureau launched a broad consultation process on the role of efficiencies under the Act. At the time of writing, this process was not complete, and the Competition Act had not been revised.

YOU DECIDE

Beer Competition
Nearly 90 percent of the beer bought in Canada is produced by just two breweries—Labatt and Molson. ▨

QUESTION
1. What could governments do to increase competition in a market that is so strongly dominated by two big firms?

Canada's Banks—To Merge or Not to Merge?

Canada's banks are big in the small Canadian market, comprising 5 of Canada's largest 22 corporations in 2004. But they are small compared to European, Japanese and American banks; the assets of Canada's largest bank (Royal Bank of Canada) are less than one-third those of the largest banks in the world. And recently, banks and financial institutions in other countries have been growing even larger as they merged as part of the process of globalization. The Dominion Bond Rating Service has observed that, "Ultimately, we believe consolidation within the Canadian banking sector is inevitable if Canadian banks are to remain globally competitive."

In January 1998, the Royal Bank of Canada and the Bank of Montreal announced their intention to merge, and in April, the Canadian Imperial Bank of Commerce and the Toronto-Dominion Bank announced similar plans. Both mergers would require the approval of the Competition Bureau and the federal minister of finance.

A flurry of controversy greeted the announcements. Critics of the mergers argued that there was already too little competition in the Canadian banking industry, and that the banks had been earning record-high profits. There was also fear of branch closings and job losses, as well as reduced competition, reduced service and higher service charges. It was also reported that the Competition Bureau had found that in nearly 40 percent of the geographical areas it examined, the merged bank would have more than a 35 percent market share, which is the "trigger" for Competition Bureau concern regarding concentration.

Defenders of the mergers argued that unless Canadian banks merged, they would be unable to compete with larger foreign banks, and noted that studies showed that Canadian banks were less cost-efficient than leading banks in the United States and the United Kingdom, presumably due to the smaller size of the Canadian banks.

At the time, Canada's banks were unpopular with the Canadian public, mainly because of their record-high profits. In December 1998, the federal government decided to disallow the two proposed mergers. However, few observers believed that this would be the end of the matter.

Within a few months of the federal government's rejection of its merger with CIBC, Toronto-Dominion announced plans to purchase Canada Trust, creating Canada's largest bank in terms of retail customers, personal deposits, and personal loans. But within three weeks, three Japanese banks added a different perspective by merging to form the world's largest bank, with combined assets more than seven times as large as the merged TD Canada Trust.

For its part, the federal government moved ahead with plans to allow increased foreign competition in the Canadian banking sector, as required by a 1997 World Trade Organization agreement. And in 2002, a technical report of the Bank of Canada[1] added weight to the banks' arguments. It found that many of the new technologies had high fixed costs and low marginal costs, which gave an advantage to larger banks in business lines that used those technologies. In the context of the worldwide trend toward mergers into larger banks, many observers believed that the government's decision to allow the mergers of Canadian banks might well be reconsidered at a future time, when there was more foreign competition in the Canadian banking sector and when the political climate was less hostile to bank mergers.

"I do think [mergers] are inevitable in the long run and they're in Canada's interest."
— CHARLES BAILLIE, CEO, TD CANADA TRUST

---

[1] Charles Freedman and Clyde Goodlet. (2002, August). *The Financial Services Sector: An Update on Recent Developments.* Bank of Canada Technical Report No. 91.

Monopoly

As we saw in Chapter 7, monopoly is the market structure under which there is the strongest market power, because the monopolistic seller has complete control over the supply of the product, and hence its price. Monopoly is therefore regarded as the least desirable of all of the market structures we have examined.

Natural Monopolies

Nonetheless, there are certain industries in which monopoly is the most logical form of organization. Generally, these industries are *public utilities and services*, such as water and public transit. The economic rationale for having monopolies in such industries starts with the fact that such utilities often require *very heavy capital investment* in facilities and equipment. This in turn results in *high fixed costs*, such as depreciation and interest on funds borrowed to finance these investments. The best way to keep these fixed costs as low as possible *to each customer* is to spread them over the maximum possible number of customers. By giving one producer a monopoly that guarantees it all of the available customers, the natural monopoly should be able to provide the service at a lower cost per customer than would otherwise be possible.

Creating a monopoly in this way will lower the production costs of the firm, but how can the government ensure that the benefits of this efficiency go to the consumer in the form of lower prices, and not to the monopoly itself? A way to protect consumers is for the government to *nationalize* the monopoly, by placing it under government ownership and having the government operate it on a non-profit basis. Canada Post is an example of this approach. Another approach is to leave the monopoly under private ownership but subject its rates (prices) to *government regulation*— Bell Canada's local telephone service is an example of this approach. The government will regulate the monopoly's rates (prices) in such a way as to permit the company to earn a reasonable rate of return on its shareholders' investment, so as to be fair to shareholders of the utility as well as to consumers.

It may seem that if natural monopolies are owned or regulated by the government, the public will be protected against overcharging. However, the matter of regulating monopolies has not turned out to be quite as simple as that. In order to regulate the prices to be charged by a natural monopoly, the people responsible for determining the regulations must possess considerable knowledge about that industry, its operations, and its costs. The most likely source of people with such knowledge is the industry itself, in the persons of former senior officials of the enterprise being regulated. Even if the regulators come from outside the industry being regulated, they must depend heavily for their information on the management of the monopoly. So the process of regulation is sometimes not the simple, objective, and effective procedure that it is intended to be. It is neither possible nor fair to generalize concerning the effectiveness of regulatory boards, since some seem to be much more effective protectors of the consumer's interests than others.

More recently, some critics have called into question the basic premise that natural monopolies are economically beneficial to consumers. One criticism is that some natural monopolies have charged *excessively high prices*, not because they earn high profits (in fact, many actually lose money), but rather because they employ excessive numbers of people and pay above-market wages and salaries. As a result, critics say, they have developed into inefficient bureaucracies with excessively high labour costs that become the justification for increasing the rates that they charge to their captive customers.

A second reason for questioning the benefits of natural monopolies is that technological progress has created the possibility of *new forms of competition* for established natural monopolies. For instance, new technology now permits competition in long-distance telephone service, and fax machines, email, electronic banking, and telecommunications technology are breaking down Canada Post's monopoly over some kinds of mail service. In a similar way, changes in communications technology are breaking into the field that once was thought to "belong" to cable television companies. These changes suggest that it may prove more beneficial to the public to open up some established natural monopolies to competition than to maintain those monopolies subject to the traditional consumer protections of government ownership or rate regulation.

Whether critics are concerned about the rates charged by natural monopolies or about making alternative technologies and services available to the public, their usual recommendations are to *open up the monopolies to competition* and possibly to *privatize* them (sell them to private investors), with the goal of making them more efficient and effective through some combination of competition and the profit motive.

In some jurisdictions, government-owned electricity generation monopolies are being replaced (or supplemented) by private firms that generate electricity and sell it to the distribution network in competition with each other. This approach brings us back in the direction of laissez-faire, as described earlier in the chapter.

Chapter Summary

1. According to the theory of laissez-faire, government should not intervene in the economy. Canadian government policy is more active, tending to be more supportive of businesses in more competitive industries, and more restrictive toward those in less competitive situations. (L.O. 1)

2. In the case of agriculture, which is the sector of the economy that most closely approximates perfect competition, government policy is quite supportive in a variety of ways intended to both increase and stabilize farmers' incomes. (L.O. 2)

3. With respect to the small business sector, which fits the description of monopolistic competition, many government programs are available, mostly to help small businesses get started. However, small businesses find that two of their main problems—taxation and governmental "red tape"—also arise from the actions of governments. (L.O. 3)

4. Industrial concentration tends to result in market power for producers, which can mean higher prices. The Canadian economy has a high degree of industrial concentration for various reasons, including competition, economies of scale, the small size of the Canadian market, and mergers of firms. (L.O. 4)

5. The purpose of the Competition Act is to promote and preserve competition. Under the Act, price-fixing is illegal and can result in heavy fines. (L.O. 5)

6. Many Canadian industrial corporations are small by international standards. As a result, while it can be argued that government policy should restrict mergers that would increase industrial concentration even further, it can also be argued that it is in Canada's best interests for some firms to merge so as to become more efficient and more competitive internationally. (L.O. 6)

7. The Competition Act is intended to provide the public with protection against anticompetitive behaviour by firms enjoying a dominant position in the

Canadian marketplace, while allowing Canadian firms to merge for the purpose of increasing efficiency and thus improving their ability to compete internationally. (L.O. 6)

8. Traditionally, it has been Canadian government policy to allow natural monopolies in many public utilities and services in order to gain cost advantages, and either to place these monopolies under government ownership or to have their rates regulated by government. (L.O. 7)

9. Recently, concerns regarding the efficiency of some natural monopolies and the rates they have been charging have led governments in the direction of opening them up to competition and/or privatizing them. (L.O. 8)

Questions

1. (a) Describe three types of government programs that are helpful to small business in Canada.
   (b) What is the opportunity cost of these government programs?
   (c) What are the benefits to Canadians that offset the opportunity costs in part (b)?

2. (a) Why is industrial concentration of concern to government policy-makers?
   (b) Is the overall degree of industrial concentration in Canada lower or higher than in the U.S.?
   (c) State four reasons for the situation described in part (b).

3. Are the following business practices in legal Canada or not? Explain the reasons for each of your answers.
   (a) actions that lessen competition substantially
   (b) price-fixing by producers
   (c) mergers of large corporations

4. Probably the most historic anti-monopoly prosecution involved Microsoft in the United States over the 1998–2002 period. Prosecutors argued that Microsoft's 80 percent share of the market for PC operating systems gave it near-monopoly power. Furthermore, they argued, Microsoft's dominant position in the market was protected by economies of scale: the fixed cost of developing an operating system such as Windows is very high, but the marginal cost of producing additional copies of Windows is very low. This facilitated business practices such as offering its Internet Explorer browser (which was tied to Windows) for free, and made it very difficult for other firms to compete.
   (a) What arguments might Microsoft use in its defence?
   (b) If the prosecution won the case, what remedies might it ask the court to award against Microsoft?
   (c) Make an argument that the facts of the situation justify declaring Microsoft a natural monopoly whose prices and/or profits should be regulated by the government.
   (d) Make an argument that government regulation of Microsoft's prices and/or profits would not only be unnecessary, but also would not be in the interests of consumers.
   (e) Do you know the outcome of the case? It's at **www.usdoj.gov/atr/cases/f200400/200457.htm**.

5. The Canadian Broadcasting Corporation (CBC) is a federal Crown corporation. Make the strongest possible argument that the CBC
   (a) should be privatized.
   (b) should continue to be a Crown corporation.

6. Which of the following two merger proposals do you think the Competition Bureau would be more likely to accept, and why?
   (a) a merger of two furniture manufacturers that would give the new company 65 percent of the Canadian market for a particular type of furniture, or
   (b) a merger of two national supermarket chains that would give the new chain nearly 50 percent of the market in many regional areas.

7. Visit the Competition Bureau's website (**www.competitionbureau.gc.ca**) and report on any significant recent developments or cases involving the Competition Act and the Competition Bureau. Click on *Law and Litigation*, then *In the Courts*. Is there any pattern to the types of cases currently being pursued in the courts by the Bureau?

8. Visit the website of the Business Development Bank of Canada (BDC) at **www.bdc.ca**.
   (a) Who owns the BDC, what is its mission, and how many branches does it operate?
   (b) What services does the BDC provide, and to whom?
   (c) What was the number and total value of loans made by the BDC last year?
   (d) Explain the difference between the activities of the Competition Bureau and the BDC.

Study Guide

Review Questions (Answers to these Review Questions appear in Appendix B.)

1. According to the doctrine of laissez-faire,
   (a) the economy functions best when government regulation and intervention are kept to a minimum.
   (b) the economy cannot function well unless the government takes over the ownership and operation of all businesses.
   (c) the economy functions best if businesses are privately owned and operated, but are subject to extensive government regulations.
   (d) all concentrated industries should be controlled by the government.
   (e) None of the above.

2. The doctrine of laissez-faire assumes that
   (a) all industries are perfectly competitive.
   (b) the economy generally consists of industries that are competitive.
   (c) businesses seek to maximize the welfare of the consumer, and government regulation is therefore unnecessary.
   (d) all business profits are reinvested.
   (e) None of the above.

3. Generally, government policy toward an industry tends to be more *supportive* of industries that are _____, and more *restrictive* toward industries that are _____.

4. *Industrial concentration* refers to
   (a) situations in which one firm controls over half of the sales of an industry.
   (b) the extent to which an industry is dominated by a few firms.
   (c) only those industries in which profits are significantly above the average for the economy as a whole.
   (d) industries in which the major firm(s) concentrate(s) on acquiring the shares of their competition.
   (e) None of the above.

5. Industrial concentration is of interest and concern to economists because
    (a) when a few firms dominate an industry, the potential exists for monopolistic practices such as price-fixing.
    (b) larger firms are sometimes more progressive technologically, and so contribute to higher productivity and living standards.
    (c) it is generally agreed that big business and the domination of industries by a few firms reduce the standard of living of the people.
    (d) Both (a) and (c) are correct.
    (e) Both (a) and (b) are correct.

6. State whether each of the following is a reason why large corporations have come to play such a large role in much of the Canadian economy. Answer *yes* or *no* to each point.
    (a) _____ Larger businesses often enjoy cost advantages due to large-scale production and are thus better able to compete.
    (b) _____ Modern manufacturing often requires such vast amounts of capital investment and large plants that large corporations are required.
    (c) _____ Government prefers large corporations to smaller businesses, and it is government policy to encourage the development of large corporations through tax advantages and other measures.
    (d) _____ Businesses often merge with their competitors.
    (e) _____ The small size of the Canadian market allows for the development of relatively few firms in some industries.

7. The most basic reason for the higher-than-average profit rates of large corporations is that oligopolists
    (a) are more efficient than the average firm.
    (b) advertise more than the average firm.
    (c) pay lower wages than the average firm.
    (d) often compete less intensely regarding prices than firms in competitive industries.
    (e) None of the above.

8. Critics of big business argue that industrial concentration tends to result in
    (a) higher prices and higher output than would be the case in competitive industries.
    (b) lower prices and higher output than would be the case in competitive industries.
    (c) higher prices and lower output than would be the case in competitive industries.
    (d) lower prices and lower output than would be the case in competitive industries.

9. Of the following, which is the *most valid argument* in defence of big business?
    (a) The profits of big businesses (expressed as a rate of return on capital) are not higher than the profits of competitive industries.
    (b) Oligopolists do not agree among themselves to raise prices and restrict output; rather, they compete vigorously on prices.
    (c) While abuses of big business's power (e.g., price-fixing) occurred in the past, these are now prevented by the government.
    (d) Oligopolists constantly strive to improve the quality of their products to the maximum extent possible and to keep their prices low.
    (e) The reinvestment of the large profits of big business in research and development, technological change, and capital investment raises productivity and thus society's standard of living.

10. In determining an appropriate government policy toward large corporations, what factors create a dilemma for Canadian authorities?

  (a) Industrial concentration in Canada is higher than in the United States and other countries.

  (b) Because Canada's largest corporations are much smaller than their foreign counterparts, they are often at a competitive disadvantage in international trade.

  (c) The profits of oligopolistic corporations in Canada are very much higher than in other countries, suggesting that price-fixing is a particularly serious problem in Canada.

  (d) Both (a) and (b) are correct.

  (e) Both (b) and (c) are correct.

11. The basic purpose of Canada's *Competition Act* (1986) is

  (a) to promote and preserve competition in Canadian markets.

  (b) to stop mergers of large corporations.

  (c) to outlaw price-fixing by businesses.

  (d) to break up corporations that are so large that they dominate markets.

  (e) to limit the market share of large corporations.

12. Two business practices that are prohibited by the Competition Act because they reduce competition in markets are

  (a) _____ and

  (b) _____.

13. The Competition Act allows firms to defend proposed mergers on the grounds that the merger would result in _____, and thereby increase the ability of Canadian industry to _____.

14. Suppose that an industry consists of four companies with the following market shares:

Company A: 30 percent of total industry sales
Company B: 26 percent of total industry sales
Company C: 24 percent of total industry sales
Company D: 20 percent of total industry sales

Suppose that Company A and Company C want to merge into one larger company that will have more than $400 million in sales or assets.

  (a) Under Canadian law, what must these companies do before they can merge into one company?

  (b) What factors will the federal Competition Bureau consider when reviewing this proposed merger?

  (c) If the Competition Bureau is not satisfied with the proposed merger, what actions might the Competition Bureau take?

15. Under the Competition Act,

  (a) the Bureau of Competition Policy has approved the vast majority of proposed mergers.

  (b) the Bureau of Competition Policy has negotiated significant modifications to some proposed mergers, mostly involving the sale of assets to competitors.

  (c) a large number of proposed mergers have been rejected by the Bureau of Competition Policy.

  (d) a large number of proposed mergers have led to disputes between the Bureau of Competition Policy and the companies involved, which have had to be referred to the Competition Tribunal for a final decision.

  (e) Both (a) and (b) have been true.

16. (a) Some industries are considered to be natural monopolies because _____ .

(b) Two examples of natural monopolies are _____ and _____ .

17. Traditionally, governments have dealt with natural monopolies by
(a) passing laws forbidding them to earn any profits.
(b) taking over the ownership and operation of them.
(c) regulating the prices that they can charge.
(d) Both (b) and (c) are correct.
(e) None of the above.

Critical Thinking Questions

(Asterisked questions 1 to 3 are answered in Appendix B; the answers to questions 4 to 7 are in the Instructor's Manual that accompanies this text.)

*1. In 2001, the Competition Bureau sought an order prohibiting Air Canada from *reducing* its fares below a certain point on certain flights in Eastern Canada that were also serviced by low-cost carriers WestJet and CanJet. Ordinarily, one thinks of the Competition Bureau as opposing the *increasing* of prices by firms. What would explain the Bureau's objection in this case to Air Canada's *lowering* of prices?

*2. Many people dislike the haggling that often characterizes the purchase of a car, and would prefer to buy a car like they buy most other items—the seller tells you the price, and you decide whether or not to buy the product. When Toyota decided to cater to such people by deciding its "best price" for its cars, and instructing its dealers to sell cars at that price, and at that price only, the Competition Bureau objected. Why do you think the Competition Bureau intervened?

*3. Following are the income statements for a manufacturing company with sales of $500 million per year and a service firm such as a restaurant with sales of $500 thousand per year:

	Manufacturing Company	Restaurant
Sales revenue	$500 million	$500 thousand
Non-labour costs	370	320
Labour costs	100	150
Profit	30	30
Payroll taxes (10% of payroll)		
Profit after payroll taxes		

(a) Why are the manufacturing company's labour costs 20 percent of sales revenue, while the restaurant's labour costs are 30 percent of sales revenue?
(b) Finish the table by calculating the payroll taxes and the profits after payroll taxes for each firm.
(c) By what percent do payroll taxes reduce the profit of each firm?

4. The development of a new drug is a very costly venture, involving years of research and testing, and possibly investment in production equipment. On the other hand, once the drug has been developed and mass-production facilities are

in place, the production of additional "copies" of the drug (pills, etc.) is often very inexpensive. Government policy regarding the drug industry is to grant a *patent* to the company that develops a new drug, which gives that company a legal monopoly for a certain number of years. After the patent expires, competing firms can also produce the drug, in generic form.

(a) Compare the drug industry's fixed costs and marginal costs.

(b) How could the situation in part (a) generate economic incentives that slow down the development of new and improved drugs?

(c) Why would the government give a legal monopoly to drug companies?

(d) Why would this legal monopoly be time-limited?

(e) After a patent expires, would you expect the price to fall significantly? Why?

5. Historically, the electricity industry has been treated as a natural monopoly. The facilities that generate electricity (such as hydro-electric plants, coal- or-gas-fired plants, and nuclear plants) and transmit it to users over complex systems of wires enjoy such large economies of scale that it was considered both inevitable and beneficial to the public that governments would own them and operate them as monopolies. More recently, however, new technologies such as windmills (visit **www.canwea.ca**) have made it economical to generate electricity on a much smaller scale, with lower fixed costs. This has led to interest in changing the electricity industry, up to and including proposals to privatize entire provincially-owned electrical utilities.

(a) Make an argument that electrical utilities should be privatized.

(b) Make an argument that electrical utilities should be continue to be government-run monopolies.

(c) Is it easier to argue for privatizing the generation of electricity or the transmission of it? Why?

(d) Can you think of some compromise between government-run monopolies and complete privatization that could be beneficial?

6. In the 1970s, Canadian governments introduced marketing boards as a new way of assisting farmers economically. In short, a marketing board is a government agency that has the authority to tell farmers that they cannot produce more than a certain amount of products such as eggs or milk or cheese or chickens. The result of such limitation of supply was, of course, that farmers received much higher prices for these products.

(a) Why would the government establish agencies whose activities would be illegal under the Competition Act?

(b) Who would object to the practices of marketing boards? Why?

7. The Bank of Canada is a federal government agency that deals with various aspects of banking in Canada, including research studies. The Bank's Technical Report No. 91 notes the significance of developments in information and communications technology, "most notably the rapid increase in processing power and the sharp decline in telecommunications costs." The report goes on to observe that "many of the new technologies have high fixed costs and low marginal costs."

(a) Why would these technologies have high fixed costs?

(b) Why would they have low marginal costs?

(c) What is the significance of Technical Report No. 91 for the banks in their efforts to convince the federal government that they need to merge?

Use the Web   (Hints for these Use the Web exercises appear in Appendix B.)

1. Visit the Competition Bureau's website (**www.competitionbureau.gc.ca**) and determine if there have been any developments concerning the efficiency exception. Go to the *News Room* and check *News Releases,* and/or search the site for "efficiency."

2. Have there been any new developments in the area of bank mergers? Keep a newspaper clippings file on these and compile a report. Also, visit the Competition Bureau at **www.competitionbureau.gc.ca** and search for "bank."

Labour Markets and Labour Unions

After studying this chapter, you should be able to

1. Explain, with the aid of a graph, how wages are determined in the nonunion sector of the labour force.

2. Give two reasons for the large differences in incomes that exist, and explain why these differences persist.

3. Explain, with the aid of a graph, the effects of a minimum wage law on a low-wage labour market.

4. Explain the purpose of each of the four steps of the collective bargaining process as described in the text.

5. Describe the results of the collective bargaining process in terms of how frequently work stoppages occur and their cost to the economy in working time lost.

6. Explain how disputes over alleged violations of a collective agreement are handled, and explain the difference between and compulsory arbitration and compulsory conciliation.

7. Describe the collective bargaining process for unionized employees in essential public services, and give two reasons why the final step in this process is not regarded as ideal.

8. State the percentage of Canada's labour force that is unionized, identify the year in which union membership as a percentage of the labour force reached its peak, and give three reasons for its decline since then.

9. Apply the concepts and facts of this chapter to various situations.

In the past few chapters, we have examined *markets for goods and services*, and how prices are determined in these markets by supply and demand, under conditions ranging from highly competitive to monopolistic. In these markets, the sellers are business firms and the buyers are mostly households, or consumers. Markets for goods and services are shown by the flows in the top half of Figure 10-1.

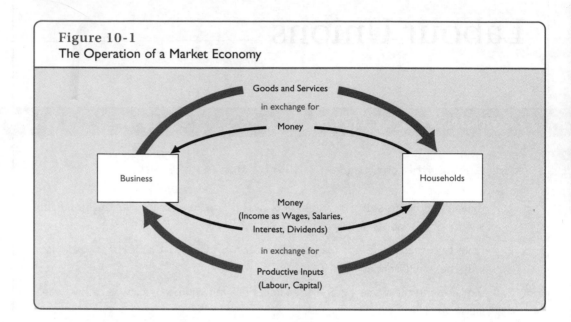

Figure 10-1
The Operation of a Market Economy

The flows in the bottom half of Figure 10-1 show *markets for labour*. In labour markets, the roles of households and businesses are reversed—the sellers are members of households (workers) seeking to sell their labour services, and the buyers are business firms who want to employ people with various skills. The items being "bought" and "sold" are the time and skills of the workers, and the "price" is the wage or salary the workers receive. In labour markets, the supply of various occupational skills interacts with employers' demand for those skills to determine the wages and salaries (or prices) of different types of labour.

In Chapter 7, we saw that markets for products could be described as *competitive* or *concentrated*. In competitive markets, sellers are not organized for the purpose of controlling supply, so prices are determined by the free interplay of supply and demand. In concentrated markets, by contrast, producers can sometimes organize themselves to restrict the supply of the product and keep its price high. These two types of product markets are shown in Table 10-1.

Table 10-1 also shows that labour markets can be characterized in the same way that product markets can. *Nonunion* labour markets are similar to *competitive* industries in that there are large numbers of sellers (workers) who are *not organized* in order to increase their market power and thus gain economically. In contrast, *unionized* groups of workers are more comparable to *concentrated* industries in which business firms are *organized* and band together to gain market power and higher incomes.

In Chapter 1, we saw that one of the three fundamental economic questions is how to divide up the economic pie among Canadians. This allocation is decided by the *incomes* of Canadians, which are mostly determined in the labour markets that we will study in Chapter 10. First, we will consider the nonunion sector of the labour market, then the unionized sector.

Table 10-1
Markets for Products and Markets for Labour

Markets for Goods and Services	Markets for Labour

(a) Competitive
    Many sellers; *not organized* to restrict competition and control supply and price. Sellers deal as *individuals*.
	(a) Nonunionized
	    Numerous workers (sellers of labour); *not organized*; deal with buyers (employers) as *individuals*.

(b) Concentrated
    A few large sellers; sometimes *organized* to restrict competition and influence price by deal *as a group*.
	(b) Unionized
	    Workers are *organized* by unions to restrict competition among themselves; deal *as a group* with employers in pursuit of higher wages, etc.

The Nonunion Sector

The nonunion sector of the labour force embraces a wide variety of people, including the self-employed, managers, most office workers, most service-industry employees (ranging from banking and finance to small-scale service firms such as restaurants and retail shops), and many part-time workers in a variety of occupations. In total, the nonunion sector accounts for about two-thirds of Canada's labour force.

The incomes of these groups, and of individuals within each group, are determined by a variety of complex factors; however, certain generalizations can be made. Broadly speaking, in the nonunion sector, the forces determining wages and salaries are the *supply of* and *demand for* various types of labour, as shown in Figure 10-2.

Tiger Woods and a gas-station attendant are both members of the nonunion sector of the labour force.

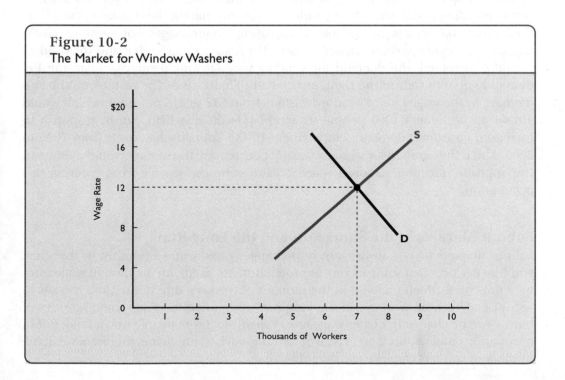

Figure 10-2
The Market for Window Washers

The supply of a particular type of labour (for instance, window washers) depends on a number of factors, such as the number of people with the required abilities and training and their willingness to work in the field. Also, as the shape of the supply curve shows, higher wages will attract more of these potential workers to actually offer their services to employers. At a wage rate of $8 per hour, 6000 people want to work as window washers, while at a wage rate of $12 per hour, 7000 people will want to work at this job. This is the same relationship that we saw in Chapter 5—higher prices (here, wages) result in a greater quantity supplied (here, labour).

derived demand
The demand for a factor of production, which is generated by (derived from) the demand for the good or service that it is used to produce.

The demand for window washers is called a **derived demand** because it is dependent on, or derived from, the demand for window washing. That is, the higher the demand for window washing is, the higher the demand for window washers will be. However, other factors, such as technological change, can also affect the demand for window washers, by altering the number of workers needed to wash a given number of windows.

Finally, as the shape of the demand curve in Figure 10-2 shows, the number of workers actually demanded (employed) by employers will depend to a significant extent on the wages of those workers—at higher wages, it will not be economical to hire as many window washers as at lower wages. Higher wages might make the price of window washing higher, reducing the "derived demand" for window washers. Also, higher wages would encourage employers of window washers to use labour-saving technology to reduce the number of employees. So a variety of factors underlie the demand and supply curves that determine the wage rate for nonunion workers. In the market for window washers depicted in Figure 10-2, the equilibrium wage rate is $12 per hour, and 7000 people will be employed.

Labour Markets

The Role of Labour Markets

Labour markets perform the important role of allocating labour to various occupations according to the demand of employers and, ultimately, the consumers who buy their products/services. In this role of allocating labour, wages—or, more precisely, *changes in wages*—play an important part. For instance, if the demand for window washing increased, the demand for window washers would increase, causing the demand curve to shift to the right, as shown in Figure 10-3. The result would be an increase in the wage rate of window washers from $12 to $16 per hour, which would attract an additional 1000 people to accept jobs in this field. So, in response to increased consumer demand, employment in this industry has risen from 7000 to 8000. And if the demand for window washing decreased, the market would operate in the opposite direction, as lower wage rates discouraged people from entering this occupation.

short run
The period of time during which the quantities of some inputs cannot be changed.

long run
The period of time after which the quantities of all inputs can be changed.

Labour Markets in the Short Run and the Long Run

Labour markets do not always adjust to changes rapidly and smoothly. In the **short run** (the period when some factors of production are fixed), an increase in wage rates may not call forth an increase in the number of workers, due to the time it takes to recruit and/or train workers. In the **long run** (the period in which the quantities of inputs *can* be changed), higher wage rates will attract more people into a field. But in occupations that require a great deal of training, such as medicine, this increase in the number of workers can take considerable time.

Figure 10-3
An Increase in the Demand for Window Washers

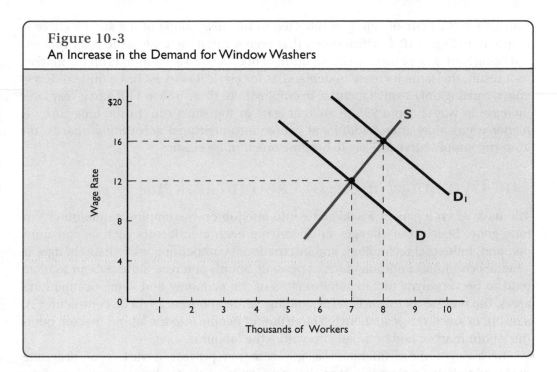

The more elastic the supply of labour is, the more smoothly a labour market will operate. Figure 10-4 illustrates this concept by comparing the response of the market for clerical workers and the market for chartered accountants to an identical increase in demand. In the case of clerical workers, homemakers provide a pool of qualified workers who are not working but available for work. This makes the supply quite *elastic*—a relatively small increase in wages and employment opportunities will attract many additional workers into the market. As a result, the increase in demand from D to D_1 causes a large increase in employment (from 100 to 130) and only a small increase in wages (from $10 to $12).

In the market for chartered accountants, the supply of labour is *inelastic*. Almost all the qualified people are already working, and due to the training period required, the number of accountants cannot be increased very much, at least not in the short

Figure 10-4
Elasticity of Labour Supply and the Operation of Labour Markets

(a) Clerical Workers

(b) Chartered Accountants

run. This inelasticity of supply is reflected in the steep slope of the supply curve in graph (b) of Figure 10-4, which shows that even a sharp increase in the wage rate will not bring forth a large increase in the number of chartered accountants on the market. As a result, the same increase in demand as for clerical workers has a quite different effect, causing only a small increase in employment (from 100 to 110) and a very large increase in wages (from $35 to $65), at least in the short run. In the long run, the higher wages may attract additional people into chartered accounting; that is, the long-run supply curve is likely to become much more elastic.

The Dynamic Nature of Labour Markets

The days when a person would settle into one job or one employer indefinitely are long gone. Because of changes in underlying economic factors such as consumer demand, industrial technology, and international competition, as well as changes in general economic conditions such as periodic booms and recessions, labour markets tend to be very dynamic. In some sectors of the economy and some occupational areas, the number of jobs will be expanding, while in others it will be contracting. As a result, in any given year, there is a large flow of people into the labour market, out of the labour market, and between jobs within the labour market.

Because of these fluctuations, governments provide a variety of programs designed to help workers adjust to changing job markets. Such programs range from the temporary income support provided by Employment Insurance to programs that retrain workers and help them to relocate in order to take new jobs.

Income Differentials

The free interaction of supply and demand in the marketplace generates a tremendous range of incomes (income differentials), from those of star athletes and entertainers to those of part-time retail workers. In competitive markets, one might wonder why such large income differentials persist over long periods of time. Chartered accountants earn far higher incomes than clerical workers. So why wouldn't more people (including clerical workers dissatisfied with their low incomes) be attracted to become accountants, thus increasing the supply of accountants and reducing the income differential between them and clerical workers?

The answer, of course, lies mainly in the fact that there are often *obstacles* to entering certain occupations. Not everyone has the abilities and skills required to become a chartered accountant, or the opportunity to pursue the education required, so the income differentials between the two groups tend to persist. Similarly, the scarcity of people with the talents to be top athletes or entertainers, or who will undertake unpleasant or dangerous jobs, causes their incomes to be very high compared to incomes for jobs that many people are able and willing to do.

Educational requirements are a major obstacle to entering certain occupations. Sometimes, educational requirements are based on specific knowledge that must be acquired in order to perform a job (such as accounting), while in other cases employers use educational requirements as a handy screening device for applicants (such as the requirement of a Bachelor of Arts degree for certain jobs).

Because of the cost of higher education, *ability to pay* is sometimes an obstacle to entering certain occupations. For instance, medical and law schools are more accessible to the children of well-off families than poor families. Because of this, many Canadians regard equality of educational opportunities as a key social policy objective, since education is the main way for the children of lower-income families to break out of the "poverty trap."

Canadians are constantly going from job to job; from job to unemployment and back; from outside the labour force to a job; and from unemployment to out of the labour force (not seeking work). In a two-year study that tracked a group of Canadians, Statistics Canada found that just 38 percent remained in the same job throughout the two years, and 48 percent averaged more than three transitions. This amounted to 7000 transitions every working hour.

Baseball player Alex Rodriguez earns over Cdn$30 million per year. A student serving fast food earns less than $7 per hour.

Obstacles to entering occupations are not the only reason for differences in incomes. Age and experience have a large influence on people's incomes, as most people's incomes are low in their early years of work and peak after age 50. Another factor is *market power*. We saw in Chapter 7 how business firms can obtain market power by acting together; in the second half of this chapter, we will see how some groups of workers do the same thing, by joining together into labour unions.

To summarize, differences in incomes are generated by various factors, including
• abilities and skills,
• educational requirements,
• age and experience, and
• market power.

Minimum Wage Legislation

The fact that, in an open labour market, some groups earn very low wages has led governments to enact minimum wage laws that set legal minimums for the wage rates that employers can pay their employees. In Figure 10-5, the equilibrium or market wage rate is $4 per hour, but the government has set the legal **minimum wage** rate at $6 per hour.

minimum wage
A legal minimum wage rate set by law.

The objective of minimum wage legislation is to increase the incomes of low-wage earners. However, as Figure 10-5 shows, minimum wage legislation also has the side effect of *increasing unemployment*. At the equilibrium wage rate of $4 per hour, 90 000 workers are employed, whereas at a legal minimum wage rate of $6 per hour, only 80 000 jobs exist (point A). There are fewer jobs because the higher wage rate reduces the number of workers that employers can and will employ. Furthermore, the higher wage rate attracts an additional 10 000 workers into the labour force who are looking for work, bringing the total number of people wanting to work to 100 000 (point B), and total unemployment of these workers to 20 000 (the distance AB).

While there is little doubt that minimum wage laws do reduce the number of jobs, there is also considerable debate as to *how much* they increase unemployment.

Figure 10-5
The Effects of a Minimum Wage

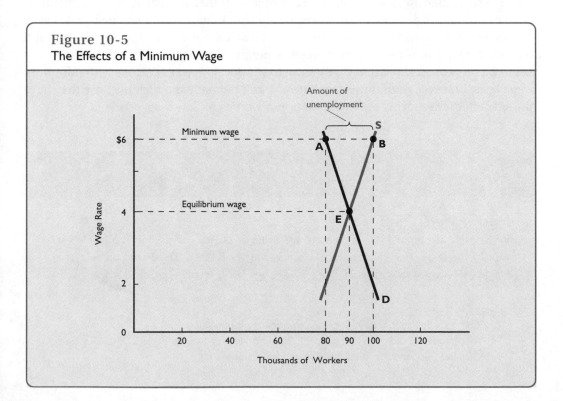

Generally, employers opposing increases in the minimum wage stress how minimum wage rates kill jobs, while labour unions and other groups that support minimum wages argue that the negative effects on employment are minimal. Supporters of higher minimum wage rates argue that past increases in the minimum wage rate have not been followed by layoffs of employees. However, the effect of higher minimum wages may be more subtle than this, as the *disemployment effect* may arise more from reduced hiring of new workers than from layoffs of existing ones. Then, as workers who left were not all replaced with newly hired workers, the total number of jobs would be reduced. According to labour economists, minimum wage laws create a sort of lottery, in which the winners are the workers who remain in (or get) jobs at the higher wage rates required by the law, while the losers are those who do not get jobs because of the minimum wage. In particular, researchers believe that minimum wages limit employment opportunities for women, many of whom work in service industries such as restaurants, and for younger workers, who are just entering the labour force and often must compete with more experienced workers for jobs.

While the extent of this disemployment effect is uncertain, the basic reality is that in order to lift low-wage earners out of poverty, the legal minimum wage rate would have to be increased substantially from the current levels. And most observers agree that such large increases in the minimum wage rate would have serious effects on the job opportunities of the very people the minimum wage was intended to help. So increasing the minimum wage rate would not in itself be an effective way to combat poverty. In Chapters 11 and 12, we will consider the problem of poverty and other ways of assisting the poor.

To summarize, in the nonunion sector of the labour force, employees' wages and benefits are largely determined by **individual bargaining** between employees and employers. Each worker is free to seek the best deal he or she can get from an employer, and employers are free (subject to legislated rules such as minimum wage laws and employment standards legislation) to seek the best deal they can obtain from workers. The forces that determine how this bargaining process works out for the participants are the supply of and demand for various productive skills. If the demand for a particular type of skill is high and the supply is low, people with that skill will have the bargaining power to obtain high incomes. In the opposite situation, incomes will be low, because supply exceeds demand. Because there are great differences in the supply/demand balance for various skills, labour markets generate some extremely high incomes and some very low ones. Governments attempt to support low-wage earners with minimum wage laws; however, minimum wage rates cannot be made too high because they have the side effect of reducing employment opportunities for low-wage workers.

In 2003, 4 percent of the work force (547 000 people) worked at or below the minimum wage rate. Most were female, young, students or part-timers working in the accommodation, food service, or retail trade industries.

individual bargaining
The process through which workers deal as individuals with employers in negotiating their terms and conditions of employment.

IN THE NEWS

Hockey Players' Salaries

In the NHL season of 1966–67, the average salary of players for the Toronto Maple Leafs was 2.7 times the average income of Canadian families. By the 2003–04 season, an average Maple Leaf player's salary was *30 times* the average family income of Canadians.

QUESTIONS
1. What explains such a large increase in hockey players' incomes?
2. What problems did such increases in National Hockey League players' incomes cause?
3. What has happened to NHL players' incomes since 2004?

The Unionized Sector

In the unionized sector of the labour force, the situation is quite different. Individual bargaining is replaced by **collective bargaining**, in which a labour union negotiates with the employer on behalf of *all* the employees represented by the union. The bargaining relationship is thereby considerably altered. The last resort of an individual bargaining on his or her own behalf is to resign (and perhaps be easily replaced, depending on his or her skills), but a union can call a *strike* of *all* the employees it represents. As a result, unionized employees are generally in a stronger position in negotiating with their employers.

collective bargaining The process through which employers and unions negotiate a new collective agreement.

Unions in Canada

As Figure 10-6 shows, the number of union members in Canada has grown substantially since 1950. However, when union membership is expressed as a percentage of the labour force, a more complex picture emerges, as shown in Figure 10-7 on page 218. As unionization spread rapidly in Canadian industry in the 1940s and into the 1950s, union membership grew much more rapidly than the labour force, causing union membership as a percentage of the labour force to increase very rapidly, from about 5 percent to nearly 25 percent. From the mid-1960s until the second half of the 1970s, union membership as a percentage of the labour force continued to grow, although less rapidly, with most growth due to the spread of unionism among government employees.

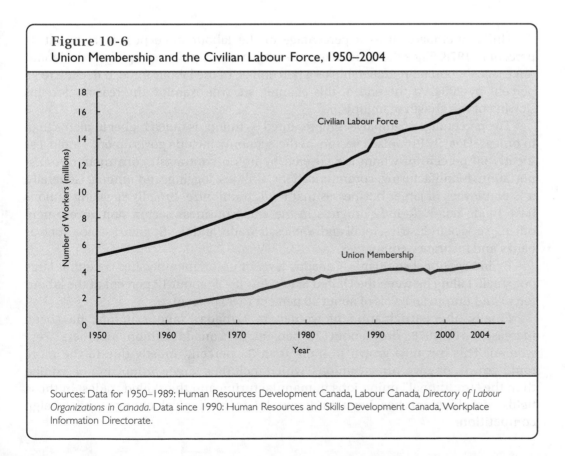

Figure 10-6
Union Membership and the Civilian Labour Force, 1950–2004

Sources: Data for 1950–1989: Human Resources Development Canada, Labour Canada, *Directory of Labour Organizations in Canada*. Data since 1990: Human Resources and Skills Development Canada, Workplace Information Directorate.

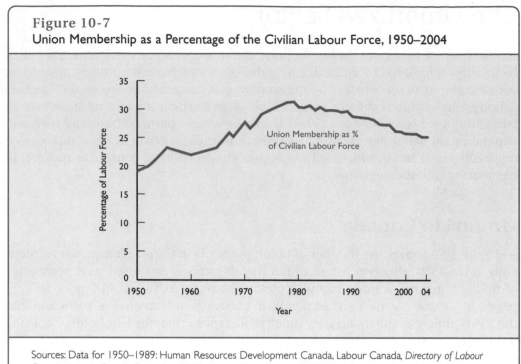

Figure 10-7
Union Membership as a Percentage of the Civilian Labour Force, 1950–2004

Sources: Data for 1950–1989: Human Resources Development Canada, Labour Canada, *Directory of Labour Organizations in Canada*. Data since 1990: Human Resources and Skills Development Canada, Workplace Information Directorate, www.hrsdc.gc.ca/en/lp/wid/union_membership.shtml.

Like corporations, unions are quite concentrated—in 2004, the largest ten unions had 49 percent of total union membership in Canada.

The largest union in Canada is the Canadian Union of Public Employees (CUPE), with 535 000 members in 2004.

www.cupe.ca

Union membership as a percentage of the labour force peaked at about 31 percent in 1978. Since then, union membership has not grown as rapidly as the labour force, causing union membership as a percentage of the labour force to decline to 25 percent by 2004. At the end of this chapter, we will examine the reasons for this slowing of the growth of unionism.

The percentage of employees represented by unions is much higher in plants than in offices. Heavily unionized sectors of the economy include government employees (nearly 90 percent of whom are covered by union contracts), construction, transportation, manufacturing, communications, utilities, logging, and mining. Generally, it is employees of larger businesses that tend to unionize. Broadly speaking, unions have made relatively little progress in the small business sector, non-government offices, service industries, retail and wholesale trade, and the financial sector, such as banks and insurance companies.

By international standards, Canada's level of union membership is neither large nor small, falling between the United States' low level (about 12 percent of the labour force) and European levels of about 40 percent to 80 percent.

Finally, the participation of women in Canada's labour unions has been increasing. In 1978, only about 28 percent of Canada's union members were women. This has now grown to more than 35 percent, mostly due to the more rapid growth of government unions, which include a larger proportion of women than the "traditional" union jobs in manufacturing and the skilled trades. In those fields, employment has been undercut by technological change and foreign competition.

Some Questions and Answers

How Do Workers Become Unionized?

A basic principle of Canadian labour law is that most workers have the right to decide democratically whether to form or join a labour union. This process often takes the form of a vote of the employees (known as a *certification vote*) that is conducted by the Labour Relations Board, a government agency that oversees industrial relations. If a majority of workers votes in favour of being represented by a particular union, that union becomes "certified" as the exclusive representative of those employees, meaning that management must deal with the employees *through the union*, rather than deal with them as individuals. (Conversely, if a group of workers no longer wishes to be represented by a particular union, they can vote to decertify it.)

About one-third of Canada's labour force is *represented* by unions. Some workers are *represented* by a union, but have not *joined* that union.

Once it has been certified, a union must by law represent all of the employees in the group for which the union is certified (the "bargaining unit"). And, since all employees in the bargaining unit receive the economic and other benefits of union representation, the general rule is that they all must pay union dues, whether they have formally joined the union or not.

How Are Collective Agreements Negotiated?

A key service provided to members by their union is the negotiation of their **collective agreement**, or labour contract. The collective agreement sets out all of the terms and conditions of employment for its duration—from wage rates and hours of work to fringe benefits and pensions. The process through which employers and unions negotiate a new collective agreement is called *collective bargaining*. The bargaining process has been compared to buying a used car—both sides open negotiations by demanding more than they are prepared to settle for, as they attempt to get the best possible deal. Then, gradually, as they both become more concerned about the possibility of a strike, the positions of the union and management teams become more reasonable and compatible. Many contract negotiations are settled at this stage. However, it is quite common for the parties to require assistance from a neutral third party before reaching an agreement.

collective agreement
A contract agreed upon by an employer and labour union, specifying the terms and conditions of employment of the employees for a specified period of time.

This assistance generally takes the form of **compulsory conciliation**, through which a government-appointed conciliator enters the negotiations. The conciliator is a neutral person who has no authority to impose a settlement on the parties; rather, the conciliator's role is to *assist them to negotiate their own agreement*. Employers and unions must go through compulsory conciliation before a work stoppage (strike by the union or lockout by the employer) can occur.

Should conciliation prove unsuccessful, there is usually a further delay (a "cooling-off period," usually of two weeks' duration) before a strike or lockout can take place. This period gives both sides an opportunity to reconsider their positions, under increasing pressure from the fact that they are facing a strike deadline that is growing closer each day. If the parties fail to reach a settlement under pressure of this strike deadline, a work stoppage can occur that will impose losses on *both* sides until an agreement is reached. In a work stoppage, the employees will lose wages, and the employer will lose sales and profits. The result is a test of the economic power of the two sides, with the side that has the greatest ability to withstand the economic pressures of the work stoppage more likely to prevail. The collective bargaining process is shown in Table 10-2 on the next page.

compulsory conciliation
A procedure, required by law before a strike is legal, in which a government-appointed officer (conciliator) attempts to help a union and employer to reach an agreement on the terms of a new collective agreement.

Table 10-2
The Collective Bargaining Process

Stage I	Stage II	Stage III	Stage IV
Union and management negotiate on their own.	Negotiations continue with the assistance of a third party.	Waiting period before a strike or lockout is legal.	Work stoppage, with economic pressure on both sides.
Negotiations Management and union negotiate from opening positions toward compromises and an agreement.	***Compulsory Conciliation*** A government-appointed neutral third party (conciliator or mediator) tries to help the parties reach a negotiated agreement. No authority to impose a settlement (not an arbitrator).	***Cooling-Off Period*** Usually two weeks: time for both parties to reconsider, under the pressure of a strike/ lockout deadline that is now (a) known and (b) close, and the knowledge that they alone can avert a work stoppage (conciliator is gone).	***Work Stoppage (Strike or Lockout)*** Economic losses suffered by both sides pressure them to compromise and settle.

Generally, somewhat less than half of contract negotiations are settled before conciliation, about the same number are settled through conciliation, and five percent or less of negotiations end in a work stoppage (usually a strike by the union, but sometimes a lockout by the employer). At whatever stage a settlement is reached, however, it must finally be approved by the membership of the union, through a *ratification vote*.

Why Permit Strikes?

Many people see strikes as a primitive way of settling labour disputes through a form of "trial by combat," and feel that the government should not permit strikes (or lockouts). They would prefer a way of settling labour disputes that is more civilized, reasonable, and fair.

However, it is important to appreciate that a basic premise of labour legislation is that industrial relations disputes are best worked out *by those directly involved*—the employer, through management, and the employees, through their union. As a result, the law does not provide for the government to intervene and impose a decision or a contract on employers and unions. Rather, the law establishes a framework within which unions and employers are expected to *negotiate their own solutions* to their problems, even if that involves a work stoppage.

The law also recognizes that work stoppages can be economically harmful not only to the employees and employer involved, but also to third parties such as customers and suppliers, and to the economy. That is why the law requires that the parties go through conciliation before a work stoppage occurs, in order to bring into the negotiations a knowledgeable and neutral third party whose expertise might help the parties to reach a settlement without a work stoppage. However, should the conciliator fail, the law leaves the parties on their own to settle—or face the consequences of failing to do so, which may include a strike or lockout.

It is also important to recognize that the threat of a work stoppage plays a very important *positive role* in the collective bargaining process. In a typical year, about 95 percent of all contract negotiations end in agreement without a work stoppage, mainly because *both* parties fear the consequences of a stoppage. So the right to strike or lock out (or, more precisely, the *threat* of a work stoppage) serves the important purpose of forcing *both* the employer *and* the union to negotiate seriously, with the usual result being an agreement *without* a work stoppage.

When Are Strikes Not Legal?

This can be a confusing matter, because there are two very different types of disputes that arise between unions and employers. In the one type of dispute, it is quite legal for a strike or lockout to occur, but in the other, it is not (see Table 10-3).

Table 10-3
Two Types of Industrial Relations Disputes

The collective agreement, or labour contract, between an employer and its union sets the terms and conditions of employment for its duration—i.e., constitutes "industrial law" for the parties.

There are two distinctly different types of disputes between employers and unions over the collective agreement:

1. Over Negotiation of the Terms of a New Collective Agreement	2. Over an Alleged Violation of an Existing Collective Agreement
e.g., union wants a 5% wage raise; management offers 1%	e.g., in firing Viv, did management violate the agreement?
➡ Union and Employer NEGOTIATE	➡ GRIEVANCE (= Appeal of Management's Decision)
If they cannot agree on terms of the new contract, A STRIKE OR LOCKOUT CAN LEGALLY OCCUR.	If they cannot agree on how to resolve the matter, A DECISION IS MADE BY AN ARBITRATOR (NEUTRAL THIRD PARTY).

The first type of dispute is the one covered in the previous section—the negotiation of a collective agreement. In such negotiations, it is generally legal to use a strike or lockout (as a last resort), although not until the previous collective agreement has expired and after the negotiations have passed through compulsory conciliation and a "cooling-off period," as required by law. The only exception is essential public services such as police and firefighters, in which work stoppages are generally not allowed by law. These are covered later in this chapter.

There is, however, a second and quite different type of union–management dispute. These are disputes not over the terms of a new contract that is *being negotiated* but rather over *alleged violations of an existing contract*. For instance, suppose that management fires a worker in a way that the worker and the union consider to be a violation of the collective agreement. How should they pursue this matter?

The law does not allow strikes (or lockouts) over such disputes. Instead, the worker must file a **grievance**, which is an appeal of management's decision on the grounds that

grievance
An alleged violation of a collective agreement by an employer.

arbitration

The resolution of union–management disputes by the decision of a third party; required by law for grievances that the union and employer cannot resolve by themselves; used to settle disputes over the terms of new collective agreements in cases where strikes of essential employees are prohibited.

it violates the collective agreement. This will lead to a series of discussions between management and the union to resolve the matter, starting at the lower levels of each organization and moving to higher levels if necessary. If these discussions fail to settle the grievance, the law requires that the dispute be taken to **arbitration**. Arbitration is a court-like process in which a neutral third party (an arbitrator) hears the evidence of both sides and decides whether the collective agreement has been violated. In the example in the previous paragraph of the grievance concerning the firing of the worker, the arbitrator might decide to uphold management's decision, or to reinstate the worker in his or her job with retroactive pay for the time missed from work during the grievance. The arbitrator's decision is binding on both the union and management, who cannot resort to a strike or lockout if they disagree with it.

Aren't Strikes Costly?

It is true that work stoppages can be costly to those directly involved—the employer loses profits and the employees lose wages. However, the effects of strikes on the nation's economy are greatly exaggerated by the general public. The working time lost due to work stoppages is an extremely small fraction of total time worked in the economy—during the 1980s, an average of less than 12 days per 10 000 days worked, or less than one-eighth of 1 percent of total time worked, as Figure 10-8 shows. In the 1990s, this figure fell to less than one-tenth of 1 percent.

This is a fraction of the working time that would be lost if all working Canadians were given one additional holiday per year. So, while industrial disputes do impose economic costs on some Canadians, it cannot be argued that strikes *in general* are ruining the nation's economy.

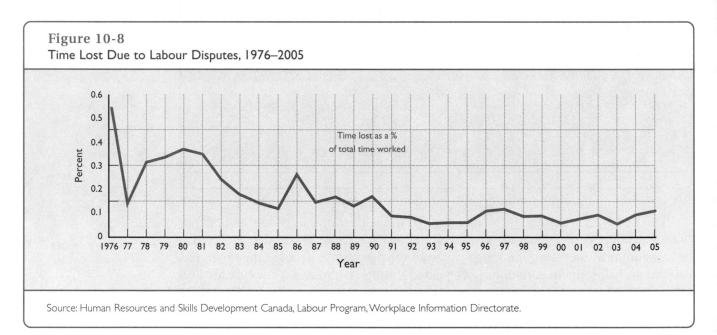

Figure 10-8
Time Lost Due to Labour Disputes, 1976–2005

Source: Human Resources and Skills Development Canada, Labour Program, Workplace Information Directorate.

But What About Public Service Strikes?

While the percentage of total time worked in the economy that is lost due to work stoppages is small, the *impact* of work stoppages on the Canadian public is probably greater than these statistics would suggest, because compared to other countries, a higher proportion of Canada's work stoppages involve *government employees* and thus the interruption of *public services*.

Government employees in Canada enjoy considerably greater rights to unionize and to strike than do their counterparts in most other countries. Since the mid-1960s, it has been a general principle of Canadian labour law that government employees should have similar rights to unionize, bargain collectively, and strike as do employees in the private sector. As a result, governments for the most part have tended to withdraw the right to strike only from employees in *essential* public services, such as police, firefighters, and some hospital workers. As a result, Canada experiences more frequent work stoppages in public services than most other nations do.

In the case of a strike by, for instance, 1500 workers at a soft-drink company, the public can continue to consume the product until inventories run out, and then can switch to other brands of soft drinks until the strike is over. However, a strike by 1500 public transit workers or garbage collectors or teachers will prove much more disruptive, because there is no alternative supplier. Work stoppages in some public services (such as postal service, education, public transit, garbage collection, and health care) have represented a difficult problem in Canadian industrial relations, because they can have a considerable impact on the public and sometimes the economy.

Some say that the solution to this problem is simply to outlaw strikes by government employees. But the matter is not nearly as simple as this. It is not sufficient merely to remove the right of employees to strike—some alternative method must be used to settle their collective bargaining disputes promptly and fairly. Usually, when the right to strike is withheld from a group of employees, the law provides for negotiations and conciliation to take place as described earlier, but requires that if the dispute is not settled through these processes, it must be submitted to *compulsory arbitration*. In arbitration, a neutral third party considers arguments from both management and the union as to what the terms of the collective agreement (wages, benefits, etc.) should be, and then makes a final decision that is binding on both sides. The union cannot strike, nor can the employer lock out the employees.

While the general public tends to see arbitration as a simple solution to the problem, those actually involved in the process are much less satisfied with it. Compulsory arbitration requires that vital decisions be made by an outsider who lacks familiarity with the problems of the employees and management, many of which are often very complex. Another problem is the long delays in the negotiation/arbitration process—it is not uncommon for settlements (and employees' wage increases) to be held up for a year or more after the previous collective agreement has expired. Without the threat of a work stoppage, neither side (particularly the employer) may feel much pressure to negotiate quickly. Also, the arbitration process itself usually lasts several months, during which both sides make extensive submissions, both in writing and at hearings, backed up by large volumes of statistical data and arguments.

Management is not always pleased with arbitration either, because it takes very important matters away from management's control. Major decisions are placed in the hands of an outsider whose decisions cannot be appealed but which may impair management's ability to deliver effectively and efficiently the public service for which the organization is responsible. So arbitration is far from the ideal and simple solution to labour disputes that it may appear to be. For another perspective on the arbitration process, see the "You Decide" box on the next page.

YOU DECIDE

Let's Play Arbitrator

If you think compulsory arbitration of labour contract disputes is a simple matter, take the following opportunity to see the kinds of challenges involved.

A married couple whom you know only slightly are having severe marital problems and disputes, largely because their marriage is not living up to the expectations that each held for it. They agree that it would have been better if, before they were married, they had written up a marriage contract specifying the rights and responsibilities of each partner. However, given the present state of deterioration of their relationship, they are unable to agree on the terms of such a contract. They have asked you, as an impartial third party, to resolve the matter for them in the following way: you will listen to the views and arguments of each of the parties, their proposals for the terms to be included in the contract, and the exact wording of each clause; then you will, on your own, *write for them a complete, detailed marriage contract* that will provide a workable basis for a renewed marriage.

Good luck! ■

QUESTIONS

1. What is your major strength as the arbitrator of these people's differences?
2. What is your major weakness as the arbitrator?
3. After listening to the positions of each of the parties, will you have a clear picture of the facts of the situation?
4. If one of the parties disagrees with your decision or part of it, how committed will that person be to trying to make your decision work?

Unionism at the Crossroads

Some observers believe that Canadian unionism is at an historic crossroads, in the sense that powerful economic forces are forcing fundamental changes upon it. In particular, unions face major challenges regarding the recruitment of members and their relationships with their employers.

Recruitment of new members has been a concern of unions since the late 1970s, when union membership, as a percentage of the labour force, peaked at 31 percent. From the 1940s well into the 1960s, the heart of Canadian unionism had been *blue-collar* workers in the manufacturing sector of the economy—workers in industries such as automobiles and steel. However, since the 1960s, the numbers of such workers—and of union members in these industries—have been undercut by a combination of technological change and international competition. These changes were very threatening to many unions. In the United States, similar trends reduced union membership in the private sector from 30 percent of employees to only 12 percent. In Canada, union membership in the private sector stagnated as it had in the United States; however, unlike the United States, unionism spread among government employees in Canada after the mid-1960s. But in the 1990s, union membership in the government sector stagnated as well, as budget problems undercut government employment. So, in the two most unionized sectors of the economy—manufacturing and government—employment growth was slow.

Where, then, were the new jobs? Since the mid-1970s, most of the newly created jobs in the Canadian economy have been in the rapidly expanding *service sector*, in industries such as retail trade, restaurants, catering, hotels, entertainment, finance, travel and tourism, recreation, day care, lawn care, home repairs, and the like. This trend poses a challenge to union recruiters for various reasons. Many service-industry employers are small businesses with only a few employees, in which owner–managers and employees often work closely together without the "us-versus-them" relationship that makes unionization easier. In addition, many employees in the service industries do not have a long-term attachment to their jobs because they are part-time and because such jobs often have a high turnover rate. As a result of factors such as these, the service sector of the economy has tended to be only lightly unionized, and quite resistant to attempts to unionize it.

Unions' relationships with employers have also been challenged by economic forces. In the past, Canadian unions in both the private and public sectors have won considerable gains for their members through the adversarial approach of hard bargaining and a willingness to resort to the strike weapon—confrontation was their style and it seemed to be effective. However, as we saw in Chapter 9, the economic environment has changed. There were growing concerns about the ability of many Canadian producers to compete internationally, as well as about the financial position of Canadian governments. In short, it was no longer as easy as it once had been for many private employers to raise prices or for governments to raise taxes in order to make peace with their unions.

During the 1990s, it became apparent that neither unions nor employers could expect past trends to continue, as both private and public employers faced strong new pressures to increase efficiency and keep costs down. These problems raised fundamentally serious questions for many unions. Similarly serious questions were also raised for management in many enterprises. Faced with strong economic pressures to increase productivity and quality, some management teams were forced to reconsider whether they could expect to achieve these goals with a traditional authoritarian management style that fostered conflict with their employees rather than the cooperation they now needed.

Had the adversarial system in which Canadian unionism was so deeply and firmly rooted become outdated and counterproductive? Would their members' interests be better served by cooperative efforts between unions and management to improve productivity and competitiveness rather than on confrontation and strikes? And, if this were the case, how could unions adjust to such a new role? Could they act more like a partner with management with respect to productivity, but as its adversary in contract negotiations and grievances?

The 1990s saw some new trends in Canadian industrial relations, such as a significant decrease in work stoppages (see Figure 10-8 on page 222) and various examples of union–management cooperation with respect to the training of workers and improvements to productivity and product quality. Some believed that the Canadian industrial relations system was evolving, as the difficult economic times of the 1990s pushed both unions and employers toward a more mature, even cooperative relationship. Others were more skeptical, and thought that unions and management would likely return to their old ways of confrontation if the pressures of the 1990s were to ease.

Chapter Summary

1. In the nonunion sector of the labour force, wages are determined by the supply of and demand for various skills. (L.O. 1)
2. Supply and demand in labour markets generate a very wide range of incomes; this is in large part due to obstacles to entering certain occupations. (L.O. 2)
3. Minimum wage laws can increase the wages of low-income groups; however, they also have the effect of increasing unemployment among those groups. (L.O. 3).
4. The terms and conditions of employment for unionized employees are negotiated by their union and employer through a collective bargaining process that generally includes requirements for conciliation and a cooling-off period before a work stoppage can take place as the final step in the process. (L.O. 4)
5. Typically, in about 95 percent of cases, collective bargaining results in an agreement without a work stoppage, and the working time lost due to work stoppages in most years is a very small percentage of total time worked in the economy. (L.O. 5)
6. For disputes over alleged violations of an existing collective agreement, the grievance procedure is used; the final step in this process is a binding decision by an arbitrator. (L.O. 6)
7. For employees in essential public services, strikes are generally not legal; instead, the final step in the collective bargaining process is compulsory arbitration. (L.O. 7)
8. Union membership as a percentage of the labour force reached its peak in the late 1970s, and has declined slightly since then, largely because employment growth has been in the service sector rather than in the more heavily unionized manufacturing and government sectors. (L.O. 8)

Questions

1. In the *nonunion sector* of the labour force, wages and salaries are basically determined by
   (a) the employer, who is free to decide the wages that will be paid.
   (b) the government, which decides what is a fair wage in each case.
   (c) the supply of, and demand for, each particular job skill.
   (d) the minimum-wage laws, as all nonunion employees would be paid less if these laws did not exist.
   (e) the economic and social contribution made by these individuals and groups.
   Explain why each answer that you did *not* select is wrong.

2. The following table shows the market for part-time student labour in Canville.

Wage Rate per Hour	Number of Workers Demanded (Jobs)	Number of Workers Supplied (Job-seekers)
11	800	1200
10	900	1100
9	1000	1000
8	1200	900

   (a) In a free market, what will the wage rate be?
   (b) If the government imposed a minimum-wage rate of $10 per hour, what would happen in this market?
   (c) Explain the reasons for the developments in part (b), with reference to changes on both the supply side and the demand side of this market.

3. Minimum-wage laws that require employers to pay wages above the market equilibrium wage rate tend to
(a) benefit *all workers*, both skilled and unskilled.
(b) benefit *all* unskilled/low-wage workers.
(c) benefit *some* unskilled/low-wage workers.
(d) increase unemployment among unskilled/low-wage workers.
(e) have both of the effects described in (c) and (d).
Explain your answer, using the table in question 2 to illustrate.

4. Suppose that the demand for dentists and house painters simultaneously increased by 25 percent over a short period of time. Which occupation would enjoy the greater increase in incomes over the next few years? Explain why this would be the case, referring in your explanation to the term *elasticity*.

5. Since the late 1970s, union membership as a percentage of the labour force has
(a) increased rapidly.
(b) increased slowly.
(c) remained stable.
(d) decreased slowly.
(e) decreased very rapidly.
Give three reasons for this trend.

6. "Strikes are an outdated 'trial by combat' approach to union–management disputes and cost the Canadian economy heavily in terms of lost work. Strikes serve no useful purpose in Canada's industrial relations system, and it would be better for all Canadians if the government simply outlawed strikes and required that all unresolved collective bargaining disputes be decided by arbitration."
Explain why you agree or disagree with this statement.

7. Both conciliators (also known as mediators) and arbitrators sometimes play a role in securing a settlement in collective bargaining between unions and employers.
(a) What is the greatest strength that helps a conciliator in playing his or her role?
(b) What is the greatest weakness that limits a conciliator in playing his or her role?
(c) What is the greatest strength that helps an arbitrator in playing his or her role?
(d) What is the greatest weakness that limits an arbitrator in playing his or her role?

8. Sometimes an approach called *med-arb* (short for *mediation-arbitration*) is used in collective bargaining in situations where a work stoppage cannot take place. In this approach, the bargaining process is the same as described in the text, except that the conciliator (mediator) and the arbitrator *are the same person*. How could this arrangement make that person more effective in both the role of the mediator/conciliator and the role of arbitrator?

9. Visit Statistics Canada's website and find StatsCan's most recent study on minimum-wage workers. A study released on March 26, 2004, is at **www.statcan.ca/Daily0/English/040326/d040326c.htm**; if there is a more recent one you could search for it at **www.statcan.ca** by clicking on *The Daily* and searching for "minimum wage."
(a) How many minimum-wage workers are there in Canada?
(b) Who are they?
(c) In which industries and in what sorts of jobs do they work?
(d) Which provinces have the highest and lowest minimum wage rates?

Study Guide

Review Questions (Answers to these Review Questions appear in Appendix B.)

Answer questions 1–4 on the basis of the following graph portraying the market for window washers.

1. If the demand for window washers is represented by the curve **D**, the hourly wage rate for window washers will be $ _____ and employment will be _____ workers.

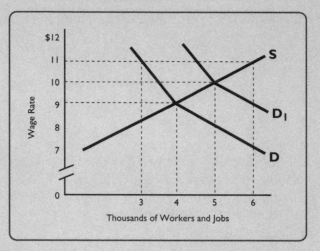

2. If the demand for window washers were to increase as shown by the curve **D₁**, the hourly wage rate would become $ _____. These changes would attract an additional _____ workers into the industry, bringing total employment to _____ workers.

3. If the government were to set a minimum wage of $11 per hour for workers such as window washers, and the demand for window washers was represented by curve **D**, the result would be that
   (a) employment would increase to 6000.
   (b) unemployment would increase to 1000.
   (c) unemployment would increase to 2000.
   (d) unemployment would increase to 3000.
   (e) None of the above.

4. The situation described in the previous question will develop for the following two reasons:
   (a) _____, and
   (b) _____.

5. Most people would agree that medical care is far more important than baseball, but baseball players are paid far more than nurses. Why is this so?
   (a) Baseball players are really entertainers rather than producers of a service.
   (b) Compared to the demand for them, good baseball players are more scarce than nurses.
   (c) Baseball players are more skilled than persons who get less pay.
   (d) The demand for baseball players is greater than for nurses.
   (e) There are fewer professional baseball players than nurses.

6. Large differences in incomes such as those in the previous question tend to persist over long periods of time, largely because
   (a) some occupations make a greater contribution to society than others.
   (b) in some occupations, the demand for labour is persistently large relative to the supply.
   (c) in some occupations, the supply of labour is persistently large relative to the demand.
   (d) there are obstacles to entering some occupations.
   (e) Answers (b), (c) and (d) are all correct.

7. By 2004, union membership amounted to approximately
   (a) 12 percent of the civilian labour force.
   (b) 18 percent of the civilian labour force.
   (c) 25 percent of the civilian labour force.
   (d) 33 percent of the civilian labour force.
   (e) 48 percent of the civilian labour force.

8. State whether each of the following types of employment is characterized by a relatively high degree of unionization (*yes* or *no*).
   (a) _____ government employment
   (b) _____ manufacturing
   (c) _____ service industries
   (d) _____ construction trades
   (e) _____ office employment

9. If an employer violates the terms of its contract (collective agreement) with its union (for instance, in the disciplining of employees), the union is legally empowered to
   (a) *sue* the employer in court for breach of contract.
   (b) file a *grievance* against the employer.
   (c) call a *strike* against the employer.
   (d) All of the above.
   (e) None of the above.

10. The final step in the process in question 9 is that
    (a) a neutral third party (an arbitrator) will make a judgment that is binding on both the employer and the union.
    (b) a court may award damages (financial compensation) to the employees.
    (c) fear of the strike or the economic losses arising from the strike will force both the union and the employer to a compromise and settle the matter.
    (d) Both (b) and (c), depending on the course of action chosen by the union.
    (e) Any of the above, depending on the course of action chosen by the union.

11. When an employer and a union are negotiating a new collective agreement, there are four stages to the negotiation process. The first step is that the union and the employer negotiate on their own. What are the other three steps that would follow, if required?
    (1) negotiations on their own, then
    (2) _____, then
    (3) _____, then
    (4) _____.

12. *Compulsory conciliation* refers to
    (a) a procedure in which, by law, government-appointed official(s) must attempt to help employers and unions avoid a work stoppage by reaching a negotiated agreement before a stoppage occurs.

(b) the legal requirement that all unresolved grievances of workers (i.e., alleged violations of the collective agreement by the employer) be submitted to a referee for a final decision, to prevent work stoppages over them.

(c) a legal requirement that a government official from the Ministry of Labour must make final decisions on all disputes between unions and employers.

(d) a procedure in which a government-appointed official makes a binding decision concerning a contract dispute involving a group of essential workers who cannot legally strike.

(e) None of the above.

13. A strike or lockout is generally legal
   (a) any time there is a dispute between a union and an employer.
   (b) only after the contract has expired, the conciliation process has concluded, and the cooling-off period required by the law has passed.
   (c) as soon as the conciliation process has concluded.
   (d) as soon as the existing contract (collective agreement) between the union and the employer has expired.
   (e) None of the above.

14. State whether each of the following statements regarding strikes is *true* or *false*.
   (a) _____ They are totally negative in character; they serve no useful purpose in our industrial relations system.
   (b) _____ They play an important role in our industrial relations system because the fear of a strike forces both the employer and the union to compromise in contract negotiations.
   (c) _____ Most employers would prefer a system in which strikes are outlawed and unresolved contract disputes are submitted to an arbitrator for a final decision.
   (d) _____ They are very costly to society in terms of lost working time and lost output.

15. The proportion of union–management contract negotiations that is settled by negotiation and without a work stoppage (strike or lockout) is generally
   (a) over 90 percent.
   (b) about 75 percent.
   (c) about 60 percent.
   (d) about 50 percent.
   (e) about 35 percent.

16. Which statement best describes the general attitude of unions and management to a legal ban on all strikes?
   (a) Both favour outlawing strikes because this would eliminate costly strikes.
   (b) Unions generally favour such a move, but employers are reluctant to accept it.
   (c) Neither favours such a move because it would require both of them to turn over to an arbitrator the right to decide issues of vital importance to them.
   (d) Employers generally favour such a move, but unions are opposed to it.
   (e) None of the above.

17. Which of the following best describes the usual way of resolving contract disputes in public services that are considered to be essential?
   (a) Contract negotiations take place as usual, including conciliation, and if no agreement is reached, a strike takes place.
   (b) Contract negotiations take place as usual, including conciliation, but if no agreement is reached the dispute is referred to an arbitrator for a final decision—a strike is not legal.

(c) Essential-service employees are not allowed to form or join labour unions or to strike; decisions regarding wages and conditions of employment are made solely by management.

(d) Strikes are not legal and no contract negotiations take place—wages and terms of employment are decided by Parliament.

(e) Contract negotiations take place as usual, except that if no agreement is reached, the dispute is referred to the government for a decision—strikes are not legal.

Critical Thinking Questions

(Asterisked questions 1 to 5 are answered in Appendix B; the answers to questions 6 to 10 are in the Instructor's Manual that accompanies this text.)

*1. Suppose that hairdressers employed by salons organized into a union in an attempt to increase their incomes. What obstacles would their effort encounter with respect to
 (a) the demand side of the market for their labour?
 (b) the supply side of the market for their labour?

*2. Visualize the sorts of developments that would probably occur within both the union and the management negotiating teams as the "cooling-off period" in the collective bargaining progresses toward its conclusion. Would these make a settlement more or less likely?

*3. Figure 10-7 on page 218 shows a gradual decline in union membership as a percentage of the labour force since the late 1970s. What would Canada's labour unions have to do in order to reverse this trend? What obstacles would unions have to overcome, and what factors might help them to recruit members?

*4. According to international statistics, Canada has one of the worst records in the world for worker-days lost due to labour disputes. Should Canadians be concerned about these statistics? Why or why not?

*5. Look at Figure 10-8 on page 222. Why do you think the time lost due to work stoppages after 1990 decreased as it did?

6. "Only a society with no sense of values would pay an uneducated goon of a hockey player fifty times the income of a police officer or a firefighter." Discuss this statement from the perspectives of *why* such income differentials exist, and whether you agree with the statement.

7. A *lockout* is a work stoppage that is initiated by the employer rather than by its union. Why would an employer lock out its employees rather than let them continue working until they decided to strike?

8. "If employers had profit-sharing with their employees and employee stock ownership plans whereby employees could become shareholders, there would no longer be any need for unions." Do you agree or disagree? Why?

9. The text refers to the *attitudes* of labour and management as an obstacle to improving Canada's labour relations environment. What are some of these attitudes, and why have they developed?

10. To resolve collective bargaining disputes in essential public services, a procedure called *Final Offer Selection* is occasionally used. Negotiations proceed as usual, but if the parties cannot agree on a new contract, each party must make a *final offer* to the other party at a final bargaining meeting, following which further

negotiations can occur. If there is no agreement, these two final offers must be presented, *unchanged,* to an arbitrator, who must select as the terms of the collective agreement the offer that is deemed the more reasonable. So *either one or the other* of the offers will become the collective agreement.

(a) How do you think Final Offer Selection is *intended* to operate in resolving collective bargaining disputes?

(b) What possible *problem*s might Final Offer Selection encounter in resolving collective bargaining disputes?

Use the Web   (Hints for these Use the Web exercises appear in Appendix B.)

1. Visit Statistics Canada's website at **www.statcan.ca** and click on, in sequence, *Canadian Statistics > Tables by subject > Labour > Salaries and wages > Average earnings of the population 15 years and over by highest level of schooling.* What do the statistics in the table tell you about the demand–supply balance at different education and skill levels of the Canadian labour market?

2. The Canadian Labour Congress (CLC) is a national federation of labour unions that represents the concerns of unions across Canada. Visit the CLC's website at **www.clc-ctc.ca**, read its home page then click on *Click, Our Newsletter.* What issues are of concern to the CLC at this time? How are these issues related to economic developments and/or government policies?

3. You can update Figure 10-8's statistics on time lost due to work stoppages by visiting **www.hrsdc.gc.ca** and searching the site for "chronological perspective on work stoppages." Has the time lost due to labour disputes decreased or increased recently? What do you think might be contributing to this trend?

Employment and Incomes in the Canadian Economy

LEARNING OBJECTIVES

After studying this chapter, you should be able to

1. Describe the trends in employment in the main sectors of the Canadian economy since 1950, explain the basic causes of these trends, and recognize the consequences of these changes.

2. Give four reasons for the increase in female participation rates and in the percentage of women in the Canadian workforce since 1950.

3. Describe the changing trends in average real family income since 1951, and explain the two basic causes of these changes.

4. Discuss the size of the male–female pay gap and the reasons for that gap.

5. Discuss the reasons for the widening pay gap between skilled workers and unskilled workers.

6. Compare the definitions of *poverty* used by Statistics Canada's Low-Income Cut-Offs (LICOs) and the market basket measure (MBM) approach, and the poverty lines and poverty rates under the two definitions of poverty.

7. Identify four groups that have a strong tendency to be poor, and explain why each group tends to be poor.

8. Apply the facts and concepts of this chapter to various situations.

In Chapter 10, we examined the operation of the labour markets in which Canadians obtain jobs and earn incomes. In this chapter, we will consider more closely two important aspects of those labour markets: (a) the current and future *trends in employment* in labour markets, and (b) two important *trends in Canadians' incomes*—the level of incomes, and how those incomes are divided among various groups, or how the economic pie is divided up.

Employment Trends in Canada

Over the past half-century, major changes have taken place in the nature of the work performed by Canadians. In the broadest terms, as Figure 11-1 shows, the number of people working in the *goods-producing sector* of the economy (industries such as agriculture, forestry, mining, fishing, manufacturing, and construction) has increased quite slowly, while there has been a dramatic increase in employment in the *services-producing sector* (industries such as business and personal services, government and community services such as health care and education, retail and wholesale trade, finance, insurance and real estate, transportation, and communication).

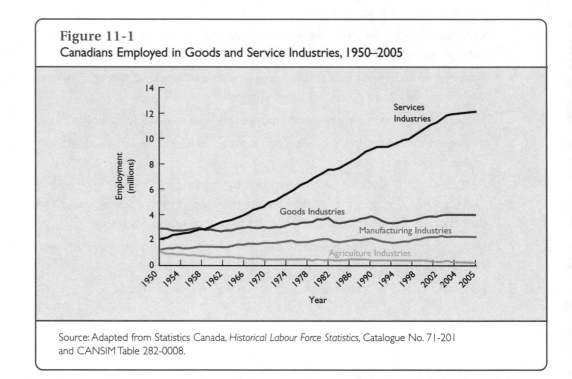

Figure 11-1
Canadians Employed in Goods and Service Industries, 1950–2005

Source: Adapted from Statistics Canada, *Historical Labour Force Statistics*, Catalogue No. 71-201 and CANSIM Table 282-0008.

The result of these trends, as Figure 11-2 shows, has been that the proportion of Canadians working in the goods-producing sector of the economy has declined from over 56 percent in 1951 to 25 percent by 2004, while there has been a corresponding increase from 44 percent to 75 percent of the work force employed in the service sector of the economy. Table 11-1 breaks this trend down into its component parts: a dramatic decline not only in the proportion but also the actual number of Canadians employed in agriculture; a steady decline in the proportion of employment accounted for by the manufacturing sector; a slight increase in the proportion of employment provided by trade, finance, insurance, and real estate; and a dramatic increase in employment in a variety of community, business, and personal service industries and public administration (or the

Figure 11-2
Shares of Total Employment of the Goods-Producing and
Services-Producing Sectors, 1950–2005

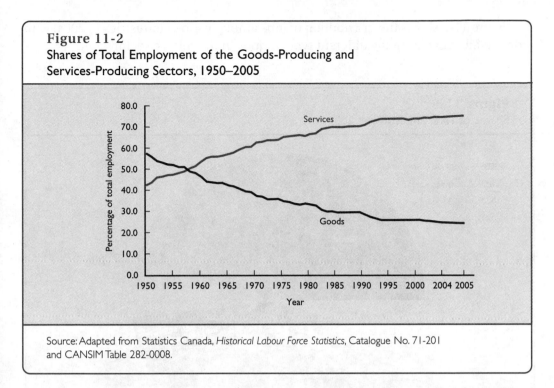

Source: Adapted from Statistics Canada, *Historical Labour Force Statistics*, Catalogue No. 71-201
and CANSIM Table 282-0008.

government sector). From 1976 to 2004, 88 percent of the increase in employment in
Canada occurred in the service sector of the economy. These trends have already caused
major changes in the ways in which Canadians learn, live, and earn their living, and will
continue to do so. In the following sections, we will examine the causes, the effects, and
the future implications of these trends

Table 11-1
The Changing Nature of Employment in Canada

	Percent of Total Employment in Each Sector in:					
	1951	1961	1971	1981	1991	2005
Agriculture	18.4	11.2	6.3	4.4	3.5	2.1
Non-agricultural primary industries	4.4	3.0	2.7	2.9	2.3	1.9
Manufacturing	26.5	24.0	21.8	19.3	15.1	13.7
Construction	6.8	6.2	6.0	5.9	5.7	6.3
Total goods-producing sector	56.1	44.5	36.9	32.5	26.6	24.8
Transportation, storage, communication and utilities	8.8	9.3	8.7	8.3	7.4	5.7
Trade	15.1	16.9	16.5	17.1	17.6	15.9
Finance, insurance and real estate	3.0	3.9	4.9	5.4	6.1	6.1
Community, business and personal services and public administration	18.0	25.3	33.0	36.6	42.2	47.5
Total service-producing sector	43.9	55.5	63.1	67.5	73.4	75.2
Total all industries	100.0	100.0	100.0	100.0	100.0	100.0

Sources: Adapted from Statistics Canada, *Historical Labour Force Statistics*, Catalogue No. 71-201 and CANSIM Table 282-0008.

www40.statcan.ca/l01/
cst01/econ40.htm

Figure 11-3 shows the distribution of jobs among various industries in 2004, with more detail concerning the different types of jobs in the service sector

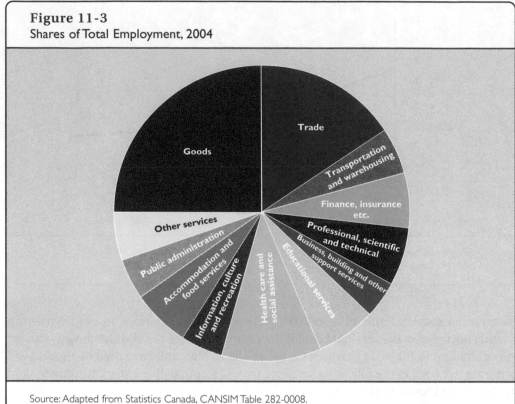

Figure 11-3
Shares of Total Employment, 2004

Source: Adapted from Statistics Canada, CANSIM Table 282-0008.

Causes of Trends in Employment

To understand why the nature of employment has changed so greatly, we must consider some fundamental changes that have occurred on both the *demand side* and the *supply side* of labour markets in Canada.

The Demand Side

Technological Change

Technological change is the most basic force underlying the changing nature of employment because it has generated major shifts in employers' demand for labour. While technology affects all industrial production methods, it has generally proven easier to apply labour-saving technology to the production of goods, which lend themselves to mass-production techniques, than to the production of services. Many services (such as haircuts, medical services, education, and legal services) are "labour-intensive"; that is, they require a person-to-person delivery. By contrast, the production of many goods can be very "capital-intensive," as the worker-hours per unit of output can be reduced considerably through using capital equipment, including computer-controlled industrial robots.

At the start of the twentieth century, most Canadians worked in the *agricultural sector* of the economy. In Canada, as in other nations, the first impact of technological change was in the agricultural sector of the economy, which is well-suited to extensive use of capital equipment. The result was a dramatic increase in agricultural productivity over that century, and a corresponding decrease in the number of workers required in the agricultural sector. Viewed differently, technological change "freed up" large numbers of workers from agriculture, making them available for work in the manufacturing and service sectors of the economy.

Many of the workers no longer needed in agriculture were able to find employment in the *manufacturing sector* of the economy, where employment increased until the late 1970s. However, much of the manufacturing sector is also quite well-suited to mass-production technology. From 1981 to 2004, the output of the manufacturing sector of the Canadian economy increased by about 90 percent, while employment in manufacturing increased by only 10.6 percent. Over the same period, employment in the service sector grew by 58 percent. So the gradual decrease in the percentage of the labour force employed in the manufacturing sector that is shown in Table 11-1 on page 235 has been mainly the result of the introduction of labour-saving technology.

From 1987 to 2003, the number of jobs for chefs and cooks grew by 51 percent. Employment of labourers increased by 5 percent.

Changes in Consumer Demand

Obviously, the rapid growth in service-industry employment shown in Figure 11-1 on page 234 could not occur without major increases in the *demand for services*. A key factor in the growth of the demand for services was the process of technological change described in the previous section. By increasing output per worker (productivity), technological change has *increased the standard of living* of Canadians. And, as their living standards rose, people spent an ever-increasing proportion of their incomes on services such as restaurants, entertainment, and travel. Since most service industries are labour-intensive, the rising demand for services generated a vast number of service-industry jobs, sufficient to allow the economy to provide work for the people freed up from the agricultural and manufacturing sectors by technological change. And so, for the most part, the shift of employment from the goods-producing sector of the economy to the service sector was achieved fairly smoothly, without excessive increases in unemployment. As a result, employment has risen very rapidly in the service sector, in fields such as retail trade, food service, sales, accounting, finance, human resources, health care, education, law, computer services, and so on.

During the twentieth century, then, the nature of the work done by Canadians underwent major changes. Early in the century, most young people stayed and worked on the farm; later, most would go to work in manufacturing plants; now, in the early twenty-first century, the vast majority find jobs in offices or service industries. Similar trends have occurred in all industrialized economies, suggesting that economic progress and change is driven by the same basic technological and economic forces that generate similar results. These forces and their results are summarized in Figure 11-4 on the next page.

International Economic Forces

A third factor that has undercut employment in some manufacturing industries has been the growth of international trade and competition since the 1970s—the process known as *globalization*. Competition from low-wage countries has been especially difficult for Canadian manufacturers in industries such as clothing, footwear, furniture, and assembly operations. Caught between low-productivity labour-intensive production methods, high Canadian wages, and low-wage import competition, many could not continue operating in Canada. Many of those that were able to survive did so through extensive "labour shedding" in order to reduce costs; the result in both cases was a reduction in manufacturing employment in some industries in Canada.

Figure 11-4
Shifts in Employment, 1951–2005

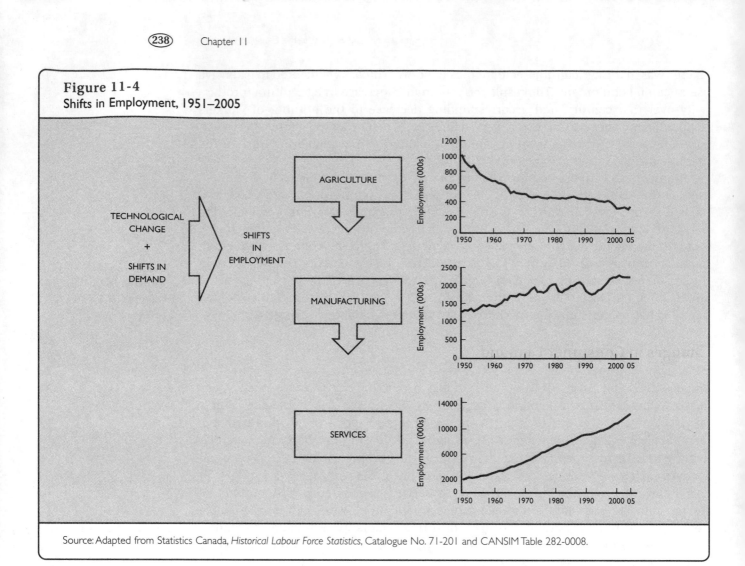

Source: Adapted from Statistics Canada, *Historical Labour Force Statistics*, Catalogue No. 71-201 and CANSIM Table 282-0008.

The Supply Side: Working Women

On the supply side of the labour market, there is no doubt that the most dramatic and important development has been the great increase in the number of working women. In 1950, the percentage of women of working age participating in the labour force—the *participation rate*—was 23 percent. By 2005, it was 62 percent. Participation rates increased most rapidly for married women, who accounted for only one-eighth of the labour force in 1961, but over one-quarter by 2005. Overall, women comprised 47 percent of the labour force in 2005, compared to less than 22 percent in 1950. These trends are reflected in Figure 11-5, which highlights the rising participation rate of women since the 1950s.

There are several reasons for this remarkable growth of the female work force. Probably the most frequently mentioned factor is the *squeeze on family incomes*. After the mid-1970s, wages and salaries in general barely kept up with inflation, making it more important for families to have a second income. However, as Figure 11-5 shows, the increase in female participation rates was underway long before this became a factor. This trend suggests that other factors were also at work.

One such factor was the *rising education levels and aspirations of women*. Many more women are completing high school and going on to college and university for

Figure 11-5
Participation Rates of Men and Women, 1950–2005

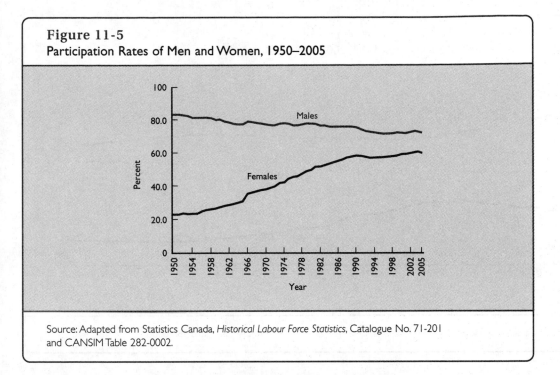

Source: Adapted from Statistics Canada, *Historical Labour Force Statistics*, Catalogue No. 71-201 and CANSIM Table 282-0002.

higher education than in the past. And, as women's education levels have risen, so have their expectations concerning their jobs, incomes, and careers.

However, these factors only increased the numbers of women *wanting* to work. For this goal to be achieved, there would have to be more *job opportunitie*s for women.

These opportunities were provided by the rapid growth of the *service sector* of the economy, as described earlier in this chapter. Many women are employed in the service sector, for various reasons. Unlike many goods-industry jobs, most service jobs do not require physical strength so much as the ability to think and to deal with people. Also, many service industries, such as retail trade, provide part-time work, which appeals in particular to working mothers. The importance of the growth of the service sector to the increase in the number of working women can be measured by the fact that, in recent years, nearly 87 percent of employed women have been working in the service sector of the economy. And this trend appeared likely to continue, as the fastest-growing areas of employment were accounting, human resource management, sales, and advertising—fields in which the number of women was increasing more than three times as rapidly as the number of men.

Finally, many more women are self-supporting than in the past. It is estimated that six in ten women at some time in their life will be self-supporting. More women are opting for careers, and more marriages break down now than in the past.

Figure 11-6 on the next page shows the changes in the composition of the labour force from 1967 to 2005. Due to the rising female participation rates already discussed, the proportion of women in the labour force rose steadily over this period. The 1970s saw a similarly rapid increase in the proportion of *young Canadians* (age 15–24) in the labour force, as the postwar "baby boom" came of working age. However, in the early 1980s, this surge of young entrants to the work force subsided, while the proportion of women in the labour force continued to rise.

On university campuses in recent years, female students have outnumbered males by roughly 4 to 3.

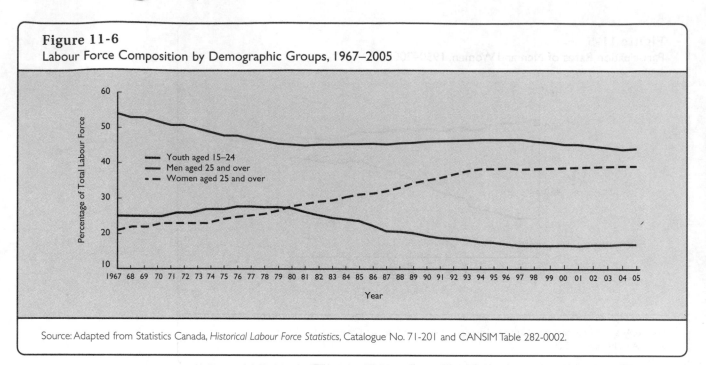

Figure 11-6
Labour Force Composition by Demographic Groups, 1967–2005

Source: Adapted from Statistics Canada, *Historical Labour Force Statistics*, Catalogue No. 71-201 and CANSIM Table 282-0002.

Adjusting to Change

The technological and economic forces discussed in this chapter—revolutionary changes in production technology, massive shifts in consumer spending toward services, and the addition of over 4 million women into the work force in 30 years—have generated and will continue to generate fundamental changes in the way that Canadians work and live. In the following sections, we will examine some of these changes in the past, the present, and the future.

The urbanization of society was one of the most dramatic effects of technological change in the first half of the twentieth century. As technology reduced the number of workers needed on the farm and drew workers into city-based manufacturing plants, Canada's population became increasingly concentrated into a few large urban areas, with all of the advantages—and disadvantages—of city dwelling. *Rising living standards* were another major result of technological progress, as the increases in output per worker generated by improved technology became the economic basis for a generally rising prosperity among Canadians.

Rising educational requirements were an inevitable aspect of this process because much work became more technical and because many of the new service-industry jobs required specialized knowledge. This trend led to the expansion of the nation's universities and to the establishment of new systems of colleges to provide the "middle-level" skills for which demand grew rapidly as the economy evolved. *Later marriages, working women,* and *higher-income but smaller families* were three other features of the modern society that emerged in the second half of the twentieth century. As noted, the rapid growth of the service industries provided women not only with greatly increased opportunities for employment but also with the prospect of fulfilling and rewarding careers. Longer periods of education and increased interest in women's careers pushed marriage back several years for many, and resulted in much higher family incomes and considerably smaller families than in the past. The *slower population growth* that resulted from these developments eventually led to a government policy of *increased immigration.*

To keep the labour force growing at a pace that would provide enough working people to support the baby boomers in their retirement years after 2010, the government increased the inflow of immigration.

Part-time work grew rapidly to over 18 percent of all jobs, in large part due to the rapid growth of service industries such as food service and retail trade, which employ part-time workers. Students and many homemakers welcomed the growth of these part-time job opportunities, but about 30 percent of part-time workers really wanted full-time jobs and were unable to find them. See the "In the News" box below for some facts about how the Canadian labour force has changed since 1976.

IN THE NEWS

Labour Force Facts

From 1976 to 2005 in the Canadian economy:
- the number of jobs increased by 6 429 800, or 66 percent;
- employment in the service sector grew by 5 784 900, or 91 percent;
- employment in the goods-producing sector grew by 644 900, or 19 percent;
- of the 6 429 800 growth in jobs, 27 percent were part-time; this brought part-time jobs up to 18.3 percent of total employment (as compared to 12.6 percent in 1976); and
- the number of part-time jobs increased by 143 percent, while full-time employment grew by 55 percent. ■

QUESTIONS
1. What do you think are the causes of part-time employment growing so much faster than full-time employment?
2. Has part-time employment's share of total jobs increased from its 2005 level of 18.3 percent? You can find updated statistics on Statistics Canada's website (**www.statcan.ca**). Click on, in sequence, *Canadian Statistics > Tables by subject > Labour > Employment > Full-time and part-time employment by sex and age group.*

Technology and Employment

After the mid-1980s, the pace of technological change in Canadian industry increased considerably. Such rapid technological change naturally raises fears that new production technology would displace people from their jobs and push ever-higher numbers of people to unemployment, creating economic and social hardship.

Economists are generally skeptical about such doomsday scenarios. They point out that similar alarms were raised in the past when new agricultural, manufacturing, and computer technologies were introduced. In fact, no long-term increase in unemployment occurred because the effects of technological change on the economy are more complex than they seem. It is generally agreed that technological change can generate *short-term* increases in unemployment by displacing some workers from their jobs. However, this displacement has not created a growing problem of *long-term* unemployment, because there are other, less-noticed aspects of technological change that have positive effects upon employment.

First, by increasing output per worker, technological progress generates *higher living standards and higher consumption of services.* As employers are able to pay higher wages to more productive workers, and as the prices of more efficiently produced goods come down, consumers have more buying power, creating jobs in other sectors of the economy, most notably the *service sector*, which has received a large share of rising consumer spending over the past quarter-century and which is generally labour-intensive.

Second, by improving productivity, technological progress enhances the *ability of Canadian industry to compete internationally*. Many Canadian jobs depend on the ability of Canadian producers to export to foreign markets or compete with imports in Canadian markets. Because of this fact, it can be argued that, by improving the efficiency and competitiveness of Canadian producers, technological change could actually increase employment.

Figure 11-7 summarizes these factors—the loss of some jobs and displacement of some workers, and the creation of other jobs through increased demand for services and improved international competitiveness. The right side of Figure 11-7 also shows the *process of change* in the labour force, as labour "shifts" from the manufacturing sector to the expanding service sector. Some of the figures shown making this shift are workers who were displaced from jobs by technology, and others are new entrants to the work force who will find work in the service sector rather than in goods-producing industries.

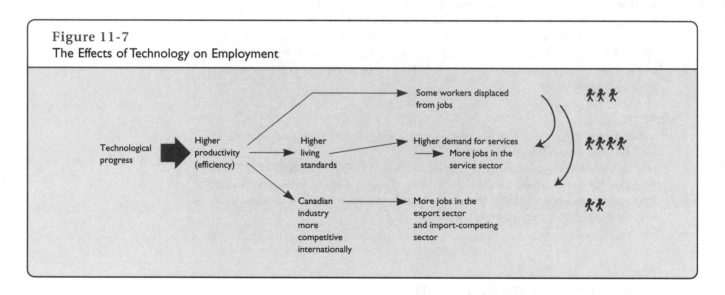

Figure 11-7
The Effects of Technology on Employment

In 2000, Canada's unemployment rate reached its lowest level in 25 years, and remained low through 2005. So, over the long term, the evidence is that technological change has tended to *change the nature of work* rather than *reduce the number of jobs*. And, as we have seen, the basic change in the nature of work has been from jobs producing goods to jobs in the service sector. However, making this type of transition to new types of work has required that the labour force adapt to change more than in the past.

Adapting to Change

The key to adapting to change is education and training. It is projected that nearly half of the new jobs created in the future will require more than 16 years of training (a combination of schooling and on-the-job experience) as compared with only 23 percent in 1986.

From the viewpoint of *the individual*, the benefits of education and training are obvious, in the form of a higher probability of finding rewarding employment. Education and training also bring benefits to *business,* in the form of higher productivity. And for *society in general,* investment in education and training is beneficial not only because it improves productivity and prosperity but also because a high-quality labour force tends to attract job-creating business investment.

It is generally agreed that education and training are areas in which Canada needs to improve. Spending on education and training by the Canadian private sector has been low compared to other industrialized countries, and Canada lacks excellent apprenticeship programs such as those of Japan and Germany. While government spending on education in Canada is among the highest in the world, and the average level of educational attainment is high, employers complain that many graduates of Canadian high schools lack the basic literacy and numeracy skills needed to make them productive workers in a modern economy.

Even when there are over a million Canadians unemployed, employers are often unable to recruit qualified workers, and it has been necessary to import certain types of skilled workers. According to a report by the Organization for Economic Cooperation and Development, Canada's weaknesses with respect to education and training were undermining Canada's international competitiveness, and educational spending should be redirected so as to place greater emphasis on the basic literacy, numeracy, and technical skills needed by a modern workforce.

www.oecdwash.org

Income Trends in Canada

As Figure 11-8 on the next page shows, the average real family income of Canadians has increased considerably since 1951.[1] In fact, average family income in 2002 was almost three times as high as it was in 1951, after adjusting for inflation.

More detailed examination of the statistics in Figure 11-8 reveals some significant facts and trends. Average family income rose most rapidly during the 1960s, when it gained almost 40 percent. The 1950s saw the second-greatest gains, of about 27 percent, with the 1970s following with 24 percent. However, most of the 1951–2000 growth in real income occurred between 1951 and 1976—the gain from 1951 to 1976 was 139 percent, while the increase from 1976 to 2002 was only 20 percent.

The rapid growth of average real family income until the late 1970s was generated mainly by two factors. The first of these was a significant increase in the number of income-earners per family, mainly the result of *more women working*. The second factor was *rapidly rising productivity*, which, as we have seen, is the most basic source of growing economic prosperity. After the late 1970s, however, the situation changed with respect to both of these factors—productivity growth slowed sharply, and the number of income-earners per family grew less rapidly (and even declined in some years) after peaking at around 1.75. And, when the growth of these two key factors slowed after the late 1970s, so did the growth of average real income per family.

---

[1] *Real income* refers to income after adjusting for inflation. Because of inflation, increases in incomes *seem* larger than they *really are.* For instance, if your income rose by 4 percent but inflation caused the prices of the things you buy to rise by 3 percent, you would be only 1 percent better off, not 4 percent. The figures used in the text and Figure 11-8 show average family income *after allowing for inflation.* For example, in 1951, average family income was about $3500 in 1951 dollars. But in those days, $3500 bought about as much as $25 500 would buy in 2002, so Figure 11-8 shows 1951 average family income as $25 500 "in constant 2002 dollars." Adjusting for inflation in this way makes it possible to compare today's incomes with incomes from long ago.

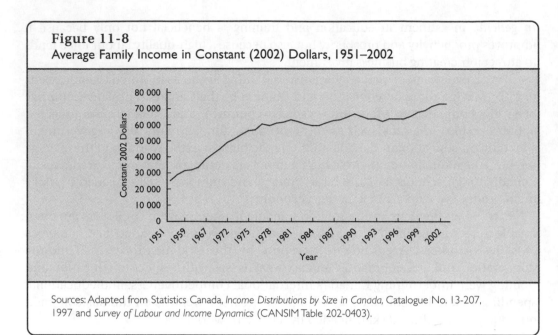

Figure 11-8
Average Family Income in Constant (2002) Dollars, 1951–2002

Sources: Adapted from Statistics Canada, *Income Distributions by Size in Canada*, Catalogue No. 13-207, 1997 and *Survey of Labour and Income Dynamics* (CANSIM Table 202-0403).

Dividing Up the Economic Pie: How Incomes Are Distributed

The previous section deals with trends in the *level* of average incomes in Canada; however, another important consideration is how incomes are *distributed* among various occupational groups and between lower-income groups and higher-income groups. This concept of distribution concerns the third of the three basic economic questions from Chapter 1—how the economic pie is divided up among Canadians.

In Chapter 10, we saw how incomes are determined in labour markets, under conditions ranging from the almost free interplay of supply and demand in markets for part-time student labour to markets in which trade unions and professional bodies regulate the supply of labour by limiting how many people can enter some occupations.

On a broader scale, there is the question of how income is distributed among different *income groups*—that is, what share of the economic pie goes to the lowest-income 20 percent of families, to the highest-income 20 percent, and to the various groups in between?

Before we start, we need to make clear exactly what is meant by "income." Statistics Canada uses three measures of income:

- **Market income**, which is income earned in the marketplace; mostly wages and salaries, but also interest, dividends, etc.,
- **Total income**, which is market income plus transfer payments received from governments, such as welfare, Employment Insurance benefits, etc., and
- **After-tax income**, which is total income less income taxes paid.

Table 11-2 is based on the total income of families of two or more people. In Chapter 12, we will look at market income and after-tax income, and the differences between them.

As Table 11-2 shows, the distribution of before-tax total income (earned income plus transfer payments from governments) between various income groups has

---

market income
Income earned in the marketplace.

total income
Market income plus transfer payments received from governments.

after-tax income
Total income less income taxes paid.

Table 11-2
Distribution of Total Family Income, 2003 (before taxes)

	Percentage of Total Income Received by Each Fifth						Average Family Income, 2003
	1951	1961	1971	1981	1991	2003	
Lowest fifth of families	6.1	6.6	5.6	6.5	6.4	6.2	$22 400
Second fifth	12.9	13.4	12.7	12.9	12.2	11.5	41 800
Third fifth	17.4	18.2	18.0	18.3	17.6	16.7	60 900
Fourth fifth	22.5	23.4	23.7	24.1	23.9	23.2	84 300
Highest-income fifth	41.1	38.4	40.0	38.3	40.0	42.4	153 900
All families	100.0	100.0	100.0	100.0	100.0	100.0	72 660

Note: Data refer to economic families of two or more people.

Source: Adapted from Statistics Canada, *Income Distributions by Size in Canada*, Catalogue No. 13-207, 1997 and CANSIM Table 202-0701.

remained remarkably steady over the years, with roughly 40 percent of total family income going to the top 20 percent of families, 24 percent of income to the second-highest 20 percent, 18 percent to the middle 20 percent, and only 12 percent and 6 percent to the second-lowest and lowest 20 percent of families, respectively. These statistics show a degree of inequality in the distribution of income that is not only *considerable*, but also *remarkably consistent* from year to year. For nearly 50 years, the top fifth of Canadian families have had a share of before-tax income roughly seven times as large as the share going to the bottom fifth.

The division of the economic pie is among the most controversial issues in the field of economics, because it raises serious issues of equity. Is the distribution of income reflected in Table 11-2 *fair*? To some, higher incomes represent a *reward* for effort and education; to them, such high incomes not only reflect those people's greater *contribution* to society but also provide *incentives* for Canadians to improve themselves and work harder. To others, these differences in income are much greater than can be explained by differing contributions or by the need to provide incentives. These people view the income-distribution process as one in which a small number of Canadians use their *economic power* to extract an excessive share of the economic pie from the system for themselves, leaving only the crumbs for the poor, who lack the market power to command high incomes.

Which view is correct? How much of this inequality is necessary in order to provide incentives? Is this distribution of income fair or not? The tools of the economist can help to explain *why* such a distribution of income exists, but are of little help in making what are, in essence, subjective value judgments as to whether it is a *fair* or an *appropriate* distribution of income.

However, the controversial nature of this matter does make it important that statistics such as those in Table 11-2 be interpreted carefully and accurately. In particular, the persistent inequality shown by the statistics—40 percent of income going to the top 20 percent of families and only 6 percent of income going to the bottom 20 percent of families, decade after decade—creates the impression that these high- and low-income groups comprise the same families, year after year. In particular, the image is generated of the same families stuck with low incomes decade after decade, without hope. While this is certainly the case with some such families, the situation is more complex than this

Statistics on incomes are collected each year by Statistics Canada through a survey of about 30 000 households that is known as the *Survey of Labour and Income Dynamics (SLID)*.

image would suggest. The lowest-income group also includes families whose income is *temporarily* low: for instance, students at school who work only seasonally or part-time, or recent graduates whose low income reflects the fact that they have worked for only part of the year. And, as we will see, the low-income group also includes some families of retired persons whose income is low but who possess considerable assets, such as a paid-for home. So the low-income group is not simply the same group of families year after year, but rather comprises to a significant extent a changing group of households, who flow into and out of the low-income group as their circumstances change.

Finally, the inequalities in the Canadian distribution of income shown in Table 11-2 are not significantly different from those in other industrialized nations. International statistical comparisons are imprecise; however, it seems that income in Canada is distributed a little more unequally than in most European countries and a little less unequally than in the United States.

The Male–Female Pay Gap

In 2004, women comprised 46 percent of Canada's labour force, but only about 10 percent of the members of the boards of directors of Canada's largest 500 companies were women.

The income differentials that have attracted the most attention in the past 35 years have been the pay differences between men and women. Different studies have estimated this pay gap differently, with most concluding that, on average, women earn roughly 70 percent of what men earn for full-time work, as shown in Figure 11-9. The existence of such a large income differential raises questions of gender discrimination in Canadian labour markets.

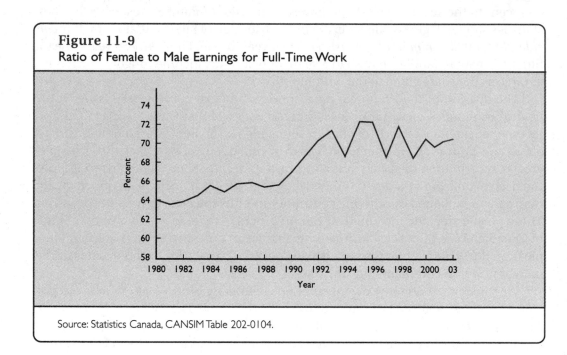

Figure 11-9
Ratio of Female to Male Earnings for Full-Time Work

Source: Statistics Canada, CANSIM Table 202-0104.

However, most of this difference between the incomes of men and women can be explained by economic factors. One such factor is the number of *hours worked*—on average, men work roughly 40 hours per week compared to about 35 hours for women, a difference of 15 percent. Most studies estimate that if differences in hours worked are considered, the male–female wage gap shrinks by nearly half. Somewhat less than another one-fifth of the gap can be attributed to "productivity factors," such as *training, education,* and *experience.* The fact that many women interrupt their career for child-raising holds back their advancement and incomes. In addition, women have shown a tendency to leave the work force earlier than men—the partic- ipation rate for women drops rapidly after age 55, depressing the average income of women by reducing the number of them working during these higher-income years.

Both *marital status* and *age* are also significant factors making women's incomes lower than men's: single women's incomes are about 91 percent of those of single men, while married women earn only 65 percent of what married men earn. And incomes of women in the 15–24 age group are 86 percent of men's, while women over 55 earn only 64 percent of what men earn.

After allowance has been made for the hours worked and productivity factors, there remains a male–female wage gap of about 10 percent that can best be explained by "gender factors." The main such gender factor seems to have been *occupational seg- regation*: approximately three-quarters of female employees work in five occupational groups—clerical, service, sales, medicine/health care, and education. Since so many women are concentrated into these occupational groups that contain many relatively low-paying jobs, the average income of women in general tends to be below average.

There seem to be at least two basic origins of this occupational segregation. One is *society's stereotypes* concerning the role of women, which probably condition many young women to think in terms of working as secretaries, waitresses, and the like. The other is *selection procedures,* for both hiring and promotion. The people in a given occupational field or workplace tend to hire and promote people with whom they are comfortable and who they believe will "fit in." So if a field is dominated by males, this makes it much more difficult for females to enter it. These two factors are illustrated in Figure 11-10.

Figure 11-10 also shows the economic effects of these forces. If large numbers of women are steered by stereotyping and deflected by selection procedures into a few occupational areas, the result will be an oversupply of (female) labour in those occu- pations, with low wages the result.

Such male–female wage gaps raise important issues of government policy. If the government wants to reduce the pay gap, one of the most basic steps would be to break down the traditional female stereotypes. The educational system attempts to do this by showing both women and men in non-traditional occupational roles in schoolbooks from the earliest grades. Another basic step would be to change hiring and promotion

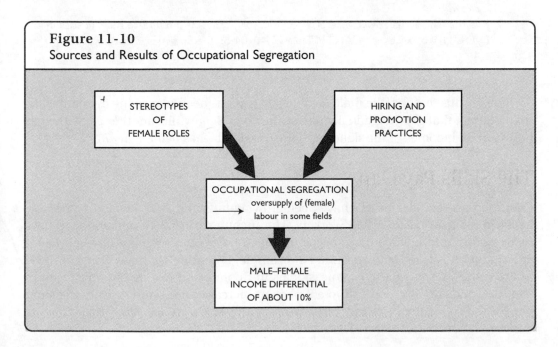

Figure 11-10
Sources and Results of Occupational Segregation

procedures through *employment equity*, either through persuasion or by legislation. And to deal with the income inequities, there is pay equity legislation. The first step toward dealing with this matter was legislation ruling that people who do the same work must receive the same pay—*equal pay for equal work* legislation. Such legislation has existed for many years in many provinces and is widely accepted. However, its effect is limited to situations where men and women are performing the same jobs. It does not address the main source of male–female wage differences—the fact that women tend to be concentrated in certain types of jobs with below-average pay.

A more controversial approach is the concept of **equal pay for work of equal value**. Under this approach, the "value" of a job is measured by a point system that takes into account factors such as skill, effort, responsibility, and working conditions. Such a system allows the pay of quite different jobs to be compared, by adding up their points: the more points a job has, the more it is "worth."

Equal pay for work of equal value legislation applies to government employees in several jurisdictions. However, the application of the same legislation to private employers is much more controversial, due to concerns regarding employers' ability to compete with other firms that are not subject to such requirements, including foreign competitors.

equal pay for work of equal value

The concept that the values of different jobs may be measured against each other using a point system that incorporates a variety of criteria, including skill levels, effort, degree of responsibility, and working conditions.

IN THE NEWS

Will the Male–Female Pay Gap Narrow in the Future?

Figure 11-9 on page 246 shows that, as of 2003, women were earning about 70 percent of what men earned for full-time work. The male–female pay gap has narrowed over the long term, but since the early 1990s, the gap has not narrowed significantly.

Nonetheless, some observers are predicting that the male–female pay gap for full-time workers will narrow further in the future. ■

QUESTIONS
1. What are some of the reasons for the expectation that the male–female pay gap will narrow?
2. Has the pay gap narrowed further since 2003 or not? (You can update the statistics in Figure 11-9 by accessing CANSIM Table 202-0104 on the Statistics Canada website.)

For various reasons, the male–female pay gap has been narrowing over time, and many expect that gap to gradually narrow further. Meanwhile, another gap—the gap between the incomes of the skilled and the unskilled—has been *widening*.

The Skills Pay Gap

Over the past few years, there have been growing indications of a widening pay gap between skilled and unskilled workers. The incomes of skilled workers have been rising quite rapidly, while those of the unskilled have been stagnant, or even falling after inflation is taken into account. For example, Figure 11-11 shows that from 1997 to 2004, the weekly wages of professionals in finance and health care increased by about 29 percent, as compared to a 9 percent increase for labourers. Over the same period, the consumer price index increased by 16 percent, so the real (after-inflation) wages of labourers actually *decreased*.

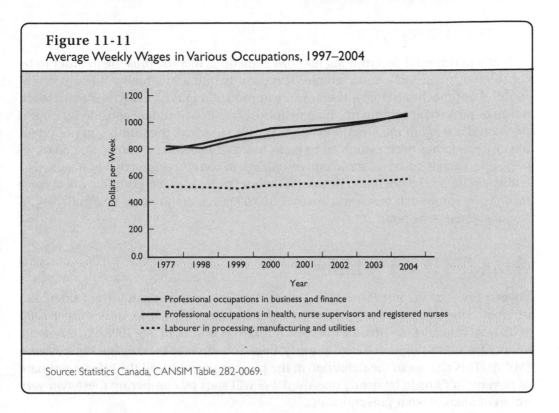

Figure 11-11
Average Weekly Wages in Various Occupations, 1997–2004

— Professional occupations in business and finance
— Professional occupations in health, nurse supervisors and registered nurses
···· Labourer in processing, manufacturing and utilities

Source: Statistics Canada, CANSIM Table 282-0069.

Many observers link this trend to the decline in lesser-skilled manufacturing jobs caused by changing technology and freer trade. According to the C.D. Howe Institute, "... there is evidence that technological change is biased in favour of skilled workers, and wage differentials between skilled and unskilled workers are widening in many industries." Also, free trade and globalization have opened Canadian markets to imports of low-cost, labour-intensive manufactured goods.

In the job market for low-skilled workers, there is an oversupply of labour relative to demand, causing incomes to increase slowly or even decrease, whereas in markets for skilled workers, the opposite is often the case. The result of these effects has been a growing gap between the incomes of skilled workers and those of less-skilled workers. The gap may also have been widened by cutbacks in the 1990s in programs such as employment insurance, which support the incomes of workers who are periodically out of work.

Poverty in Canada

On average, Canadians enjoy one of the highest standards of living in the world, but we have seen that this prosperity is *distributed* far from evenly among Canadians.

How many Canadians have such low incomes that they are living in poverty? According to some estimates, from 5 000 000 to over 7 000 000 Canadians (over 20 percent of the population) are "poor." But other estimates place the number as low as 2 000 000, or even 1 000 000 (3 to 6 percent of Canadians). These widely varying estimates of the extent of poverty arise from the fact that there are very different ways to just *define* what *poverty* actually means.

This is an important debate. By some definitions, poverty is a national crisis that demands massive government action, while according to others, it seems to be a much less widespread problem. First, we will consider the challenges in defining what "poverty" is and measuring how many people are living in poverty.

What Is Poverty?

Defining *poverty* and determining how low someone's income must be in order to be considered "poor" is far from simple. There are two fundamentally different philosophical approaches to this question. One approach might be called a *physical* definition of poverty, according to which people or families would be considered poor *if they could not afford the necessities of life.* By this standard, the number of poor people in Canada has been estimated to be as low as 1 000 000 to 1 500 000. The other basic approach is based on *social and psychological considerations;* that is, a person or family would be considered to be poor if their income were *too far below the average income.* By some such measures, nearly 7 000 000 Canadians—over one in five—can be considered to be poor.

Canada's Poverty Lines

Poverty lines are income levels below which families or individuals are considered to be poor. The statistics that have most commonly been used for this purpose are Statistics Canada's **Low-Income Cut-Offs** (LICOs). However, in late 1998, governments adopted a quite different set of poverty lines based on a **market basket measure** (MBM). This change in the definition of the poverty line reduced the official estimate of poverty in Canada by nearly one-third. We will start by comparing these two very different ideas of what *poverty* means.

Using Statistics Canada's Low-Income Cut-Offs (LICOs) as poverty lines reflects the view that people are poor if their income is too far below the average income. Statistics Canada's purpose in developing the LICOs was not to define *poverty* but rather to identify low-income Canadians so as to gather statistics on this group. Nonetheless, many groups, including the **National Council of Welfare** (NCW), consider the LICOs to represent poverty lines, and use them to estimate how many Canadians are poor.

There are two sets of LICOs—one that uses before-tax income and one that uses after-tax income. According to the before-tax LICOs, 4 393 000 Canadians (14.4 percent of the population) were living in poverty in 2001. (The actual before-tax incomes that these LICO-based poverty lines represent are shown in Table 11-3.) But according to the after-tax LICOs, 3 163 000 Canadians, or 10.4 percent of the population, were poor.

The use of the LICOs as poverty lines has been criticized for exaggerating how many Canadians are poor. The main criticism has been that the LICOs *measure inequality rather than poverty.* Critics argue that if the incomes and living standards of all Canadians, including the poor, were to double, it would seem logical that the number of poor people would decrease considerably. However, according to the LICOs, the percentage of people who are poor would not decrease, because there would still be as many people whose incomes were *far enough below the average* to be classed as poor. This is one reason why, despite generally rising living standards, the percentage of Canadians who are poor has not decreased by much, and has even increased in some years.

Market basket measure (MBM) poverty lines reflect the view that poverty means the inability to afford the necessities of life. MBM poverty lines are based on the cost of a "basket" of goods and services that a family requires in order to live above the poverty line.

Many people regard MBM-based poverty lines as more realistic and more understandable than the LICOs. But using MBMs as poverty lines is not as simple as it might seem. The most basic problem is deciding just what should go into the basket in order to keep people above the poverty line. Deciding this takes us back to the problem of defining *poverty* that we discussed at the beginning of this topic—in a wealthy society, what should be considered a necessity of life? Establishing MBM

poverty lines
Income levels below which families or individuals are considered to be poor.

Low-Income Cut-Offs
Income levels below which the income of families or individuals are less than the average income by more than a certain amount.

market basket measure
Poverty lines based on the cost of a "basket" of goods and services that a family requires in order to live above the poverty line.

National Council of Welfare
A citizens' advisory body to the Minister of Human Resources Development Canada on matters of concern to low-income Canadians.

www.ncwcnbes.net

"Statistics Canada has clearly and consistently emphasized . . . that the LICOs are quite different from measures of poverty."
— FROM STATISTICS CANADA, *INCOME DISTRIBUTIONS BY SIZE IN CANADA*, 1997.

Table 11-3
National Council of Welfare Estimates of Statistics Canada's Pre-Tax
Low-Income Cut-Offs for 2004*

Size of Family Unit	Rural Areas	Community Size			
		Less than 30 000	30 000 to 99 999	100 000 to 499 999	500 000 and over
1 person	13 892	15 932	17 122	17 241	20 101
2 persons	17 364	19 915	21 402	21 551	25 127
3 persons	21 596	24 767	26 617	26 803	31 249
4 persons	26 141	29 981	32 220	32 445	37 828
5 persons	29 223	33 513	36 017	36 269	42 285
6 persons	32 304	37 045	39 813	40 093	46 742
7 or more persons	35 385	40 577	43 610	43 916	51 199

* Based on an estimated inflation rate of 1.5 percent in 2004.

Source: National Council of Welfare, *Poverty Profile 2001* (Autumn 2004). Reproduced with the permission of the Minister of Public Works and Government Services Canada, 2005.

poverty lines is further complicated by the fact that the cost of the same basket of items (especially shelter) varies widely from place to place across Canada.

New Poverty Lines for Canada

Finally, governments concluded that as long as the LICOs were used as poverty lines, the poverty rate would not only be exaggerated, but also unlikely to decrease in the future. So in late 1998, Canadian governments adopted a new definition of poverty and new poverty lines based on the MBM approach. As an example of the meaning of this change, a family of four would be considered to be poor if it did not have enough income to

- eat nutritious meals as defined by Health Canada,
- buy clothing for work and social occasions,
- rent a median-cost three-bedroom apartment, plus
- have additional income equal to 60 percent of the combined cost of the food and clothing budgets, for the purchase of other necessary items such as personal care, household needs, furniture, telephone service, public transit, reading, recreation, and school supplies.

The poverty lines were to be adjusted for family size and for variations in living costs in different regions.

The adoption of these new poverty lines had significant effects. Since the MBM poverty lines were roughly 20 percent lower than the LICOs, the number of Canadians classed as poor fell by about 1.5 million and the poverty rate (the percentage of the population considered to be poor) was reduced by nearly one-third.

Other Measurement Problems

Critics argue that both the LICOs and the MBM poverty lines exaggerate the extent of poverty, due to problems in actually estimating the number of poor people.

One problem is that the income statistics on which estimates of poverty are made come from surveys, and some people will *underreport their income*, usually to evade income taxes. One example would be people in the food service industry who earn minimum-wage incomes that are supplemented significantly by cash tips, much of which is not reported. Studies have also found that when surveyed, people tend to underreport their employment insurance benefits by about 40 percent and their welfare benefits by about 20 percent.

Another measurement problem arises from the fact that the poverty lines consider *money income only*. For instance, there are retired people who have low money incomes but a reasonably comfortable lifestyle because they possess assets bought earlier in their lives, especially a *paid-for house*. Not having to pay rent or mortgage payments represents a major economic benefit for such people, often the equivalent of several thousand dollars per year of additional income that does not get counted when money income is the only factor considered in defining *poverty*.

Also, poverty statistics include people in transition, whose incomes are *only temporarily low*. This group would include some new entrants to the work force who only worked part of the year, some immigrants (only income earned in Canada is counted), some people following marital breakups, and others whose low-income situation is only temporary, but who are counted as living in poverty. Also included are college and university students, whose low earned income may not be reflective of their lifestyle if they share rent or live rent-free at home when not at school.

When all is said and done, defining poverty and developing accurate estimates of the number of Canadians who are poor is a task that is complex, difficult, and controversial. As a result, estimates of the number of poor Canadians continue to vary widely, from as low as 3 percent of the population to over 20 percent.

Who Are the Poor?

These difficulties in measuring the number of poor people do not mean that there is no poverty problem in Canada, only that we are uncertain as to its extent. There certainly are many Canadians who are poor, and it is important to know who they are. This will help us to understand the nature and causes of poverty, and to develop effective policies for addressing this problem.

In the following sections, statistics from the National Council of Welfare (NCW) are used. Because the NCW uses the LICOs as poverty lines, the poverty rates will be higher than those using the new MBM poverty lines; however, these statistics will provide the best available estimates of the characteristics of those Canadians who are poor.

According to the National Council of Welfare, probably the most important overall factor influencing the risk of poverty is *family type*. This refers to the subcategories of families and unattached individuals shown in Figure 11-12. These are arranged according to the poverty rate (the percentage of each group that is below the LICOs) for each group. Figure 11-12 uses the poverty lines established by the *after-tax* LICOs.

Figure 11-12 shows that unattached women under 65 (most of whom were young women), had the highest poverty rate, with 36.2 percent of this group having low after-tax incomes in 2001. The second-highest poverty rate (31.9 percent) was for single-parent mothers. They were followed by unattached men under 65 (again, mostly the young) with a poverty rate of 26.5 percent. Unattached women over 65 had the fourth-highest poverty rate at 20.5 percent, followed by unattached men over 65 at 16.4 percent. By far the lowest poverty rates were among couples, with couples over 65 and childless couples the least prone to low incomes.

Statistics on poverty can also be analyzed according to *age* and *sex*. These statistics show that poverty rates are highest among young people in general, and among older unattached individuals. The high poverty rates among young people reflect factors such as the lower pay earned by newer entrants to the work force due to lack of

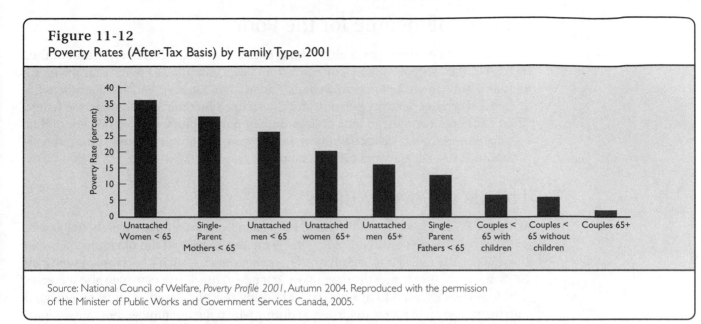

Figure 11-12
Poverty Rates (After-Tax Basis) by Family Type, 2001

Source: National Council of Welfare, *Poverty Profile 2001*, Autumn 2004. Reproduced with the permission of the Minister of Public Works and Government Services Canada, 2005.

experience and seniority, as well as the intermittent work and high unemployment rates experienced by many in this group. Causes of low incomes among older unattached individuals include the fact that this group includes a large number of widows, as well as the low pensions received by some older people and problems finding work. However, it should also be noted that the poverty rate among seniors has declined sharply, from 33.9 percent in 1980 to less than 17 percent in 2001.

Across all age groupings, *women* have a higher poverty rate than men, with poverty rates for young women being particularly high. Most of the high poverty rate for women under 65 can be attributed to the high poverty rates of two subgroups within this group: unattached women and single-parent mothers.

Poverty rates can also be analyzed according to the *education* of those with low incomes. As would be expected, poverty rates are generally higher for those with less education; for people with less than a high-school diploma, the poverty rate is roughly two or three times as high as for people with a post-secondary diploma or degree.

The Working Poor

While many poor people do not work, a large low-income group that deserves attention is the *working poor*. For this group, low wages and/or intermittent employment mean low incomes despite the fact that they do work considerably.

In 2001, 50 percent of poor families with children and 43 percent of poor couples without children and 43 percent of poor unattached individuals under 65 relied entirely on their earnings, rather than transfer payments from governments. These figures show that many of the poor had considerable attachment to the labour force.

Many of these working poor earn the minimum wage. Most minimum-wage earners are women, young people, students, and part-time workers; however, some 27 000 heads of families with no spouse were working for the minimum wage or less in 2003. Many of the working poor live on incomes that are actually lower than they would receive if they were on welfare. Nonetheless, the social welfare system has provided little help for these people, because their work activity often makes them ineligible for assistance. People working for the minimum wage rate generally fall below the poverty line, but as we saw in Chapter 10, if the minimum wage rate were increased to above-poverty-line levels, job opportunities for the low-income group could be reduced.

Sources of Income for the Poor

Low-income Canadians, particularly those over 65, receive a high proportion of their income in the form of *transfer payments* from governments. These transfer payments include Employment Insurance, welfare, Canada and Quebec Pension Plan benefits, the federal Old Age Security pension and Guaranteed Income Supplement, the federal Child Tax Benefit and the federal GST credit. For poor seniors, over 90 percent of their income comes from transfer payments, while younger poor people rely upon transfer payments for 40–50 percent of their incomes.

Trends in Poverty Rates

As Figure 11-13 shows, the poverty rate has generally followed quite closely the general condition of Canada's economy. When the economy grows and the unemployment rate falls, the poverty rate falls as well; however, when recessions such as occurred in the early 1980s and early 1990s cause the unemployment rate to rise, the poverty rate also increases.

However, Figure 11-13 also shows that during the 1990s a different trend emerged, with the poverty rate *rising* over a period during which the unemployment rate *declined*. One possible explanation of this trend is the growing gap between the incomes of highly skilled workers and the less skilled that was described earlier in this chapter. It is too early to determine whether this is a longer-term trend or a temporary aberration.

Finally, it can be seen from Figure 11-14 that poverty rates vary quite widely across the country, ranging in 2001 (on a before-tax basis) from a low of 11.7 percent in Ontario to 17.6 percent in Newfoundland and Labrador and 17.2 percent in Quebec.

In Conclusion

While there are different views as to how *poverty* should be defined and how many poor people there really are, there are some matters upon which there is fairly broad agreement. The risk of having a low income is greatest among single-parent mothers and unattached young people, and lower levels of education increases the risk of poverty considerably.

Women have a higher risk of poverty than men, especially single mothers, younger unattached women with low levels of education, and elderly women living on

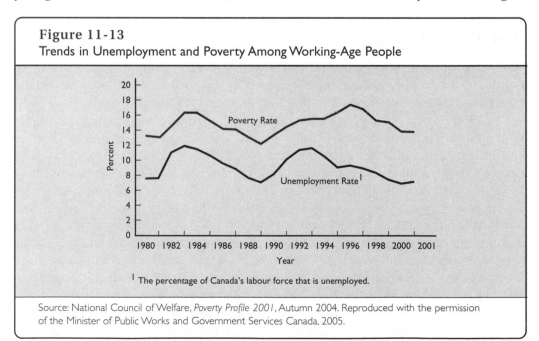

Figure 11-13
Trends in Unemployment and Poverty Among Working-Age People

[1] The percentage of Canada's labour force that is unemployed.

Source: National Council of Welfare, *Poverty Profile 2001*, Autumn 2004. Reproduced with the permission of the Minister of Public Works and Government Services Canada, 2005.

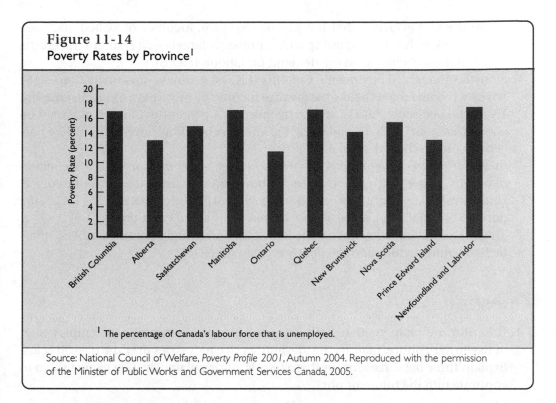

Figure 11-14
Poverty Rates by Province[1]

[1] The percentage of Canada's labour force that is unemployed.

Source: National Council of Welfare, *Poverty Profile 2001*, Autumn 2004. Reproduced with the permission of the Minister of Public Works and Government Services Canada, 2005.

their own. In the past, seniors have had a high incidence of poverty due to the inadequacy of many pension plans. However, as pensions and government assistance to seniors have improved, and many retirees have benefited from selling their homes at high prices, poverty has become much less of a "seniors' problem" and more of a "youth problem" and "women's problem." Also, child poverty has become more of an issue in Canada in recent years, in large part due to the persistently high poverty rates of younger parents, especially single mothers.

Chapter Summary

1. Due to changes in technology and demand, the composition of Canada's labour force has changed greatly since 1950. Employment in the goods-producing sector has increased only slightly, whereas employment in the services sector has increased greatly. (L.O.1)

2. The increased participation of women in the labour market has been the outstanding trend in the labour force since 1950. This trend is due to various factors, including higher education levels and aspirations among women, the need to add to family incomes, the need of more women to be self-supporting, and the growth of job opportunities in the service sector. (L.O. 2)

3. The average real family income of Canadians in 2002 was almost three times as high as in 1951, with most of the increase occurring by 1976. Since then, family income has grown more slowly, due to slower growth of both productivity and the number of income-earners per family. (L.O. 3)

4. There exists a pay differential between men and women of about 10 percent that is attributed to gender factors. In particular, women have tended to be concentrated in certain occupational groupings within which many jobs have below-average incomes. (L.O. 4)

5. There is some evidence that the gap between the incomes of skilled and less-skilled workers has been growing wider, probably largely as a result of the effects of technological change on the demand for labour. (L.O. 5)

6. Statistics Canada's Low-Income Cut-Offs (LICOs) estimate how many Canadians have an income that is below the average income by more than a certain amount. Using the before-tax LICOs as poverty lines, 14.4 percent of Canadians would be classed as "poor" in 2001, and using the after-tax LICOs as poverty lines, 10.4 percent would be classed as poor. (L.O. 6)

7. In 1998, Canada's governments adopted a *market basket measure* (MBM) definition of poverty, under which poverty lines are based on the cost of the necessities of life. Under the MBM poverty lines, which are roughly 20 percent lower than the LICOs, the number of Canadians classed as poor decreased by about one-third. (L.O. 6)

8. The risk of having a low income is highest among single-parent mothers, unattached young people, and the poorly educated. (L.O. 7)

Questions

1. Describe the changes that have occurred in the distribution of employment between agriculture, manufacturing, and service industries over the past 50 years. Explain three basic reasons for these trends, and explain why you expect them to continue into the future or not.

2. Most observers expect that the rapid increase of the labour force participation rate of women will level off, or at least increase much more slowly in the future. What explains the rapid increase of the female participation rate of the past few decades, and why would it be expected to increase more slowly or level off in the future?

3. After the late 1970s, the growth of real average family income in Canada slowed considerably. What is "real" income, and why did it grow more rapidly before the late 1970s, then much more slowly since then? In the future, what would be the most likely cause of any increases in the real average family income of Canadians?

4. The text describes the pay gap between males and females for full-time work.
   (a) How large is this gap, and what are the reasons for it?
   (b) Would you expect the male–female pay gap to widen or become smaller in the future? Why?

5. The text refers to indications of an increasing gap between the incomes of people with higher levels of education and skill and those with less education and skill. Why has this pay gap been widening? If this gap were to continue to grow, what would be the implications for social trends and problems in Canada? How might government policies help to reduce or ease any such problems?

6. Explain the reasoning behind the following statement: "If Canada were to continue to use the LICOs as its measure of poverty, Canada's poverty problem would not only appear to be larger than it really is, but also would quite likely appear to be *becoming larger* in the future."

7. Would using market basket measure poverty lines reduce or eliminate the problems described in question 6? Why?

8. Visit the Statistics Canada website (**www.statcan.ca**) and click on, in sequence, *Canadian Statistics > Tables by subject > Labour > Labour force characteristics > Employment by industry*.

   What are the recent trends regarding employment by industry in Canada, and what might explain these trends?

Study Guide

Review Questions (Answers to these Review Questions appear in Appendix B.)

1. State whether each of the following accurately describes trends in the distribution of employment in Canada over the past half-century. (Answer *yes* or *no* for each.)
   (a) _____ Employment in the service industries has increased much faster than employment in the goods industries.
   (b) _____ Manufacturing workers comprise a smaller proportion of the work force than 50 years ago.
   (c) _____ Agricultural employment has remained almost stable.
   (d) _____ Employment in the service-industry sector of the economy has grown at about the same pace as total employment in the economy.

2. The changes in the labour force described in question 1 have been caused by
   (a) changes in production technology.
   (b) changes in government policies.
   (c) changes in consumer demand patterns.
   (d) increasing international trade and competition.
   (e) Answers (a) and (c) and (d) together.

3. As living standards have increased, the average Canadian family has tended to
   (a) spend more on services, thereby creating more jobs in service industries.
   (b) increase the percentage of its income spent on food products, thereby creating more jobs in the agricultural sector.
   (c) reduce its spending on manufactured goods, which explains the slow growth of employment in the manufacturing sector.
   (d) spend about the same percentage of its income on food, manufactured goods, and services as it always did.
   (e) None of the above.

4. Which of the following are results of the changes in technology and living standards that occurred over the past century? (Answer *yes* or *no* for each.)
   (a) _____ the growth of large cities
   (b) _____ great increases in employment in the manufacturing sector
   (c) _____ rising educational requirements for workers
   (d) _____ larger families
   (e) _____ fewer jobs in the agricultural sector
   (f) _____ increased employment of women
   (g) _____ growth of part-time work
   (h) _____ government policies to restrict immigration

5. If a country's population is 13 million and there are 10 million people of working age and 6.5 million of them participate in the labour force (by either working or seeking work), the labour force participation rate for that country is
   (a) 89 percent.
   (b) 77 percent.
   (c) 65 percent.
   (d) 50 percent.
   (e) None of the above.

6. What has been the trend in male and female labour force participation rates over the past 50 years?
   (a) a slight decrease in the male rate and a large increase in the female rate
   (b) a large decrease in the male rate and a slight increase in the female rate
   (c) an increase in both the male rate and the female rate
   (d) a slight decrease in both the male rate and the female rate
   (e) a slight decrease in the female rate and a slight increase in the male rate

7. In the 1950s, 1960s, and 1970s, average real family incomes in Canada increased quite rapidly, due to
   (a) lower unemployment.
   (b) increases in the number of hours worked per week.
   (c) rising worker productivity.
   (d) increases in the number of income earners per family.
   (e) Answers (c) and (d) together.

8. After the late 1970s, the growth of average real income per family slowed, due to _____ and _____.

9. Most studies show that women earn about
   (a) 50 percent of what men earn for full-time work.
   (b) 63 percent of what men earn for full-time work.
   (c) 70 percent of what men earn for full-time work.
   (d) 80 percent of what men earn for full-time work.
   (e) 90 percent of what men earn for full-time work.

10. If pay differences due to hours worked, and productivity factors such as training, education, and experience are eliminated, the remaining male–female wage gap that is best explained by "gender factors" is estimated to be roughly _____ percent.

11. The pay gap in question 10 is mainly the result of
    (a) pay discrimination.
    (b) many women having part-time jobs.
    (c) the average age of working women being lower than that of men.
    (d) women interrupting their careers to have babies.
    (e) many women being concentrated in a few job areas that are relatively low-paying.

12. The *poverty line* is
    (a) the percentage of people who are considered to be poor.
    (b) people waiting at the welfare office for their welfare cheques.
    (c) an income that is 50 percent below the national average.
    (d) the income level below which people are considered to be poor.
    (e) None of the above.

13. The *poverty rate* is
    (a) the percentage of any group that has an income below the poverty line.
    (b) the hourly wage rate below which a person is considered to be poor.
    (c) the percentage of families whose income is below the Canadian average income.
    (d) an income less than $20 000 per year.
    (e) None of the above.

14. The use of Statistics Canada's Low-Income Cut-Offs (LICOs) as poverty lines is an illustration of defining the poverty line as an income that is
    (a) not large enough to purchase the necessities of life.
    (b) too far below the average income.
    (c) less than one-half of the national average income.

(d) less than one-third of the national average income.

(e) None of the above.

15. If Statistics Canada's before-tax Low-Income Cut-Offs (LICOs) are used as poverty lines, the conclusion would be that, in 2001, approximately

(a) 5–6 percent of the population had incomes below the poverty line.

(b) 10 percent of the population had incomes below the poverty line.

(c) 14–15 percent of the population had incomes below the poverty line.

(d) 20–21 percent of the population had incomes below the poverty line.

(e) 29–30 percent of the population had incomes below the poverty line.

16. In late 1998, Canada's governments adopted a new definition of *poverty* and new poverty lines based on the *market basket measure* (MBM) approach. Under the MBM approach, a family would be considered poor if its income was

(a) not large enough to purchase the necessities of life.

(b) less than one-quarter of the national average income.

(c) less than one-third of the national average income.

(d) less than one-half of the national average income.

(e) None of the above.

17. The poverty-line incomes under the market basket measure (MBM) definition are

(a) lower than the LICO-based poverty lines.

(b) about the same as the LICO-based poverty lines.

(c) higher than the LICO-based poverty lines.

18. If the market basket measure (MBM) poverty lines are used, the poverty rate is

(a) higher than if the before-tax Low-Income Cut-Offs are used as poverty lines.

(b) about the same as if the before-tax Low-Income Cut-Offs are used as poverty lines.

(c) lower than if the before-tax Low-Income Cut-Offs are used as poverty lines.

19. Three groups with a high risk of poverty are

(a)

(b) _____

(c) _____

Critical Thinking Questions

(Asterisked questions 1 to 5 are answered in Appendix B; the answers to questions 6 to 10 are in the Instructor's Manual that accompanies this text.)

*1. "One of the fundamental underlying causes of the great increase in the role played by women in the labour force was technological change." Explain the reasoning behind this statement. Do you agree? Why or why not?

*2. In 2001, poor women over 65 outnumbered poor men over 65 by about 4 to 1 (365 000 women to 95 000 men, based on before-tax incomes). What might explain why so many more of Canada's older poor people are women than are men?

*3. Some of the *working poor* earn less than they would receive if they went onto welfare and did not work at all. Why, then, do you think they decide to work?

*4. Under many social assistance (welfare) programs, the benefits that people receive are *below* the Low-Income Cut-Offs that many regard as the *poverty line*. What might explain this seeming inconsistency?

*5. Write an explanation of why some people think that poverty is a very serious problem in Canada, while others believe that it is a relatively small problem. Why is the debate over the extent of poverty an important matter?

6. The labour force participation rate of women decreases quite sharply after age 55.

(a) Why do you think so many women leave the labour force after 55?

(b) What effect would this tendency have on the average incomes of women as compared to men?

(c) Would you expect the participation rate of women over 55 to increase or decrease in the future? Why?

(d) How would the change in part (c) affect the male–female pay gap?

7. Why do you think women outnumber men by about four to three in university undergraduate programs, and what are the implications of this for the labour force and the male–female pay gap of tomorrow?

8. Look at the poverty lines in Table 11-3 on page 251.

(a) To you, do these incomes seem to be reasonable approximations of what individuals and families need in order to barely escape poverty? Why or why not?

(b) Why do you think the poverty line for a single person living in a city of over 500 000 is $20 101, while for a couple in the same city it is only $25 127?

9. Unattached men and women under 65, most of them young people, account for about 23 percent of all poverty in Canada. For such individuals living in cities of over 500 000, the National Council of Welfare's poverty line in 2004 was a before-tax income of $20 101 per year, and an after-tax income of $16 600.

(a) What does the fact that the after-tax poverty line is $3500 less than the before-tax poverty line tell you about Canada's personal income tax system? What might explain this aspect of the personal income tax?

(b) Would you support changes to the personal income tax that would mean that no taxes were payable on incomes up to $20 000? Explain the reasons for your answer.

(c) "If the poverty line for these people is $20 101, the government should do whatever it takes to guarantee that these people receive an annual income of at least $20 101." (This would be the equivalent of working 40 hours per week for 50 weeks at a wage rate of just over $10 per hour.) Explain why you agree or disagree with this statement.

10. If we use the *before-tax* LICO incomes as poverty lines, 14.4 percent of Canadians are classed as poor in 2001. If we use the *after-tax* LICOs as poverty lines, only 10.4 percent of Canadians are classed as poor. But the poor do not pay much if any income tax. So why are so many fewer Canadians classed as poor if we use after-tax incomes as the measuring stick?

Use the Web (Hints for these Use the Web exercises appear in Appendix B.)

1. Visit the Statistics Canada website (**www.statcan.ca**) and click on, in sequence, *Canadian Statistics > Tables by subject > Labour > Labour force characteristics > Labour force and participation rates by sex and age group.*

What are the recent trends regarding the labour force participation rates of various groups, and what might explain these trends?

2. Visit the Statistics Canada website (**www.statcan.ca**) and search *The Daily* for "family income."

What are the most recent trends regarding family income in Canada, and what might be the reasons for these trends?

3. Visit the Statistics Canada website and search *The Daily* for "university enrolment."

What are the most recent trends regarding male and female university enrolment in Canada, and what might explain these trends?

The Government Sector

After studying this chapter, you should be able to

1. Describe the three key types of programs that comprise Canada's social welfare system.

2. List the four main sources of government tax revenue, and explain the advantages and disadvantages of each of these.

3. Explain the difference between progressive and regressive taxes, and identify taxes as either progressive or regressive.

4. Given data concerning a person's income and income taxes payable, calculate the marginal tax rate paid by that person, and explain how marginal tax rates affect incentives.

5. Summarize how Canadian governments' transfer payments and income taxes redistribute income among Canadians.

6. Describe the purposes of federal government transfer payments to the provincial governments.

7. Distinguish between reasonable and unwise uses of debt, and explain the relationship between a government's budget deficits and its debt and the dangers of excessive deficits.

8. Summarize the problems of growing federal government budget deficits and debt after 1975, how this problem reached a crisis point in 1993, and how measures to resolve it affected health care, education, and income support programs.

9. Explain how government income support programs can create disincentives to work.

10. Identify the three basic alternative uses for the federal government budget surpluses that developed after 1997, and state the arguments in favour of each of these.

We have seen how, in a market economy, the incentives of profits and competition will lead privately owned businesses (the *private sector*) to do a very good job of providing high living standards, by producing goods and services both effectively and efficiently, without government guidance.

However, a market economy will not automatically provide accessible public services such as health care and education, and it generates extreme inequalities in the distribution of income. In addition, a market system provides incentives for various socially undesirable actions by businesses, such as misleading consumers, exploiting workers, using unfair competitive tactics, monopolizing markets, polluting the environment and so on. These problems mean that while the marketplace is the source of many economic benefits, it also has weaknesses, so there is a role for government in a market economy. In this chapter, we will consider various aspects of that role.

As discussed in Chapter 2, the Canadian economy is characterized as a *mixed free-enterprise* economic system. With about 80 percent of economic activity being carried out by private businesses in response to the demand of buyers, the economy is basically "market" in nature. However, there is also a substantial amount of *government involvement* in the economy. As we saw in Chapter 2, governments provide extensive *public services*, such as health care and education, and they own and operate various enterprises, such as the Canadian Broadcasting Corporation and Canada Post. In addition, government taxation and transfer payment programs *redistribute income* from those with higher incomes to those with less, and *government regulations* establish in countless ways the economic "rules of play" for Canadian businesses, workers, and consumers, from advertising practices to employment standards.

Furthermore, the role of government in the Canadian economy has grown considerably over the years. While the federal government attracts the most public attention, spending by *provincial* and *local (municipal)* governments has exceeded federal government spending since the mid-1960s. The reason is that the provinces have the primary responsibility for education and health care, both of which have expanded greatly since the 1960s.

Figure 12-1 shows the growth of the grand total of spending by all three levels of government—federal, provincial, and local—on all government programs, such as

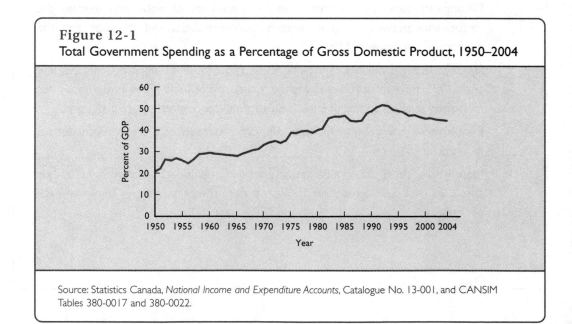

Figure 12-1
Total Government Spending as a Percentage of Gross Domestic Product, 1950–2004

Source: Statistics Canada, *National Income and Expenditure Accounts*, Catalogue No. 13-001, and CANSIM Tables 380-0017 and 380-0022.

health care, education, employment insurance, welfare, pensions, national defence, police, firefighters, subsidies to businesses, plus interest on government debt. After many years of growth, total government spending reached a peak in 1992 of 52 percent of Canada's Gross Domestic Product. Figure 12-1 shows another important aspect of government spending—its decrease as a percentage of GDP since 1992, a development that we will examine later in this chapter.

Impressive though they may be, these spending statistics understate the role of government in the economy by a considerable amount. They do not include the activities of government-owned *Crown corporations* such as Canada Post and the Canadian Broadcasting Corporation, nor do they include the myriad of *government regulations* of economic activity that have been enacted over the years.

So, the role of government in the Canadian economy has expanded greatly over the past half-century. In this chapter, we will examine the reasons for this growth, and look at recent developments and possible future trends with respect to the role of government in the Canadian economy.

The Growth of Canada's Social Welfare Programs

As we have seen, Canadian governments spend substantial amounts of money on social welfare programs, with most of it going to the three key areas of *income security* (such as Employment Insurance, welfare, and pensions), *health care,* and *education.* Government spending on these programs has risen dramatically during the twentieth century. Why has this happened?

In the most basic sense, the growth of the social welfare system was brought about by the transition from a rural farming society of small communities to a modern, urban society with a large industrial work force. In the earlier society of small, closely knit, and stable communities, traditional institutions such as the family, the church, the local community, and private charity were able to provide for the needs of those who required assistance. However, as Canada evolved into an urban society with a large, mobile work force of industrial employees, the situation changed significantly. People and families were exposed to increased risks of loss of income due to unemployment (or layoff), illness, disability, and old age. And as the traditional social institutions became less able to provide for Canadians' social needs, it became increasingly necessary for governments to provide assistance to those who needed it.

The growth of the government's role acquired considerable momentum from the Great Depression of the 1930s. The Depression destroyed faith in the laissez-faire philosophy that the economy could be counted upon to automatically provide employment for all who wanted it and that people could therefore be expected to take care of themselves economically. By doing so, the Depression made much more acceptable the idea that the government should provide assistance to the victims of economic forces beyond their control in the form of benefits for those without jobs and incomes of their own.

"Income security, health, and education represent central supports of the welfare state."
— ROYAL COMMISSION ON THE ECONOMIC UNION AND DEVELOPMENT PROSPECTS FOR CANADA (OTTAWA, MINISTER OF SUPPLY AND SERVICES, 1985).

Income Security Programs

In the decades that followed the Great Depression, Canada's social welfare programs expanded greatly. In the field of *income security programs*, unemployment insurance was introduced in 1942, Family Allowances in 1945, Old Age Security in 1952, various social assistance programs in the 1950s, the Canada and Quebec Pension Plans in 1965, the Canada Assistance Plan for social welfare and the Guaranteed Income Supplement in 1966, the Spouses' Allowance in 1975, and the Child Tax Credit in 1978. Also, in the 1970s, benefits under the Unemployment Insurance and Family Allowance programs were increased significantly.

Another important, although less visible, way in which governments support people's incomes is through **tax credits** in the income tax system. These tax credits reduce the income taxes payable by Canadians in order to offset a variety of factors that adversely affect their living standards, from children and other dependants to sales taxes and property taxes. Some of these tax credits are structured so that they benefit only lower-income individuals and families, partly by reducing the taxes that they pay, and in some cases entitling them to tax refunds.

tax credits
Credits that reduce the income taxes payable by Canadians in order to offset a variety of factors that adversely affect their living standards, including dependants, property taxes, and sales taxes.

www.cihi.ca

Health Care

Health care represents the second key element of Canada's social welfare system. Health care can be extremely expensive, exposing individuals and families to the risk of heavy costs and even financial ruin. As a result, it was decided as a matter of social policy that all Canadians should have access to health care without having to pay the costs themselves, giving Canadians one of the most liberal health-care systems in the world. Following the introduction of hospital insurance and medicare programs, government expenditures on health care grew to one of the largest government-spending programs. The Canadian Institute for Health Information (CIHI) estimates total government spending on health care in 2003 to be almost $85 billion.

Education

Education, which represents the third pillar of Canada's social welfare system, is completely financed by tax revenues in the case of primary and secondary education. Post-secondary education is subsidized by governments through grants to colleges and universities that allow them to charge tuition fees that represent a relatively small proportion of the cost of students' education. These government expenditures are justified in part on economic grounds, as an investment in the "human capital" needed by a modern economy. Also, government support of education is seen as a key aspect of social policy, as a means of providing equality of opportunity for all Canadians to obtain the education needed for their lives and careers. Canadian governments spend about 6 percent of GDP on education ($69 billion in 2003-04), which is fairly high by international standards.

Taken together, these programs involve a great deal of government spending. In 2004, program spending (spending on all items other than interest on government debt) by all levels of government in Canada amounted to $443 billion, or more than $13 800 for every Canadian man, woman, and child. This brings us to the question of how governments raise all the revenues to pay for these expenditures.

Paying For It: Sources of Government Revenues

consumption taxes
Taxes levied when consumers buy goods and services; for example, sales taxes.

In 2004, Canadians paid about $424 billion in taxes of various sorts.

There are four basic types of taxes that pay for government spending:
- taxes on *incomes* (personal and business income taxes),
- taxes on *spending* (sales taxes, or **consumption taxes**),

- taxes on *assets* (mainly, property taxes), and
- taxes on *employers' payrolls* (such as Canada Pension Plan and employment insurance premiums).

These taxes raise the funds that provide us with government services and benefits. But each type of tax also brings its own type of costs to the economy, as we will see in the following sections.

Taxes on Incomes

Taxes on incomes such as personal income taxes and business profits taxes are the largest tax source in Canada, mainly because they can be applied to millions of people and businesses. The personal income tax alone raises about 34 percent of all tax revenues collected by governments in Canada.

A key feature of the personal income tax is that the rate of taxation (the percentage of income taken by taxes) can be tailored to people's ability to pay. People with low incomes can pay a low percentage of their income to taxes or none at all, while people with high incomes can be taxed at much higher rates. Taxes that take a higher percentage of the incomes of the "rich" than of the "poor" are known as **progressive taxes**. The most prominent of these is the personal income tax, and in the view of many, this makes the personal income tax a particularly fair tax. And the personal income tax is more progressive than many Canadians believe: according to Statistics Canada, in 2002 the 10 percent of Canadian tax filers with the highest incomes paid almost 53 percent of all federal income taxes paid.

The major limitation regarding income taxes is that if the rate of taxation becomes *too* high, it can have a negative effect on incentives to work, save, and invest. The key here is what economists call the **marginal tax rate**, which is the tax rate payable on any *additional* income that is earned over and above one's present income.

progressive taxes
Taxes that take a higher percentage of high incomes than of low incomes.

marginal tax rate
The percentage of any additional income that is earned that goes to taxes.

The Marginal Tax Rate

Let's illustrate with an example. If Fred earns $40 000 per year working in a library and pays income taxes of $8000, he is paying a 20-percent tax rate on his income—on average, he pays 20 cents in taxes on every dollar he earns. This, however, is not Fred's marginal tax rate—his *marginal* tax rate is the percentage of any *additional* income that he earns that goes to taxes. For instance, suppose that Fred works nights as a professional wrestler and earns *an additional* $10 000. If he has to pay $3500 in income taxes *on this $10 000 of extra income*, his marginal tax rate is 35 percent.

It is the marginal tax rate that affects Fred's incentive to work, because it applies to extra income that Fred can decide to earn or not earn. Even if the tax rate on Fred's main income as a librarian is increased sharply, he has little choice but to continue working—he needs this main source of his income. But a sharp increase in the marginal tax rate on his *extra* income as a wrestler might cause him to decide to retire from the ring, or wrestle less often.

High marginal tax rates can generate disincentives in various ways. As the example of Fred shows, high marginal tax rates can discourage people from working overtime or at a second job, or from saving and investing money in order to earn investment income. High marginal tax rates on business profits can discourage the capital investment that improves efficiency, or even discourage businesses from investing in the country or province with those high tax rates. So marginal tax rates that are high enough to create disincentives to work, save, and invest will have negative effects on productivity and on the economic prosperity of society.

Taxes on Consumption

Another basic type of tax is *taxes on spending* by consumers. The most visible such taxes are of course provincial sales taxes (PST) and the goods and services tax (GST); however, the very high taxes on tobacco, alcohol, and gasoline are also consumption taxes. By taxing a broad base of consumer spending, sales taxes can be a significant source of revenue for governments—for instance, revenues from the GST alone amount to roughly $30 billion per year.

The main disadvantage of sales taxes is that they are **regressive**—that is, they take a higher percentage of the incomes of low-income earners than from those with high incomes. Certainly, the rich pay *more dollars* in sales taxes than the poor do, because they buy much more. But the poor pay *a higher percentage* of their income to sales taxes, because their incomes are so low. This is why sales taxes are more burdensome to lower-income people than to those with higher incomes.

Taxes on Assets

The third major source of tax revenue is *taxes on assets*. The largest of these is *property taxes*, which are a major source of revenue for local governments—about $35 billion in 2003.

Because they apply to fewer people (those who own particular types of assets, mainly real estate), these taxes raise less revenue than either income or sales taxes. In addition, property taxes often are regressive, in that they take a larger percentage of the incomes of low-income people than of those with high incomes. As with sales taxes, the rich pay more dollars in property taxes, but people with low incomes pay a higher percentage of their income to these taxes, as illustrated by the case of Pat and Patricia.

Taxes on Payrolls

Payroll taxes are levied on employers, based on the *size of their payroll*. These taxes include employment insurance premiums, Canada Pension Plan premiums, workers' compensation premiums, and, in some provinces, a tax to help pay for the costs of health care and post-secondary education. These taxes must be paid whether the employers make a profit or not.

The problem with payroll taxes is that they amount to taxes on employing people, in the sense that the more people a firm employs, the higher the taxes it must pay. Studies estimate that, on average, payroll taxes add close to 8 percent to Canadian employers' payroll costs—that is, to the cost of employing people. Furthermore, the burden of these taxes falls especially heavily on small businesses, many of which are much more labour-intensive than most larger businesses. As a result, payroll taxes are criticized for discouraging hiring by the small business sector, which has created a high proportion of new jobs in Canada in recent years.

How Much Do Government Programs Redistribute Income?

One major aspect of Canada's social welfare system is *public services* such as health care and education, as described earlier in this chapter. The other major component of the social welfare system is *redistribution of income* from people with higher

regressive tax
A tax that takes a higher percentage of low incomes than of high incomes.

Patricia earns $40 000 and owns a house on which she pays property taxes of $2000 per year. Her property taxes amount to 5 percent ($2000 ÷ $40 000) of her income. Pat earns $24 000 and lives in an apartment that he rents for $600 per month, or $7200 per year. Of this, approximately 20 percent, or $1440, goes to cover the property taxes paid by the landlord. Pat's property taxes amount to 6 percent ($1440 ÷ $24 000) of his income. In this case, the property tax is regressive—the person with the lower income pays a higher percentage of that income to property taxes than the higher-income person pays.

payroll taxes
Taxes paid by employers based on the number of their employees or the amount of their payroll.

In 2003–04, the federal government collected $17.5 billion in employment insurance premiums (taxes) and paid out $15.1 billion in Employment Insurance benefits.

incomes to those with low incomes. Income is redistributed by both the tax system and government transfer payments. Those with higher incomes pay a larger percentage of their incomes to taxes, mainly due to the progressive nature of the personal income tax. And those with lower incomes receive various types of transfer payments, such as welfare, pensions, and employment insurance benefits. The overall result of these programs is the redistribution of income that is reflected in Table 12-1.

There are three definitions of *income* used in Table 12-1:
- *Market income*, which is income earned in the marketplace (wages, salaries, investment income, etc.),
- *Total income*, which is market income plus government transfer payments, such as welfare or employment insurance benefits, and
- *Income after transfers and taxes*, which is total income less income taxes paid.

Table 12-1 shows that in 2003 an average family in the lowest 20 percent of income-earners earned $8600 in market income and received $13 800 in transfer payments, for a total income of $22 400. It paid income taxes of $900, leaving it with an income after transfers and taxes of $21 500. So, on balance, transfer payments and income tax *added* $12 900 to its income. At the other extreme, an average family in the highest 20 percent group earned $150 700 in market income, received $3200 of transfer payments, and paid $35 800 in income taxes and, so it *contributed* $32 600 to these redistribution programs.

Table 12-1
Redistribution of Income by Transfer Payments and Income Taxes, 2003
(for economic families with two or more people)

	Lowest 20% of incomes	Second 20% of incomes	Middle 20% of incomes	Fourth 20% of incomes	Highest 20% of incomes
Average market income	$8600	$31 900	$53 800	$79 400	$150 700
Average transfer Payments received	+13 800	+9900	+7100	+4900	+3200
Average total Income	22 400	41 800	60 900	84 300	153 900
Average income tax paid	−900	−4100	−8600	−14 500	−35 800
Average income after transfers and taxes	21 500	37 700	52 300	69 800	118 100
Net effect of transfers and taxes	+12 900	+5800	−1500	−9600	−32 600

Source: Adapted from Statistics Canada, CANSIM Table 202-0701.

Table 12-2 on page 268 summarizes the redistribution of income shown in Table 12-1, in terms of each group's share of total income before and after the government programs that redistribute income. The share of total income going to the lowest-income 20 percent of families was increased from 2.7 percent to 7.2 percent by the government's income taxes and transfer payments. At the other end of the scale, government programs decreased the share of total income going to the highest-income 20 percent of families from 46.4 percent to 39.4 percent. The impact on the middle three groups was relatively small, so the main effect of the governmental programs was to redistribute income from the highest group to the lowest group.

Table 12-2
Shares of Total Income Before and After Government Programs, 2003

	Share of Total Income, 2003[1]	
Income Group	Market Income	Income After Transfers and Income Taxes
Lowest 20%	2.7%	7.2%
Second 20%	9.8%	12.6%
Middle 20%	16.6%	17.5%
Fourth 20%	24.5%	23.3%
Highest 20%	46.4%	39.4%

[1] Economic families with two or more people.

Source: Adapted from Statistics Canada, CANSIM Table 202-0701.

Problems Financing Government Programs

As noted earlier, government social service programs (such as health care and education) and income redistribution programs (such as welfare and employment insurance) are costly to operate. And much of the burden of financing these programs is the responsibility of the provincial governments.

Under the Constitution, health care, education, and welfare are the responsibility of the provincial governments, not the federal government. After the mid-1960s, the rapid growth of spending on health care, education, and welfare put severe strains on the finances of provincial governments. By contrast, the federal government possesses greater taxation powers than the provinces, mainly because it levies the personal income tax, the largest single source of government revenue in Canada.

Federal Transfer Payments to the Provinces

One way that was developed to deal with this imbalance in taxation powers and spending responsibilities was for the federal government to transfer some of its revenues to the provinces to help to finance their programs in health care, post-secondary education, and welfare. These federal–provincial transfer payments grew rapidly, from about $1 billion in 1967 to nearly $27 billion in 1993, when they comprised almost 23 percent of total provincial government revenues. In the first half of the 1990s, the provinces were receiving transfer payments from the federal government amounting to almost $1000 per citizen per year, which the provincial governments were spending on health care, post-secondary education, and welfare.

Budgeting Basics

A government uses its budget to plan its revenues (mostly taxes) and expenditures for the next year, much as a family's budget is its financial plan for its income and spending. In 2004, the budgets of all levels of Canadian governments (federal, provincial, and local) involved nearly $500 billion of revenues and expenditures. These budgets had a significant influence on the key "what to produce" decision that we saw in Chapter 1, by directing resources into the production of social services such as education and health care. And as we have just seen, government budgets have considerable influence on the "how to divide it up" question, by transferring income from higher-income Canadians to those with lower incomes.

Uses and Misuses of Debt

In some years, a family may spend more than its income. For instance, a family may buy an asset such as a house or a car, and borrow money to finance this purchase. Provided that the asset is not too costly for debt repayments to be made out of the family's annual income, such borrowing is considered to be a reasonable decision. After all, the asset will last for years, so it is reasonable to pay for the asset over its lifetime. As shown in Figure 12-2, a decision to borrow to finance the purchase of an asset involves a *one-time* increase in debt, followed by a decrease in indebtedness as the debt is repaid over the life of the asset.

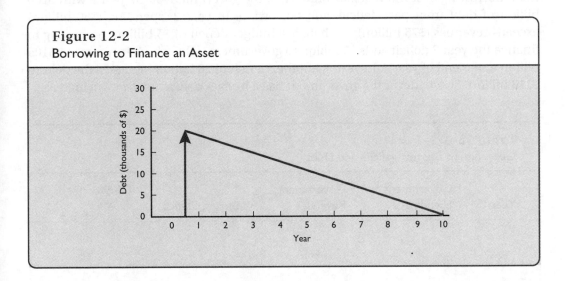

Figure 12-2
Borrowing to Finance an Asset

Borrowing to finance a one-time expenditure on an asset such as a car is one thing, but borrowing to pay ongoing expenses is a very different matter. For instance, if you borrowed to pay the costs of operating the car (say, $300 per month for gas, insurance, etc.), you would be adding to your debt every month. The result would be a steadily rising debt, as shown in Figure 12-3. The situation would be made worse by interest on the debt pushing your debt higher, in a sort of spiral that is the opposite of the well-managed debt portrayed in Figure 12-2.

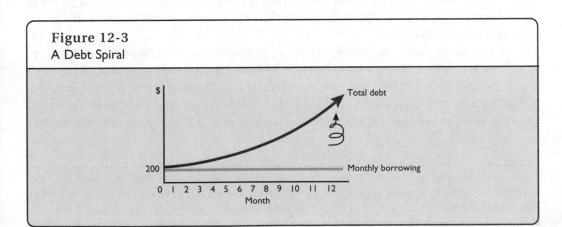

Figure 12-3
A Debt Spiral

Government Budget Deficits and Debt

Budget deficit
An excess of government spending over government revenues.

When a government's spending exceeds its revenues, it is said to have a **budget deficit**. If the extra spending is for the purpose of building "social assets" such as hospitals or schools, it can be compared to a family's borrowing to buy a house—the government is borrowing to acquire a long-term asset.[1] The government borrows by *selling government bonds*, most of which are long-term in nature—that is, repayable in 10 years or more. Such bonds are mostly bought as long-term investments by large institutional investors, such as pension funds, mutual funds, banks, and so on, although individuals buy them as well. Mostly, they are sold to Canadian investors, although foreign lenders can and do buy them as well.

The relationship between government budget deficits and government debt is shown in Table 12-3. The budget *deficit* is the excess of government spending over revenues for a year. Government *debt*, on the other hand, is the grand total of government borrowing over the years. In Table 12-3, the government starts year 2 with $100 billion of debt from past deficits and borrowing. In year 2, spending ($80 billion) exceeds revenues ($75 billion), so there is a budget deficit of $5 billion. Borrowing to finance the year 2 deficit adds $5 billion to government debt, which increases to $105 billion at the end of year 2. In year 3, another deficit of $8 billion increases the debt to $113 billion. So whenever the government has a budget *deficit*, its *debt* will increase.

Table 12-3
Government Budget Deficits and Debt

Year	Government Spending	Government Revenues	Budget Deficit	Government Debt
1	n.a.	n.a.	n.a.	$100
2	$80	$75	$5	105
3	88	80	8	113

A Brief History of Federal Budgets

During the 1970s, the federal government made a series of policy decisions that caused deficits and rising debt, as shown in Table 12-3. First, the government increased spending on various social programs, such as unemployment insurance and pensions, and made commitments to transfer large amounts of federal funds to the provincial governments to help finance their spending on health care, welfare, and post-secondary education.

At the same time, the federal government introduced various tax reductions, which had the effect of depressing its tax revenues. These spending and taxation decisions by the government caused an imbalance to develop between government spending and revenues, so that federal government spending regularly exceeded the government's revenues. Figure 12-4 shows that the federal government's budget

[1] It is also considered reasonable for the government to have budget deficits when the economy is in a recession, in order to increase spending in the economy; this is covered in my macroeconomics text, *Canadian Macroeconomics: Problems and Policies*, Eighth edition.

deficits after 1974 became not only *large*, but also a *regular annual event* until the late 1990s. This was a borrowing situation like the dangerous one shown in Figure 12-3, not the well-planned one in Figure 12-2.

To finance these large annual budget deficits, the federal government sold large volumes of bonds each year. In the process, the government's debt grew rapidly, as Figure 12-4 also shows. By the mid-1980s, both the size and the rate of growth of the federal government's debt were becoming serious concerns.

In the second half of the 1980s, the government restrained its spending and increased various taxes in an attempt to reduce its budget deficits. But by this point another factor was driving the federal budget deficit upward—*interest payments on the government's massive and growing debt.*

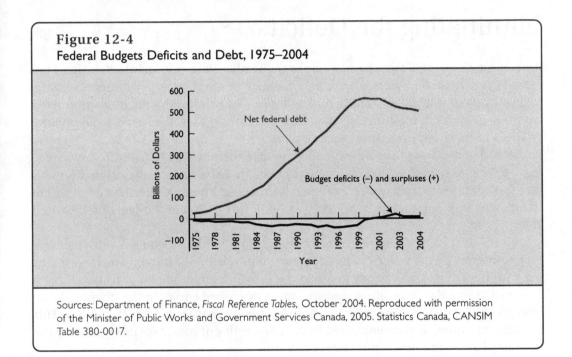

Figure 12-4
Federal Budgets Deficits and Debt, 1975–2004

Sources: Department of Finance, *Fiscal Reference Tables*, October 2004. Reproduced with permission of the Minister of Public Works and Government Services Canada, 2005. Statistics Canada, CANSIM Table 380-0017.

Provincial Budget Deficits

One way in which the federal government tried to reduce its budget deficits after 1985 was by limiting its transfer payments to the provincial governments for programs such as health care, welfare, and post-secondary education. The reduction in these transfer payments left the provinces with growing budget deficits of their own. When the recession of the early 1990s undercut provincial tax revenues and increased provincial spending on welfare, the combined budget deficits of the provincial governments soared to about $20 billion.

The Critical Point

Ultimately, a borrower can only borrow for as long as lenders are willing to lend. By 1993, the situation was becoming critical for Canada's governments. The combined budget deficits of the federal and provincial governments amounted to over $50 billion per year. The total net debt of all Canadian governments was over 90 percent of the GDP, and interest payments on the debt were driving it higher, in an upward spiral.

To finance their massive budget deficits, Canadian governments (mostly the provinces) had for several years been borrowing heavily from foreign lenders. Canada's debt to foreign lenders, about half of which was owed by Canadian governments, was by far the largest in the world and was rising rapidly.

But by the early 1990s, foreign lenders were becoming concerned about the very heavy debt of Canadian governments. The credit ratings of some provinces deteriorated, forcing the provinces to pay higher interest rates on their bonds in order to attract lenders. These developments forced both the provincial and federal governments to finally confront their budget problems and to make some difficult choices.

Eliminating the Deficits

As noted at the start of this chapter, Canada's social welfare system is built around the three keystones of *income security programs* (such as employment insurance, welfare, and pensions), *health care*, and *education*. The financial problems of governments were so great that they forced governments to consider the most fundamental changes to these key programs in many years.

"For years, governments have been promising more than they can deliver, and delivering more than they can afford. That has to end. We are ending it."
— FINANCE MINISTER PAUL MARTIN, 1994.

The only two ways for governments to reduce their budget deficits are to *increase taxes* or *reduce spending*. Taxes had already been increased so much during the 1980s that further tax increases were considered impossible. The only alternative left was to reduce government spending, which was done in the federal budgets of 1994 and 1995.

From 1993 to 1997, annual federal program spending (which is all spending except interest on the government's debt) was cut by over $11 billion. The largest cuts were to the federal transfer payments to the provinces that helped to finance health care, post-secondary education, and welfare as described earlier in this chapter. From 1993 to 1997, these transfer payments to the provinces were cut by 21 percent. This reduction in provincial revenues led in turn to a series of major spending cuts by the provincial governments on their own programs.

Health Care

Of all of Canada's social welfare programs, reform of the health-care system probably confronted governments with the most politically difficult challenge. Canadians have a strong attachment to their system of universal free health care, which they regard as both a major protection and a fundamental right. On the other hand, escalating health-care costs were pushing government budget deficits higher. After the federal government reduced its transfer payments to the provinces, the provincial governments cut back on health-care services in various ways, such as closing hospital beds, eliminating coverage for certain procedures, and restricting health-care coverage for Canadians outside the country. As the resources of the health-care system were unable to keep up with the demand for services, Canadians faced longer waits for many types of operations. A variety of other measures were proposed to control health-care costs, including reduced use of hospitals (the most costly method of health-care delivery), increased emphasis on prevention of health problems, and encouragement to doctors to help to curb excessive use of the health-care system.

Post-Secondary Education

Chapter 11 stressed the importance of education not only to the individual, in terms of access to better jobs and a rewarding career, but also to the economy, in terms of the higher productivity of a trained and educated work force. In addition, access to post-secondary education is a significant social issue: with post-secondary education so often the gateway to better jobs and careers, it is considered important as a matter of social policy that high costs not present an unfair barrier to members of lower-income families.

As a result, governments subsidized post-secondary education, so as to keep its cost within reach of people of modest means. This was done mainly through grants to colleges and universities that enabled them to keep tuition fees low; in addition, student loan programs were available to those who needed them. But as with health care costs, the cost of subsidizing education was contributing to government budget deficits.

When the federal government cut its transfer payments to the provinces, this forced very difficult choices upon colleges and universities. Various adjustments were made, including increasing students' tuition fees, limiting enrolment, and increasing class sizes, none of which were regarded as satisfactory.

Income Support Programs

By the mid-1990s, government transfer payments to persons were approaching $100 billion per year, and absorbing over one-quarter of government revenues. Such a large component of government spending could not escape the fight to eliminate budget deficits.

Faced with reductions in federal transfer payments, provincial governments reduced welfare benefits, in some cases by more than 20 percent. Various benefits payable to higher-income Canadians were reduced or eliminated, and the federal government reduced the benefits available under the employment insurance program.

In 2004, the average recipient of employment insurance benefits received $296.87 per week.

Incentives to Work

The question of transfer payments was complicated by the fact that there was reason to believe that Canada's income support programs were reducing the incentive to work. While many people feel that welfare recipients are simply lazy and prefer welfare to working, the situation is usually more complex than this.

A welfare system will discourage welfare recipients from working if for every dollar a welfare recipient earns by working, his or her welfare benefits are reduced by so much that there is little or no incentive to work. It is not the *intention* of the welfare system to kill incentives. Rather, the system tries to focus benefits on those who need them—and the more a recipient earns, the less welfare he or she needs. So as earned income rises, welfare benefits will be reduced. But to welfare recipients, this can mean that if they earn some income by working, their welfare benefits will be reduced by so much that it is not worth working. This has the same effect as a *very high marginal tax rate* on their income: it reduces the incentive to earn income and to get off the welfare system (see the cases of Joan and Sandy in the "You Decide" box on the next page).

YOU DECIDE

The Marginal Tax Rate and the Economic Incentive to Work

The *marginal tax rate* is the percentage of any extra income that is earned which goes to taxes. Because it determines how much of any additional income a person gets to keep, the marginal tax rate is very important to the incentive to work; specifically, the higher the marginal tax rate, the lower the economic incentive to do additional work.

We will consider the marginal tax rates of two people. Joan, a teacher, is wondering whether to teach a night course. The course would pay her $1000, but after taxes, Joan would receive only $600, because her marginal tax rate is 40 percent. Joan complains that there is little incentive for her to teach the night course because of these high taxes, which go to support people whom she describes as "lazy welfare bums."

Sandy is on welfare, receiving $800 per month. If she earns $100 per month working part-time, her welfare will be reduced to $720 per month, leaving her $20 better off for having earned $100. In other words, Sandy's marginal tax rate is 80 percent. Sandy declines the job on the grounds that it's not worth the trouble. ■

QUESTIONS

1. Is Sandy just being "lazy"?
2. If we want to get Sandy off welfare and working, what kinds of changes do we need to make to the welfare system?

Studies of this problem have estimated that many recipients of social welfare gain so little by working that if they do work, they are in a similar position to someone who is paying a marginal tax rate of *from 80 to 100 percent*. In some cases, this can work as a "trap" in which welfare recipients become caught indefinitely. To escape from this trap, a person usually has to find a reasonably steady full-time job, so as to break completely clear of the welfare system. But unless one has skills and experience, it is unlikely that this can be achieved, so the welfare cycle tends to go on and on, from year to year, and even from generation to generation.

In an attempt to improve work incentives, some social assistance plans have been modified to allow recipients to earn at least some income without suffering a reduction in their welfare benefits. Such changes do help to improve the incentive for welfare recipients to earn some income by working at part-time jobs. But beyond a certain level of earned income, their welfare benefits are reduced, and if this reduction occurs too rapidly, the same disincentive effect will occur, although at a higher level of earned income.

Advocates of reform to the social welfare system argue that there are real benefits in improving the work incentives in the system. This would help to keep welfare recipients in the work force (even if only combining part-time work with their welfare) and earning both income and self-esteem, rather than passively relying on welfare. Also, by encouraging welfare recipients to earn more, it could actually reduce their reliance on welfare and thus reduce the total amount of welfare benefits that governments pay out, thus helping to reduce the cost to society.

On the other hand, improving incentives is not a simple matter. The more people earn, the less welfare they need, so it is reasonable to reduce benefits as earned income increases. The key is to not reduce benefits so rapidly that there is little or no incentive for welfare recipients to earn income.

After the Deficits: How to Use the Surpluses?

The cuts to government spending brought the spending side of government budgets under control, as can be seen in Figure 12-1 on page 262. Over the same period, government tax revenues increased considerably. This was not due to increases in tax rates, but rather to rapid economic growth, which generated not only jobs, incomes, sales and profits, but also tax revenues on all of these.

With spending down and tax revenues up, the federal deficit was eliminated by 1998, when the federal government posted its first budget surplus since 1970. This was followed by surpluses over the next seven years, which led to an unexpected turn of events—the next public debate would be over how to use government budget *surpluses*!

The deficits of the past and the battle to eliminate them had left various scars on Canadians: heavy government debt, reduced public services, and high taxes. There were therefore three basic ways to use the government surpluses: *reduce government debt, increase government spending,* or *reduce taxes.*

Reduce Government Debt?

Federal and provincial government deficits had left Canada with a massive government debt that was costing taxpayers $75 billion per year in interest in the late 1990s. This burden made it attractive for the government to use part of its budget surpluses to reduce its debt. The federal government's net debt was reduced from a peak of $588 billion in 1997 to $524 billion by 2004. This is reflected in Figure 12-5, which shows federal debt as a percentage of the size of the country's economy (Gross Domestic Product, or GDP).

But by 2004, debt reduction had become a less urgent priority. Interest on its debt was absorbing only 19 percent of the federal government's revenues, as compared to 38 percent in 1996. And projections showed that if the government reduced the debt

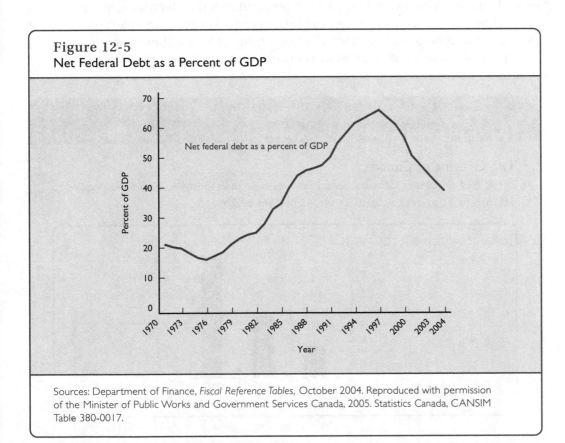

Figure 12-5
Net Federal Debt as a Percent of GDP

Sources: Department of Finance, *Fiscal Reference Tables*, October 2004. Reproduced with permission of the Minister of Public Works and Government Services Canada, 2005. Statistics Canada, CANSIM Table 380-0017.

by \$5 billion each year, the debt would be about 10 percent of GDP by 2028, as compared to 13 percent if the government did not reduce the debt at all. (With debt constant, debt as a percent of GDP would decrease as GDP grew.) This raised the question of other uses for those federal surpluses.

Increase Government Spending?

Reductions in federal transfers to the provinces had undercut the nation's social welfare system in ways that concerned many Canadians. The cuts to health care spending had left hospitals with inadequate staffing and many Canadians waiting for medical care that they required. There was concern whether the nation's health care system would be able to deal with Canadians' needs as the baby boomers aged. Public opinion polls showed that Canadians placed the highest priority on health care, and were very concerned about the effects of spending cutbacks. In the field of education, cuts in grants to colleges and universities had led to large increases in tuition that left graduates with heavy debt loads from student loans. And cuts to the social welfare system had left many worse off than before, and had turned onto the streets people who had previously been cared for in public institutions.

Reduce Taxes?

Finally, the tax increases that had been a major aspect of the deficit reduction program since the mid-1980s had placed a heavy tax burden on Canadians. Canada's personal income taxes were the highest of all major nations, and taxes on Canadian businesses were also high by international standards. Such high taxes raised concerns that both business investment and skilled people would choose to locate elsewhere, to the detriment of Canada's economy.

In summary, good arguments could be made in favour of all three basic uses for federal budget surpluses: debt reduction, program spending increases, and tax reductions. However, the surpluses were not large enough to be an economic "cure-all"—for example, the reportedly "enormous" 2005 surplus of \$7.8 billion amounted to only \$243 per Canadian for the year, or 67 cents per day.

IN THE NEWS

The Greying of Canada

In 1999, 12 percent of Canada's population was over the age of 65. This was forecasted to increase to 22 percent by 2030, and to 42 percent by 2050. ▪

QUESTIONS
1. Why are such large increases in the seniors population forecasted?
2. What are the implications of this trend for the living standards of Canadians?
3. What could the government do to reduce the negative economic effects of an aging population?

Government Benefits and Services in Perspective

Underlying the debate over government benefits and services is the basic economic reality of *scarcity*, as discussed all the way back in Chapter 1, when the people in the island mini-society had to deal with the reality that they did not have the economic resources to produce all of the food, fuel, and security that they needed and wanted. If they decided to produce more of any one item, the *opportunity cost* would be that they would have less of the others.

Concerning government social welfare programs, the situation is essentially the same—more resources being employed in the government sector of the economy means that less is available for private consumption by Canadians. So, the opportunity cost of having improved health care or educational services might be that people have to make do with fewer restaurant dinners and video rentals. Viewed from the opposite perspective, if Canadians want lower taxes so that they can have more restaurant dinners and video rentals, the opportunity cost will be reduced government services and benefits.

For nearly two decades after the early 1970s, Canadians seemed to have avoided these realities, as they enjoyed higher levels of *both* private consumption *and* government benefits and services. However, much of this was made possible by borrowing that could not go on forever. By the mid-1990s, economic reality had asserted itself, and Canadians were forced to decide what balance between their private consumption and the level of government benefits and services they wanted for their society. The choice was not an easy one, and ensured difficult decisions and controversy for years to come.

Chapter Summary

1. The three main aspects of Canada's social welfare system are income security programs, health care, and education. (L.O. 1)
2. The four main sources of tax revenues for governments are taxes on incomes (personal and business), consumption taxes, property taxes, and payroll taxes. (L.O. 2)
3. Progressive taxes take a higher percentage of the incomes of the rich than of the poor, while regressive taxes have the opposite effect. (L.O. 3)
4. The marginal tax rate, which is the percentage of additional income that goes to taxes, has important effects on economic incentives to work, save, and invest. (L.O. 4)
5. The effect of Canadian governments' transfer payments and income taxes in 2003 was mostly to redistribute income from the highest-income 20 percent of families to the lowest-income 20 percent of families. (L.O. 5)

6. The federal government transfers large amounts of revenues to the provincial governments to help pay for the health-care, post-secondary education, and welfare programs for which the provinces are constitutionally responsible. (L.O. 6)

7. If the government has a budget debt, it must borrow money, and its debt will increase. Borrowing is considered to be a reasonable way to finance the purchase and construction of assets, but not a sound way to finance operating costs. (L.O. 7)

8. After 1975, the federal government had large annual budget deficits, and accumulated a large and growing debt. By 1993, the situation was so severe that it forced cuts to spending on key government programs such as health care, education, and income support. (L.O. 8)

9. Government income support programs can create disincentives to work if recipients lose too much of their benefits when they earn additional income. (L.O. 9)

10. By 1997, the federal government had budget surpluses, which could be used for paying down government debt, for spending on programs, and/or for tax reduction. (L.O. 10)

Questions

1. (a) What are the three basic types of social welfare programs in Canada, and what are the benefits that they provide for Canadians?
   (b) What is the opportunity cost of these programs?
   (c) How could you assess whether Canadians believe that the benefits of these programs are worth their costs?

2. Suppose the government needs more tax revenue. List the economic and political advantages and disadvantages of increasing each of the following taxes:
   (a) personal income taxes
   (b) corporate income taxes
   (c) gasoline taxes
   (d) consumption taxes (such as the GST)
   (e) payroll taxes

3. Ernie, an accountant, earns $60 000 per year, on which he pays income taxes of $10 000. If Ernie takes on extra work as a night school teacher, his income will increase to $68 000, and his income taxes will increase to $12 800. Ernie's *marginal tax rate* is _____ percent. Show your calculations.

4. Create your own example of how a social welfare system can redistribute income from families with high incomes to families with low incomes. In your example, use the terms *market income*, *total income*, and *income after transfers and taxes*, and compare the effects of transfer payments and income taxes on a family with a market income of $10 000 and a family with a market income of $100 000. Your example must reduce the annual income gap between these families from $90 000 to $50 000.

5. Sally is on welfare of $700 per month. She has been offered a part-time job that would pay her $300 per month. If she takes this job, her welfare would be reduced to $500 per month. If Sally took the job, her income from working would in effect be subject to a marginal tax rate of _____ percent. Show your calculations.

6. (a) At the start of this year, the government's debt is $300 billion. If the government's spending this year is $220 billion and its tax revenues are $200 billion,

the government's budget deficit for the year will be $ _____ billion, and the government's debt at the end of the year will be $ _____ billion.

(b) Would the building of a hospital be considered a reasonable purpose for the government to borrow money? Why or why not?

(c) Would paying the salaries of hospital workers be considered a reasonable purpose for the government to borrow money? Why or why not?

7. Make the strongest possible argument for each of the following possible uses of the budget surpluses of Canada's federal government:
(a) reduction of government debt
(b) increased spending on government programs (health care, education, etc.)
(c) reductions in taxes

8. Statistics Canada has statistics on "consolidated government spending," which show the combined spending of all levels of government. Visit **www.statcan.ca**; click on, in sequence, *Canadian Statistics > Tables by subject > Government > Consolidated government > Consolidated government revenue and expenditures > Expenditures and surplus or deficit.* Calculate the percentage increase for each category of government spending over the years shown in the table.
(a) Which programs seem to have enjoyed the highest priority in recent years? What might explain the emphasis being placed on these programs?
(b) On which programs has government spending lagged, and what might explain the lower emphasis on these programs?

Study Guide

Review Questions   (Answers to these Review Questions appear in Appendix B.)

1. Which of the following are considered to represent the three "keystones" of Canada's social welfare system?
(a) employment insurance, welfare, and pensions
(b) education, income security programs, and pensions
(c) income security programs, education, and health care
(d) education, welfare, and pensions
(e) employment insurance, welfare, and government jobs

2. What are the four basic types of taxes listed in the text?
• Taxes on _____
• Taxes on _____
• Taxes on _____
• Taxes on _____

3. A *progressive tax* is defined as
(a) a tax that takes a lower percentage of the incomes of the rich than of the poor.
(b) a tax that takes a higher percentage of the incomes of the rich than the poor.
(c) a tax that takes an equal percentage of everyone's income.
(d) a tax that is increased year after year.
(e) None of the above.

4. Which of the following is an example of a *progressive tax*?
   (a) the personal income tax
   (b) property taxes
   (c) provincial sales taxes
   (d) payroll taxes
   (e) None of the above.

5. A *regressive tax* is defined as
   (a) a sales tax based on the value of goods and services.
   (b) a tax that takes a higher percentage of the incomes of the poor than of the rich.
   (c) a tax that takes a lower percentage of the incomes of the poor than of the rich.
   (d) a tax that takes an equal percentage of everyone's income.
   (e) None of the above.

6. Last year, Nadia's income was $40 000 and her income taxes were $8000. This year, her income is $50 000 and her income taxes are $11 500. Nadia's marginal tax rate is ____ percent.

7. There is a saying among factory workers that "If you work 5 hours of overtime, the first 2 hours are for the government." This indicates that they believe their marginal tax rate to be about _____ percent.

8. In their song "Taxman," the tax collector tells the Beatles "one for you, nineteen for me." The marginal tax rate implied by this reference is _____ percent.

9. Generally speaking, high marginal tax rates tend to
   (a) reduce the incentive to work.
   (b) not affect the incentive to work.
   (c) reduce the incentive to save and invest.
   (d) increase the incentive to work.
   (e) Both (a) and (c) together.

10. Government tax collection and spending on social welfare redistributes income from Canadians with higher incomes to those with lower incomes. In broad general terms, which of the following best describes the overall effect of these programs on how income is distributed in Canada?
    (a) Income is transferred from the highest-income 40 percent of families to the lowest-income 40 percent of families.
    (b) Income is transferred from the highest-income 20 percent of families to the lowest-income 20 percent of families.
    (c) Income is transferred from the middle-income 20 percent of families to the lowest-income 20 percent of families.
    (d) Income is transferred from the middle-income 20 percent of families to the lowest-income 40 percent of families.
    (e) Income is transferred from the highest-income 40 percent of families to the rest of Canadian families.

11. The federal government transfers some of its revenues to the provincial governments in order to support their spending on three major types of social programs, which are
    (a) health care, education, and public security.
    (b) health care, education, and the environment.
    (c) health care, post-secondary education, and welfare.

(d) health care, welfare, and public security.

(e) post-secondary education, welfare, and public security.

12. State whether each of the following would be an economically reasonable purpose for financing expenditures by borrowing money. (Answer *yes* or *no* for each.)

(a) ____ the purchase of a house by a family

(b) ____ the weekly purchases of food by a family

(c) ____ the purchase of machinery by a corporation

(d) ____ the building of a college by the government

(e) ____ the payment of the monthly expenses of operating a college (wages, supplies, etc.)

(f) ____ the purchase of a car by a family

(g) ____ weekly payments for the costs of operating the car (gas, insurance, etc.)

13. A government *budget deficit* exists if

(a) the government's spending is less than its tax revenues.

(b) the government's spending and tax revenues are equal.

(c) the government's spending exceeds its tax revenues.

14. The government raises the money to finance its budget deficits by _____.

15. Suppose the government's debt at the end of last year was $400 billion. If its spending for this year were $170 billion, and its tax revenues for this year were $130 billion,

(a) its budget deficit for this year would be $_____ billion, and

(b) its debt at the end of this year would be $_____ billion.

16. The main reason that Canada's welfare system reduces the incentive to work is that

(a) welfare benefits are so high that many people are encouraged to quit full-time jobs and go on welfare.

(b) people on welfare are not permitted to seek work.

(c) when a welfare recipient earns money by working, his or her welfare benefits are reduced, often by so much that there is little or no economic incentive to work.

(d) there are no government agencies to help those on welfare to find work.

(e) welfare agencies and social workers encourage people to remain on welfare rather than to seek employment.

Critical Thinking Questions

(Asterisked questions 1 to 5 are answered in Appendix B; the answers to questions 6 to 10 are in the Instructor's Manual that accompanies this text.)

*1. Would tariffs (import duties) on imported goods be a regressive or progressive tax? Explain the reason for your answer.

*2. Which do you think would have more negative effects upon the productivity of the economy and the prosperity of Canadians—a 50-percent marginal tax rate on personal incomes, or a 50-percent marginal tax rate on business profits?

*3. "The government should never borrow money. Borrowing only leads to debt, and debt leads to trouble." Do you agree with this statement? Why or why not? Why might the speaker believe this?

*4. (a) Fill in the columns in the following table for budget deficit/surplus and government debt for each year through 20X4.

Billions of Dollars

Year	Government Spending	Government Tax Revenues	Budget Deficit (–) or Surplus (+)	Government Debt
20X1	$110	$100	– $10	$310
20X2	117	105	———	———
20X3	125	110	———	———
20X4	132	114	———	———
20X5	———	———	———	———

(b) Develop a combination of spending reductions and/or tax increases for 20X5 that eliminates the deficits (balances the budget) in 20X5.

(c) What obstacles would the government probably encounter in its efforts to balance its budget in part (b)?

(d) If the budget were to remain balanced in each year *after* 20X5, what would happen to the level of government debt?

*5. If you are receiving employment insurance (EI) benefits, you are allowed to earn up to $50 per week or 25 percent of your regular benefits (whichever is higher) without facing any loss of EI benefits. But all earnings above that limit will be deducted *dollar for dollar* from your weekly EI benefits.

(a) What is the purpose of allowing people receiving EI to earn this income?

(b) What is the marginal tax rate on earnings above the limit?

6. "The government should significantly decrease taxes on *incomes* (both personal incomes and business profits), and make up the lost revenue by significantly increasing taxes on *consumption*, such as the goods and services tax." Explain why the speaker believes that this proposal would improve the operation of the economy in terms of productivity and the standard of living.

7. An alternative to the progressive personal income tax is the *flat tax*, under which everyone pays the same marginal tax rate. Few deductions are permitted, and the tax system is greatly simplified by the elimination of the large number of deductions, exemptions, and tax credits that now exist. Advocates of the flat tax argue that the elimination of deductions, exemptions, and credits enables the tax system to have relatively low *tax rates* but still collect adequate amounts of *tax dollars*. The table below shows a flat tax system with a marginal tax rate of 25 percent and with the first $20 000 of personal income exempt from income tax.

(a) Complete the table.

Income	Taxable Income	Income Taxes	Taxes as a Percent of Income
$ 0	$ 0	$ 0	0
20 000	0	0	0
25 000	5 000	1 250	5%
30 000	———	———	———
50 000	———	———	———
100 000	———	———	———
200 000	———	———	———
300 000	———	———	———

(b) Is the flat tax progressive, regressive, or neither? Why?

(c) If a flat tax were introduced, what do you think would be the keys to making it a tax that would be acceptable to the general public as a reasonably "fair" tax?

(d) What political obstacles would there be to introducing a flat tax in Canada?

8. "The 'disincentive problem' with welfare in Canada is that welfare benefits are so generous that people would rather sit on their chairs at home and take welfare than get up and go to work." Is this an accurate description of the problem of disincentives in Canada's income support programs as described in this chapter? Explain the reasons for your answer.

9. What do you think would have happened after 1993 if Canadian governments had *not* reduced their spending and deficits?

10. One proposed reform for health care is to charge a *user fee* of perhaps $5 to $10 for every visit a person makes to a doctor or a hospital emergency room. What would be the main arguments in favour of such user fees, and why do many people oppose them?

Use the Web (Hints for this Use the Web exercise appear in Appendix B.)

1. From 1998 to 2005, the federal government used its budget surpluses to pay down its debt by an average of about $8 billion per year. But by 2005, critics were saying that federal budget surpluses should be used for other purposes such as spending programs or tax reductions. Since 2005, has the federal government continued to pay down its debt at the same pace as from 1998 to 2005? Updates are available on Statistics Canada's website (**www.statcan.ca**); click on, in sequence, *Canadian Statistics > Tables by subject > Government > Federal government > Federal government debt.*

13

Environmental Economics

For over 40 years, the environment has been a public issue in Canada and other nations. More recently, however, the growing seriousness and the scale of environmental problems such as global warming and the depletion of the ozone layer have made earlier concerns over air and water pollution seem minor by comparison. According to some projections, the environmental side effects of our economic growth and prosperity might even threaten our very existence.

Environmental concerns are not a new phenomenon. During the late 1960s and early 1970s, concerns over air and water pollution led to the first legislation governing automobile emissions and air pollution. From the mid-1970s to the mid-1980s, however, environmental issues took second place to "bread and butter" economic issues, such as unusually severe inflation and unemployment. During the second half of the 1980s, a combination of better economic times and serious pollution problems brought these environmental issues back to the forefront. And while other concerns, most notably unemployment, dominated much of the 1990s, environmental issues remained a high priority.

But much public discussion of environmental issues is not productive. Rather than focusing on the *causes* of environmental problems and setting realistic *objectives* and effective *strategies* for dealing with it, discussion of environmental issues too often focuses on predictions of catastrophe and on *fixing blame*, usually on someone else. Often, the problem is simply blamed on "industry," with the implication that if industry (that is, someone else) behaved more responsibly, there would be no environmental problems.

A more productive approach is to analyze the *causes* of environmental problems. By doing so, we can not only gain a better understanding of these problems, but also formulate government policies that are most likely to be effective in dealing with them.

Economic analysis of this sort shows that environmental problems are much more than the result of industrialists' negligence. Environmental problems are deeply rooted in the very nature of our society and our economy, in at least two fundamental ways. The first of these is our desire for material benefits. To a significant extent, pollution is a by-product of the high levels of consumption and production that we have come to enjoy. One of the most telling illustrations of this reality is the fact that the largest single source of air pollution in North America is not industry, but rather our own automobiles. And the fact that about half the new vehicles sold in North America in recent years have been "light trucks" (SUVs, pickups, and minivans) provides an indication of consumers' true concern about the environment. The second reality is that there are strong *economic incentives to pollute* the environment. Whether you are a corporation dumping waste into the water and air, or a driver disconnecting the emission controls on your car to save on gas, it is to your short-run economic advantage to pollute the environment. From the viewpoint of the *individual* person or business, pollution pays. However, the *collective* effect of millions of individuals behaving in this way can be serious—even catastrophic—environmental damage in the longer run.

SUVs consume two-thirds more fuel than small cars.

The Economic Incentive to Pollute

As noted in Chapter 2, in a market system, the profit motive provides important economic incentives for businesses to produce what consumers want and to produce it as efficiently as possible. These incentives contribute greatly to the economic prosperity of consumers.

But the profit motive also generates socially undesirable incentives. One of these is for producers to join together in price-fixing agreements, as discussed in Chapter 7. Another is the economic incentive to pollute the environment.

In discussing this problem of incentives, economists distinguish between two types of costs of producing a product:

(a) private (internal) costs, and

(b) social (external) costs.

private (internal) costs
Production costs, such as labour and materials, that are paid by producers and ultimately included in the price paid by the consumer.

Private costs are ordinary production costs such as labour and materials. These costs are paid by producers, and are ultimately included in the price paid by the consumer. Because these costs are contained *within* the production/consumption system, they are called *internal costs.*

Social costs are the costs to the environment, and thus to society at large, of actions such as the dumping of industrial wastes into the air and water. These costs may or may not be measurable in dollar terms, but they are real and often high, including health problems and costs for those affected. Because they are not paid for by the business that *produces* the product and not included in the price of the product paid by the consumer who *uses* the product, but rather are *passed on* to the environment and to society at large, they are called *external costs.*

social (external) costs
Costs that are not paid by producers, but rather passed on to society at large.

The economic incentive is for producers to *minimize* their internal costs by being as efficient as possible. This encourages them to use economic resources such as labour and materials as efficiently as possible. It also encourages them to *maximize* their external costs by dumping as much of their waste as possible into the environment rather than paying to prevent or clean up the resultant pollution. It is important to note that such behaviour is economically beneficial (in the short run) not only to the *producer* (who gets higher profits) but also to the *consumer* (who gets the product at a lower price). But the result can be serious effects upon the environment.

Externalities

externality
An incidental cost, or side effect, inflicted on others by the production or consumption of a product. Also known as a *spillover effect.*

When the production or the consumption of a product inflicts incidental costs such as pollution on others, and these costs are not paid by those who inflict them, economists say that an **externality** exists. This is also known as a *spillover effect,* because the effects of some people's actions spill over onto others. Pollution is among the most serious of these effects. In our pursuit of material prosperity, we—consumers as well as producers—are choosing to avoid paying some important costs of our prosperity, and choosing to pass these on instead to our environment, with potentially serious results.

As we have seen, the marketplace can solve many important economic problems. However, pollution is not a problem that the marketplace will solve on its own—the incentives within the market system tend to generate pollution, not reduce it. As a result, government action will be required to deal with this problem.

The Cost of a Cleaner Environment

Another fundamental reality of environmental economics is that pollution is mostly the by-product of the consumption and production of goods that most people are fond of having and reluctant to do without. You may be upset about the quality of air in your community, but are you willing to reduce your driving by one-third and do without your air conditioning in order to reduce air pollution from cars and electrical generating plants? Alternatively, would you be willing to pay significantly more for these and other consumer products in order to pay for the costs of making the producers' plants and the products themselves less damaging to the environment?

Many people have been reluctant both to accept these realities and to pay the cost, preferring instead to view the situation with alarm while blaming others. Such attitudes could explain the reluctance of many politicians to mount an effective attack on environmental problems. If government leaders believe that voters are unwilling to pay the cost of a cleaner environment, their efforts will tend to consist of strong words but weak action. For instance, they will tend to pass impressive-sounding legislation, but enforce it ineffectively.

At the most basic economic level, a cleaner environment is like any other good or economic benefit: we can have more of it if we are prepared to accept less of other things. As we saw in Chapter 1, the fact that society has limited economic resources means that using more of these resources to produce one thing necessarily means having less available to produce other things. The people of the island mini-society of Chapter 1 could have used one of their workers to clean up the island, but that would have meant they would have to do without the food, fuel, or security that this person could have provided. A cleaner environment does have opportunity costs.

Similarly, if in our modern economy we choose to devote more of our economic resources, such as capital and labour, to producing pollution control equipment and thus a cleaner environment, we will have less of other products, or a lower standard of living. Viewed from a different perspective, if producers have to install costly pollu-tion-control equipment, their production costs and the price consumers pay for their products will be higher. For instance, the cost of capping greenhouse gas emissions at 1990 levels has been estimated to be an additional 8 cents per litre on the price of gasoline—$300 to $400 per year for an average driver. This is a trade-off, like other economic choices, that we somehow have to make.

The trade-off between consumer goods and a cleaner environment can be shown with a production-possibilities curve of the sort discussed in Chapter 1 and illustrated in Figure 13-1. We could choose point A, at which we would have the maximum possible amount of consumer goods but devote no resources to pollution control and therefore have the dirtiest possible environment—perhaps one in which we would have to wear gas masks to work. At the other extreme, we could choose point B, at

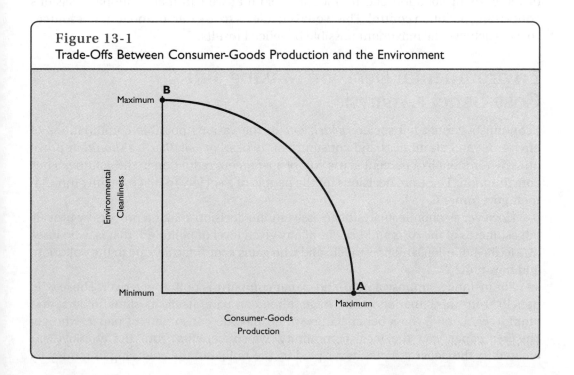

Figure 13-1
Trade-Offs Between Consumer-Goods Production and the Environment

which we would have the cleanest possible environment, but a very low standard of living due to extremely strict environmental controls that highly restricted the production of consumer goods and made them more costly.

Points A and B represent the two extremes of environmental decision making. In reality, it would be reasonable to expect a choice somewhere between A and B that represents an *acceptable balance* between our material wants and the quality of our environment.

The trade-off between a cleaner environment and fewer consumer goods is the way that *the economist* sees the issue. *The consumer* sees it in terms of having to *pay higher prices* for products in order to cover the costs of pollution control measures and equipment used in their production, leaving the consumer with less money to spend on other things. The result is the same—a trade-off in which the outcome is a cleaner environment and a lower standard of living (consumption per person). The money that consumers must pay for emission controls on their automobiles cannot be spent on other consumer goods and services.

Diminishing Returns and the Environment

As with other economic benefits, the cleanup of the environment is subject to the Law of Diminishing Returns described in Chapter 8. That is, it may prove quite easy to reduce the level of pollution by, say, 20 percent, through relatively simple and inexpensive measures. However, to achieve a further 20-percent reduction of pollution may well involve higher costs, while improvements beyond this are likely to prove even more costly. To reduce pollution to very low levels could prove so costly that it might well be considered not worth doing.

This reality makes it all the more important that we have reasonable estimates of the costs of pollution (and thus of the benefits to be gained by reducing pollution) and of the costs of pollution-control measures, so that we can make rational decisions concerning pollution control. This would enable us to use our antipollution resources so as to achieve the maximum possible beneficial results.

Environmental Decision Making and Cost–Benefit Analysis

Economists cannot tell society *which one* of the various possible combinations of environmental cleanliness and consumption is best, or *whether we should* improve our environment by x percent at the cost of a y-percent reduction in the volume of our consumption. These are decisions for the people of a society to make, mainly through their governments.

However, economic analysis can assist in the decision-making process by providing estimates of the *costs* and *benefits* of any given level of pollution; that is, who loses due to the pollution, and how much, and who gains economically due to the pollution, and how much?

For instance, suppose a pulp-and-paper company is polluting a river. Those who benefit from this situation would include the company itself, its shareholders, and employees. Less obvious beneficiaries would include consumers of paper, who get cheaper paper, and the local community, which benefits from the employment created by the paper mill, the taxes paid by the mill, and the spending of money by mill employees. Some of the social costs of the pollution could be estimated, such as damage to commercial fishing and tourism, water purification costs, and health costs. Other costs, such as damage to wildlife and the quality of the environment, would be more difficult to determine. However, it would be possible at least to estimate the costs and benefits of the situation as it is now, and estimate the benefits and costs of reducing the volume of pollution.

Such estimates can help in making decisions concerning the following matters:

(a) *The objective of the pollution control program:* Is the target the total elimination of the pollution, or would the Law of Diminishing Returns make this target too costly? What would be the benefits and the costs of reducing the pollution by 90 percent? 80 percent? 70 percent? Having estimates of the costs and benefits of these decisions can be quite helpful in setting targets for pollution control programs.

(b) *How to attack the problem:* As we will see shortly, there is a variety of possible approaches to protecting the environment. If we know who benefits and who loses from the situation, and the economic incentives involved, we should be better able to devise the most effective approach.

(c) *Who should pay the costs of attacking the problem:* Depending on the costs and benefits involved, it may be appropriate for the cost to be paid by the producer and/or the consumer and/or the government. Economic analysis can help to determine who should pay these costs.

The Current Environmental Situation

Until the late 1960s, the environment *seemed* capable of handling most industrial by-products—those that were not recycled by natural processes seemed to be spread sufficiently thinly so as not to constitute a serious concern. During this era, the prevailing attitude was summed up in the catchphrase "the solution to pollution is dilution." By the early 1970s, however, growing problems of air and water pollution made it clear that dilution was *not* the solution. Growing public concern led to legislation providing some protection for the environment, but this movement lost momentum in the second half of the 1970s and the first half of the 1980s, when public concern over severe inflation and high unemployment pushed economic concerns ahead of the environment.

www.ec.gc.ca

After the mid-1980s, environmental concerns again came to the fore. Not only was the volume of waste larger than ever, but also much of it was more toxic than before, and included a variety of new chemicals. Most seriously, however, environmental concerns moved to a global scale. Problems such as *acid rain*, the *greenhouse effect*, and the *depletion of the ozone layer* were said to threaten worldwide disaster.

While the marketplace will solve many economic problems, environmental pollution is not one of these. So, environmental problems call for action by governments, not only on a national level but also internationally.

What Can Governments Do?

We have seen that the basic reason for pollution is that there is an incentive for producers and consumers to pass on the external costs of their activities to the environment and to society at large. From the economic viewpoint, then, the objective of antipollution policy should be to *internalize* the external costs of pollution, so that those who benefit from pollution are forced to *pay all of the costs* arising from their activities. Then polluters will have an incentive to take steps to reduce or eliminate their pollution. The following sections describe four ways of doing this: *direct regulation and fines, taxes, tradable pollution credits*, and *legal liability*. In addition, we will consider the possibility that, in some cases, governments should pay for, or *subsidize*, pollution control. Finally, we will examine the question of *waste management*.

Direct Regulation

By far the most common form of government antipollution action is *direct controls*. Under this approach, the polluter is required by law, or by a government agency empowered by law to set pollution standards, to reduce the pollution to a certain level. The emission controls set by governments for automobiles are probably the best-known form of pollution control by direct regulation. The most common penalty for violating the law is fines.

While regulations appear to be simple ("pollution is bad, so make it illegal"), in practice, matters are more complex. The main problem is the setting of the limit, or standard, for the pollution. From the environmental viewpoint, it would seem desirable to set a standard of zero pollution, or ban pollution outright. However, as we have seen, it would prove extremely costly (and in some cases technically impossible) to achieve zero pollution. So outright bans are used only for substances that have such extremely severe environmental effects that they must be banned at virtually any cost. Generally, direct controls allow some pollution, but specify the acceptable limits. Setting such standards is a difficult and controversial matter, especially when the environmental costs and the costs of pollution control are not completely known. Almost always, polluters complain that the costs of meeting the standards are excessive and will result in lost jobs, while environmentalists complain that the standards are so lax that serious pollution will continue.

Once the standards have been set, there remains the problem of enforcing them. Enforcement of complex regulations requires considerable resources, mainly in the form of qualified inspectors. Environmentalists argue (often with justification) that governments tend to pass environmental legislation but fail to provide the resources to enforce it effectively.

Because they are classed as "trucks," SUVs are exempt from government fuel-efficiency laws that apply to cars.

On the other hand, very strict enforcement of some environmental laws can generate problems of a different sort. An example is provided by California, where the city of Los Angeles and farmers in the state's central valley depend upon water pumped from the San Joaquin River in Northern California. Because of this pumping of water, the delta smelt, a small fish that inhabits the San Joaquin River, became a candidate for the endangered species list. To save the delta smelt would require very costly changes to the complex systems that deliver water from Northern California to the south. When a proposal was made to build a reservoir that would hold winter rain runoff and reduce the amount of water that had to be pumped from the delta smelt's habitat, environmentalists discovered on the site of the proposed reservoir the home of a single family of rare kit foxes—another endangered species. This was not a unique case—residential and commercial/industrial developers found that governments frequently stopped their projects when antigrowth activists discovered some rare animal or plant on the site. While California had led the way in the environmental movement of the 1980s, there was by the 1990s a political backlash against excessive regulation, which was perceived as preventing socially and economically desirable projects. In economic terms, the regulations were considering only the *benefits* of measures to protect the environment, and not taking into account their *costs*.

Finally, it is essential that the penalties for violating environmental protection laws be sufficiently high to discourage polluters. Often, both the risk of prosecution for violating pollution control legislation and the fines levied on violators have been so low that the economic incentive is to take one's chances by ignoring the law, and pay the fines if caught.

Notwithstanding these difficulties, direct controls are the most common form of pollution control. When properly set and enforced, and with adequate penalties, direct controls can force polluters to pay the costs of pollution prevention or cleanup. By forcing producers—and consumers of the products, if their prices rise—to pay these costs, direct controls have the effect of internalizing at least some of the previously external costs that had been passed on to the environment and society at large, thus providing incentives to stop or at least reduce the pollution.

Taxes on Pollution

Another approach to pollution control is to levy a *tax on polluters* (a *pollution tax*) equal to the external costs caused by their pollution. Such a tax would force polluters to pay the full external costs of their activities. More importantly, it would provide an incentive for polluters to invest in pollution control equipment. For instance, suppose that a firm is paying pollution taxes of $150 000 per year. If by investing $1 million in pollution control equipment, it can cut its pollution so as to pay no pollution tax, it would save itself $150 000 per year—a rate of return of 15 percent (after tax) on the investment of $1 million. Such a rate of return would warrant investing the $1 million in pollution control equipment.

While attractive in theory, this approach also has certain disadvantages. In many cases, it may be difficult if not impossible to measure the external costs imposed by a polluter, making it very difficult to establish the amount of pollution tax to be paid. In addition, the pollution control authorities would have to monitor each polluter's performance so as to levy the appropriate taxes. Finally, there are political obstacles to this approach. While economists see pollution taxes as an incentive to invest in pollution control equipment, the public tends to see them as a licence to pollute that wealthy firms will cheerfully pay while continuing to destroy the environment. As a result of these problems, governments have seldom employed this approach, and have relied mostly on direct controls.

Tradable Pollution Credits

The objective of a system of *tradable pollution credits* is for an industry to achieve an acceptable level of pollution at the lowest possible cost. Under this system, the government establishes an overall acceptable level of pollution for an industry—say, 100 000 tonnes of sulphur dioxide (SO_2) emissions per year into the air. Each producer in the industry is then allocated a share of the total credits, which gives each producer the legal right to emit a certain amount of SO_2. Older plants, which are the most difficult and costly to upgrade environmentally, will tend to pollute in excess of the amount permitted by their credits, while newer plants with better equipment will pollute less than allowed by their credits, giving them surplus credits. Rather than invest in very costly pollution-control equipment, owners of the older plants can buy pollution credits from newer, cleaner plants. Over a period of time, the government will reduce the total allowable pollution limit for the industry, which will increase the value (price) of the tradable pollution credits. This will give producers increased incentives to develop pollution-cutting innovations, so as to provide themselves with

On the Chicago Climate Exchange, companies buy and sell pollution credits.

www.chicagoclimatex.com

more surplus pollution credits that they can sell at higher prices to firms with higher pollution levels. In effect, *overall* emissions targets for the industry are met, while *within* the industry emissions are shifted from plants where the unit cost of pollution control is low to plants where it is high.

Advocates of tradable pollution credits argue that not only is this system a more efficient way of controlling pollution, but it also provides the best *incentives for firms to develop continual improvements in pollution-reducing technology*, by literally creating a profitable market for pollution-control technology. By contrast, they say, direct regulation tends to freeze pollution control technology, by dictating that firms use certain equipment to control pollution, without providing incentives to do better. This system is used in the United States to reduce emissions from over 100 coal-burning electrical utilities in the Midwest, and the U.S. Environmental Protection Agency has auctioned 150 000 one-tonne pollution permits to electrical utilities for about US$21 million.

Environmentalists and much of the public tend to dislike tradable pollution credits, on the grounds that this policy seems to make pollution socially acceptable, through the government selling licences to do it and promoting a market for those licences. The main limitation on this approach in Canada is that much of Canadian pollution comes from relatively few sources, making it more difficult to establish an effective market such as could exist among over 100 U.S. electrical-generating utilities. On a smaller scale, Ontario Hydro practised something like this by shifting sulphur dioxide emissions between its power stations in order to minimize the cost of meeting increasingly lower emission limits set by the government.

Lawsuits for Damages

Another way to force polluters to pay for the external or social costs of their activities is to allow the victims of their pollution to *sue them* for damages. If damages could be proven and the amount established, such lawsuits—whether by groups of citizens, other businesses, or governments—could provide an incentive for polluters to invest in pollution-control equipment, in the same way as pollution taxes can. This approach is seen as a useful part of antipollution policy, but the complexities, cost, and time involved in taking a lawsuit to court have tended to restrict it to a minor role.

Subsidies

Much of Canadian industry operates in highly competitive world markets, which require that the industries manage costs very effectively. Canadian businesses often argue that if Canada forces them to invest in costly pollution control equipment, they will be placed at a competitive disadvantage vis-à-vis foreign competitors who are not subject to such requirements. In the extreme, these costs might become so high that Canadian producers are unable to compete and must close. A variation of this argument is that corporations—both Canadian and foreign—will tend to establish new plants outside of Canada, where pollution controls are less strict and costly. This argument can be quite telling, because it places protection of the environment in direct conflict with another very high policy priority—jobs for Canadians. Such concerns are particularly high in communities that rely on one industry for employment, such as pulp-and-paper towns.

"If you want this town to grow, it's got to stink."
— MAYOR OF A NORTHERN ONTARIO TOWN, IN THE 1970s.

If pollution control regulations would really seriously impair a firm's competitive position, government policy-makers are faced with a difficult choice—should they allow the firm to continue to pollute at an unacceptable rate, or impose regulations that might cost the firm's employees their jobs? In either case, an undesirable social effect will result. In such circumstances, it may be justifiable for society at large, through the government, to use public funds to subsidize the cost of pollution control equipment, so as to permit businesses to reduce their pollution without causing severe economic hardship.

Waste Management

Each year, Canadians dispose of about 790 kilograms per person, for a total of about 25 million tonnes per year, of which 64 percent consists of paper and food wastes. Where should all this garbage *go*?

There are three basic alternatives for dealing with the vast amounts of waste generated by a modern industrial society: *landfills*, *incineration*, and *recycling*. Each of these has its own advantages and disadvantages, from the perspective of economics and the environment.

Landfills

Landfills (less elegantly known as garbage dumps) occupy a somewhat paradoxical position because while they are the *least costly* way of dealing with waste, they are very *unpopular politically*. Few issues will generate hostility in a community more quickly and strongly than the prospect of becoming host to a garbage dump. Consequently, there are few tasks for a government as politically awkward as finding a location for a new landfill site.

Notwithstanding its unpopularity, landfilling is clearly by far the lowest-cost means of disposing of waste. In most countries, even with rising government standards required for landfill sites, the cost of dealing with waste through landfilling is between 40 and 75 percent of the cost of incineration, the next-cheapest method. At least, then, the cost savings associated with landfilling raises the possibility of governments offering remuneration to communities that agree to provide landfill sites.

The problem of landfill space is more a matter of politics than geology. It is estimated that if Canada continued to produce municipal waste at the present rates of use for 1000 years, the total waste could all fit into a space less than 50 kilometres square and 10 metres deep.

Incineration

As noted, incineration is the second-cheapest method of disposing of waste. Even if incineration produces energy that can be sold, it is still one-third to one-half more costly than landfilling. This is partly because government standards for incineration have also been rising, to protect against air pollution from incinerators. Rules governing air emissions from incinerators can require that as much as half the capital cost of a new incineration plant consist of air-pollution control equipment.

Recycling

In a sense, recycling is the opposite of landfilling, in that it is the most politically popular but least economical means of dealing with waste. Despite the popular appeal of recycling, the economics of recycling have often not worked out very well. Many recycling schemes have (at least so far) been costly money-losers, largely due to a lack of planning on the part of governments.

Seizing upon recycling as a popular way to reduce the volume of garbage to be sent for landfilling or incineration, governments have often established very ambitious recycling targets. The result has been mountains of recyclable materials—more than

"Many people love recycling. It seems to meet some deep need to atone for modern materialism, by saving some of the materials from the rubbish bin."
— *THE ECONOMIST*

can be sold to recyclers. This oversupply of recyclables—collected at considerable cost to the government—drives the market price of recyclable materials to very low levels. As a result, the governments lose money when they sell the materials to recyclers. In the case of household waste, which requires extensive collection and sorting, the price that can be gotten for the recyclables rarely covers even a fraction of the cost of collecting and sorting them. In the case of some waste plastic, the price has been negative; that is, the governments have had to pay companies to take the waste for recycling.

In part, the costs of the recycling process itself are a problem. The collection and sorting of recyclable materials is a labour-intensive and therefore quite costly process. Then there are the costs of recycling the waste into usable materials. Even when the waste "raw materials" are very cheap, the cost of processing them into finished products is often higher than producing products from new materials. For recyclers, the "bottom line" is that they must compete with companies that produce materials from virgin raw materials. This is a particularly serious problem if new raw materials are available at a low price, as many have been in recent years.

As a result of factors such as these, while recycling has certainly grown, it has not yet been able to play the role in waste management that was hoped for or expected. There is nothing inherently faulty with recycling; indeed, it is conceptually the most attractive way of dealing with waste. However, recycling can become economical enough to play its potential role in waste management only if the right combination of technology, labour costs, and materials costs occurs.

Recycling: The Government at Work

One area in which recycling can be helpful is with respect to household garbage. The recycling of some types of garbage, including paper, tin cans, and bottles, not only provides reusable materials but also reduces the volume of garbage and the strain on disposal facilities.

A major obstacle to recycling household garbage is sorting it into different categories, such as paper, glass, cans, and other materials. This task is most easily and economically done at the household level, but there is no direct economic incentive to do so. In fact, such sorting involves a cost to householders: the opportunity cost of the time spent to sort the garbage.

Some municipalities encourage households to recycle by providing free containers for recyclable garbage (a form of government subsidy) and by providing considerable publicity stressing the advantages to their community of using these containers. So, by spending a relatively small amount of public money, governments have been able to promote environmentally beneficial recycling.

Recycling: The Market at Work

A Japanese scientist projects that more than half of the world's consumption of paper could be produced from the waste of banana plantations, rather than by cutting down trees.

A major environmental concern is the exhaustion of certain types of nonrenewable natural resources, such as minerals. Some futurists have painted economically disastrous scenarios in which the world runs out of many such resources.

However, market forces appear to be capable of dealing, at least in part, with this concern. As the most attractive low-cost sources of some minerals have depleted, their prices have risen. These rising prices have provided incentives for both consumers and producers of these minerals to do some useful things. Faced with higher prices, users of these minerals have found ways to economize on their use and/or find substitutes. Meanwhile, rising prices have not only encouraged the development of new sources of such materials, but also have made it more economical to *recycle* them. In effect, higher metal prices can change scrap metal into an economically viable alternative to mining.

In such circumstances, the market provides the necessary economic incentives for recycling, as recycled metals become cheaper than newly mined minerals. Even 20 years ago, the Western world was obtaining 48 percent of its lead, 38 percent of its copper, 25 percent of its aluminum, 24 percent of its zinc, and 21 percent of its tin from recycling.

The Environment Industry

While many people see private industry and the environment as being in direct conflict with each other, the fact is that Canada is developing a significant *environment industry*. One rapidly growing part of this industry is waste collection. In part, this is due to the lower costs of private waste management firms as compared to government operations.

Other aspects of the environment industry involve consulting and equipment installation and maintenance. Statistics on the waste management industry are not easy to come by, but by some estimates there are more than 3500 environmental equipment and service firms operating across Canada, employing more than 110 000 people and generating sales of about $7 billion annually. Furthermore, the environmental sector is regarded as a growth industry, with projected growth rates of 20–40 percent per year. Nonetheless, compared to European nations, Canada's environment industry has been described by knowledgeable observers as "less developed."

Making Polluters Pay

In the previous sections, much has been made of the costs of waste disposal. This has led to proposals that would require polluters themselves to pay for the amount of garbage that they generate. In theory, such schemes would not only force polluters to pay, but would also provide incentives for them to reduce the amount of their pollution.

At the household level, this approach takes the form of pay-to-throw schemes for garbage collection of the type run in over 200 U.S. cities. Most such plans charge a fixed fee for a basic garbage collection service (say, two cans or bags per week) and extra fees for additional garbage (say, $1.00 per can or bag).

On the face of it, such schemes appear rather successful. One study for the World Resources Institute estimated that a fee of $1.50 on each 32-gallon (145-L) garbage container would cut the volume of waste by 18 percent.

But where does this 18 percent of volume of garbage *go*? A good deal of it still went out in people's garbage containers, but in a more compressed form. This compression was achieved by a manoeuvre known as the "Seattle stomp," after that city introduced a pay-to-throw scheme. In one city, the average weight of a container filled with garbage rose by 42 percent. Worse, however, was an increase in illegal dumping, as people threw their garbage onto public (and private) property and into ditches and rivers in order to avoid extra charges. And when Seattle's pay-to-throw plan was introduced, local charities found their drop-offs and doorsteps swamped with bags of unwanted "donations" that often seemed to resemble garbage.

Ultimately, then, a policy that seeks to force polluters to pay high costs through what amounts to a "garbage tax" will encounter the problem that it gives them a strong incentive to dump their garbage illegally. A more logical policy would be to tax not garbage, but rather consumption. The tax revenues could then be used to subsidize recycling and proper garbage disposal, giving people an incentive to use these socially beneficial methods rather than an incentive to dump illegally.

Global Warming and the Greenhouse Effect

www.ccme.ca

In recent years, global warming has emerged as the major environmental issue. Environmentalists claim that greenhouse gases generated by humans are driving temperatures upwards, with potentially catastrophic effect. The Canadian Council of Ministers of the Environment (CCME) reports that the area of the Canadian Arctic permanently covered by sea ice has decreased by one-quarter since the late 1960s, and that a shorter ice season has made survival more difficult for polar bears in Hudson Bay. Skeptics assert that global warming concerns are the result of "junk science" and are completely unwarranted.

Out of all this confusion, a few facts can be gleaned. The most basic fact is that greenhouse gas emissions are mainly (about 80 percent) generated *by consumers*, not by producers (industry). Per person energy consumption in 2002 was almost 60 percent higher than in 1967, and in the 1990s, energy consumption per Canadian increased by 5.5 percent, while the amount of energy used to produce $1.00 of output actually *decreased*.

What is Canada's contribution to greenhouse gas emissions? *In total*, not much—only 2 percent of world emissions. But that is not because Canadians are virtuously thrifty with energy; it is simply because Canadians represent only one-half of 1 percent of the world's population. On a *per person* basis, Canadians are just about the biggest energy consumers in the world. And as we will see, we have a poor track record of improvement.

Our lifestyle is tied to high energy consumption. We use energy to transport ourselves, to heat us in winter and cool us in summer, to fuel our industrial activity, and to operate the myriad of electrical appliances that we use daily. Even much of our leisure time is spent consuming energy through travel, the use of recreational vehicles, equipment that uses electricity, and so on.

The simple fact is that current large-scale energy sources generate significant amounts of pollution. The main problem is the burning of fossil fuels, mainly gasoline. The automobile is the largest single source of air pollution, accounting for about 40 percent of greenhouse gas emissions. It is followed by the coal and oil burned to generate much of the electricity that our lifestyle requires.

Some of the pollutants from the burning of fossil fuels can be controlled, but not all. The most intractable pollutant is *carbon dioxide*, which, unlike other pollutants from automobiles, cannot be controlled with pollution-control equipment. The resultant ongoing large-scale emission of carbon dioxide into the air has contributed to the **greenhouse effect**—the global warming trend that environmentalists fear will cause disastrous climatic changes around the world, including the raising of ocean levels, widespread flooding of coastal areas, and weather changes such as hurricanes.

Unless technology can solve the carbon dioxide problem, the fundamental conflict will remain between our high-energy-consumption lifestyle and the environment in which we live. At present, the only way to control carbon dioxide emissions is through conservation: that is, by controlling and reducing our energy consumption (see the "In the News" box on the next page). This approach would require changing from a value system based on economic growth and high and rising living standards to one that embraces conservation and quality of life, and accepts limits on our lifestyles and energy consumption. The problem is that this would mean such a drastic change in people's attitudes and lifestyle that political leaders are reluctant to confront the problem.

greenhouse effect

The global warming trend that environmentalists fear will cause disastrous climatic changes around the world, including the raising of ocean levels, widespread flooding of coastal areas, and weather changes such as hurricanes.

The Outlook for the Environment

What is the outlook for improving our environment? Certainly, public concern has increased the pressure on both governments and business to pay more attention to protecting the environment. However, there remains the reality of the trade-off discussed earlier in this chapter—that there are real costs to be paid in order to achieve a cleaner environment. The key to an effective attack on pollution, then, is not whether the public is *concerned* about the environment, but whether people are *willing to pay* to protect and improve the environment.

The evidence and the performance on this key matter has been somewhat mixed. During boom periods when economic concerns are distant, the public seems more concerned about the environment and more willing to pay the costs of environmental protection. However, when recessions increase unemployment and concerns about making ends meet, public concerns about the environment diminish. The track record of governments is also somewhat mixed; for instance, for years Ontario claimed to have exemplary environmental legislation, but a report found Ontario's actual pollution record to be the third-worst of all Canadian provinces and American states (Texas was the worst; Ohio second). Similarly, the performance of industry has been mixed. While some industries remained serious polluters, there were also examples of real concern and progress on the part of the private sector.

The glaciers of the Himalaya Mountains are melting at such a rapid pace that the long-term water supply of much of India and China is threatened.

According to the Canadian Wind Energy Association, Canada could meet 20 percent of its electricity needs from wind energy.

www.canwea.ca

IN THE NEWS

Higher Taxes on Gasoline?
Gasoline prices in North America are much lower than in Europe and Japan, mainly because Canadian and U.S. governments do not tax gasoline as heavily as other countries.

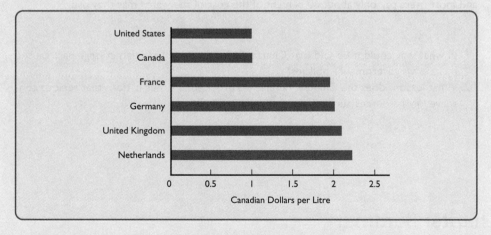

Canadian Dollars per Litre

Considering the serious concerns regarding emissions from automobiles, air quality, global warming, and dependence on oil from the Middle East, some observers argue that the single most logical policy for the Canadian and U.S. governments would be to increase the taxes on gasoline considerably. ■

QUESTIONS
1. What is the logic of proposing higher gasoline taxes and prices?
2. Why do the Canadian and U.S. governments seem unwilling to even consider this proposal?
3. Would you vote for a political party that made this proposal a keystone of its election platform?

In recent years, much attention focused on the Kyoto Accord, under which nations pledged to reduce their greenhouse gas emissions. In Canada's case, emissions of carbon dioxide and other ozone-depleting pollutants were to be cut, over a 10-year period, by nearly 30 percent from their 2002 levels.

This led to a storm of controversy, with opponents of Kyoto arguing that meeting such targets would cost nearly half a million jobs and boost gasoline prices by 80 percent, and Kyoto supporters asserting that these were wild exaggerations. As matters unfolded, it seemed that the economic costs to Canada of meeting its Kyoto undertaking were almost as unknown as the federal government's plans for actually meeting those targets.

It soon became apparent that the federal government's commitment to Kyoto was minimal, perhaps because the United States had refused to ratify the Kyoto agreement, which could leave Canadian producers at a competitive disadvantage if they had to bear the higher costs of Canada's Kyoto undertakings. But the situation was not that simple. While the U.S. *federal* government was uninterested in pollution emissions, significant progress was in fact being made in the United States at the *state* government level. According to the Commission for Environmental Cooperation (CEC), Canada was actually lagging behind the United States in the control of greenhouse gas emissions. This left Canadians in the unenviable position of being not among the largest energy consumers in the world, but among those making the least progress toward improvement.

www.cec.org

IN THE NEWS

Wasting Water in China

China is suffering from severe water shortages, with over 100 big cities short of water and half of these seriously threatened. Prices in China are set by the government, and until 1985, most users paid nothing for water. Today, water is still heavily subsidized by the government, and most users pay only about 60 percent of the cost of the water that they use. ■

QUESTIONS
1. In what way could it be said that China's water shortage has been in large part caused by its own government's policies?
2. What lessons does the Chinese experience provide for other nations that seek to conserve key resources such as water and electricity?

Chapter Summary

1. There are economic incentives for both producers and consumers to pollute, by passing the external costs of their production or consumption on to the environment. (L.O. 1)
2. There is an economic trade-off in which society can have a cleaner environment if it is willing to accept a lower level of production and consumption of goods and services. (L.O. 2)
3. As with other economic benefits, the cleanup of the environment is subject to the Law of Diminishing Returns: as the level of pollution is lowered, it becomes increasingly costly to reduce it further. (L.O. 3)

4. Economic analysis of the costs and benefits of pollution control can help in making decisions concerning the objectives of a pollution control program, how to attack the problem, and who should pay the costs of the program. (L.O. 4)
5. Some types of action that can be taken to protect the environment are direct regulation, taxes on pollution, tradable pollution credits, lawsuits for damages due to pollution, and government subsidies to help pay the cost of pollution controls. (L.O. 5)
6. With respect to waste management, landfilling is the lowest-cost disposal method, incineration is second-lowest, and recycling the highest-cost way of dealing with waste. Taxes on consumption and subsidies for proper garbage disposal and recycling are considered more environmentally effective than taxes on garbage itself, which tends to generate environmentally damaging illegal dumping. (L.O. 6)
7. The burning of fossil fuels generates *greenhouse gases*, which environmentalists believe are contributing to the potentially serious problem of global warming. (L.O.7)

Questions

1. "The pollution problem is most fundamentally a problem of economic incentives leading people to behave self-destructively, and the solution to pollution is for governments to change those incentives so that people behave environmentally responsibly."

   Explain the speaker's viewpoint, using the terms *private costs*, *social costs*, and *externalities*.

2. (a) Draw a production-possibilities curve to illustrate that a cleaner environment can be viewed as involving similar "trade-offs" to those involved with increasing the production and consumption of any other good.
   (b) How does the curve show the opportunity cost of a cleaner environment?
   (c) How does the Law of Diminishing Returns complicate the task of seeking a cleaner environment?

3. (a) Which method of handling household and industrial waste is the most politically popular—landfills, incineration, or recycling?
   (b) Why, then, is this method not used more frequently?

4. A city is suffering from severe air quality problems, mostly due to emissions from cars.
   (a) Who benefits from this emissions/pollution situation?
   (b) Who bears the costs of the pollution?
   (c) The city's residents are pressuring the city government to "pass a law" limiting the pollution, but why is direct regulation not a simple solution to this problem?
   (d) Using the concepts of costs, benefits, and incentives, explain how a road toll system could be used in a situation such as this.
   (e) Is this a situation in which government subsidies for public transit should be considered? What would you like to know before using taxpayers' money to reduce the cost of public transit to riders?

5. "Setting pollution-control standards is simple—the standards should require that pollution be reduced to the maximum extent possible using modern technology. In fact, the objective of any pollution-control program should be to reduce pollution to zero."

   Do you agree with the above statement or not? If not, how should pollution-control standards be determined?

6. One approach to waste management is to charge householders a fee for every bag of garbage that is collected.
   (a) How is this policy intended to work?
   (b) Explain some unintended negative environmental effects that this policy is likely to have, and why these effects would probably occur.
   (c) The effects in (b) would not occur if governments collected garbage for free and paid for this service by taxing products when they were purchased rather than when they were thrown away, by increasing the sales tax. Why do you think that governments have not implemented such an alternative policy?

7. Visit the website of the Canadian Wind Energy Association at **www.canwea.ca** and read the *Why Wind?* brochure and frequently asked questions.
   (a) What percentage of Canada's electricity is presently generated by burning coal, and what percentage is generated by wind power?
   (b) What is estimated to be the potential percentage of Canada's electricity that could be generated by wind power? Does experience in other countries suggest that this goal could be attainable?
   (c) What would be the environmental benefits of Canada's reaching its potential for generating electricity from wind power?
   (d) Would you say that the government should consider subsidizing the development of wind energy? What key fact would the government need to know before deciding whether to subsidize this industry?

Study Guide

Review Questions (Answers to these Review Questions appear in Appendix B.)

1. State whether each of the following is an example of a *private cost* or a *social cost*.
   (a) Wages paid to employees
   (b) The effects of sulphur dioxide emissions from a plant
   (c) Interest payments to bondholders
   (d) The cost of the company's annual social event
   (e) Traffic congestion caused by a company's warehouse

2. In attempting to maximize its profits by reducing costs, a producer is likely to conclude that
   (a) minimizing social costs is less important than minimizing private costs.
   (b) private costs should be replaced by social costs whenever possible.
   (c) social costs should be minimized.
   (d) Both (a) and (b).
   (e) None of the above.

3. The basic reality is that a cleaner environment is like any other good: if we want more of it, we will have to accept _____.

4. Because of the Law of Diminishing Returns,
   (a) pollution will diminish to nearly zero if you keep coming back at the problem.
   (b) technology has made it easier to push pollution to very low levels.
   (c) the cost of reducing pollution by a given amount increases, the further pollution is reduced.

(d) it is often not economically feasible to reduce pollution to zero.

(e) Both (c) and (d) are correct.

5. Direct regulation of polluters

(a) is not a policy that is popular with the general public.

(b) is the most common form of government antipollution policy.

(c) will only be effective if there is adequate enforcement and penalties for violators are sufficiently heavy.

(d) is a relatively rare form of government antipollution policy.

(e) Both (b) and (c) are correct.

6. Taxes on pollution

(a) can create an incentive for polluters to invest in pollution control equipment.

(b) are not a policy that is popular with the general public.

(c) are the most common form of government antipollution policy.

(d) Both (a) and (b) are correct

(e) None of the above.

7. Tradable pollution credits

(a) are a commonly-used approach to reducing pollution.

(b) can provide incentives for firms to improve their pollution-reducing technology.

(c) are not a policy that is popular with the general public.

(d) Both (b) and (c) are correct.

(e) None of the above.

8. Lawsuits for damages from pollution

(a) are costly and difficult to organize and win.

(b) are very seldom pursued.

(c) are a major concern of companies with bad pollution records.

(d) Both (a) and (b) are correct.

(e) None of the above.

9. Which method of handling household and industrial waste is least costly?

(a) landfills

(b) incineration

(c) recycling

(d) Both (b) and (c).

(e) None—all methods cost roughly the same.

10. State whether each of the following statements concerning recycling is *true* or *false*.

(a) T or F

It is by far the most economical method of dealing with waste.

(b) T or F

Most recycling projects have proven to be very profitable.

(c) T or F

The large quantities of recyclable materials collected have often driven the prices at which they can be sold to recyclers to very low levels.

(d) T or F

Recycling is a very popular concept with the public and with governments.

(e) T or F

Producers often find it less costly to use virgin raw materials than recycled materials.

11. The *greenhouse effect* refers to

(a) the use of carbon dioxide to grow plants.

(b) a global warming trend.

   (c) the political impact of the Green Party on election results.
   (d) the environmental impact of the clearing of the Amazon rain forest.
   (e) None of the above.

12. Of all greenhouse gas emissions,
   (a) about 20 percent come from consumers and 80 percent from producers (industry).
   (b) about 40 percent come from consumers and 60 percent from producers (industry).
   (c) about 50 percent come from consumers and 50 percent from producers (industry).
   (d) about 60 percent come from consumers and 40 percent from producers (industry).
   (e) about 80 percent come from consumers and 20 percent from producers (industry).

13. Canada is the source of about
   (a) 2 percent of the world's greenhouse gas emissions.
   (b) 5 percent of the world's greenhouse gas emissions.
   (c) 10 percent of the world's greenhouse gas emissions.
   (d) 20 percent of the world's greenhouse gas emissions.
   (e) 25 percent of the world's greenhouse gas emissions.

14. On a per person basis,
   (a) Canadians consume much less energy than people in other countries.
   (b) Canadians consume slightly less energy than people in other countries.
   (c) Canadians consume about the same amount of energy as people in other countries.
   (d) Canadians consume slightly more energy than people in other countries.
   (e) Canadians are among the biggest consumers of energy in the world.

15. In making progress regarding the control of greenhouse gas emissions,
   (a) Canada is ahead of the United States.
   (b) Canada is lagging behind the United States.
   (c) Canada and the United States are making similar progress.
   (d) Canada was behind the United States until recently.
   (e) Both (a) and (d) are correct.

Critical Thinking Questions

(Asterisked questions 1 to 4 are answered in Appendix B; the answers to questions 5 to 8 are in the Instructor's Manual that accompanies this text.)

*1. "The real problem with pollution is that people do not understand the side-effects of their actions. What is needed to combat pollution, therefore, is a comprehensive educational program pointing out how pollution is caused and the threat it is to all of us." Do you agree or disagree with this statement? Why?

*2. "The real problem with pollution is that it pays to pollute. And as long as it pays to pollute, consumers and producers will continue to foul our environment."
   (a) Do you agree or disagree with this statement? Explain fully.
   (b) What are the implications of this reality for government environmental policy?

*3. "The thing that people just have to learn to accept is that if we want more of a cleaner environment, we will have to put up with less of something else."

(a) Explain what the speaker means, using the term *opportunity cost.*

(b) Why do you think many people are reluctant to accept these realities?

*4. One source of pollution is throwaway drink containers.

   (a) Identify some of the costs and the benefits of using such containers.

   (b) Identify the advantages and disadvantages of each of the following approaches to the problem of throwaway drink containers:

      (i) prohibition of throwaway containers

      (ii) taxes on throwaway containers

5. In many cities, the problems of both traffic and pollution from automobile emissions are made worse by high numbers of cars with only one occupant. An interesting approach to managing this problem is *HOT lanes*, which stands for a combination of high-occupancy (HO) and toll (T) lanes. Certain traffic lanes are reserved for the use of cars with multiple occupants (HO), which pay no toll. Single-occupant vehicles can also use these lanes, but only if they pay a toll. *HOT* lanes are primarily a traffic management strategy, but also deliver environmental benefits.

   (a) In what ways would *HOT* lanes reduce air pollution?

   (b) What factors would have to be taken into consideration when deciding the toll rate for single-occupancy vehicles?

   (c) Modern computer technology allows the toll rate for single-occupancy vehicles to be different at different times of the day. How would you expect the toll rate to change during heavy-traffic periods, and why would this be done?

6. The text notes that the Law of Diminishing Returns leads to the logical conclusion that beyond a certain point, rising costs of additional pollution reduction tend to make it not worthwhile. Under what circumstances would this generalization *not* be an appropriate guideline for government policy concerning the environment?

7. Norway has perhaps the highest gasoline prices in the world (Cdn$2.30 per litre in 2005), due to its very high taxes on gasoline.

   (a) Explain how such high gasoline prices would have positive effects on the environment.

   (b) How does Norway provide an excellent example of the trade-off between a cleaner environment and a higher standard of living?

   (c) Higher taxes on gasoline would not only benefit the environment, but also would provide governments with much-needed funds for key social programs such as health care and education. Why, then, have governments in Canada and the United States not imposed higher taxes on gasoline?

8. Do you believe that the values of your generation concerning the environment and material goods and services are different from those of your parents' generation? Would you be more prepared than your parents were to reduce your standard of living in order to create a cleaner environment? If your answer is *yes*, what might explain why your views are different? What might explain an answer of *no*?

Use the Web   (Hints for these Use the Web exercises appear in Appendix B.)

1. To gain an impression of the scope of the market for recyclable materials, visit the Global Recycling Network (GRN) at **www.grn.com**.

   (a) What is the Global Recycling Network?

   (b) Go to GRN's Main Menu and select *Paper Recycling*. What does the table tell you about the most recent change in the price for *Baled Waste Paper*? Why is this information very important to the recycling of baled waste paper?

(c) Now click on *Baled Waste Paper*, then *View Listings*. Go to *Wanted and Available Listings*, and beside *Display Listings*, click on *Wanted*, then click on *Available*. Describe what you have just seen in terms of the supply side and the demand side of a market.

(d) How do markets for recyclable materials and organizations such as GRN contribute to a cleaner environment for all of us?

2. Visit the Statistics Canada website (**www.statcan.ca**) and search *The Daily* for "energy supply and demand."

(a) What have been the most recent trends in Canadian energy production and consumption?

(b) Do these trends represent progress in dealing with greenhouse emissions? Why or why not?

3. Visit the website of the Chicago Climate Exchange (**www.chicagoclimatex.com**).

(a) What is the mission statement of the Chicago Climate Exchange?

(b) What are some of the current developments in the marketplace for tradable pollution credits?

14

The Agricultural Sector

After studying this chapter, you should be able to

1. Describe the effects of technology in the twentieth century on agricultural productivity, output, and employment.

2. Explain why farm incomes have tended to be both low and unstable.

3. Using a graph to illustrate, explain the effects of an *offer-to-purchase* support program (for farms).

4. Using a graph to illustrate, explain the operation of an *acreage restriction* program.

5. Using a graph to illustrate, explain the operation of a *deficiency payments* program.

6. Describe the approach taken by marketing boards to try to increase and stabilize farm prices and incomes.

7. Identify three groups that are critical of Canada's marketing boards, and give the reason for each group's stance.

8. Describe the impact of freer trade on Canada's agricultural sector.

9. Apply the facts and concepts of this chapter to various situations.

The agricultural sector of the Canadian economy stands in sharp contrast to the large corporations and labour unions of earlier chapters. In those sectors, the spotlight was often on the market power of corporations and unions, but in the agricultural sector the situation has generally been very different. In agriculture, there are large numbers of producers, many of which have no real market power. Farmers have suffered so much from strong competition, overproduction, and low returns that governments have felt compelled to *support* them in order to maintain long-term stability in this industry. To understand the nature of the Canadian agricultural problems, we must first consider the nature of the industry, as well as the changes that have swept through it over the past few decades.

Profile of Agriculture

In 2001, there were over 90 000 female farm operators in Canada—26 percent of all farm operators in Canada.

Agriculture is an extremely varied sector of the Canadian economy. Canadian farms range from highly mechanized prairie wheat farms of over 1000 hectares (ha) to small vegetable farms of less than 40 ha. The one feature that is common across all of Canadian agriculture is that most operations are *family farms*. According to the 2001 census, 98 percent of Canada's 246 923 farms were operated by families, the vast majority being sole proprietorships.

A look at a map may suggest that Canada has vast amounts of land available for agriculture, but this is not the case. Eighty-nine percent of Canada's land is not suitable for agriculture of any kind, and less than 0.5 percent is rated as class one— suitable for all types of crops. And not all suitable land is being used for agriculture— 37 percent of all class-one land can be seen from the top of Toronto's CN Tower, and is within commuting distance of Canada's largest and fastest-growing city.

While the agricultural sector's production amounts to less than 4 percent of the total output of the Canadian economy, and employment in primary agriculture is only 2 percent of total employment in Canada, the performance of the agricultural sector is of great importance to Canadians. Agricultural exports such as wheat make an important contribution to Canadians' economic prosperity, and the typical Canadian family spends about 16 percent of its budget on food.

The Agricultural Revolution

The changes that occurred in the agricultural sector during the twentieth century were so sweeping that they have been called *the agricultural revolution*. The driving force behind the agricultural revolution has been *technological change*, such as improved equipment and fertilizers, improved strains of crops, better farming techniques, and so on. All of these have generated tremendous increases in *farm productivity*, as measured by output per hectare and output per farm worker. One result of these changes, as Figure 14-1 shows, has been a long-term trend toward fewer but larger and more mechanized farms, producing food much more efficiently.

Another result of the agricultural revolution has been a sharp decline in the number of Canadians living and working on farms. In 1950, there were 1 018 000 Canadians working on farms. By 2005, there were only 344 100 Canadians working on farms, a decrease of 66 percent from 1950.

Figure 14-2 shows the decrease in the number of workers and in the percentage of the labour force employed in agriculture from 1950 to 2005.

Figure 14-1
Number of Census Farms and Average Farm Size, Canada, 1871–2001

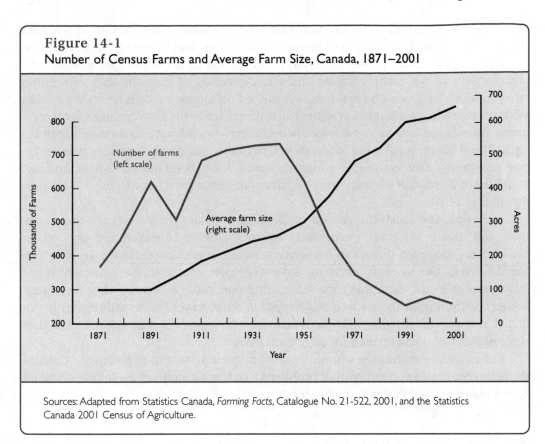

Sources: Adapted from Statistics Canada, *Farming Facts*, Catalogue No. 21-522, 2001, and the Statistics Canada 2001 Census of Agriculture.

Figure 14-2
Employment in Agriculture, 1950–2005

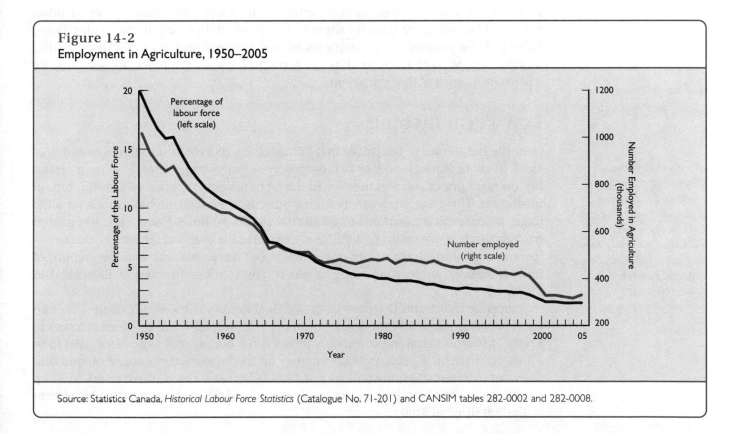

Source: Statistics Canada, *Historical Labour Force Statistics* (Catalogue No. 71-201) and CANSIM tables 282-0002 and 282-0008.

The agricultural revolution has provided the economic basis for Canadians' high standard of living. As we saw in Chapter 11, technology has "freed up" large numbers of workers from employment in agriculture and has thus made them available for employment in the manufacturing and service sectors of the economy, where they can produce the goods and services that make Canadians' present lifestyle possible. Without these improvements in agriculture, nearly three million Canadian workers—about nine times as many as now work on farms—would have to be working in the agricultural sector producing food rather than other goods and services that add to our prosperity. Our economic progress would have been much slower and our standard of living much lower, and Canadian families would have to pay much more for their food.

Economic and social changes on such a large scale naturally lead to concerns that they will create hardship, particularly unemployment. However, the agricultural revolution proceeded remarkably smoothly. With the economy usually growing reasonably well, the workers freed up from the agricultural sector generally found employment in the expanding manufacturing and service sectors. This very large-scale transition from the farm to other types of employment was made easier by the fact that it was mostly the *children* of farmers who made the transition, rather than their parents who had farmed for all of their lives.

But while these changes did not create an unemployment problem for Canada, they *did* contribute to certain other problems that the agricultural sector experienced. These are discussed in the following section.

The Farm Problem

Despite the impressive improvements in technology and productivity described in the previous sections, the agricultural sector of the Canadian economy, as in other nations, has had more than its share of economic difficulties. In particular, many farmers have suffered from problems of *low incomes* and *unstable incomes* that together are often characterized as the *farm problem*. In the following sections, we will examine each of these problems.

Low Farm Incomes

Over the past 50 years, the prices that farmers have received for their crops and livestock have increased less than half as rapidly as prices in general. The main reason for low farm prices and incomes lies in the technological progress of the agricultural revolution. The great productivity improvements in agriculture have made possible large increases in the supply of agricultural products. But farmers have not gained from this improvement in their efficiency, because the demand for food is *inelastic*—increases in supply have driven prices down, but have not increased the amount of food demanded by consumers by as much. The farmers' problem is illustrated in Figure 14-3.

Suppose that S and D represent the original demand and supply curves, with an equilibrium price of $10 and sales of 100 units for a total revenue (farm income) of $1000. If technological improvements increase the supply to S_1, the price will fall to $7—a decrease of 30 percent. Unfortunately for the farmers, the amount of food sold does not increase by as much as its price has fallen. As a result, the farmers wind up selling 120 units of food for $7, for total revenues of $840—a decrease of 16 percent from their original $1000.

About 40 percent of farms have a computer to help manage the farm.

In 2004, there was one farm worker for every 98.5 Canadians, as compared to one for every 13.5 Canadians in 1950.

"Farms that occupied 65 percent of America's workers in 1850 use 3 percent today, and the only worry is keeping even that dwindling band of gross over-producers artificially solvent."
— *THE ECONOMIST*

Figure 14-3
With an Inelastic Demand, Rising Supply Means Lower Farm Incomes

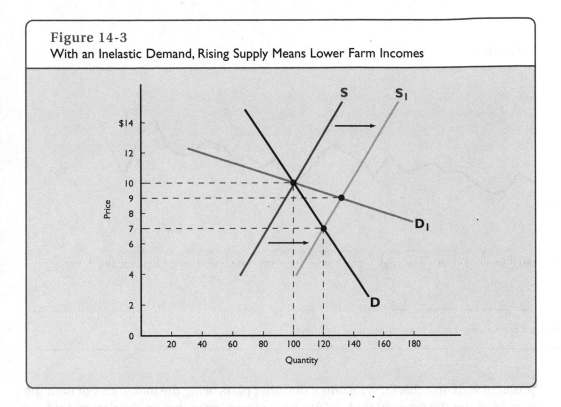

Clearly, the problem is that the demand for food is *inelastic*: people do not buy much more food simply because its price is lower. So when there is an increase in supply, prices are forced downward. Demand curve D_1 shows what would have happened if the demand had been *elastic*—with consumers eager to buy more at lower prices, the price would have only had to fall to $9, rather than $7, in order to sell off the increased supply. Unfortunately for farmers, the demand for food generally is inelastic. So farmers' efforts to increase productivity tend to be self-defeating, in that the increased supply drives farm prices—and incomes—downward.

To make matters worse for farmers, the *income elasticity of demand* for farm products is also quite low. This means that, as consumers' incomes have risen, the amount of food that they buy has not increased as rapidly; rather, they have spent most of their increased income on other things, such as services and durable goods. As a result, farmers have not benefited as much as other Canadians from the economic progress of their nation. This slow growth of demand has combined with rising supply to generate surpluses of many farm products, together with low prices and low farm incomes. Figure 14-4 on the next page shows farm net cash income from 1971 to 2004. Over this period, farm income rose only about one-third as fast as labour income.

Unstable Farm Incomes

Low incomes are only part of farmers' economic difficulties. Farm prices (and thus farm incomes) are also notoriously *unstable;* that is, they fluctuate sharply from year to year. As Figure 14-4 also shows, it is not unusual for the incomes of Canadian farmers to vary greatly from year to year. Also, Figure 14-4 shows *total* farm income; for *individual* crops and *individual* farmers, the fluctuations are often much more severe.

Why are farm incomes so unstable? It is a well-known fact that variations in the weather cause fluctuations in crop sizes (the supply of particular agricultural products) and thus in farm incomes. But varying weather conditions are only part of the

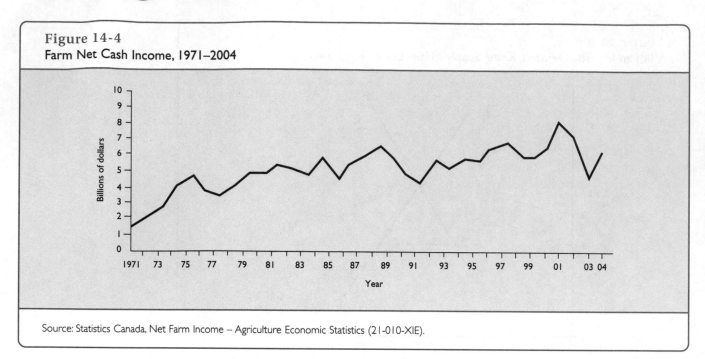

Figure 14-4
Farm Net Cash Income, 1971–2004

Source: Statistics Canada, Net Farm Income – Agriculture Economic Statistics (21-010-XIE).

problem with unstable farm incomes, the other parts being the inelasticity of both the supply of and the demand for food. We have already seen that on the demand side of the market, consumers' demand for food tends to be quite inelastic; that is, changes in prices will not change the amount of food that they buy by much. The supply side of the market is also inelastic—once a crop is harvested, the supply cannot readily be increased or reduced. Figure 14-5 shows how this inelasticity of both demand and supply generates instability in farm prices and incomes.

Graph (a) of Figure 14-5 portrays the market for agricultural products. Both demand and supply are inelastic—in fact, the supply curve (S) is perfectly inelastic. This means that 70 000 units have been harvested and must be sold, regardless of how high or

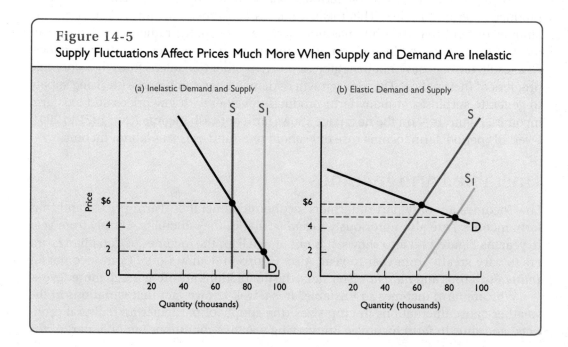

Figure 14-5
Supply Fluctuations Affect Prices Much More When Supply and Demand Are Inelastic

how low the price goes. With demand as shown by the demand curve D, the price will be $6. However, if good weather conditions result in a much larger crop next year, so that supply increases by 20 000 units as shown by S_1, the price of this product will plunge to $2. The reason for such a large decrease in price is not merely the increase in supply—the inelasticity of both the demand and the supply play a big part in the price decline as well. This is shown by graph (b), in which the price starts out at the same $6 and the supply increases by exactly the same 20 000 units as in graph (a), *but* both the demand and the supply are elastic. The result, as graph (b) shows, is very different—the price decreases by only about $1.

In summary, due to a combination of high and fluctuating supply, and inelastic demand and inelastic supply, farm prices and incomes tend to be both *low* and *unstable*. And because it is rooted in the very nature of agricultural markets, this "farm problem" exists not only in Canada but also in other countries.

Dealing with the Farm Problem

Since there is nothing farmers can do about the inelastic nature of the demand for farm products, the key to supporting and stabilizing farm prices and incomes lies in *controlling the supply* of farm products. In other words, farmers would benefit greatly from an oligopolistic price-and-production agreement among themselves, as described in Chapter 7.

The major obstacle to such action has, of course, been the very nature of farming (and, some would add, farmers). Farming is an excellent illustration of a highly competitive industry such as we saw in Chapter 7: it consists of many small, independent-minded producers selling substantially similar products in a highly competitive marketplace.

Given these realities, it has proven very difficult to achieve any kind of agreement or coordinated action on the part of farmers, even when it would be in their best interests to do so. Attempts have been made to use *farm cooperatives* (co-ops) to restrict production and support and stabilize prices, but these efforts have seldom been successful. Such agreements are voluntary and lack any means of enforcement; as a result, too many farmers tended not to participate or to break the agreements. Consequently, co-ops have tended to be of more benefit to farmers in areas such as research, advertising, and securing volume discounts on purchases of supplies and equipment, rather than in restriction of supply.

When such efforts at self-help proved largely unsuccessful, farmers turned to *government assistance* with their problem of low and unstable incomes. Such government assistance can take various forms, the main ones of which are presented in the following sections.

Government Programs to Support and Stabilize Farm Incomes

Offers to Purchase

Under the **offer-to-purchase** method, the government establishes the price of the farm produce and undertakes to purchase from the farmers any produce that is unsold at that price. As we saw in Chapter 6, and as Figure 14-6 shows on the next page, the result of farm price supports will be *surpluses* of farm produce.

offer to purchase
A farm-income support program under which the government establishes the price of the farm produce and undertakes to purchase any unsold produce at that price.

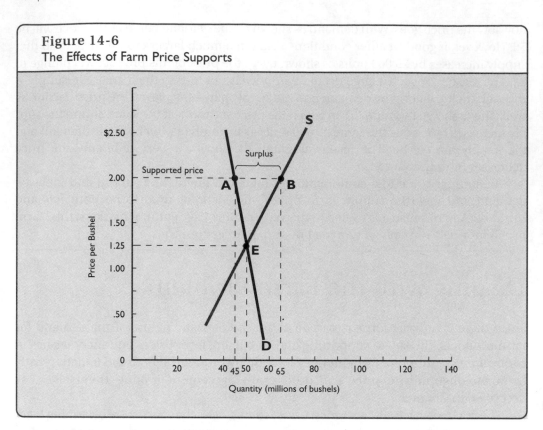

Figure 14-6
The Effects of Farm Price Supports

At the government-supported price of $2 per bushel, farmers will produce 65 million bushels but only 45 million will be purchased. The result is a surplus of 20 million bushels that the government will have to buy from the farmers and store. Unless market conditions turn favourable, the government will likely accumulate quite large crop surpluses that are costly to store and difficult to dispose of, which explains why the offer-to-purchase approach is no longer widely used.

Acreage Restrictions

To avoid the problem of crop surpluses, governments have sometimes employed **acreage restrictions**. Under such a program, farmers are either required to reduce their acreage under cultivation or are given financial incentives to do so; that is, they are *paid to not grow crops* on part of their land.

The result, as shown in Figure 14-7, is that the supply is reduced, shifting the supply curve left to S_1 and increasing the price from $1.25 to $2.00. Acreage restrictions have not always proven a reliable method of restricting supply, however, because farmers often take their least productive land out of cultivation and cultivate the remainder more intensively.

Deficiency Payments

Under the previous two programs we have examined, crop prices are increased by reducing the amount of food available to consumers—either by the government buying surplus produce and holding it off the market, or by causing less produce to be grown. A completely different approach, which does *not* reduce the amount of food available to consumers, is known as **deficiency payments**. Under this approach, the government sets a *target price* for the produce. If the actual market price is lower than

"To prevent 'overproduction' of food the (United States) Agriculture Department ordered farmers to let land lie fallow. Roughly 60 million acres (24 million hectares), an area the size of Britain, stand idle."
— *THE ECONOMIST*

acreage restrictions
A crop supply management program that either forces farmers to reduce their acreage under cultivation, or gives them financial incentives to do so.

deficiency payments
Programs for supporting farm incomes under which the government guarantees farmers a target price for a crop by subsidizing all sales of that crop that fall short of the target price.

Figure 14-7
The Effects of Acreage Restrictions

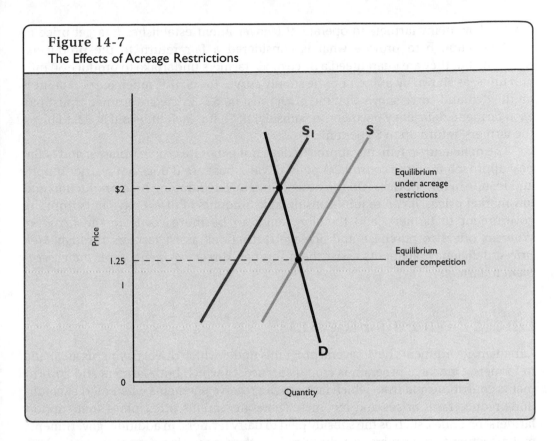

the target price, the government will pay the farmers the difference between the target price and the market price.

Figure 14-8 shows how a deficiency payments plan works. In a free market, supply and demand would establish an equilibrium price of $3. Since this price would be too

Figure 14-8
The Effects of Deficiency Payments

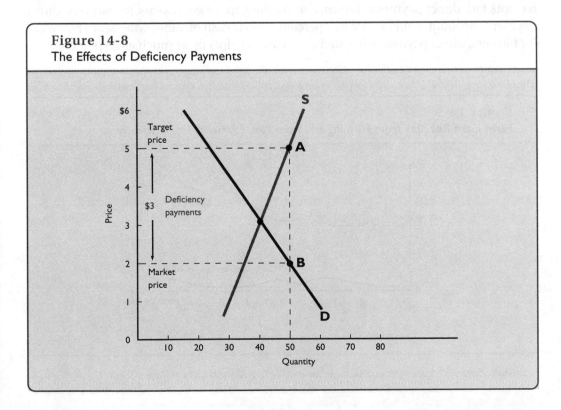

low to allow many farmers to operate, the government establishes a target price of $5—high enough to provide what is considered a fair return to the producers. Knowing that they are guaranteed a price of $5, farmers undertake to produce 50 million units, as shown by point A on the supply curve. To sell this much output, point B on the demand curve shows that the price must be $2. So the government must pay each farmer a deficiency payment (or subsidy) of $3 for each unit sold at $2, to bring the farmers' return up to $5 per unit.

The deficiency-payments approach does not generate crop surpluses, and is the best approach from the *consumer's* point of view, because it does not restrict supply, and results in lower prices. On the other hand, by encouraging high production and low market prices, it can require considerable amounts of direct payments from the government to farmers, and therefore tends to be more costly to the *taxpayer*. Whereas offers to purchase and acreage restrictions assist farmers through *high prices*, deficiency payments assist them through direct *payments from the government* to farmers.

Direct Payments Programs

Canadian governments have several programs under which direct payments are made to farmers. One large program is crop insurance, to which both farmers and governments contribute and from which farmers can receive payments when market conditions reduce farm prices and incomes. There are various other plans that support farmers' revenues, such as the subsidy paid to dairy farmers. In addition, governments make payments to farmers to help to reduce their operating expenses, particularly interest on loans and property taxes.

Figure 14-9 shows farm cash receipts from farming and direct payments from government programs (net of farmers' contributions to those programs). Note how when farmers' cash receipts are high, direct payments are low, and when farmers' cash receipts fall, direct payments increase to fill the gap. In good years for farmers, direct payments accounted for as little as 2 percent of their cash receipts, whereas in bad years for farmers, direct payments boosted their cash receipts by as much as 20 percent.

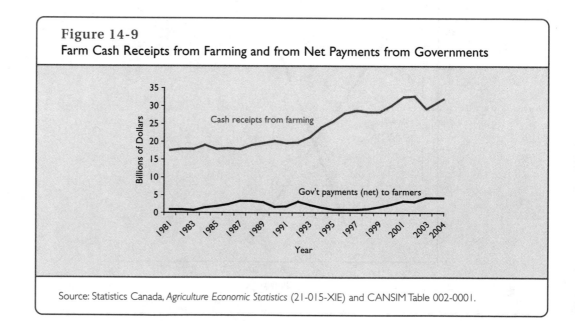

Figure 14-9
Farm Cash Receipts from Farming and from Net Payments from Governments

Source: Statistics Canada, *Agriculture Economic Statistics* (21-015-XIE) and CANSIM Table 002-0001.

Direct payments such as these do not comprise nearly all of the assistance given Canadian farmers by governments. Another major type of government assistance takes the form of the higher prices for farm products sold through government-sponsored *marketing boards*.

Marketing Boards: From Competition to Monopoly

In certain sectors of Canadian agriculture, a quite different approach to agricultural policy was initiated in 1972—the concept of *supply management* through marketing boards. **Marketing boards** are government-sponsored organizations of farmers that are intended to regulate the production and price of various farm products, such as poultry and dairy products.

marketing boards
Government-sponsored organizations of farmers that support farm incomes by restricting the supply of produce, usually through a system of quotas on individual farmers.

The objective of marketing boards is to ensure that farmers receive a fair profit, by both *raising* and *stabilizing* the price of farm products. To do this, the marketing board establishes a price for a particular product (say, eggs), using a formula based on the costs of production of an average farm. The marketing board estimates the size of the market for a particular farm product at the price it has established, then *restricts the supply* of that product so as to keep the price at the level established by the board. The marketing board does this by assigning production quotas (limits) to individual farmers so that they will not produce more than the market can absorb. Individual farmers sell their production to the marketing board, which acts as a monopoly sales agent on their behalf, selling at the price established by the marketing board. For marketing boards to be able to control markets in this way, it is essential that the government *control imports* of those items so as to keep lower-price foreign produce out of the Canadian market. Originally, this was done through *import quotas* that strictly limited the amount of foreign products that could enter Canada.

Because they have the legal power to set production quotas for individual producers and so control supply and prices, marketing boards are in effect *monopolies*. Unlike other monopolies, however, marketing boards have been encouraged by the government, and exempted from anti-monopoly legislation. After 1972, when federal legislation paved the way for marketing boards, several sectors of Canadian agriculture (including eggs, chickens, turkeys, and dairy products) went through a dramatic transformation from highly competitive industries to virtual monopolies. By the mid-1990s, marketing boards covered nearly 80 000 Canadian farmers, and accounted for about 20 percent of total farm cash receipts.

Rose Acre Farms Inc. is one of the three largest egg producers in the United States. In its high-tech farms in Indiana, Missouri, and Iowa, Rose Acre Farms has 12 million hens. Canada's 1435 egg farmers have a total of 17.2 million hens. Referring to Canada, Marcus Rust of Rose Acre Farms observed that "big (U.S.) producers could do very well up there."

Marketing boards seem quite simple in theory, but in practice they have become controversial. The main criticism of marketing boards is that they cause excessively high prices, because their formulas for calculating prices are often heavily weighted toward the higher production costs of smaller, less efficient producers. According to critics, the result of such calculations is not only high prices for consumers but also windfall profits for more efficient producers with lower-than-average production costs.

Related to the question of high costs and prices is the complaint that marketing boards *foster inefficiency* in farming. Because of the high prices established by marketing boards, many small, inefficient producers are kept in business. Furthermore, marketing boards' production quotas discourage farmers from expanding and consolidating into larger, more efficient units. In order to expand, farmers must *buy production quotas* from other farmers. Since the production quotas issued by marketing boards are in effect a piece of a monopoly, they can be quite expensive to buy. For instance, Ontario dairy farmers have had to pay as much as $25 000 for the fluid milk quotas required in order to add just one additional cow to their herds. Not only does the cost of quotas discourage growth, but also the quotas themselves can prevent farms from growing to efficient sizes. For instance, while production costs per dozen eggs decrease substantially for operations with 50 000 or more hens, marketing boards in some provinces would not allow flocks that large. Finally, by forcing farmers to operate below their capacity levels, marketing boards reduce efficiency and add to costs and prices.

The result of these factors was that the prices of farm products produced under Canadian marketing boards were often 50 to 100 percent higher than U.S. prices for the same products. So, while marketing boards proved effective in raising farm prices and incomes, they became quite controversial, mainly because of their effect on agricultural efficiency and consumer prices.

Farm Family Income

Since the surge in farm prices of the early 1970s, average farm family income has been quite close to the average income of husband–wife families in Canada. In recent years, farm family income has been about 90 percent of non-farm family income.

However, these figures are somewhat misleading. A growing proportion of "farm" family income has been coming *from non-farm sources*, as farm families have increasingly supplemented their farm income with off-farm earnings. As Figure 14-10 shows, the share of farm income derived from non-farm sources has increased from about 50 percent in the mid-1960s to over 70 percent today. In part, this reflects the economic problems of farmers, as they increasingly rely on sources of income other than their farm incomes.

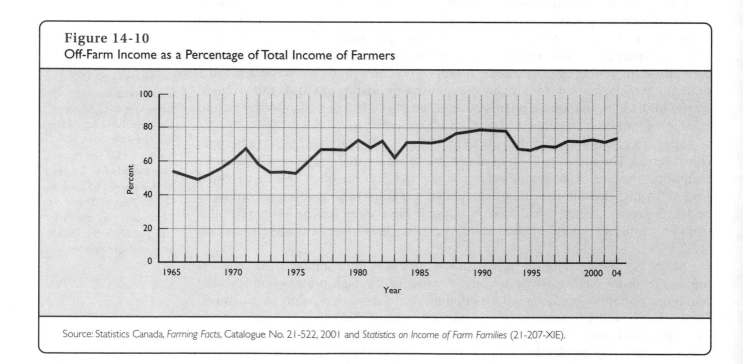

Figure 14-10
Off-Farm Income as a Percentage of Total Income of Farmers

Source: Statistics Canada, *Farming Facts*, Catalogue No. 21-522, 2001 and *Statistics on Income of Farm Families* (21-207-XIE).

Pressures for Change to Canadian Farm Policy

In recent years, there has been growing pressure on Canadian governments to make changes to their farm income-support programs, especially to marketing boards. This pressure has been coming from consumer groups, food processors, and Canada's trading partners.

Consumer groups have argued for many years that government farm programs were excessively costly to consumers. For lower-income families, who spend a higher proportion of their budget on food, the burden was greater. And the benefits of government programs were also questioned: for each farm job saved by government assistance, the cost to consumers was estimated to be over $140 000.

Canadian food processors were another source of complaints. Their concern was that, under Canada's marketing boards, much government assistance to farmers took the form of higher prices, which translated into higher production costs for Canadian food processors. For example, prices of chicken, turkey, eggs, cheese, and industrial milk in Canada were higher than U.S. prices by 50 percent or more. For Canadian food processors that must compete with American processors who use low-priced American food inputs, this was a serious problem. (Because the United States was using deficiency payments more than Canada, U.S. farmers got their government support more through payments from governments than through the higher prices that occur under Canadian marketing boards.)

However, the most serious pressures on Canada's farm policies were generated by *Canada's trading partners*, through international trade negotiations. As noted earlier, the key to protecting the high prices charged by marketing boards is to keep imports of cheaper products out of the Canadian market, and Canada had used import quotas to do this. However, this policy conflicted with the 1995 agreement under the **World Trade Organization (WTO)**, which made the first serious attempt to reduce trade barriers between countries for agricultural commodities.

Under the WTO agreement, Canada could no longer use import quotas to bar imports; instead, the quotas had to be converted to the equivalent level of protection in tariff form ("tariffied"). Initially, these tariffs were to be extremely high. Such high tariffs would keep imports out of Canada as effectively as the quotas that had preceded them; however, under the WTO agreement, the tariffs were to be reduced by 15 percent over six years. This new approach would gradually reduce prices, bringing benefits to Canadian consumers; however, many farmers who had been operating under the protection of marketing boards and import quotas found it threatening. The government reassured them that it intended to preserve marketing boards; however, whether this would be possible was uncertain as the tariffs on agricultural imports decreased.

www.wto.org

World Trade Organization (WTO)
An international organization through which 149 member nations negotiate and enforce rules for international trade.

Trade in Agricultural Products

Free trade has influenced Canadian agriculture considerably in recent years. As Figure 14-11 shows, both exports and imports of agricultural products have grown considerably in recent years. For some farmers, freer trade meant increased competition. But free trade also brought export opportunities, not only for Canada's traditional exporters of wheat, oilseeds, beef, and pork, but also for niche producers

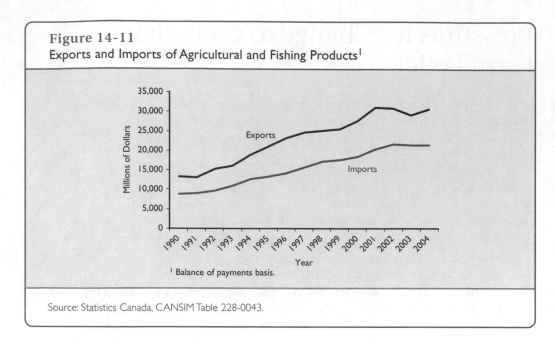

Figure 14-11
Exports and Imports of Agricultural and Fishing Products[1]

Millions of Dollars

Exports

Imports

[1] Balance of payments basis.

Year

Source: Statistics Canada, CANSIM Table 228-0043.

selling value-added products into smaller segments of large export markets. From 1990 to 2001, Canada's trade surplus (of exports over imports) in agricultural and fish products grew from $4.6 billion to $10.7 billion, before decreasing in 2002–03 due to mad cow disease and drought on the Prairies. Despite these setbacks, many observers predicted growing world food demand and a favourable outlook for many Canadian farmers.

Agricultural Policy in Perspective

As we have seen, Canada has a variety of programs to support and stabilize farm prices and incomes, including price supports, acreage restrictions, deficiency payments, and supply management through marketing boards. As with all government programs, there are benefits and costs associated with agricultural programs.

Ultimately, of course, the cost of agricultural programs falls upon the public, through *higher food prices* and/or *taxes* to finance subsidies to farmers. On the other hand, there are various economic and social benefits associated with programs to support and stabilize farm incomes. Support of farmers ensures a *healthier agricultural sector*, not only today, but well into the future, because producers are protected against adverse economic conditions beyond their control, and there are sufficient economic incentives to attract young, capable people into farming. Another argument on behalf of farm support programs is that they help to *preserve farmland.* By making farming a more economically attractive use of land, they reduce the incentive for farmers to sell their land for industrial or residential use, and thus help to preserve the amount of good agricultural land available to Canadians in the future. In these ways, it can be argued that agricultural support programs represent a trade-off, in which consumers pay higher food prices today in exchange for a more stable and healthier agricultural sector in the future.

Finally, assistance to farmers can be defended on grounds of *equity*, or fairness. Because farming is one of the most competitive sectors of the economy, farm incomes have tended to be lower than the incomes of other Canadians, many of whom belong

The 11-percent decrease in the number of farms between 1996 and 2001 was the fastest decrease since 1971.

to labour unions or professional associations, or are employed by large corporations or governments that have the means to pay higher incomes. Consequently, it can be argued that it is only fair that farmers have some protection against the harshness of a marketplace that is not only extremely competitive, but also quite unstable.

While support of farmers is widely accepted as a policy *objective*, there has been criticism of some of the support *methods* used in Canada. In particular, there are concerns about supply management and the operation of marketing boards, which restrict output and tend to foster inefficiency and high prices. With the trend toward freer international trade generating stronger international competition, Canada has been pushed in the direction of agricultural policies that do not restrict efficiency, supply, and imports, but rather promote efficiency.

According to many agricultural economists, the approach that is likely to achieve increased efficiency and output while still protecting farmers against periodic price and income declines would be some form of deficiency payments or crop insurance, as described earlier. While this approach stabilizes farm incomes to a significant degree (subsidized by the government if necessary), it does not reduce production or discourage the development of improved efficiency, as marketing boards do.

Chapter Summary

1. During the twentieth century, technological progress has greatly increased agricultural productivity, generating plentiful supplies of farm products despite agricultural employment declining to about 2 percent of the labour force. (L.O. 1)
2. Farm incomes have tended to be low, due to growing supply interacting with an inelastic demand, and unstable, due to fluctuating supply interacting with an inelastic demand. (L.O. 2)
3. One type of government program to support and stabilize farm incomes is the offer to purchase, under which the government establishes the price of the farm produce and purchases any unsold produce at that price; however, this program tends to result in crop surpluses. (L.O. 3)
4. Under acreage restrictions, the government either requires or pays farmers to reduce the amount of land under cultivation, so as to reduce the supply of produce and increase its price. (L.O. 4)
5. With a system of deficiency payments, supply is not restricted; rather, the price of the produce is directly subsidized by the government up to the target price level. (L.O. 5)
6. Marketing boards are government-sponsored organizations of farmers that increase farm incomes by restricting the supply of produce through production quotas for individual farmers and restrictions on imports. (L.O. 6)
7. Pressures for changes to Canada's marketing board system have come from consumer groups and Canadian food processors due to high prices, and from Canada's trading partners due to marketing boards' restrictions on imports. (L.O. 7)
8. Free trade has presented Canadian farmers with both challenges in the form of competition from imports, and opportunities in the form of opportunities to export. Overall, Canada exports more agricultural products than it imports. (L.O. 8)
9. Government assistance to farmers is defended on the grounds that (1) it ensures a healthy agricultural sector, (2) it preserves farmland, and (3) because farming is so extremely competitive, it is fair for the country to assist it. (L.O. 9)

Questions

1. Describe the effects of *the agricultural revolution* in the twentieth century, and how the agricultural revolution contributed to the growth and development of the Canadian economy.

2. "Farmers can't be blamed for their own economic troubles, nor can they be expected to solve these without government assistance. The problems of both low and unstable farm incomes have their origins in the very nature of both the supply side and the demand side of their industry and in changes in technology." Explain what the speaker means, with respect to the problems of
   (a) low farm incomes and
   (b) unstable farm incomes.

3. From the viewpoint of low-income families, which would be the most desirable approach to supporting and stabilizing farm incomes?
   (a) marketing boards
   (b) offers to purchase
   (c) acreage restrictions
   (d) deficiency payments
   Explain your answer.

4. "Why should farmers get special treatment in the form of financial assistance from governments? Why shouldn't they have to take their chances in the free market, just like other businesses do?"
   On behalf of Canada's farmers, explain why you disagree with the speaker.

5. As Figure 14-4 shows on page 310, farm net cash income fell sharply in 2002–03 as a result of mad cow disease and droughts in the Prairies. For recent statistics, visit the Statistics Canada website (**www.statcan.ca**) and click on, in sequence, *Canadian Statistics > Tables by subject > Agriculture > Farm finance > Income of farm operators.*
   Have farm cash receipts recovered since 2002–03?

6. Visit the Statistics Canada website (**www.statcan.ca**) and click on, in sequence, *Canadian Statistics > Tables by subject > Agriculture > Farm finance > Net cash receipts.*
   Have government direct payments to farmers increased or decreased in recent years?

Study Guide

Review Questions (Answers to these Review Questions appear in Appendix B.)

1. As a result of the agricultural revolution of the twentieth century,
   (a) the number of farms in Canada has increased.
   (b) fewer people now live on farms.
   (c) the productivity of farms has increased.
   (d) the proportion of Canada's labour force employed on farms has decreased.
   (e) Answers (b), (c), and (d) are correct.

2. The effects of the agricultural revolution on the development of Canada's economy are considered to be
   (a) unfavourable, because they increased unemployment.
   (b) beneficial, because with fewer workers needed by the agricultural sector, more workers became available for other sectors of the economy, such as manufacturing and services.
   (c) neutral, in that they have benefited one sector of the economy at the expense of another sector.
   (d) unimportant, because agricultural production is now only a small part of Canada's economy.
   (e) None of the above.

3. Which of the following describes the historical *farm problem*?
   (a) Farm efficiency has been high, but farm prices and incomes have been low.
   (b) Farm prices and incomes have been unstable, with a tendency to decrease periodically.
   (c) Low efficiency and high-cost-per-unit operations have caused profits and farm incomes to be low.
   (d) Because farm efficiency has steadily improved, profits and farm incomes have risen faster than those in other industries.
   (e) Both (a) and (b) are correct.

4. State whether each of the following has been a factor contributing to the problem(s) referred to in the previous question. For each item, answer *yes* or *no*.
   (a) _____ Farm technology has not improved significantly over the past 50 years.
   (b) _____ Farming is a highly competitive industry.
   (c) _____ The demand for farm products is elastic.
   (d) _____ Variations in weather conditions can cause considerable fluctuations in the supply of particular crops from year to year.
   (e) _____ The supply of farm products is relatively inelastic.

   Answer the following four questions on the basis of the following graph of the market for wheat:

5. The change in supply represented by the shift from **S** to S_1 would be caused by
   (a) higher prices for wheat.
   (b) a larger crop of wheat.
   (c) a smaller crop of wheat.
   (d) lower prices for wheat.
   (e) a marketing board restricting how much farmers can produce.

6. The change in supply from **S** to **S₁** would cause
    (a) the price of wheat to change from $ _____ to $ _____, and
    (b) the total revenue of wheat farmers to change from $ _____ to $ _____.

7. The decrease in price is as large as it is because
    (a) demand is unstable.
    (b) demand is elastic and supply is quite stable.
    (c) demand is elastic.
    (d) demand is inelastic and supply is unstable.
    (e) supply is elastic.

8. If the demand for wheat were more elastic, fluctuations in the price of wheat would be
    (a) more extreme.
    (b) less extreme.
    (c) the same—elasticity of demand has no impact on price fluctuations.

9. In the market represented by the graph below, if the government were use an *offers to purchase* program to support the price at $6, the result would be

    (a) a surplus of 10.
    (b) a surplus of 20.
    (c) a surplus of 30.
    (d) a shortage of 30.
    (e) neither a surplus nor a shortage—just higher incomes for farmers.

10. Under an *acreage restriction* program,
    (a) the government restricts what types of crops farmers can grow.
    (b) the government pays farmers to reduce the amount of land they use to grow crops.
    (c) the price of crops subject to acreage restrictions increases.
    (d) the government guarantees farmers a fair price for their crops.
    (e) Both (b) and (c) are true.

11. State whether each of the following statements concerning a system of *deficiency payments* is *true* or *false*.
    (a) T or F
        The government offers to buy farm products at predetermined prices, and absorbs any surpluses that might occur.
    (b) T or F
        The government does not attempt to determine the *prices* of farm products—prices are determined by supply and demand in the marketplace.

(c) T or F

The government sets a target price for farm products that would give the average farmer a reasonable income.

(d) T or F

If the market price falls below the target level, the government pays the farmers the difference between the market price and the target price.

(e) T or F

The government establishes production quotas that restrict the amount of output that each farm can produce.

12. The following graph represents the market for a particular crop.

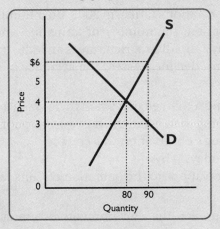

(a) The market price is $ ____, and _____ units are being produced and sold by all of the farmers of this crop.

(b) Under a deficiency payments program with a target price of $6, _____ units will be produced and the government will pay a total of $ _____ to the farmers.

13. (a) The basic objective of marketing boards is to _____.

(b) In order to achieve this objective, marketing boards _____.

14. Is each of the following a criticism that has been made of marketing boards? For each item, answer *yes* or *no*.

(a) _____ They have failed to increase either farm prices or incomes.

(b) _____ Their monopolistic power has increased prices well above the levels that would exist in a competitive marketplace.

(c) _____ They encourage the consolidation of farms into larger, more efficient units.

(d) _____ They have resulted in windfall profits for some producers.

(e) _____ They keep small, inefficient farms in operation.

15. Freer trade between countries has presented

(a) a threat to all Canadian farmers.

(b) a threat to some Canadian farmers.

(c) an opportunity for all Canadian farmers.

(d) an opportunity for some Canadian farmers.

(e) Both (b) and (d) are correct.

16. Is each of the following a reasonable defence of government assistance to farmers? For each item, answer *yes* or *no*.

(a) _____ These programs help to ensure that Canada will have a healthy agricultural sector in the future.

(b) _____ It is economically beneficial to Canada to keep as large a proportion of the labour force as possible employed in the agricultural sector.

(c) _____ These programs help to preserve farmland that otherwise might be sold for industrial, residential or commercial purposes.

(d) _____ Since farmers lack market power and are more exposed to economic insecurity than most other Canadians, it is only fair to provide farmers with government assistance when it is needed.

Critical Thinking Questions

(Asterisked questions 1 to 4 are answered in Appendix B; the answers to questions 5 to 8 are in the Instructor's Manual that accompanies this text.)

*1. In 1950, 1 018 000 Canadians worked on the nation's farms; in 2005, their numbers were down to 344 100. Over the same period, the number of farms in Canada decreased by more than 50 percent. Clearly, Canadian agriculture is an industry in serious and probably irreversible long-term decline." Assess the accuracy of this statement.

*2. In the 1600s, the English writer Gregory King remarked that when there was a good harvest, farmers actually received *less* income than when the harvest was poor.
(a) Explain the economic reasons why King's observation was correct.
(b) Are King's observations still relevant today? Why?
(c) Explain the relationship of King's observations to the operation of Canada's agricultural marketing boards today.

*3. Marketing boards are a controversial approach that governments use to assist farmers economically.
(a) What do marketing boards do that makes them controversial?
(b) Who would object to the practices of marketing boards? Why?
(c) To be effective, marketing boards must limit the production and supply of products. Why might this sometimes prove difficult?
(d) How could imports create problems for marketing boards, and how could they deal with this problem?
(e) Since marketing boards were introduced in the 1970s, Canada has entered into various free trade agreements. What are the implications of free trade for marketing boards?

*4. If the government wanted to encourage farmers to produce more food more efficiently, which of the following would be the most logical way to provide government assistance to farmers in those cases in which assistance was necessary?
(a) marketing boards
(b) acreage restriction
(c) deficiency payments
(d) Any of the above—none would be more advantageous than the others. Explain your answer.

5. As noted in this chapter, the production quotas assigned by marketing boards acquire market values, so that new or expanding producers must buy them in order to make their production legal.
(a) Why would quotas acquire prices in this way, and what would determine their price?
(b) Explain why some farmers have come to regard their production quotas as a key factor in their retirement plans.
(c) How would freer imports of agricultural commodities affect the value of quotas?

6. Suppose that governments had decided long ago that they would provide no financial assistance to farmers, and had left the fate of Canada's farmers to the marketplace. What do you think would have been the market solution to the problems of the country's agricultural sector?

7. Many of Canada's farmers are growing older, and have children who are not interested in carrying on the management and operation of the family farm. How might these facts influence the evolution of Canada's agricultural sector in the future?

8. For decades, improvements in agricultural productivity have assisted the development of Canada's economy by making available to the manufacturing and service sectors of the economy large numbers of workers who are no longer needed on the farm. Now, however, with only about 2 percent of Canada's labour force employed on the farm, there is little scope for continuing this process. In the future, what will the manufacturing and service sectors have to do in order to keep their output increasing?

Use the Web (Hints for this Use the Web exercise appear in Appendix B.)

1. As Figure 14-11 shows on page 318, both exports and imports of agricultural and fish products decreased in 2003. For updates to the statistics, visit the Statistics Canada website (**www.statcan.ca**) and click on, in sequence, *Canadian Statistics > Tables by subject > Trade > Exports > Exports of goods on a balance-of-payments basis, by product*; and then *Canadian Statistics > Tables by subject > Trade > Imports > Imports of goods on a balance-of-payments basis, by product*. Since 2003, what have been the trends in exports and imports of these products?

15

Into the Future

After studying this chapter, you should be able to

1. Define the term *resource wealth mentality* and explain how this term could be applied to Canadian attitudes and government policies in the past.

2. Provide three reasons for the phenomenon known as *globalization*, and explain how it has presented Canada with major economic challenges and opportunities.

3. State three characteristics that help to make a nation's economy attractive to investment in high-technology industries in the globalized world economy.

4. Describe changes that Canada made to its policies regarding trade, government finances, and other matters in response to globalization, and explain how these changes were intended to help Canada to prosper in the globalized world economy.

5. Apply the facts and concepts of this chapter to various situations.

For many years, Canada was an economically comfortable country, with high living standards and extensive government social programs for its people. In fact, Canada was consistently rated as one of the best countries in the world in which to live.

However, in the period from the late 1980s through the much of the 1990s, Canadians experienced considerable economic change and discomfort as the country grappled with some major economic challenges. The most fundamental of these challenges was the changing international economic environment known as *globalization.* In addition, there were the problems of *government deficits* and *debt,* and the related problem of *high taxes.* Another basic problem was the *slow growth of productivity* in the Canadian economy, which threatened both the standard of living of Canadians and the ability of Canadian industries to compete in the globalized world economy. How Canada addressed these issues would largely determine the economic prosperity of Canadians in the future.

Dealing with these challenges would involve fundamental changes in both government policies and in the Canadian economy itself. Before we consider these changes, however, we will review the background to this situation—the basic nature of the Canadian economy and government policy orientation that existed in the past.

Canada Before the 1990s

Economically, Canada is a relatively small country, with an economy about one-tenth the size of the United States' economy and a population similar to California's. From Canada's very beginning as a nation, its economic prosperity was largely due to exports of natural resources and resource products, mainly to the United States.

Canada used its prosperity to develop quite an extensive social welfare system, as was described in Chapter 12. Canadian governments established a broad range of social welfare programs for individuals and families (such as education and health care), an extensive support system for weaker and less efficient producers (including tariff protection for manufacturers, subsidies for farmers, and assistance of various sorts for many corporations in difficulty), and various forms of aid to economically weaker regions (including equalization payments, regional development grants, and subsidies to people and businesses in those regions). In the words of Professor Michael Porter,

> Traditionally, Canadians have lived in a relatively insulated environment brought about by paternalistic government policies, a history of market protection, and the accumulated attitudes and experiences of both individuals and businesses.
>
> This old economic order, as we call it, was a system where many prospered. However, because the old order generally provided insulation from external pressures and fostered limited internal pressures, many of the critical requirements for upgrading to more sophisticated and sustainable competitive advantages in Canadian industry have been missing or are only weakly present.[1]

Porter describes a Canada that had traditionally relied upon exports of natural resources and resource products as its basic source of economic prosperity. These exports, together with substantial inflows of foreign (mainly U.S.) business capital investment, provided Canadians with the foreign currency with which they purchased the imported goods and services that supported their high living standards.

---

[1] Michael E. Porter, *Canada at the Crossroads: The Reality of a New Competitive Environment* (October 1991; a study prepared for the Business Council on National Issues and the Government of Canada).

resource wealth mentality
The view that society's economic wealth is derived mainly from the sale of natural resources, as opposed to efficiency in the production of goods and services.

According to some critical observers, Canada had developed a **resource wealth mentality**—the view that wealth is not so much something that you *create* as something that *happens to you* through processing and selling resources that you are fortunate enough to own. With economic wealth so readily provided by resource exports and foreign investment, government policy in Canada tended to be less concerned with *creating wealth* than with promoting a *fair distribution of wealth*, by providing assistance to individuals, businesses, and regions that needed it.

In short, with high living standards supported by their exports of natural resources and by foreign investment, with tariffs to protect much of their manufacturing sector from import competition, and with government social welfare programs that sheltered them from competition and economic hardship, Canadians were able to enjoy a comfortable and secure economic prosperity.

Pressures for Change: Globalization and Competition

During the 1980s, a variety of factors combined to generate such a large increase in international trade, investment, and competition that this phenomenon would come to be known as *globalization*. The main source of globalization was *freer trade*, as nations lowered tariff barriers and markets were opened to international competition. Other important factors were improved computer, communications, and transportation technology that lowered the costs of doing business internationally and facilitated trade and investment on a global scale. With new technology, came worldwide markets for many more goods and services. Designers, manufacturers, and retailers became able to communicate with each other more quickly and more effectively all around the world than was possible in the past within one country. And, with increased international competition came higher productivity and lower costs and prices.

Challenges and Opportunities

The increased competitiveness of the new global economy presented Canada with some major challenges. The most basic of these was the problem of Canada's lagging productivity growth, which was noted earlier. Much of Canada's manufacturing sector was not very efficient, having produced only for the small Canadian market and with tariff protection against foreign competition. Such industries were ill-prepared for the stronger international competition associated with globalization. And, despite the importance of trade to the domestic economy, Canadian producers and governments were slow to adapt to this new, more competitive international environment. Rather than look outward to the opportunities presented by the global economy, Canada sought to maintain the old order described above, by protecting its less efficient producers against competition, with tariffs and government subsidies. Partly as a result of this protectionism, the efficiency, or productivity, of much of the Canadian economy failed to keep pace with improvements in other nations. As the 1980s progressed, Canada became less and less internationally competitive, especially in manufacturing.

But globalization brought tremendous opportunities as well as threats. For Canadian producers that *could* compete, there was the opportunity to break out of the small Canadian market and into much larger foreign markets. The Canada–U.S. Free Trade Agreement of 1989 alone secured Canadian firms' access to a market *ten times* the size of the small Canadian market.

Coping with Change

In the new, globalized world economy, it is more important than ever for a nation to be efficient and competitive and to be an attractive location for business investment. Multinational corporations, including Canadian firms, search the world for the most economical locations for their activities. If a country can attract business investment and the jobs and production that this investment brings, that country will prosper economically. If it fails to attract investment, it will fall behind economically.

What makes a country an attractive location for business investment? Many people think that the answer is cheap labour, but this is not usually the case. Low-wage labour is only important for labour-intensive manufacturing industries such as clothing and footwear. But in many industries, such low-wage, semi-skilled labour has already been replaced to a great extent by technology.

To modern, high-technology industries, the key attraction is not cheap labour, but rather *skilled people* with *specialized knowledge*. In addition, a nation needs to have excellent *transportation and communication links* to the rest of the world, in order to function effectively as part of the new world economy.

From this perspective, a nation's key strategic assets economically are no longer its cheap labour or its natural resources, but rather the *quality of its labour force* and its transportation/communications *infrastructure*—the knowledge and skills of its people, and the support systems for linking the productive use of those skills into the global economy so that they can access markets and partners around the world. In addition, a nation's taxation system must be attractive to employers, investors, and skilled workers.

If a country has these qualities, it will tend to attract business investment and prosper economically. Its productivity will be high, the standard of living of its people will be high, and its industries will be internationally competitive. Its skilled work-force will earn high incomes and its government will have a strong tax base, which can be used to invest further in better schools, research, and transportation and communications systems. These features will attract more investment, and the cycle of prosperity can be continued. For an economically small nation such as Canada, globalization offers the additional opportunity of increasing its exports into larger foreign markets, if its producers are able to compete.

For nations that lack a skilled workforce and communications and transportation infrastructure, the opposite kind of cycle can take place. Unable to attract capital with their labour forces' skills and their infrastructure, such nations would be forced to resort to low wages and low taxes as inducements for businesses to invest there, and would be able to compete only in labour-intensive, low-wage industries.

Into the Future

The mid-1980s witnessed the beginning of a gradual but persistent and significant shift in the emphasis of government policy in Canada, a key purpose of which was to adapt to the globalized world economy. Less emphasis was placed on government support for individuals and industries, and increased emphasis was being placed on market forces, private enterprise, entrepreneurship and incentives for work, investment, productivity, and the creation of wealth. In short, the policy emphasis shifted from the *redistribution* of wealth toward the *creation* of wealth.

In this context, the 1989 Free Trade Agreement with the United States represented a landmark decision for Canada, by signalling Canada's intention to participate more fully in the increasingly globalized markets of the world. As such, it was the most visible part of a basic shift in Canadian policy toward an emphasis on productivity, competitiveness, and an outward-looking internationalism rather than on more inward-looking nationalistic policies that sheltered Canadian industries from international competition. The Free Trade Agreement was regarded not as an end in itself, but rather as the first step toward Canada's becoming productive and competitive on a global scale. In 1994, another step was taken as the North American Free Trade Agreement (NAFTA) added Mexico to the North American free trade market.

Another major policy change occurred after 1993, when Canadian governments began to seriously address the problem of their budget deficits through reductions in government spending. And as government deficits decreased, the confidence of lenders in Canada recovered. This allowed interest rates to fall to their lowest levels in many years, and business confidence in the future improved, laying the groundwork for better economic performance. The other side of these deficit-reduction policies was, of course, that cuts in government spending forced some basic and painful changes to Canada's social welfare programs, as discussed in Chapter 12.

And after the federal government's budget deficits were turned into surpluses, the government introduced a series of cuts to personal and business income taxes that totalled roughly $100 billion over the 2001–05 period.

In addition to these major initiatives of NAFTA, deficit reduction, and tax cuts, a variety of smaller policy changes occurred. These policy changes had the same objective: to improve the efficiency—and with it the competitiveness—of the Canadian economy.

One such policy thrust was to *increase competition* in the Canadian economy, so as to increase efficiency. The first step in this direction had been taken in 1986 with the new Competition Act. As we saw in Chapter 9, the new law made it more difficult for businesses to reduce competition through tactics such as mergers with competitors and agreements to avoid price competition, or price-fixing. However, the new law specifically *allowed* mergers that would increase the efficiency and international competitiveness of the firms involved. The free trade agreements also exposed Canadian industries to increased foreign competition, forcing them to become more efficient.

deregulation
Policies to reduce government regulation of business, with the intention of promoting efficiency.

Another policy change aimed at increasing competition was the **deregulation** of some industries. Over the years, Canada had accumulated a large body of government regulations of industries, many of which controlled prices and production and/or restricted the entry of new competitors into industries. Many of these regulations had the unintended effect of reducing competition and efficiency in the regulated industries. To improve productivity performance, the government deregulated some industries, such as airlines, financial services, and communications (most notably, long-distance telephone service).

Another change was *reductions in government subsidies* to business, which forced businesses to improve efficiency rather than rely on government subsidies. In addition, there was the *privatization,* or sale to private interests, of several Crown corporations (including Air Canada and Canadian National), forcing them to operate more efficiently and without the subsidies that they had received when owned by the government. Changes were made to the *social welfare system,* especially employment insurance; these included reductions in benefits, restrictions on frequent claimants, and a shift in the nature of EI toward retraining of the unemployed rather than simply supporting their incomes.

Government policy-makers also increasingly emphasized the *small business* sector of the economy, which as we saw in Chapter 3 had provided a high proportion of the new jobs created in the recent past and was expected to play a large role in the future. Unlike resource and heavy manufacturing industries, the emerging high-tech and service industries are not dominated by giant corporations; in fact, small size, innovation, and flexibility are often seen as advantages in these fields.

Taken together, these new policies represented a significant shift in Canadian economic policy. As noted earlier, government policies had traditionally been directed largely toward *redistributing economic wealth*, through an extensive social welfare system. But to improve productivity and competitiveness, the new Canadian policies emphasized the *creation of wealth*. This required incentives for enterprise, entrepreneurship, and investment, as well as increased emphasis on competition and efficiency.

In a broad strategic sense, the new direction of government policy was to shift the emphasis in the Canadian economy from *security and consumption* toward *efficiency and investment*—or from benefits that exist mainly in the present to longer-term gains.

Canadians want a great deal from their economic system. They want prosperity for themselves in the form of high levels of private personal consumption, high levels of government services (including a strong social welfare system, health care, and education), economic security, and protection of the environment. To provide of all these, the Canadian economy must be prosperous and productive. Only by becoming more productive, more efficient, and more competitive will Canadians find it possible to achieve all their economic and social goals.

Chapter Summary

1. Traditionally, Canada relied heavily upon natural resource exports to create much of its economic wealth, while government policies aimed more at redistributing income and providing social welfare programs than at promoting productivity, the creation of wealth, and competitiveness. (L.O. 1)
2. The increasing globalization of the world economy presented Canada with major economic challenges, the main one being the need to become more efficient and internationally competitive than in the past. Globalization also offered opportunities, as large markets outside of Canada opened up. (L.O. 2)
3. In the globalized world economy, a knowledgeable and skilled labour force and excellent transportation and communication links to the rest of the world are important in attracting business investment and the jobs and economic wealth such investment brings. (L.O. 3)
4. After the mid-1980s, in an attempt to improve the nation's productivity and competitiveness, Canadian government policy shifted away from redistribution of wealth and protection of industries from foreign competition, and more toward wealth creation and economic internationalism. (L.O. 4)
5. Specific government policies in pursuit of these objectives included

   (a) the free trade agreements with the United States and Mexico,
   (b) reductions in government budget deficits, mainly through reductions in spending,
   (c) reductions in personal and business income taxes, and
   (d) various other policies to improve productivity and economic performance, including new competition legislation, deregulation of some industries, reduction of government subsidies to business, privatization of some Crown corporations, changes to the employment insurance system, encouragement of small business, and increased emphasis on investment in human resources. (L.O. 4)

Questions

1. Briefly describe Canada prior to the 1990s in terms of
   (a) the basic source of its economic wealth, and
   (b) the general thrust of its government economic policies.

2. (a) What is the phenomenon known as *globalization*?
   (b) How did globalization present Canada with both threats and opportunities economically?

3. (a) In what ways would Canada have to change its government economic policies in order to take advantage of the opportunities of globalization and deal with the threats that it presented?
   (b) Describe at least four changes that Canada made to its government economic policies in response to globalization, and explain the intended results of each of these policy changes.

4. In the fall of 2005, the federal minister of finance announced that the government was making the improvement of Canada's productivity performance an important priority of government policy, and was planning a "productivity budget."
   (a) How could the Department of Finance use federal budgets to improve productivity?
   (b) Visit the Department of Finance website at **www.fin.gc.ca**. What indications do you see of policies to improve productivity, and how are these intended to work?
   (c) Canada's productivity performance had been disappointing for nearly 30 years. Why do you think the government made it a policy priority in 2005?

Study Guide

Review Questions (Answers to these Review Questions appear in Appendix B.)

1. Canada's traditional source of economic prosperity was in the
   (a) exporting of manufactured goods.
   (b) exporting of resource-based raw materials.
   (c) establishment of social welfare programs.
   (d) earning of income from investments in other countries.
   (e) Both (a) and (c).

2. A *resource wealth mentality*
   (a) refers to the view that in order to prosper economically, a society must use *all* of its economic resources (labour, capital and land) efficiently and effectively.
   (b) refers to the view that economic prosperity comes mainly from processing and selling natural resources, rather than efficient and effective production of goods and services.
   (c) can lead to the belief that the government's role is to ensure that the country's economic wealth is distributed fairly among its citizens.
   (d) Both (b) and (c) are correct.
   (e) None of the above.

3. In the *globalization* process of the 1980s and 1990s, international trade increased greatly due to various forces, including

(a) _____

(b) _____

(c) _____

4. Globalization presented Canada with both

(a) opportunities, in the form of _____ and

(b) threats, in the form of _____ .

5. In the globalized world economy, Canada's major *disadvantage* was _____ .

6. Which of the following factors is most important to multinational high-technology corporations in deciding in which countries to locate their production facilities?

(a) sources of cheap raw materials

(b) low wage rates

(c) a highly educated and skilled work force

(d) Both (a) and (b).

(e) None of the above.

7. To improve Canada's ability to compete in the globalized world economy, it was necessary for governments to place more emphasis on policies that would

(a) improve the productivity of Canadian industry.

(b) control the growth and market power of large corporations.

(c) redistribute income from the rich to the poor.

(d) provide more protection for Canadian jobs against foreign competition.

(e) None of the above.

8. In the following table, match each of the government policy initiatives undertaken since the mid-1980s (in the left column) with the intended results of those policies (in the right column). (Note: Each policy can have **more than one** intended result.)

Government Policy	Intended Result of Policy
1. The 1989 Free Trade Agreement with the United States	(a) to push businesses to improve efficiency, rather than rely on government assistance
2. Action to keep the rate of inflation low	(b) to keep prices competitive
3. Tax reductions	(c) to improve productivity and competitiveness
4. Deregulation of some industries	(d) to make Canada's labour force more productive
5. The new Competition Act (1986)	(e) to increase incentives to work, save, and invest
6. Reductions in government subsidies to business	(f) to increase competition in Canadian economy
7. Reform of the employment insurance program	(g) to improve the confidence of investors and multinational corporations in Canada
8. Increased investment in human resources	(h) to keep interest rates low
9. Elimination of federal government budget deficits	

Critical Thinking Questions

(Asterisked questions 1 to 3 are answered in Appendix B; the answers to questions 4 to 7 are in the Instructor's Manual that accompanies this text.)

***1.** How did the 1989 Canada–U.S. Free Trade Agreement symbolize a fundamental shift in the direction and goals of Canadian economic policy, and how did the new policy objectives differ from those of the past?

*2. What role can improvements in productivity play in helping Canada to meet its economic challenges and achieve its potential?

*3. How could the budget surpluses of Canada's federal government be used to promote more rapid increases in Canadian productivity?

4. In the view of economists, the game (industry) of professional hockey provides a good example of how globalization, or the internationalization of markets, presents Canadians with both challenges and opportunities. Explain why this is the case, taking into account the perspectives of both players and teams.

5. What role can the internet play in helping Canada to meet its economic challenges and achieve its potential?

6. What changes to Canada's educational system would you suggest in order to help Canada to meet its economic challenges and achieve its potential?

7. If you could make *one* change to Canadian government economic policies aimed at increasing productivity in the Canadian economy, what would that change be?

Use the Web   (Hints for this Use the Web exercise appear in Appendix B.)

1. Visit the Industry Canada website at **www.ic.gc.ca**. What services and programs do you see that are intended to help Canadian industry to be more efficient and competitive? Explain how each service or program could help Canada to meet the challenges of being competitive in the globalized world economy.

The Politics of Economics

LEARNING OBJECTIVES

After studying this chapter, you should be able to

1. Summarize the major economic goals of right-wingers, and explain how they believe these can best be achieved.

2. Summarize the major economic goals of left-wingers, and explain how they believe these can best be achieved.

3. Explain why it is generally believed that the most effective approach to economic issues involves government policies that contain a balance of the left and right approaches.

This chapter

The Politics of Economics

can be found on the Companion Website at www.pearsoned.ca/lyons.

Answers to Boxed Questions

Chapter 1: What Is Economics?

YOU DECIDE: The Scarcity Problem on a Personal Level

1. As the situation is described, most people would say "no" to this question because the opportunity cost is too high. Because you have borrowed a total of $400 at the high interest rates that are charged on credit cards, the repayments will cut into your future spending on consumer goods and services by considerably more than $400. These high interest rates add so much to the cost of buying things on credit cards that they should make people more careful when "paying with plastic." But for many people, the opposite happens—buying on credit is so easy that they do so without considering how costly it is. Buying on credit is simply paying for things out of your future income, and paying the lender for the use of the money in the meantime. This does not mean that one should never buy on a credit card—just that, before doing so, one should consider whether getting the item sooner is worth paying so much extra for it. Finally, if you conclude that getting the item right away is important to you, are there other ways to borrow the money and at a lower rate of interest?

2. Most personal finance advisers suggest paying the outstanding balance on credit cards on time each month, to avoid interest charges. Then the credit card becomes a convenience rather than a burden. But this requires that you restrain your credit card spending each month to the amount that you can afford to repay. If this sort of self-discipline is not your style, the safest type of card to carry is a debit card that allows a vendor to take the money directly from your account.

YOU DECIDE: Measuring Your School's Performance

1. To measure the *effectiveness* of a school, you need to first consider the real *goal(s)* of the school. For a community college whose programs are geared to the job market, the success of graduates in finding jobs and rewarding careers would be a good indicator of effectiveness. A transfer institution would consider the success of graduates in securing admission to university as a key indicator of effectiveness. High schools might place more importance on graduation rates, as well as graduates' success in securing admission to postsecondary education.

2. Measuring the *efficiency* of a school could involve *physical* or *financial* measures. Physical measures would include statistics such as number of students per teacher, class size, and number of classes per teacher. The efficiency with which the facilities are used could be measured by statistics on number of teaching hours per day/week/year, and by data on square metres per student. Financial measures of efficiency would include things such as cost per student, cost per student/hour taught, etc.

3. Some ways to increase the efficiency of a school would be to increase the number of students per teacher, by increasing class sizes and/or the number of classes that each teacher must teach in a week or year. Also, longer school hours and longer school years would increase efficiency in the use of facilities.

4. This question is intended to raise the question of whether pursuing one goal (in this case, efficiency) might have negative effects upon the achievement of the other goal (here, effectiveness). The potential for conflicts between the goals of efficiency and effectiveness arises from the possibility that larger classes and

heavier class loads for teachers would make it more difficult for students to get the feedback and assistance that is important to their learning.

Chapter 2: Canada's Economic System

YOU DECIDE: To Subsidize or Not to Subsidize?

1. The opportunity cost of subsidizing public services depends on what one assumes would have been done with the funds if they had not been used to subsidize those services. If one assumes that the funds would have been spent on other government programs, the opportunity cost would be less of other government services, such as health care or education. If, on the other hand, one assumes that the funds would have been returned to the public via tax reductions, the opportunity cost would be the goods and services that the public could have bought with those funds.

2. A good case can be made that public transit and college programs in business and technology should be selected for subsidization. As noted in the text, a market system will tend to under-produce such public services, because people will only pay as much for them as warranted by the benefits that they receive from them *as individuals*, whereas the purchase and provision of these services bring *broader social benefits*. Specifically, the more people use public transit, the less traffic and pollution there will be, to the benefit of *all* of the people of the city. Also, such basic infrastructure makes the city more attractive for businesses to locate and invest. And a more educated work force contributes to higher productivity and economic prosperity, not only for the graduates but also for society at large.

It is more difficult to claim widespread social benefits for the other two items listed. Government support for a symphony orchestra does bring cultural benefits, but these are enjoyed by a smaller segment of society than the beneficiaries of public transit and education. The same can be said of subsidizing campsites, which primarily benefits citizens who like to camp, at the expense of those who choose not to camp.

The "bottom line" regarding subsidization may be this: how convincingly can you explain to some who does *not* use the subsidized service (public transit, education, orchestra or campsites) that using their tax money to subsidize it actually does *benefit them*?

Chapter 3: Business Organization in Canada

YOU DECIDE: Update to the Saga of Dan's Doughnut Dens

1. *Sole proprietorship:* This is easy to start, and provides the owner-manager with strong incentives as well as independence. On the other hand, sole proprietorships tend to suffer from a lack of management expertise since few individuals are strong in all aspects of management; partly for this reason, the workload of the owner-manager is often very heavy. If the business earns a high income, taxes on this income will be high since it will be taxed as the personal income of the owner. If, on the other hand, the business is unsuccessful, the personal liability of the owner can place his or her personal assets at risk.

Partnership: The partnership has advantages and disadvantages similar to the sole proprietorship's, except that a partnership can add management talent and capital. However, there is the disadvantage of potential conflict between the partners. In the event that the business fails, general partners have unlimited liability.

Corporation: Limited liability is a major advantage in two ways. First, the owners' (shareholders') personal assets are not at risk, but more importantly, this makes it much easier for a corporation to raise capital by selling shares to the public. Beyond a certain level of profits, tax rates on corporations are lower than on the personal income(s) of the owner(s). However, the process of incorporating a business is costly, and a possible risk (that Dan experienced) of selling shares is that control of the corporation may be lost.

2. $45.0\% + 5.1\% = 50.1\% =$ control of the corporation by Dan and Ermyntrude.

3. First, Dan should determine his *objective(s)*—what does he want to accomplish through this business? For instance, does he want to become the biggest doughnut shop operator in the city or the country (or in the world), or would he be happy to be a small independent player in this market? From this starting point, logical *strategies* can be developed for achieving his objective(s). Throughout the story, Dan seemed

to let himself be carried along by events or be reacting to situations, rather than proactively pursuing strategies in order to reach objectives.

4. Mainly because larger businesses generally need to raise considerable amounts of capital, and the corporate form of organization is best suited to this task due to its ability to issue shares to the public.

IN THE NEWS: Self-Employment in Canada

1. A key factor in the growth of self-employment (and small business generally) has been the growth in the *service sector* of the economy. A modern economy is capable of producing large volumes of *goods* with relatively few workers by using high-technology production methods. The high output per worker generated by this technology also increases people's standard of living, and consumers with higher living standards tend to buy more services, such as travel, entertainment, restaurants, and so on. And while the production of *goods* is often best suited to large mass-production facilities (big business), *services* are generally most effectively delivered by smaller enterprises that are convenient to the consumer. For instance, your car may have been built in a mass-production plant in Kansas City, but you get it repaired and washed by small business operators near your home.

   Much of the growth of self-employment has been associated with the growth of the service sector, described above. In addition, the downsizing of many Canadian corporations and government agencies during the mid-1990s forced many people into self-employment. Also, some employers laid off employees and then re-engaged them as self-employed "contractors," which saved the employers from having to pay payroll taxes and allowed the employees-turned-contractors to deduct work-related expenses from their incomes for tax purposes.

2. The rapid growth of employment opportunities in the service sector coincided with greater social and economic self-sufficiency among women, a result of their increased levels of education and career expectations. Growing numbers of women entrepreneurs have successfully established themselves in the expanding service sector, because it is so well suited to small businesses and self-employment.

3. There is a general expectation that these trends will continue. The driving forces behind these trends—technological advances and rising demand for services—seem likely to continue.

YOU DECIDE: Sales and Jobs

1. General Motors is a *manufacturing* company that is "capital-intensive"—it uses a great deal of capital equipment and relatively little labour in its production of automobiles. McDonald's, on the other hand, is a *service* company (the serving of fast food) that is "labour-intensive" in nature: it takes a lot of worker-hours to operate a business that prepares and serves food to people. Put differently, there are a lot more worker-hours in a million dollars worth of hamburgers served than there are in a million dollars worth of cars built.

YOU DECIDE: A Competitive Market for Education?

1. The pressure of competition could push schools to improve the quality of the education they offer in order to attract students and "sales income," much as many private schools do.

2. There might be a "quality control" problem. Some schools might offer education that *looks* attractive, but is in fact inferior in order to attract business.

3. The main thing would be *consumer knowledge*; the better-informed parents are about the educational "product" being offered, the more likely they are to make good choices, thus placing more pressure on schools to provide high-quality education.

   It should be noted that in school systems in which students are free to attend the school of their choice and in which schools' operating grants from government(s) vary directly with enrolment each year, there is already a de facto "market system" in operation.

Chapter 4: The Demand Side of Markets

YOU DECIDE: The Economics of Smoking

1. Demand is more inelastic for adults than for youths, because the same price increase causes a smaller reduction in smoking by adults.

2. There are two logical explanations for the more inelastic demand of adults. First, having smoked for longer, they are more addicted to tobacco. And second, adults generally have more disposable income than youths.

3. IF—and this is a *big* if—the same coefficient of elasticity applies to a very large price increase as applies to a 10 percent price increase, a price

increase of more than 60 percent would be required. (Since a 10 percent price increase cuts youth consumption by 8 percent, the price increase would have to be a little more than six times as large.)

Chapter 5: The Supply Side of Markets

IN THE NEWS: Price and Supply

1. Price increases are leading producers to increase production. Rising demand for oil (much of the increase coming from developing countries such as China) has been driving its price higher, and the market is telling producers (through higher prices that make it more profitable to produce oil from costly sources such as the Tar Sands) to produce more of it, as they did in the 1970s.

2. Various adjustments are possible, so it helps to organize your ideas into "supply side" factors and "demand side" factors.

   On the supply side, various higher-cost sources of crude oil would be made economical by higher prices. These include not only the oil sands, but also more remote and less accessible sites. On the demand side, the high price of gasoline and heating oil would drive consumers and businesses to economize on their use of these products in various ways, as they did in the 1970s. They would buy more fuel-efficient cars, turn thermostats down, switch to other sources of home heating, and so on.

Chapter 6: The Dynamics of Competitive Markets

IN THE NEWS: Golf Fees

1. (a) On the demand side of the market, the demand for golf in the Greater Toronto Area (GTA) has risen rapidly, due to a combination of rising population, rising incomes, and the aging of the population.

   (b) On the supply side of the market, there are only so many golf courses in the GTA, and a limited amount of land has been available for building new courses. In addition, competition from housing developers has driven the cost of land to very high levels.

2. It would be logical to expect that the prices at the GTA courses would be more likely to increase further. As the population continues to age, the demand for golf will continue to increase (at least for a while), placing growing pressure on existing golf courses in the Greater Toronto Area. And many well-off older golfers would probably be willing to pay more to golf near home rather than drive to more distant courses with lower fees. On the supply side of the market, the lack of suitable open land in the GTA, plus the very high cost of land, would reduce the number of new golf courses being opened within the GTA. In fact, such high land values would create pressure to either sell some existing golf courses to housing developers, or to increase fees further. The main asset of a golf club is its land, and as land values rise, the opportunity cost of keeping it as a golf course increases. In these circumstances, the logical decision is to either increase golf fees or sell the land and invest the proceeds.

IN THE NEWS: World Oil Prices

1. Beyond output of 85 million barrels per day, the supply curve becomes *steeper*, or *more inelastic*. This indicates that there were obstacles to increasing the quantity of oil supplied, at least at the prices of the past. (It should be noted that in mid-2005, most oil producers were pumping at or near their capacity.) So if demand continued to rise, the prospect was for quite sharp price increases.

2. Using the technique suggested in the question generates a price in the range of $75 per barrel. The significance of this increase is that an increase in demand of just 10 percent would cause a price increase of about 50 percent.

3. Anything that would increase the supply of oil would help to restrain price increases. This could include new oil fields, technology for extracting more oil economically from existing fields, and the like. The problem was that such developments usually take some time.

4. If buyers of gasoline and heating oil reduced their purchases (i.e., if demand decreased), the price increases would be smaller. If the high price of gasoline and heating oil drove consumers and businesses to economize on their use of these products in various ways, as they did in the 1970s, by buying more fuel-efficient cars, turning thermostats down, switching to other sources of home heating, and so on, the price would rise by less. As question 2 showed, the price in this market is quite sensitive to changes in buyer behaviour.

IN THE NEWS: Commercials During the Super Bowl

1. Advertisers buy *exposure to an audience* who will see their commercials. The Super Bowl draws a massive audience of over 130 million people, which makes sponsors willing to pay extremely high rates to advertise on the show; that is, it increases the demand for advertising time greatly.

2. On the supply side, the supply of commercial time is obviously both *low* (there are only so many minutes of commercial time during a football game) and extremely *inelastic* (the amount of commercial time cannot be increased even if the price rises to very high levels).

YOU DECIDE: The Internet and Markets

1. Buyers should pay lower prices, because the internet in effect brings more competing sellers into the market, as anyone who has used bizrate.com knows very well.

2. The experience has been the opposite of question 1: people who have posted their garage sales on the internet have received *higher* prices. The generally accepted reason is that the internet postings attract more competing buyers to these "mini-markets."

3. The purpose of this question is to focus back onto the *market basics* involved in this item: in question 1, the effect of the internet is to bring *more sellers* into the marketplace, which depresses prices. In question 2, the internet brings *more buyers* into the marketplace, which supports higher prices. That is, the key is not the internet per se, but rather how the internet affects the marketplace.

Chapter 7: Market Structures

IN THE NEWS: VoIP Price Wars

1. The industry was in a very early stage of development in the early 2000s, rather like the automobile manufacturing industry in the early 1900s. A large number of providers had entered the market, many of them quite small, and larger players had announced plans to wade in on a large scale. The price competition appeared likely to become so intense that only larger providers with advantages in operating costs seemed likely to survive.

3. One line of thought was that, following the competitive "free-for-all" described in question 1, only one company would be left standing. Another (related) argument could be made that this industry had a cost structure that made it a sort of "natural monopoly," as was the case with regular telephone service for many years.

YOU DECIDE: Coffee Crop Control

1. The seemingly strange behaviour of farmers (plantation owners, actually), burning part of their crop distracts from the simple reality that this is merely a measure to restrict the supply of coffee on world markets so as to secure a higher price for it. Economically, it is the same tactic as OPEC's pumping less crude oil, or car companies shuttering plants and laying off workers a few months before the end of a model year. The difference is that in agriculture, weather and other uncertainties mean that producers cannot effectively control production as required over the course of the year. Rather, they have to wait until the end of the crop year, *then* control the supply.

2. For such a plan to achieve its objective, *all* the major players in the world market would have to agree to participate in restricting the supply. There would have to be a reasonable amount of trust among them, such that none would "chisel" on their agreement. And, of course, the demand for coffee would have to be inelastic.

3. As usual, we should consider both the demand side and the supply side of the market. If the demand for coffee were elastic, the plan to raise prices would fail—but have *you* ever seen someone stagger into a Starbucks or Tim Hortons in the morning, review the prices posted on the wall, deliberately count his or her money, and depart? So the only problems that could arise are on the supply side, and the main ones are that some producers might fail to stick to the agreement to destroy part of their crops, and that an "outside" producer might enter the market. This is what actually did happen when Vietnam became the world's second-largest coffee producer in the late 1990s.

IN THE NEWS: OPEC

1. For such a small reduction in supply to cause such a large increase in price, demand must be very *inelastic*. This behaviour is what one

would expect of the demand for oil, at least in the short run. Buyers of gasoline and fuel oil are not in a position to quickly change the equipment (vehicles and furnaces) in which they use petroleum products, so demand would be inelastic.

2. The key to achieving higher prices is to restrict the production (supply) of oil. But OPEC only controls 35 to 40 percent of world crude-oil production. If the higher prices that OPEC was seeking were to lead non-OPEC producers to increase their production, OPEC's price objective would not be achieved. In addition, the objective of a higher price would necessarily involve lower production quotas for each member of OPEC. But members of OPEC have often been known to cheat on their production quotas. If some OPEC members were to pump oil in excess of their quotas, the world supply of oil would be higher than OPEC had planned—and the price would be below OPEC's target.

YOU DECIDE: The International Diamond Monopoly

1. There is a real possibility that more diamonds will be found than can be absorbed by the market at current prices. Furthermore, the high prices of diamonds create an incentive to find more of them. If De Beers were to be unable to buy all such newly found diamonds, they might be sold on the open market, driving prices downward.

2. If the monopoly is charging high prices, its high profits will attract competitors. These could take the form of new firms producing the same product or substitutes. The change in DeBeers' strategies over the years supports this view; on the other hand, BeBeers did manage to exercise monopoly power for a long time.

Chapter 8: The Costs and Revenues of the Firm

YOU DECIDE: Ebusiness Costs

1. The marginal cost of additional units is *very* low; selling additional units does not require paying for any more labour or materials.

2. Such a combination of high fixed costs and low marginal costs supports a very aggressive pricing strategy, for two reasons. First, such low marginal costs mean that additional

units can be priced very low and still sold profitably. And second, such low prices would increase sales volume, which would spread the firm's high fixed costs over a larger number of units. High fixed costs tend to dictate a fairly high break-even point, and low prices help the firm to achieve this level of sales.

Chapter 9: Government Policy Toward Business

YOU DECIDE: Beer Competition

1. Even with assertive monitoring by the Competition Bureau, there would still be only two major competitors. With the aging of the population, the beer market has been growing very slowly, so there is no room for more Canadian breweries as competitors. So if the government really wanted to increase competition, the best way would be to open up the Canadian beer market to foreign competitors. This is in fact what did happen, thanks in large part to free trade agreements.

Chapter 10: Labour Markets and Labour Unions

IN THE NEWS: Hockey Players' Salaries

1. The "short answer" to this question is that the demand for NHL hockey players grew by a factor of 5 (from 6 teams to 30), while the supply of players of NHL calibre did not. However, this explanation seems insufficient to account for such a massive increase in players' salaries.

According to people who follow the National Hockey League, the reasons for the rapid increase in salaries were more complex, and were rooted in a combination of free agency, salary arbitration, and a very wide gap in the financial conditions of the rich (big-market) teams and the poor (small market) teams. Under their collective bargaining agreement (CBA or labour contract), at a certain stage in their respective careers, players who had been tied to one team could become *free agents* and sign with the team that bid the most for their services. In this free agent market, some rich teams (most notably the New York Rangers) were willing to pay extremely high salaries for a few key players who might help them to win the Stanley Cup.

The NHL's labour contract also provided that at an earlier point in their careers, players who were not yet free agents and who had salary disputes with their team could apply for *salary arbitration*, in which an arbitrator would decide the player's salary. In these arbitrations, players were able to use the salaries paid by rich teams to key free agents as benchmarks for their own salary claims. For example, if the New York Rangers signed free agent Pierre Slapshotte for $10 million a year, Yuri Skormor could argue to an arbitrator that the Calgary Flames should have to pay him $8 million because he scored 80 percent as many points as Slapshotte. So the huge salaries paid to a few key players by a few rich teams spread to players on the poor teams.

2. Before long, many of the smaller-market "poor" teams were losing large amounts of money. This problem was made worse by the fact that the league did not have a revenue-sharing plan whereby the big-market rich teams shared their revenues with the small-market teams. The league had overexpanded and had brought in teams that could not live with its combination of free agency, salary arbitration, and lack of revenue-sharing.

3. In a free-market situation, perhaps 10 of the teams would have gone bankrupt. But the NHL would not let this happen, perhaps because it believed that its image could not withstand such a blow. So, in the negotiations for a new labour contract with its players, the league decided that there must be a dramatic decrease in players' salaries—a decrease large enough to keep the small-market teams in business. The players refused to accept this, so the 2004–05 season was lost when the league locked the players out. The final settlement included many concessions by the players, including salary rollbacks of 24 percent.

YOU DECIDE: Let's Play Arbitrator

1. You are neutral, and because of this neutrality, both sides accept you as arbitrator.

2. You are still an "outsider"—you have not actually *lived with* the problems that you are trying to resolve.

3. No. You will only know *what you have been told* by two people who are probably not interested

in the facts so much as in getting a decision from you that suits them.

4. There is a real risk that this person will feel no commitment to making your decision work. It is too easy for this person to rationalize that the decision was made by someone else.

Chapter 11: Employment and Incomes in the Canadian Economy

IN THE NEWS: Labour Force Facts

1. In large part, the growth of part-time employment is the result of the growth of the *service sector* of the economy. While the production of goods lends itself to full-time work such as in manufacturing plants, services such as retail trade, restaurants, and entertainment often tend to be delivered at peak periods, making part-time employment particularly well suited to these industries.

However, financial pressures on employers also seem to be a factor in decisions between hiring full-time and part-time employees. During the economic boom of the second half of the 1980s, part-time employment *decreased* from 17.0 percent of all jobs to 16.6 percent. During the recession of the early 1990s, part-time employment increased to 19.1 percent by 1993, but in the boom of the late 1990s, it *fell again*, to 18.1 percent. So at least in some cases, employers seem to prefer full-time workers, but will hire more part-timers when pressed financially.

2. The Statistics Canada's webpage also contains some interesting breakdowns of part-time employment by age and sex.

IN THE NEWS: Will the Male–Female Pay Gap Narrow in the Future?

1. The main reason for expecting that the male–female pay gap will narrow in the future is that more young women than men are pursuing post-secondary education. On university campuses today, women outnumber men by about four to three, and young males are particularly likely to become high school dropouts. Another important factor will be the retirement of older women, for whom the pay gap is largest (33 percent for women aged 45–54) and their replacement by younger women, for whom the pay gap is smaller (19 percent for women aged 15–24).

Chapter 12: The Government Sector

YOU DECIDE: The Marginal Tax Rate and the Economic Incentive to Work

1. No. She is merely responding logically to the incentives presented to her by the system. If Joan faced a marginal tax rate of 80 percent and decided not to teach night school because of it, her middle-class friends would probably say that she was behaving rationally and that the tax system was virtually forcing her to turn down this extra work.

2. Sandy needs to be allowed to keep a higher proportion of any income that she manages to earn. In other words, her welfare benefits should not be reduced so rapidly when she earns money that her incentive to work is destroyed.

IN THE NEWS: The Greying of Canada

1. The increase in the seniors population reflects the aging of the *baby boomers*—the large number of Canadians who were born from 1946 to 1966. The oldest baby boomer turns 65 in 2011; the youngest turns 65 in 2031. Many of these baby boomers will live to about 80 or more.

2. The implications of this trend for the living standards of Canadians are not positive. With so many more people retired, Canadian society will have a lower proportion of its total population working than in the past. Another way of looking at it is that a smaller proportion of working Canadians will have to produce enough to provide for themselves plus a larger proportion of non-working Canadians.

   To illustrate, imagine a deserted island economy with 20 people. Two are too young to work, 16 are of working age, and 2 are too old to work. If 10 of the 16 work (62.5 percent), then *10 workers have to support 2 retired people.* If 4 more retire, then 6 will be too old to work. If 2 are still too young to work, that leaves 12 of working age. Even if 8 of them work (66.7 percent), *8 workers have to support 6 retired people.*

3. One major thing that governments could do to reduce the negative economic effects of an aging population would be to increase the age of retirement. This would keep more older people working, so fewer would be in retirement. Another key policy would be to increase immigration of young people with the skills required by Canadian employers, so as to replenish Canada's labour force as the baby boomers retire. Also, any government policies that would encourage more Canadians of working age to work would help, as would policies that would increase productivity. The more each working Canadian produces, the less serious would be the problem of supporting the increased number of retired people. One way or another, the key is to keep output as high as possible despite the loss of so many baby boomers from the workforce.

   Other approaches are less attractive, as they would require either that retired Canadians accept a lower living standard in the form of reduced pensions, or that working Canadians accept a lower living standard because of higher taxes to support the retirees.

Chapter 13: Environmental Economics

IN THE NEWS: Higher Taxes on Gasoline?

1. The argument is that higher gasoline taxes and prices would discourage excessive consumption of gasoline, and that the resultant conservation of gasoline would reduce the automobile emissions that are the main source of air pollution. (In the short run, the demand for gasoline would probably be inelastic—people would not suddenly sell their SUVs and buy more fuel-efficient vehicles. In the longer run, more adjustments are possible—in the 1970s and 1980s, people did in fact switch to more fuel-efficient vehicles following the very large increases in gasoline prices.)

2. There are three answers to this question— politics, politics, and politics. Consumers love cheap gasoline, and are very hostile to taxes that increase the price of their gas. Politicians will never forget that, in December of 1979 the fledgling Progressive Conservative government of Joe Clark was defeated after it proposed an 18-cent-per-litre tax on gasoline that would have benefited both federal finances and the environment.

IN THE NEWS: Wasting Water in China

1. By underpricing water, the Chinese government has encouraged not only excessive consumption of water, but actual wasting of

water by China's consumers and producers. There is so little opportunity cost from misusing water that people are given an incentive to misuse it.

2. If a society wants its citizens to *conserve* a resource (be it water, or electricity, or oil), it has to place an appropriate *price* on that resource— a price that is high enough to impose a sufficiently high opportunity cost that people will use less of it. Government policies that keep prices low in order to gather the support of voters in the short term will only cause environmental problems and resource depletion in the longer term.

APPENDIX B
Answers to Study Guide Questions

Chapter 1

1. e
2. b
3. b
4. d
5. b
6. e
7. a
8. b
9. a
10. d
11. c
12. a
13. (a) 2 kg of vegetables
    (b) 4 kg of vegetables
    (c) 6 kg of vegetables
    (d) 6 kg of vegetables
    (e) 12 kg of vegetables
    (f) 8 kg of vegetables
    (g) 20 kg of vegetables
14. d
15. b

CRITICAL THINKING QUESTIONS

1. (a) Your car will not be fixed, so the opportunity cost will be whatever the use of your car would have provided for you. Maybe you'll forgo the income you could have earned if you had been able to get to work, or maybe you'll miss out on some social or recreational opportunities.
   (b) Your mother will be very disappointed about not getting to go to the concert. The opportunity cost of getting your car fixed will be whatever the consequences of her disappointment are for you. (You know these better than anyone else. . . .)

2. The obvious opportunity costs are related to the cost of your attending school—the things that you could have bought with the money spent on tuition, books, and so on. The less obvious opportunity cost is the foregone income that you could have earned if you had not gone to school.

3. Not at all—Rajinder has many more dollars, but still has only has a limited number of dollars. Every dollar that Rajinder spends on one thing means that there is one less dollar available to spend on other things.

4. (a) This is intended to improve effectiveness, by telling management what customers like and dislike about the company's products and services.
   (b) This is intended to improve efficiency, by motivating workers to produce products at a faster rate.
   (c) This is intended to improve both effectiveness and efficiency. If the robots produce products with precision, they will be more effective than workers, and if they produce products rapidly enough, the cost per product will be lower than with workers.

5. (a) This is intended to improve effectiveness, by telling the college what students like and dislike about the college's programs, courses, and services.
   (b) This is intended to improve efficiency, by increasing the number of students taught by each teacher. The increase in efficiency could be measured by an increase in teacher productivity (output per worker), or by a decrease in the cost per student.

USE THE WEB

1. In answering this question, don't look for the words *effectiveness* and *efficiency*; articles are unlikely to use these exact terms. Instead, look at an item and ask yourself whether you can apply the concepts of effectiveness and efficiency to it.

Chapter 2

REVIEW QUESTIONS

1. e
2. e
3. c
4. c
5. d
6. c
7. e
8. c
9. c
10. e
11. (a) T
    (b) T
    (c) F
    (d) T
    (e) F
12. (a) F
    (b) T
    (c) T
    (d) F
    (e) T
13. (a) T
    (b) T
    (c) T
    (d) F
    (e) T
14. c
15. c
16. e
17. e
18. b
19. c

CRITICAL THINKING QUESTIONS

1. (a) Market element: Consumers are directing the use of economic resources by buying more goat meat, which will cause its price to increase, which will encourage more production of goat meat. No government action is involved.
    (b) Command element: Governments are directing the use of economic resources toward education by using tax funds to finance education at no cost to users.
    (c) Market element: The oversupply will drive prices down, which will encourage buyers to buy more computers, and producers to adjust their production. No government action is involved.
    (d) Command element: Due to concerns that the merger of two such large firms would create monopoly-like power in the marketplace, the government is directing that the merger not take place.
    (e) Command element: The government is directing that the market's distribution of income (division of the economic pie) be altered so that lower-income citizens receive a larger share.
    (f) Market element: This situation was essentially the negotiation of a price (the compensation of players) by private buyers (the hockey clubs) and private sellers (the players). The decision was made by these parties, not the government.
    (g) Command element: The tax system established by governments is directing that higher-income citizens pay a larger share of the cost of government programs.

2. Assuming no changes in production costs per product,
    (a) the price of product A would rise by $2, and the profit per product would increase by $2/$7, or 29 percent.
    (b) the price of product B would fall by $1, and the profit per product would decrease by $1/$7, or 14 percent.
    (c) produce more of product A and less of B. Note how relatively small changes in *prices* can have significant effects on *profits* and on producers' *incentives*.

3. Corporations—this is merely one form that business enterprises can assume. But for a market system to function properly, there must be markets and prices. It is through price changes in markets that producers are given incentives to adjust production in response to the demand of buyers. And, of course, it is the profit motive that gives producers the economic incentive to do so.

4. (a) Competition among producers not only pushes producers to use resources effectively and efficiently; it forces them to *keep prices down*. If there were no competition

(that is, a monopoly), the producer could charge much higher prices. The same idea applies to producers getting together and agreeing on their price, which is illegal in Canada. Probably the most attractive aspect of the market system is that it does a good job of benefiting consumers, who are portrayed as "kings of the marketplace."

(b) However, if there were no competition, producers, not consumers, would be the dominant force in markets.

USE THE WEB

1. and 2. These questions are intended to show how a sophisticated information system such as the internet can improve how markets function, by making communications between buyers and sellers easier and faster.

Chapter 3

REVIEW QUESTIONS

1. T
2. F
3. T
4. T
5. T
6. T
7. T
8. F
9. T
10. T
11. F
12. F
13. F
14. T
15. T
16. F
17. F
18. T
19. T
20. e
21. c

CRITICAL THINKING QUESTIONS

1. CFIB provides two important services for its members that they could not afford to do on their own. The first of these functions is political lobbying to persuade governments to consider the concerns of the small business community when deciding their economic, taxation, and other policies that affect small business. Another function is the conducting of research of interest and value to the small business community.

2. The most frequently cited reason for people wanting to be in business for themselves is psychological rather than economic—they are independent in nature and prefer working for themselves, even if this involves less income and security than working for a large corporation. For some people, another reason is the possibility of striking it rich by establishing a very successful business.

3. Payroll taxes are taxes based on the size of an employer's payroll, or the number of its employees. Small businesses are particularly concerned about payroll taxes because small businesses tend to be more *labour-intensive* than larger businesses, often because small businesses provide services and/or use less high-technology production methods.

    This means that for labour-intensive businesses, labour costs are often a higher percentage of their total costs than for large firms such as big manufacturers. In turn, this means that payroll taxes, which in effect add to a firm's labour costs, are often more burdensome for small businesses than for large ones.

4. In support of government ownership and operation of such enterprises, it can be argued that they have contributed greatly to the economic development and unity of Canada, by providing energy (especially electricity) and key transportation and communication infrastructure such as railways, air service, postal service, and radio and television. In addition, it can be argued that these government enterprises made these services available to all Canadians, whether or not the size of their communities was large enough to make it profitable to provide that service.

5. Critics of government-owned-and-operated enterprises argue that they are inefficient and ineffective, largely because they lack a profit motive and have no competition. In addition, critics say, many government enterprises pay above-market wages to their employees, which adds to their inefficiency and costs. In turn, this means that many of these enterprises lose money and have to get subsidies

from governments, which involves opportunity costs because those governments could have spent those taxpayers' funds on other important public services, such as health care or education.

USE THE WEB

1. This is another example of how the internet makes vital information about markets readily available to people.
2. This question relates to the section in Chapter 3 about the problems of small business, and how various agencies offer assistance of different sorts to small businesses. For an idea of how an incubator works, visit the various sections of the website, such as the one on success stories.

Chapter 4

REVIEW QUESTIONS

1. a
2. decrease
3. (a) unwilling
   (b) unable
4. (a) substitute
   (b) do without (buy less)
5.

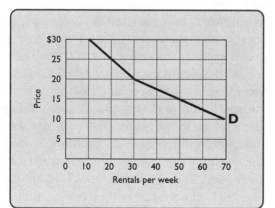

6. b
7. a
8. a
9. c
10. a
11. b
12. a
13. a
14. b
15. b

16. Neilson's chocolate ice cream
    chocolate ice cream
    ice cream
    dairy products

CRITICAL THINKING QUESTIONS

1. Note that in both graphs, the quantity demanded is 100 units per week at a price of $5. So our starting point is that, in both graphs, total revenue is $500 per week at a price of $5. Next, we check what would happen to total revenue if the price increased to $8.

    Graph A shows an elastic demand, because at a price of $8, total revenue *decreases* to $400 per week ($8 x 50 units). And graph B shows an inelastic demand, because at a price of $8, total revenue *increases* to $640 per week ($8 x 80 units).

2. (a) From $2 to $3: inelastic—total revenue increases, from $100 to $120 thousand
    From $3 to $4: unitary elasticity—total revenue is unchanged at $120 thousand
    From $4 to $5: elastic—total revenue decreases, from $120 to $100 thousand
   (b) At a price of $2 per dozen, most consumers seem to be willing to accept a price increase to $3, probably because they do not see attractive substitutes at a price of $3 for cobs of corn. However, when the price reaches $5, buyer resistance increases, as more people are unwilling to pay such a price. When a dozen cobs of corn costs you $5, substitutes seem more attractive than when it costs you $3.

3. (a) inelastic—the tradition of the Christmas turkey dinner would make price less of a consideration at Christmas.
   (b) elastic—with the alternative of DVDs available, people would become more resistant to increases in the price of movie tickets.
   (c) elastic—this adds another substitute for the products of the existing pizzerias, which would make it more difficult for them to increase their prices.

4. (a) air conditioners—these are less of a necessity than furnaces (in Canada's climate); it is easier to do without them or substitute for them.
   (b) automobiles—if the price of both autos and licences rose 20 percent, the fact that in some cases the purchase of a car can be postponed would cause their sales to decrease more than those of licences,

which are *required* in order to drive a car. Another factor would be the high price of a car as compared to a licence.

(c) telephone service—while the demand for both these items would be inelastic, there are more substitutes for telephone service than for electricity—for example, instant messaging on the internet.

(d) new autos—see (b) above; plus, when you need a replacement part in order to get the use of your car back, are you going to refuse to buy it because it is expensive?

5. (a) The demand for SUVs would decrease, so the demand curve for SUVs would shift to the left.

(b) These are complementary goods, because gasoline is bought in combination with an SUV.

6. (a) When the price of gasoline goes up sharply, most consumers complain loudly but keep buying nearly as much gas as before. At this point in time, they are trapped—they already own (or are leasing) their vehicle, and it would be costly to change to a more fuel-efficient one. These facts keep the demand for gas high (inelastic, really), which in turn contributes to high gas prices.

(b) If the price of gas *remains* high (which would lead more drivers to expect that it would continue to be high), the behaviour of consumers changes. When the time comes to replace their vehicle, more drivers buy a fuel-efficient one. This decreases the quantity of gasoline that they buy, which could be regarded as a decrease in demand and/or more elastic demand. In addition, people discover alternatives that economize on gas, such as carpooling, which they can exercise if the price of gas goes up.

USE THE WEB

1. To monitor trends over the five years shown, calculate the *percentage increase* for each year over the previous year. Doing this will allow you to easily compare the trend in the statistics for your province with the trend in the much larger statistics for Canada as a whole. Trends in new housing starts are affected by various factors, including mortgage interest rates, the condition of the economy (boom or recession), and population growth.

2. *The Daily* is used by Statistics Canada to release new statistics on all sorts of matters, which are kept in an archive. Its releases often contain both up-to-date statistics and explanations for recent trends shown by the data.

3. This question is another example of how the internet contributes to the functioning of markets.

Appendix 4A

REVIEW QUESTIONS

1. (a)

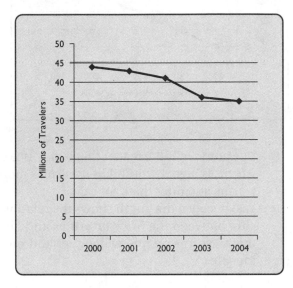

(b) The graph tells the reader that the number of American travellers entering Canada decreased from 44 million in 2000 to 35 million in 2004.

(c) No, the graph shows only *what* happened, not *why* it happened.

2. (a)

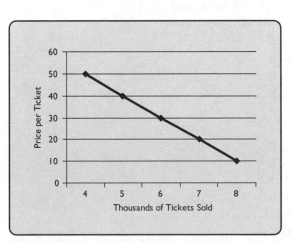

(b) The graph tells the reader that if the price of tickets is higher, people will buy few tickets, and at lower prices they will buy more tickets.

(c) Yes, because the graph shows the relationship between the price of tickets and how many tickets people will buy.

3. (a)

(b) The graph tells the reader that if the price of worms is higher, the children will pick more worms and offer them for sale.

(c) Yes, because the graph shows the relationship between the price of worms and how many worms people will gather and offer for sale.

Chapter 5

REVIEW QUESTIONS

1. b and e
2. c
3. d
4. (a) concentrated
   (b) competitive
   (c) concentrated
   (d) competitive
5. d
6. a
7. e
8. b
9. a
10. a
11. b
12. b
13. d
14. c
15. c
16. d

17.

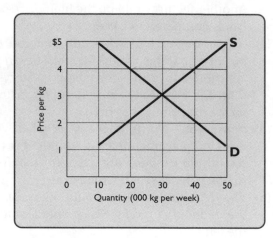

18. (a) $3
    (b) 30 000
19. c
20. b

CRITICAL THINKING QUESTIONS

1. The supply curve would shift from S to S1, as shown in the following graph.

Assume that retailers have 100 000 pairs of unsold summer shoes. Earlier in the season, they were charging $50 a pair for these shoes, but now that the season is nearly over, they reduce the price to $25. This reflects an increased willingness to sell this product, which takes the form of a price reduction rather than the increase in the amount offered for sale that is usually associated with such a shift in the supply curve.

2. The supply of retail clerks would be more elastic. If the price (that is, the wage rate) of retail clerks increased, the quantity of "clerk labour" supplied could increase considerably. Sources of labour could include young people who have left school, part-time student workers (more of them plus longer hours of work), homemakers, retired people, and so on. An increase in the incomes of doctors would also bring forth more doctors, but not nearly so readily—it takes years to educate and train new doctors, and most doctors are already working full-time.

3. (a)

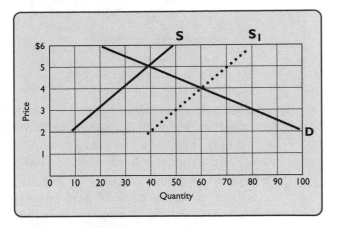

The equilibrium price is $5.

(b) See the dotted supply curve (S1); the new equilibrium price is $4.

4. (a) The supply curve would become much steeper for quantities beyond 85 million barrels per day. It would not become vertical, because *some* more crude oil could be squeezed out of existing oilfields if higher prices warranted the cost of doing so; however, not much oil could be obtained this way. Over the longer term, the supply curve would be kept quite steep by the fact that while additional crude oil could be obtained from those more remote and costly sources, the high cost of producing it would mean that its price would be high.

(b) The implication is that if the demand for oil continues to increase, the price is likely to not only stay high, but probably increase further.

(c) If something were to happen that increased the supply of crude oil, the price of oil would not increase, and could even fall. A similar development could occur if a substitute for oil (or for the gasoline that is made from oil) were developed.

5. This is a situation in which supply becomes inelastic because of limited plant (refinery) capacity. The problem in this case is an *inelastic supply of gasoline*, rather than a limited supply of crude oil (which has usually been the reason for rapidly rising gasoline prices).

Unless refinery capacity were increased, even large increases in the price of gasoline would fail to bring forth a larger quantity of gasoline supplied.

USE THE WEB

1. Clicking on the "New and Used" section beside a book will show you a list of a number of sellers of used copies of that book. The more sellers there are, the more competitive that market should be.

2. Check how many dealers are offering that particular car for sale; more sellers in a particular market area indicates a more competitive market.

Chapter 6

REVIEW QUESTIONS

1. increase, increase
2. decrease, decrease
3. decrease, increase
4. increase, decrease
5. b
6. a
7. $3, 50 units per week
8. c
9. (a) The quantity supplied would increase to 80 per week.
   (b) The quantity demanded would decrease to 20 per week.
10. b
11. (a) The quantity demanded would increase to 70 per week.
    (b) The quantity supplied would decrease to 30 per week.
12. b
13. c
14. d
15. a

CRITICAL THINKING QUESTIONS

1. (i) This would cause the demand for the product to increase. The demand curve would shift to the right, causing both price and quantity to increase.
   (ii) This is an increase in supply. The supply curve would shift to the right, causing the price to decrease and the quantity to increase.
   (iii) The demand curve would shift to the left (and become more elastic), so both price and quantity would decrease.

(iv) This is a decrease in supply, so the supply curve would shift to the left (or upwards, depending on how you look at it), which would cause the price to increase and the quantity to decrease.

(v) A shortage would develop, as in Figure 6-9.

(vi) Demand would decrease, so the demand curve would shift to the left. Both price and quantity would decrease.

(vii) The tax adds to the cost of producing and selling the product, so the supply curve would shift upwards by $2, reflecting the added cost. The result would be an increase in the price and a decrease in the quantity.

(viii) The supply curve would become vertical or nearly vertical at an output of 70 units per week, and the price would increase to where the new supply curve intersects the demand curve.

(ix) A surplus would develop, as in Figure 6-8.

(x) Both the demand curve and the supply curve would shift to the right; the equilibrium quantity would rise but the result could be either an increase or a decrease in the equilibrium price, depending on whether the demand or the supply increased by more.

2. (a) an increase in supply—a large harvest of corn has generated lower prices that are encouraging higher consumption.

(b) an increase in demand—a cold winter has increased the demand for natural gas and caused prices to rise.

(c) a decrease in demand—the demand for boat rentals is down, possibly due to bad weather; and marinas have cut rental rates in an attempt to offset this.

(d) a decrease in supply—a poor harvest of strawberries has caused higher prices for the reduced amount on the market this year.

3. (a) The starting point in the graph is that the market is represented by demand curve D and supply curve S, and the equilibrium price (rent) is $1000 per month and the equilibrium quantity is 500 apartments. The influx of renters increases the demand from D to D1, which causes rents to increase from $1000 per month to $1300.

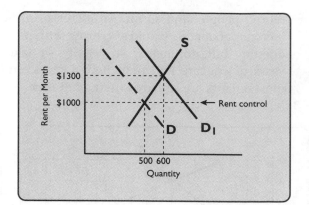

(b) If monthly rents are allowed to rise to $1300, the supply curve tells us that the quantity of apartments supplied will increase from 500 to 600. But if the town limits rents to $1000, the quantity supplied will only be 500, and there will be a shortage of apartments. Builders will build apartments in other towns, where they can charge the market rate for rent.

4. This is an interesting phenomenon that has been observed in various centres. The most common explanation for it is that early in the morning the demand for gas is more inelastic, because most buyers of gas are commuters who are in a hurry and, if they need gas, do not shop around for the best price—they just stop at the first station they see, or go to their usual station. Later in the day, more gas is bought by people who are not in such a hurry, and can take more time to compare prices.

5.

Initially, demand is represented by D and supply by S, and the equilibrium price is $300 000. Let's assume that because there is a general expectation that housing prices are going to rise rapidly, two things happen in this market:

(a) more buyers want to buy now, to beat the price increases, which increases demand to D1, and

(b) some sellers decide to postpone putting their houses onto the market for a while, hoping to get considerably higher prices at that time. This will decrease the supply (temporarily) to S1.

The combined effect of *expected* rising prices on the demand side and the supply side of the economy can cause prices to actually increase sharply (in this example, from $300 000 to $400 000).

USE THE WEB

1. The statistics that you will see are not *prices*, but rather something that statisticians call "indexes." These are averages of the prices of items in each category (food, shelter, etc.), statistically adjusted so that the average for each category = 100.0 in 1992. So what these index numbers measure is not prices as such, but rather how much prices have increased from any one year to any other year. For example, the index for shelter was 120.5 in 2004 and 117.5 in 2003, so in 2004, the average price of items comprising "shelter" increased by 2.6 percent (120.5 minus 117.5, divided by 117.5). In looking for explanations of price changes, watch for factors such as changes in taxes (on tobacco and/or alcohol) and the effect of low-priced imports (such as clothing and footwear).

Chapter 7

REVIEW QUESTIONS

1. (a) many small firms
   (b) easy to enter
   (c) identical products
2. a
3. c
4. d
5. e
6. d
7. b
8. a
9. increase their prices
10. (a) The producers make an agreement concerning price and output.
    (b) The producers maintain that agreement.
    (c) Newcomers and foreign competitors are kept out of the market.
    (d) The demand for the product is inelastic.
11. a
12. e

13. e
14. there is only one producer of a product.
15. c
16. control the supply of its product.

CRITICAL THINKING QUESTIONS

1. (a) Perfect competition
   (b) He is one of many small producers of identical products.
   (c)

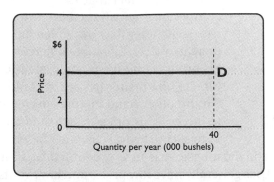

   (d) 40 000 bushels (as much as he can)
   (e) His sales would fall to zero.
   (f) No. He can already sell all that he can produce at the market price, so cutting his price would serve no purpose.
   (g) No. His product is identical to that of all the other farmers, so advertising would serve no purpose.
   (h) He should increase the efficiency of his farm, so as to get his cost of producing a bushel of wheat down. That would increase his profit per bushel sold.
2. (a) monopolistic competition
   (b) His business is one of many small firms in an industry that is easy to enter, and his product is not identical to those of his competitors—it is differentiated.
   (c)

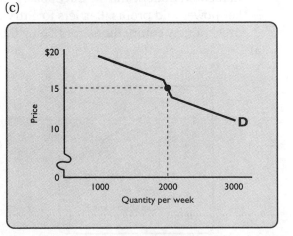

(d) (i) He should differentiate his product from those of his competitors.

(ii) He should make his production methods as efficient (low-cost) as possible.

(iii) Advertising makes sense, so as to bring the features of his products and services to people's attention.

(iv) His product differentiation gives him the opportunity to increase prices a little, but the fact that there are many competitors to whom his customers can switch limits how much he can increase prices. The more differentiated his product and the more loyal his customers, the higher his prices could be. On the other hand, he may decide not to increase his prices much or at all, so as to secure a loyal customer base.

3. The most basic reason why competitive industries generally have low prices and low profits is that producers are unable to control or restrict the supply of their product or service. And the main reason why they cannot restrict supply is that it is *easy for new firms to enter* their industry. This is very much in contrast with the situation in the next question.

4. (a) Barriers to entry are factors that prevent new firms (competitors) from starting up in an industry in competition with established firms. Examples of barriers to entry include the amount of capital needed to start a business, consumer acceptance and problems achieving the level of sales needed to operate profitably, and various other factors described in Chapter 7.

(b) The above-average profit rates of oligopolists will tend to attract new competitors that could undermine the oligopolists' market power and profits. Barriers to entry can prevent new competitors from doing this.

5. (a)

Since there are only a few firms in the industry, what will happen when this one firm increases its price will depend on what the other firms do with *their* prices.

(b) If this firm increases its price and the other firms do not increase their prices, this firm's sales will fall considerably. Its demand will be *elastic*, and a price increase will cause its sales revenue to decrease.

(c) If this firm decreases its price, we have to assume that the other firms will decrease their prices, too. In this case, this firm's price will be lower but its sales will only be slightly higher, so its sales revenue will decrease. For a price decrease, demand will be *inelastic*.

(d) The situations in parts (b) and (c) create an incentive for firms in this industry to agree on the price that they will all charge; then, the incentive for each firm is to neither increase nor decrease its price until all the firms agree upon a new price.

USE THE WEB

1. Be sure to select *Dealer Listing*—the objective is to see how many dealers are offering each car, not how many private sellers there are. Then be sure to count the *number of dealers* offering that car, not the number of vehicles for sale.

Chapter 8

REVIEW QUESTIONS

1. (a) fixed
   (b) variable
   (c) variable
   (d) fixed
   (e) fixed
   (f) variable

2. b

3. c

4. d

5. a

6. Law of Diminishing Returns

7. a

8. d

9. c

10. (a) $24

(b) Yes. Producing and selling the twenty-sixth product adds more ($24) to the firm's revenues than it adds to its costs ($23).

11.

Units of output per day	Fixed Costs	Variable Costs	Total Costs	Average Fixed Cost per Unit	Average Variable Cost per Unit	Average Total Cost per Unit	Marginal Cost per Unit
0	$600	$ 0	$ 600	n.a.	n.a.	n.a.	n.a.
5	600	150	750	$120	$30	$150	$30
10	600	200	800	60	20	80	10
15	600	225	825	40	15	55	5
20	600	300	900	30	15	45	15
25	600	550	1150	24	22	46	50

(a) (i) Average fixed cost per unit decreases as fixed costs are spread over more units.

(ii) Average variable cost per unit decreases at first, then increases, as the Law of Diminishing Returns causes average output per worker to increase at first, then decrease.

(iii) Average total cost per unit decreases at first as fixed cost per unit and variable cost per unit fall, but, after output reaches a certain level, will increase as a result of rising variable costs per unit due to the Law of Diminishing Returns.

(b) Marginal cost per unit is the cost of producing one additional unit.

As output increases, the Law of Diminishing Returns causes marginal cost per unit to decrease at first, then to increase.

CRITICAL THINKING QUESTIONS

1. The longer tubes are used commercially; consequently, they are mass-produced to a greater extent than the smaller ones. As a result, the large tubes have the lowest production costs (particularly fixed costs) per unit, despite their larger size and the greater amount of materials in them.

2. In publishing, there are *heavy fixed costs* associated in the development and production of a book. Books with high sales volume such as Dr. Spock's spread these fixed costs over a very large number of copies, making the fixed cost *per copy sold* lower than for books with shorter print runs.

3. (a)

Output (units per week)	Fixed costs	Variable costs	Total costs	Total revenue	Profit
0	$500	$ 0	$ 500	$ 0	–$ 500
100	500	500	1000	1000	0
200	500	1000	1500	2000	500
300	500	1500	2000	3000	1000
400	500	2000	2500	4000	1500
500	500	2500	3000	5000	2000

At sales of 400 products per week, the weekly profit will be $1500.

(b)

Output (units per week)	Fixed costs	Variable costs	Total costs	Total revenue	Profit
0	$800	$ 0	$ 800	$ 0	–$ 800
100	800	600	1400	800	–600
200	800	1200	2000	1600	–400
300	800	1800	2600	2400	–200
400	800	2400	3200	3200	0
500	800	3000	3800	4000	200

At sales of 300 products per week, fixed costs of $800 per week, variable costs of $6 per product and a price of $8, the firm will have a weekly loss of $200.

4. (a)

Units of output per day	Fixed Costs	Variable Costs	Total Costs	Average Cost per Unit	Average Revenue per Unit	Marginal Cost per Unit	Marginal Revenue per Unit
0	$ 200	$ 0	$ 200	——	——	——	——
10	200	170	370	$ 37.00	$ 22.00	$ 17.00	$ 22.00
20	200	320	520	26.00	22.00	15.00	22.00
30	200	440	640	21.33	22.00	12.00	22.00
40	200	580	780	19.50	22.00	14.00	22.00
50	200	800	1000	20.00	22.00	22.00	22.00
60	200	1100	1300	21.67	22.00	30.00	22.00

4. (a)

(b)
(c) (i) 50 units
(ii) $100 (average revenue = $22.00; average cost = $20.00, so profit is 50 units x $2.00 each)
(d) Yes, as indicated by the perfectly elastic demand curve.
(e) The price would be forced downward by competition, reaching an equilibrium level of about $19.50, where the AC curve is at its lowest point. Profits would then be zero, having been eliminated by competition.

USE THE WEB
1. This is a good practice exercise in working with the concepts of this chapter.

Chapter 9

REVIEW QUESTIONS
1. a
2. b
3. competitive; concentrated
4. b
5. e
6. (a) yes
(b) yes
(c) no
(d) yes
(e) yes
7. d

8. c
9. e
10. d
11. a
12. (a) price-fixing
(b) mergers of firms, *if* they would lessen competition substantially
13. increase efficiency; compete internationally
14. (a) They must secure approval from the federal Competition Bureau.
(b) The Competition Bureau will consider whether the proposed merger would lessen competition substantially. In addition, it will consider whether the proposed merger would likely result in gains in efficiency that would increase the ability of the merged companies to compete internationally.
(c) The Competition Bureau would seek to negotiate changes to the proposed merger that would preserve competition in affected markets, such as the sale of some operations and assets to competing firms. If the Bureau and the companies proposing the merger cannot agree, the matter is taken to the Competition Tribunal for a decision.
15. e
16. (a) The very heavy capital investment in these industries makes their fixed costs so high that in order to keep costs to users down, they should be made monopolies so that they can have the maximum number of users
(b) public transit, water utilities, postal service
17. d

CRITICAL THINKING QUESTIONS
1. The key to understanding this matter is that the basic goal of the Competition Act is to promote *and preserve* competition in Canadian markets. Smaller regional airlines had made several complaints that Air Canada was pricing its flights *below its costs*, with the objective of driving the smaller airlines out of business. This sort of practice (described in Chapter 7 as "predatory pricing") does indeed reduce prices in the very short run, but by driving competitors out of business, it reduces competition and makes it easier to increase prices after that.

2. The Competition Bureau objected because, by in effect dictating the price that dealers could charge for its cars, Toyota was interfering with competition in the marketplace. This is different from price-fixing, which is an offence that involves competing producers agreeing on a price. In cases such as the Toyota one (known as *resale price maintenance*), a producer takes action that prevents retailers from competing regarding the price of its producer—an action described in law as "maintaining the resale price" of the product.

3. (a) The restaurant is labour-intensive; that is, it needs a lot of labour in order to cook and serve food and beverages. The manufacturing firm, on the other hand, is capital-intensive: many of its operations are carried out by machinery rather than by labour. As a result, labour costs are a higher proportion of the restaurant's total costs than of the manufacturer's total costs.

(b)

	Manufacturing Company	Restaurant
Sales revenue	$500 million	$500 thousand
Non-labour costs	370	320
Labour costs	100	150
Profit	30	30
Payroll taxes (10% of payroll)	10	15
Profit after payroll taxes	20	15

(c) Payroll taxes reduce the manufacturing firm's profits by 33 percent ($10/$30), and they reduce the restaurant's profits by 50 percent ($15/$30).

USE THE WEB

1. Developments concerning the efficiency exception were expected by mid-2005 but had not materialized as of the fall, so there should be some news in this area by 2006 at the latest.

Chapter 10

REVIEW QUESTIONS

1. $9 per hour; 4000 workers
2. $10 per hour; 1000 workers; 5000 workers
3. d
4. (a) the number of people seeking work would increase to 6000, while
   (b) the number of jobs would decrease to 3000

5. b
6. e
7. c
8. (a) yes
   (b) yes
   (c) no
   (d) yes
   (e) no
9. b
10. a
11. (b) conciliation
    (c) cooling-off period
    (d) work stoppage (strike or lockout)
12. a
13. b
14. (a) false
    (b) true
    (c) false
    (d) false
15. a
16. c
17. b

CRITICAL THINKING QUESTIONS

1. (a) On the supply side of the market for hairdressers, the union's problem would be that it could not prevent lower-price competition from non-union hairdressers who refused to join the union, and from self-employed hairdressers.

   (b) On the demand side, the key factor would be the elasticity of demand for hairdressing. If the demand were relatively elastic (for instance, if higher prices caused people to go to the hairdresser less often), a union could only achieve large increases in hairdressers' incomes if it were prepared to accept a significant reduction in the number of (unionized) jobs in the industry. And a larger problem could be that the presence of non-union hairdressers as a substitute would make the demand for unionized hairdressers more elastic, which would further reduce the number of jobs for unionized hairdressers.

2. When the "cooling-off period" begins, two important changes come into play in the negotiating process. First, after the conciliator departs, the two negotiating teams are *completely on their own*, and second, they are both

keenly aware that they are facing a strike deadline that is *both known and getting closer.*

Regarding the first point, there is no longer any hope that the conciliator will come up with some way to get a negotiated settlement; if a work stoppage is to be averted, the bargaining teams themselves will have to do whatever it takes to negotiate a settlement. So if either negotiating team has anything more to offer, the pressure to make that offer is growing.

Regarding the second point, the pressure to negotiate an agreement grows as the strike deadline approaches. Both parties have been aware from the start of negotiations that a work stoppage *could* occur, but that prospect was off in the future somewhere. Once the conciliator is gone and the "cooling-off period" begins, that deadline is now known (e.g., midnight on Thursday, May 28), *and* it is getting closer.

By placing strong and growing pressure on *both* negotiating teams, these factors make a negotiated settlement more likely, particularly near the end of the cooling-off period.

3. Chapter 10 notes that a major reason for the decline in union membership as a percentage of the work force has been *changes in the nature of employment.* In highly unionized fields such as manufacturing and government, job growth has been slow. In contrast, most of the growth of employment has been in the service sector, which is not highly unionized. Unions cannot change these trends in the types of work, so for union membership to grow again as a percentage of the labour force, unions would probably have to recruit more members in the service sector of the economy. Many service industries are not easy to unionize. Often, firms are small in size, much of the work is part-time, and worker turnover is high. Unions would probably target service industries in which employers are larger, such as banking and big retailers; however, most of these firms tend to resist union recruiting efforts very strongly. If employees of these firms felt that they were being underpaid and/or treated unfairly by management, they would be more likely to join a union, as groups of employees at some Wal-Marts have periodically tried to do.

4. The main reason for concern is not the loss of working time and economic output; these are both very small as a percentage of time worked and the economy's output. According to most observers of the labour scene, the main concern is that a reputation for labour strife could cause multinational corporations to see Canada as a less attractive place in which to locate, invest, and create jobs. In many cases, the facilities of such multinational firms are very costly, and the prospect of down time due to work stoppages could be of concern to them.

5. Unions tend to strike more frequently when the economy is booming and employers are more anxious to avoid a work stoppage; also, low unemployment improves a union's bargaining power. Strikes also tend to be more frequent when inflation is rapid, since workers demand larger pay raises because they fear that prices will rise rapidly in the future.

In the early 1990s, there was a recession that was followed by several years of high unemployment. These economic conditions are believed to explain much of the reduction in strike activity, as workers were reluctant to risk going on strike. Over the same period, the fact that inflation slowed down also contributed to the reduced strike activity—with less fear of their earnings being eroded by rapid inflation, workers were prepared to settle for relatively modest increases.

USE THE WEB

1. Many people think that having a high level of education more or less entitles someone to a higher income, but people's incomes are determined by supply and demand. So, when you compare the income figures for different education and skill levels, think in terms of the supply of and demand for the services of people who possess that education or skill level.

2. The CLC takes positions on a wide range of economic, social, and political issues. In reviewing the CLC's position on any given issue, ask yourself how the CLC's recommendations would affect union members.

3. The most useful column is the one on the far right, which shows the percentage of working time lost due to work stoppages. One important

factor that affects the number of strikes is the overall condition of the economy. Unions tend to strike more frequently during economic booms, when busy employers are more anxious to avoid a work stoppage and have good profits, and less often when high unemployment and a sluggish economy create a less favourable environment.

Chapter 11

REVIEW QUESTIONS

1. (a) yes
   (b) yes
   (c) no
   (d) no
2. e
3. a
4. (a) yes
   (b) no
   (c) yes
   (d) no
   (e) yes
   (f) yes
   (g) yes
   (h) no
5. c
6. a
7. e
8. slower increases in the number of income earners per family and in worker productivity
9. c
10. 10 percent
11. e
12. d
13. a
14. b
15. c
16. a
17. a
18. c
19. (a) single-parent mothers
    (b) young people
    (c) elderly women living alone

CRITICAL THINKING QUESTIONS

1. The reasoning behind this statement is that most women work in service industries and office work rather than in goods-producing industries such as manufacturing, construction, and agriculture, and that because of technology, job growth has been much more rapid in service industries than in service industries. Chapter 11 describes how employment in goods industries has grown only slowly, while employment in service industries has grown very rapidly, creating growing numbers of job opportunities for women. One obvious reason for these trends is changes in production technology, which has cut into employment in goods industries. A less obvious but equally important effect of technological change has generated a much higher standard of living, which in turn has increased consumer demand for the services that provide employment for many women. The argument is that without technological change, most jobs would still be in the goods-producing industries, which tend to be male-dominated.

   That said, another perspective is that, for various reasons, the time had come for women to insist on a role in the workforce, and that they were going to go out and compete with men for jobs in any case, whether those jobs were in traditional goods-producing industries or in service industries.

2. The main reason for such a striking statistic is probably the demographic fact that women live significantly longer than men, so that there are many more women than men in the over-65 population. Also, in part, these statistics reflect the fact that women past retirement age have lower incomes than men. Many of those with their own pensions have lower pensions than men because their incomes were on average lower than men's, while widows often live on two-thirds or one-half of their husbands' pensions.

3. For most of the working poor, it is a matter of pride—they do not wish to be dependent upon social assistance. Does this make them noble contributors to society or illogical people who don't exercise their most economically advantageous alternative? And what does it say about the economic alternatives offered to them by society?

4. There are three alternatives here, the last two of which seem the most likely:
   - governments know that the LICO poverty lines are valid and have decided to provide welfare benefits that are too low for people to live on,

- governments believe that the poverty lines are not valid and that people can live on less, and/or
- governments believe that if they provide welfare benefits equal to the LICOs, these will be so high that many people will choose to remain on welfare, creating financial problems (and political problems with taxpayers) for the government.

5. This question addresses the very real problems of defining and measuring poverty. First, people who define poverty as the state of having an income that is too far below the average income (the LICO approach) will see the poverty problem as much more serious than people who believe that poverty means having an income too low to buy the necessities of life (the MBM approach). Second, there is the problem of how to measure poverty. If we simply use people's reported income as the measurement, everyone with an income below the poverty line is counted as poor. But if we do not count as poor those people who have unreported cash income such as tips, people whose incomes are only temporarily low, and people who have considerable paid-for assets such as a house, the number of poor people decreases considerably. This is not a matter of who is right and who is wrong, but rather of different ways of looking at the matter of poverty.

USE THE WEB

1. Participation rates are affected by economic conditions—when a booming economy creates more job opportunities, participation rates tend to increase, while the opposite tends to happen when unemployment increases and job opportunities are scarce.
2. *The Daily* often includes both statistics and the causes of changes in the statistics.
3. *The Daily* often includes both statistics and the causes of changes in the statistics.

Chapter 12

REVIEW QUESTIONS

1. c
2. (a) taxes on incomes (personal and business)
   (b) taxes on spending (sales taxes, or consumption taxes)
   (c) taxes on assets
   (d) taxes on payrolls

3. b
4. a
5. b
6. 35 percent ($3500/$10 000)
7. 40 percent (2/5)
8. 95 percent (19/20)
9. e
10. b
11. c
12. (a) yes
    (b) no
    (c) yes
    (d) yes
    (e) no
    (f) yes
    (g) no
13. c
14. borrowing money (mostly by selling government bonds)
15. (a) $40
    (b) $440
16. c

CRITICAL THINKING QUESTIONS

1. They would be regressive, because import duties add to the prices of imported products, in the same way as sales taxes do. And sales taxes take a higher percentage of the incomes of the poor than they take of the incomes of wealthier Canadians.
2. The key to this question is not which of these choices one might prefer, but rather what the effect of such tax rates on the economy would be, particularly in terms of their effect on incentives to work and to invest. To answer this question requires looking beyond the fact that higher personal income taxes would leave people with less take-home pay, and asking what effects these scenarios would have on productivity and therefore on living standards.

   A 50-percent marginal tax rate on personal incomes would represent a significant increase (the average marginal tax rate is now around 40 percent). The key question is whether such a marginal tax rate would cause many people to refuse to do additional work, such as overtime or a second job. To the extent that people declined to do additional work, efficiency would be impaired.

   A 50-percent marginal tax rate on business profits would represent an even larger increase than for workers in the previous paragraph. The key question here is how such a marginal tax rate would affect the decisions of businesses— would they reduce their investment in equipment that increases efficiency, or, even worse, would some multinational businesses decide not to invest in Canada?

We know from experience that marginal tax rates in the 50-percent range do not kill the incentive to do additional work for most Canadians. We do not know how similar tax rates would affect business decisions to make investments that would increase their efficiency, only that the potential for negative effects could be considerable. And if business investment were severely affected, the impact on the Canadian economy could be serious.

3. The statement is a very simplistic one, based on the notion that debt is bad. As the text points out, there are situations in which borrowing by governments is certainly reasonable. The clearest such case is when a government borrows in order to purchase or build a costly asset, such as a hospital or a college; by borrowing, the government can provide the public with the use of the asset much sooner, and the public's taxes can pay off the debt over a period of time. Households can make good use of debt in this way (e.g., to buy a house), so can businesses (e.g., to acquire plant or equipment), and so can governments.

The speaker might be (mistakenly) comparing all government borrowing to the misuse of credit cards by some consumers, who go excessively into debt not to acquire assets, but rather just to increase their consumption spending beyond their income. Or perhaps the speaker is thinking back to Canada's experience of the 1975–93 period, as described in Chapter 12. Or maybe the speaker does not trust elected governments to manage their finances soundly in the face of political pressures to give voters benefits above and beyond the taxes that they pay.

4. (a)

(b) The figures in year 20X5 (1) balance the budget solely by reducing spending so that spending and tax revenues are both $114 billion. The budget is balanced.

The figures in year 20X5 (1) balance the budget solely by increasing tax revenues so that tax revenues and spending are both $132 billion. The budget is balanced.

These are just examples. Any combination of spending cuts and tax increases that added up to a total of $18 billion in 20X5 would also balance the budget.

(c) The spending reductions and tax increases in part (b) are *big*. The spending cuts amount to nearly 14 percent of all government spending, and the tax increases require boosting the tax burden by nearly 16 percent. Changes in government spending and/or taxes on such a large scale would inevitably generate a great deal of political opposition from groups that would be adversely affected.

(d) The government's debt would remain stable (in this example, at $355 billion).

5. (a) The purpose is to provide people who are receiving EI benefits with an incentive to work, at least to a certain extent. There had been many complaints from employers that EI was creating an incentive for people to *not* take jobs that were available, especially if these might be short-term jobs that would leave the worker unqualified to go back on EI when the job ended. For example, fish canneries in communities with very high unemployment rates sometimes found themselves unable to recruit workers.

(b) 100 percent—for every dollar that you earn over the limit, your EI benefits are reduced by one dollar. You get to keep none of your earnings, which is a marginal tax rate of 100 percent.

Billions of dollars

Year	Government Spending	Government Tax Revenues	Budget Deficit (–) or Surplus (+)	Government Debt
20X1	$110	$100	– $10	$310
20X2	117	105	– 12	322
20X3	125	110	– 15	337
20X4	132	114	– 18	355
20X5 (1)	114	114	0	355
20X5 (2)	132	132	0	355

1. Use the "Net federal debt" statistics at the bottom of the table on the Statistics Canada website.

Chapter 13

REVIEW QUESTIONS
1. (a) private cost
   (b) social cost
   (c) private cost
   (d) private cost
   (e) social cost
2. d
3. less of other things (goods); that is, a lower standard of living
4. e
5. e
6. d
7. d
8. d
9. a
10. (a) F
    (b) F
    (c) T
    (d) T
    (e) T
11. b
12. e
13. a
14. e
15. b

CRITICAL THINKING QUESTIONS
1. The problem with this view is that it assumes that, once educated about the negative social effects of their actions, people and businesses will willingly take actions that cost them economically in order to live up to their social obligations. In other words, it does not really address the problem that there are economic incentives to pollute. So, for this approach to be effective in dealing with pollution, people would have to be persuaded to voluntarily accept the costs of reducing their pollution, without any assurance that others would do the same.
2. (a) This is an unattractive statement, but it is accurate. As Chapter 13 notes, both producers and consumers of a product gain economically from not having to pay the social costs of their actions. If a company saves $1 per product by dumping waste into the air or water, the company will save on the costs of disposing of the waste, and consumers of the product will probably enjoy lower prices as well.

   (b) This reality means that governments must actively intervene in order to protect the environment; the marketplace and the incentives of the marketplace will make pollution problems worse, not better. So government environmental policy needs to start from the realization that it must overcome the economic incentive to pollute, using incentives and/or penalties that change people's behaviour.

3. (a) In effect, we can "produce" a cleaner environment by investing in pollution-control equipment. And since the resources used to produce a cleaner environment cannot be used for other purposes, there is an opportunity cost of improving the environment in terms of lower production of other things. For consumers, this opportunity cost takes the form of higher prices for the products that they buy, leaving them less money to spend on other things.

   (b) In general, people dislike the economic reality of opportunity cost; they would rather be able to have more of all things, and not have to face the reality that more of one thing means less of others. Regarding the opportunity cost of a cleaner environment, there are probably other factors. Most individuals do not see themselves as benefiting from pollution (unlike some industries, for example), so they cannot see why they should pay for cleaning it up. And many people feel that pollution is caused by others (mostly industry), so others should bear the costs of cleaning up and protecting the environment.

4. (a) The main benefit is simply convenience and cost, for both consumers and producers. For consumers, the main cost saved is the time and effort of carting empties around, while for producers the collection and recovery/reuse of reusable containers is a labour-intensive task that can be quite costly. All of these are private costs.

   The main costs are social costs, such as the economic costs of cleaning up all the discarded throwaways and the extra use of scarce landfill sites, and the littering of the environment with throwaways.

(b) (i) Prohibition would eliminate the costs in a quite simple manner. It would also eliminate the consumer's having any choice in the manner (such as paying a higher price for the convenience), and may seem to some to be a somewhat drastic approach to dealing with a problem that generates litter but is not life-threatening.

(ii) Taxes on throwaways could discourage the use of these containers, depending on how high the taxes were. They would leave consumers the choice of paying more for the convenience of throwaways (i.e., "internalize" the external costs), and the tax revenues could be used to pay for cleanups, to subsidize recycling, etc. However, they would not completely eliminate the problem.

USE THE WEB

1. By following the directions in the question, you can get a good idea of how the internet can contribute to a cleaner environment by helping to create an effective and efficient market for recyclable materials. By moving materials from sellers to buyers, this market increases the amount of recycling that is done.

3. This is another example of how markets (in this case, markets for tradable pollution credits) can contribute to improvement of the environment.

Chapter 14

REVIEW QUESTIONS
1. e
2. b
3. e
4. (a) no
   (b) yes
   (c) no
   (d) yes
   (e) yes
5. b
6. (a) from $6 to $4
   (b) from $360 ($6 x 60) to $320 ($4 x 80)
7. d
8. b

9. c
10. e
11. (a) F
    (b) T
    (c) T
    (d) T
    (e) F
12. (a) $4; 80
    (b) 90 units; $270 (90 units x $3 per unit [$6 target price minus the $3 market price])
13. (a) increase and stabilize farm prices and incomes
    (b) limit the amount that farmers can produce
14. (a) no
    (b) yes
    (c) no
    (d) yes
    (e) yes
15. e
16. (a) yes
    (b) no
    (c) yes
    (d) yes

CRITICAL THINKING QUESTIONS

1. The decrease in the number of people working on farms does not indicate that farming is in serious decline; rather, it reflects the tremendous increase in agricultural productivity that has occurred as technology allows more food to be produced with fewer workers. Similarly, the decrease in the number of farms is largely due to the consolidation of small farms into larger ones, often to take advantage of the economies of scale made possible by capital equipment. This is not to say that Canadian farmers do not face economic problems—just that these statistics do not show these problems. Statistics on farm incomes would be a better indicator of the economic health of the industry.

2. (a) King's observations reflected the fact that because the demand for food is inelastic, an increase in supply can cause a decrease in the incomes (total revenue) of farmers. The connection goes like this: the higher supply causes a considerably lower price, but the lower price does not generate significant increases in sales, so the farmers wind up selling a little more food at considerably lower prices, and receive less income.

(b) Yes. These are basic economic realities that have not changed over several centuries. And so a basic problem of farmers continues to be oversupply and low prices and income.

(c) Marketing boards work to overcome the problem first identified by King, by restricting the amount that farmers produce.

3. (a) A marketing board acts as a sort of monopoly that limits the amount that farmers can produce, in order to increase prices. The prices of products under the jurisdiction of Canadian marketing boards are usually much higher than the prices of the same products in the United States.

(b) Because marketing boards increase food prices, most objections come from buyers of food. The largest such group is of course consumers, as represented by the Consumers' Association of Canada (**www.consumer.ca**; see **www.consumer.ca/1630** for a specific example). Objections also come from industrial buyers of food, because the higher prices of marketing boards add to their production costs. Their problem can be especially serious if they must compete with producers in the United States, who can buy food inputs at lower prices in that country.

(c) It is not a simple matter to monitor the activities of large numbers of producers spread out over a wide area. Most marketing boards exempt small producers from limits on production, and the high prices that marketing boards generate creates an incentive for people to produce those products and sell them, legally or not.

(d) Imports of lower-price foreign products could represent a real threat to marketing boards. In the past, marketing boards were protected against foreign competition by government quotas that nearly banned imports.

(e) Free trade agreements have made the long-term future of marketing boards uncertain, since unrestricted imports of lower-price food would make it impossible for marketing boards to operate as they

have in the past. However, this prospect is far in the future; at present, the products covered by marketing boards are protected by very high tariffs on imports, which are scheduled to come down only gradually under trade agreements.

4. Deficiency payments tend to encourage efficiency more than marketing boards or acreage restrictions do. Under a system of deficiency payments, farmers are guaranteed a target price for their crops, but there are no restrictions on how much they can produce. So under a system of deficiency payments, the incentive for farmers is to produce as efficiently as they can in order to reduce costs, and to produce as much output as they can. Marketing boards and acreage restriction programs limit how much farmers can produce, which increases fixed costs per unit of output. Also, the cost of quotas under marketing boards can prevent farms from expanding and achieving economies of scale.

USE THE WEB

1. Keep track of not only exports and imports of agricultural and fish products, but also the gap between them, or the amount by which exports exceed imports.

Chapter 15

REVIEW QUESTIONS

1. b
2. d
3. (a) trade agreements that reduce barriers to trade
   (b) improvements in communications technology
   (c) improvements in transportation technology and costs
4. (a) improved access to larger foreign markets
   (b) increased competition from foreign imports
5. Much of its industry was not efficient enough to compete internationally.
6. c
7. a

8.

Government Policy	
1. The 1989 Free Trade Agreement with the United States	a, c, f
2. Action to keep the rate of inflation low	b, h
3. Tax reductions	c, d
4. Deregulation of some industries	a, b, f
5. The new Competition Act (1986)	b, f
6. Reductions in government subsidies to business	a
7. Reform of the Employment Insurance program	c, d, e
8. Increased investment in human resources	c, d
9. Elimination of federal government budget deficits	g, h

CRITICAL THINKING QUESTIONS

1. In the past, government policy had stressed the goal of a fairer distribution of economic wealth, and had sheltered Canadian manufacturing industries from international competition—the "resource wealth mentality" described in Chapter 15. The 1989 Free Trade Agreement with the United States signalled a basic shift in Canadian policy toward an emphasis on creating economic wealth and competing internationally. This shift in policy increased the importance of goals such as increasing productivity and improving the ability of Canadian industry to compete internationally.

2. As a small country that relies heavily on exports for its economic prosperity, Canada needs its industries to be able to compete internationally. And a key to competing internationally is to have high productivity, since high output per worker per hour helps to keep production costs low.

3. Budget surpluses could be used to finance tax reductions that were meant to increase incentives for businesses to invest in productivity-increasing equipment, and for people to work, save, and invest. Budget surpluses could also be a source of funds for government spending programs that would increase productivity; these could include programs such as research and development and education and training.

USE THE WEB

1. Click on "Programs and Services," and look for programs that are intended to improve the ability of Canadian industry to compete internationally; these could range from skills training for workers to assistance with developing export markets.

Glossary

acreage restrictions A crop supply management program that either forces farmers to reduce their acreage under cultivation, or gives them financial incentives to do so.

administered prices A term used to describe prices that have been fixed by sellers. See price-fixing.

after-tax income Total income less income taxes paid.

arbitration The resolution of union–management disputes by the decision of a third party; required by law for grievances that the union and employer cannot resolve by themselves; used to settle disputes over the terms of new collective agreements in cases where strikes of essential employees are prohibited.

board of directors A group of people elected by the shareholders of a corporation to provide direction to the management of the corporation.

budget deficit An excess of government spending over government revenues.

capital (equipment) The tools, equipment, machinery and factories used to increase production per worker.

cartel A formal agreement among producers to coordinate their price and output decisions for the purpose of earning monopoly profits.

coefficient of elasticity The percentage change in quantity demanded that results from a 1-percent change in price.

collective agreement A contract agreed upon by an employer and labour union, specifying the terms and conditions of employment of the employees for a specified period of time.

collective bargaining The process through which employers and unions negotiate a new collective agreement.

command system An economic system in which economic decisions are made mainly by the government, in a centralized manner.

competitive industry An industry that consists of many small firms and is easily entered by new competitors.

complementary good A good that is bought in combination with another good.

compulsory conciliation A procedure, required by law before a strike is legal, in which a government-appointed officer (conciliator) attempts to help a union and employer to reach an agreement on the terms of a new collective agreement.

concentrated industry An industry that is dominated by a few large firms and is not easily entered by new competitors.

consumption taxes Taxes levied when consumers buy goods and services; for example, sales taxes.

corporation A business firm that is a separate legal entity from its owners, or shareholders, each of whose liability is limited to the amount of his or her investment in the firm.

Crown corporations Corporations owned by a government and that are ultimately responsible, through a cabinet minister, to that government.

deficiency payments Programs for supporting farm incomes under which the government guarantees farmers a target price for a crop by subsidizing all sales of that crop that fall short of the target price.

demand The entire relationship between the various possible prices of a product or service and the quantity demanded at each price, expressed through either a schedule or a graph.

deregulation Policies to reduce government regulation of business, with the intention of promoting efficiency.

derived demand The demand for a factor of production, which is generated by (derived from) the demand for the good or service that it is used to produce.

ebusinesses Businesses using processes and activities based on electronic information and data exchanges via the internet and the World Wide Web.

economics The study of the decisions a society makes concerning the production of goods and services and the division of these among its people.

economies of scale Lower production costs per unit made possible by higher volumes of production that permit the achievement of increased efficiencies.

effectiveness A measure of how well an economy performs in terms of producing goods and services that are needed and wanted.

efficiency A measure of how well an economy performs in terms of producing high volumes of goods and services at a low cost per item.

elastic demand The term used to describe demand if a price increase causes a reduction in total sales revenue.

elastic supply A situation in which the quantity supplied increases readily when the price increases.

equal pay for work of equal value The concept that the values of different jobs may be measured against each other using a point system that incorporates a variety of criteria, including skill levels, effort, degree of responsibility, and working conditions.

equilibrium price A price determined in the marketplace by the interaction of supply and demand.

equilibrium quantity The quantity sold (bought) at the equilibrium price.

externality An incidental cost, or side effect, inflicted on others by the production or consumption of a product. Also known as a spillover effect.

fixed costs Production costs that remain constant, regardless of the level of output (for example, rent).

general partners Partners who take an active part in the management of the business and who have unlimited personal liability for its debts.

globalization The growing internationalization of business, trade, and finance that has characterized the period since the early 1980s.

greenhouse effect The global warming trend that environmentalists fear will cause disastrous climatic changes around the world, including the raising of ocean levels, widespread flooding of coastal areas, and weather changes such as hurricanes.

grievance An alleged violation of a collective agreement by an employer.

Gross Domestic Product (GDP) A measure of the total value of goods and services produced and incomes earned in a country in one year.

individual bargaining The process through which workers deal as individuals with employers in negotiating their terms and conditions of employment.

industrial concentration The degree to which an industry is dominated by a few firms.

inelastic demand The term used to describe demand if a price increase causes an increase in total sales revenue.

inelastic supply A situation in which quantity supplied does not increase readily when the price increases.

inputs Economic resources, such as labour, capital equipment, and natural resources, that are used to produce goods and services.

labour The largest single productive input available to any economy, labour includes all of the productive talents of the people of a society, mental as well as physical.

laissez-faire The doctrine or philosophy that from the viewpoint of the public interest, it is neither necessary nor beneficial for governments to intervene in the operation of the economy.

land Short form for all the natural resources available to a society's economy as economic inputs.

Law of Diminishing Returns A physical law stating that, if additional units of one productive input (such as labour) are combined with a fixed quantity of another productive input (such as capital), the average product per unit of the variable input (labour) will increase at first and then decrease.

limited partner A partner who invests in a business but takes no active part in the management of it, and whose liability is limited to the amount invested.

long run The period of time after which the quantities of all inputs can be changed.

Low-Income Cut-Offs Income levels below which the income of families or individuals are less than the average income by more than a certain amount.

marginal cost per unit The addition to total costs resulting from the production of one more additional unit of output.

marginal productivity (per worker) The increase in production resulting from the hiring of one additional worker.

marginal revenue per unit The addition to total revenue resulting from the sale of one additional unit of output.

marginal tax rate The percentage of any additional income that is earned that goes to taxes.

market basket measure Poverty lines based on the cost of a "basket" of goods and services that a family requires in order to live above the poverty line.

market income Income earned in the marketplace.

market power The ability to raise one's prices; usually associated with a dominant or monopolistic position in the market.

market structure Term used to describe the organization and nature of a market or an industry, particularly whether it is competitive or concentrated in nature.

market system An economic system in which economic decisions are made mainly by consumers and privately owned producers, in a decentralized manner.

marketing boards Government-sponsored organizations of farmers that support farm incomes by restricting the supply of produce, usually through a system of quotas on individual farmers.

minimum wage A legal minimum wage rate set by law.

monopolistic competition A term describing industries that consist of many small firms, where entry to the industry by new firms is easy, and where the products or services of individual firms, while basically similar, are differentiated from each other to a degree.

monopoly A situation in which there is only one seller of a particular good or service.

National Council of Welfare A citizens' advisory body to the Minister of Human Resources Development Canada on matters of concern to low-income Canadians.

natural monopoly An industry, such as public utilities, that by its nature lends itself to a monopolistic form of organization.

non-price competition Competition between sellers based not on price but rather on factors such as product differentiation and advertising.

offer to purchase A farm-income support program under which the government establishes the price of the farm produce and undertakes to purchase any unsold produce at that price.

oligopoly A situation in which four or fewer firms account for at least half of the sales of an industry.

opportunity cost The concept that the real economic cost of producing something is the forgone opportunity to produce something else that could have been produced with the same inputs.

output The goods and services produced by a society using its productive inputs.

partnership A business firm owned by two or more persons, with each person bearing full legal liability for the firm's debts.

payroll taxes Taxes paid by employers based on the number of their employees or the amount of their payroll.

perfect competition A term describing industries that consist of a large number of small firms, where entry to the industry by new firms is easy, and where all firms in the industry sell identical products.

perfectly elastic demand A situation in which any price increase above the market price will cause a firm's sales to fall to zero; represented by a horizontal demand curve.

poverty lines Income levels below which families or individuals are considered to be poor.

price-fixing Agreements among oligopolists to raise their prices above levels that would prevail in a competitive situation.

price-maker Term used to describe the position of the dominant firm(s) in a concentrated industry, which can influence the price of the product.

price-taker Term used to describe the position of the individual small firm in a competitive industry, which is unable to influence the price of its product and is forced to accept (take) whatever price is determined in the market.

price control (ceiling) A legal limit on a price or on increases in a price, which holds the price below its equilibrium level.

price leadership A technique of price-fixing in which one firm (the price leader) sets its price and the rest of the firms in the industry follow suit.

price support (floor) An artificially high price, held above the equilibrium level by the government.

private (internal) costs Production costs, such as labour and materials, that are paid by producers and ultimately included in the price paid by the consumer.

private corporation A private corporation has fewer than 50 shareholders.

Privatize The process of selling government enterprises (usually Crown corporations) to private interests.

product differentiation Attempts by individual firms to distinguish their products or services from those of their competitors.

production-possibilities curve A curve that shows the economy's potential output, assuming that economic inputs are fully employed and efficiently utilized.

productivity Output per worker per hour; a measure of efficiency.

profits Those funds left from a business's sales revenues after all expenses have been paid; such funds are therefore available (after taxes have been paid) for dividends to shareholders and reinvestment in the business.

progressive taxes Taxes that take a higher percentage of high incomes than of low incomes.

proxies Legal instruments that allow a shareholder's right to vote at shareholders' meetings to be delegated to another person, either with or without specific instructions as to how that vote will be exercised.

public corporation A public corporation has 50 or more shareholders.

recession A period during which the economy's output is falling and unemployment is high.

regressive tax A tax that takes a higher percentage of low incomes than of high incomes.

resource wealth mentality The view that society's economic wealth is derived mainly from the sale of natural resources, as opposed to efficiency in the production of goods and services.

scarcity The problem that, while economic inputs (and thus potential output) are limited in availability, people's wants and needs are apparently unlimited.

shareholders The owners of shares (stocks) in a corporation; shareholders may or may not have voting rights and their liability is limited to the amount invested.

short run The period of time during which the quantities of some inputs cannot be changed.

social (external) costs Costs that are not paid by producers, but rather passed on to society at large.

sole proprietorship A business firm owned (and usually managed) by a single person who bears full legal liability for the firm's debts.

standard of living A measure of the economic prosperity of the people of a society, usually expressed in terms of the volume of consumer goods and services consumed per household or per person per year.

subsidies Payments by the government of part of the cost of a service in order to reduce the cost to the user of the service.

supply curve A graphical representation of a supply schedule.

supply schedule A table depicting the relationship between the price of a product and the quantity supplied (offered for sale).

tax credits Credits that reduce the income taxes payable by Canadians in order to offset a variety of factors that adversely affect their living standards, including dependants, property taxes, and sales taxes.

total income Market income plus transfer payments received from governments.

variable costs Production costs that vary with the level of output (for example, direct labour and materials).

World Trade Organization (WTO) An international organization through which 149 member nations negotiate and enforce rules for international trade.

Index

MICROECONOMICS SCOREBOARD

CANADA'S LARGEST 10 CITIES

SOURCE: STATISTICS CANADA, *CANADA AT A GLANCE*, 2005.

	POPULATION
Toronto	5 101 610
Montreal	3 574 516
Vancouver	2 134 286
Ottawa	1 132 181
Calgary	1 016 616
Edmonton	990 525
Quebec	705 898
Hamilton	702 917
Winnipeg	698 210
London	457 233

EDUCATIONAL ATTAINMENT, (POPULATION AGE 15+, 2003)

SOURCE: STATISTICS CANADA, *CANADA AT A GLANCE*, 2005.

Number:	25 250 700
Education:	
0–8 years	9.1%
Some secondary	16.0%
Graduated from high school	19.2%
Some post-secondary	9.7%
Post-secondary certificate or diploma	28.8%
University degree	17.1%

PERSONS PER SQUARE KILOMETRE (2001)

SOURCE: STATISTICS CANADA, *CANADA AT A GLANCE*, 2005.

	PERSONS PER SQUARE KILOMETRE
Japan	337
United Kingdom	244
Germany	228
Italy	190
France	108
Mexico	50
United States	30
Canada	3